The Strike-Threat System

THE ECONOMIC CONSEQUENCES
OF COLLECTIVE BARGAINING

W. H. Hutt

Arlington House   NEW ROCHELLE, N.Y.

Contents

Preface

ONE OF this book's conclusions is that *fear* of strikes inflicts far greater damage on the economic system than actual strikes. That is why its title is *The Strike-Threat System,* not *The Strike System.* The harmful consequences upon the capital structure alleged here may all be experienced without actual strikes. The mere right to disrupt the continuity of the productive process is having deplorable effects, regarding both the size of real income and equity in the distribution of that income.

In 1930 I published a small book entitled, *The Theory of Collective Bargaining* (London: P. S. King). In 1954 it was republished, unchanged, in the United States (Glencoe, Ill.: The Free Press). This early contribution of mine argued that, while the power to strike can redistribute income in favor of the members of particular unions, it cannot redistribute income in favor of labor in general at the expense of capital in general. Despite so clear a thesis, it has yet to be successfully refuted. Yet if the argument is valid, its importance for the contemporary world can scarcely be exaggerated.

The present work advances a wholly new exposition in which the same conclusion is reached via a somewhat different route. Its purpose is to analyze the nature, distributive consequences, policy implications and ethical significance of the strike-threat in modern societies. During this analysis, it examines typical arguments which are used, especially by "labor economists," to justify notions of the kind that I challenged in 1930.

Already in the late 1920s I had reached the conclusion that all the textbook treatments I could find of this important subject were—superficially considered—definitely indefensible or inadequate and unconvincing.[1] For instance, the great Alfred Marshall's treatment of what he appeared to regard as the crucial issue—bilateral monopoly—was illustrated by his famous example of the barter of nuts and apples; yet as I saw the problem, the circumstances he was thus postulating were, for a variety of reasons, of negligible practical significance.[2] And Marshall was widely regarded as the greatest economist of his age.

I expected that the obvious challenge of my book would prompt a major contribution, from economists better qualified than myself, to deal with the questions I raised. During my entire academic life I have been expecting an authoritative book. But although there have been many splendid contributions, mainly in the form of articles that have given more or less the same answers that I myself have given, they have had hardly any policy impact. The following economists have all written cogently on aspects of the problems discussed here, and I have gained something substantial from each of them (although some might differ—or would have differed—sharply on certain issues): Fritz Machlup, Ludwig von Mises, Milton Friedman, Friedrich A. Hayek, Aaron A. Director, M. Reder, Goetz A. Briefs, John Van Sickle, Armen A. Alchian, William R. Allen, Marshall Colberg, Yale Brozen, Arthur A. Shenfield, S. Rottenberg, H. Gregg Lewis, Gottfried Dietze, Clarence Philbrook, Henry Hazlitt, H. Demsetz, F. A. Harper, A. Rees, P. Sultan, V. Orval Watts, C. E. Lindblom, C. H. Cooley, Henry Simons, W. Eucken, E. H. Chamberlin, Wilhelm Röpke, David McCord Wright, Gottfried Haberler, Sylvester Petro, N. J. Simler, Ben Rogge, Helmut Schoeck, H. G. Johnson, and P. Mieskowski.[3] Of course, there are many others who would share some or most of my conclusions. Yet these economists have not yet succeeded in making their convictions on the strike-threat issue influential. They have failed, particularly, to win the sympathy even of those of their academic colleagues whose minds are not closed (which, unfortunately, I often think today is a small proportion).

It seems almost arrogant of me to attempt to achieve what I feel economists of such eminence have failed to achieve. Yet try I must. I speak to those who do not refuse "dialogue." But I am hopeful, above all, that this contribution will have some influence among that small but active group of young, skeptical, independent-minded students in colleges and universities whose misgivings cause them to see further than their teachers. These students discern, I know, that something is more fundamentally wrong in the labor market than they are being taught, while the conventional diagnoses of today (they perceive) go disastrously astray.

There is of course today an enormous literature on "labor economics." I find it for the most part tendentious, often derivative, and usually devoid of any original or independent thinking. Much of it has been written, I guess, to satisfy the imperative in American universities to "publish or perish." Trying to judge whether there is anything worthwhile in all these volumes has been exasperatingly time-consuming and unrewarding. But it is the bias of most of this literature which is most disturbing. In an article published a few years ago, I ventured a diagnosis.[4] I said that most books on "labor economics" have been by labor consultants, arbitrators, conciliators, mediators, labor attorneys, labor correspondents; and that such "economists" cannot think or write dispassionately on matters affecting their incomes.

Two decades ago, a leading member of the British Labor party, Lady Wootton (Barbara Wootton), stated quite categorically, that it is "the business of a union to be anti-social; the members would have a just grievance if their officials and committees ceased to put sectional interests

viii

first."[5] F. A. Hayek, commenting on this passage, noted "few liberal sympathizers of the trade unions would dare to express . . . [this] obvious truth."[6] But why should trade union sympathizers, including their academic advisers, not *dare* to refer to such a truth unless they felt that their political ambitions or prospects as consultants, or advisers, or labor journalists would be jeopardized by so frank an admission?

Having referred to a mass of works on "labor economics," which I judge to be worthless *on the topics to be discussed here,* I must make it clear that I am *not* referring to a relevant field in which research in the best sense of the word "scientific" has occurred. Especially since World War II, there has been a considerable output of scholarly statistical and empirical studies in the sphere of wage-rates and income distribution, including some books and articles by the economists I mentioned on p. viii. These works, of which some of the most impressive have been published under the auspices of the National Bureau of Economic Research, have bolstered my confidence in the conclusions I have reached. Their investigations have convinced me that the opinions I had formed at the beginning of my academic life, and to which I find myself adhering (dogmatically or steadfastly) toward its end, are consistent with the findings of empirical research.

In Chapters 15 and 16 I discuss the limits to which studies of measurable "economic quantities" can be useful on the particular topics I have covered. But I ought at this stage to express my indebtedness to all those who have explored the statistical material with such care, patience and ingenuity. Apart from the contributors mentioned on p. viii, the economist-statisticians whose works have contributed most to my confidence are those quoted in Chapter 16 although I must not claim (for I do not know) that they would all agree with the inferences I draw from their research.

Teachers of economics in the "classical tradition" often warn their readers that economic science is not concerned with moral valuations but simply with explaining the causes of exchange values and prices and the actions that create them and respond to them. Nevertheless, ethical speculation can seldom occur usefully unless the economic implications of human interaction are understood. The purpose of my analysis is to assist those who are genuinely concerned with building "the good society." I want to help them to think rigorously about what I myself have come to regard as the crucial issue respecting interpersonal relations.

I have tried to write for the layman *and* the economist. Where I have found it expedient to use the technical jargon of economics, the reader will usually find a paraphrase which avoids such terminology or that I have provided simple definitions, either in the text or in footnotes. And I have throughout found it useful to disclose the general trend of my argument as early as possible, developing my case as I meet objections or after meeting predictable objections. If readers who are shocked by the thesis outlined in Chapter 1 will patiently withhold judgment, they will I think discover that the grounds for their initial dissent (and in some cases expostulations) will be dispassionately examined in the appropriate context later on. Often I repeat points made earlier because, despite many cross-references, repetition has seemed to be the most effective way of reminding the reader of what has already been shown.

Although I shall most often enunciate what I myself judge to be the accepted principles of "classical economics," I shall at times argue for propositions which some *economists* would be inclined to challenge. When I resort to the first person, it will indicate that I do not wish to leave any impression of reliance on authority. That is, without making claim to originality, I want to stress at that point that economists in general might not necessarily accept my logic or premises.

The branch of economic relations on the operation of which I am trying to throw light is one of which, because the fortunes of men may be influenced by what is clarified, the findings (not assumptions or logic) may be bitterly challenged. A century and a half ago the logician Whately pointed out that if the teachings of Euclid had borne on human affairs they would have been subject to violent controversy down to his day. My own crucial thesis, sketched in Chapter 1, will be praised or damned for this reason whether it is right or wrong. Self-interest (including supposed self-interest) tends to warp even the most sincere judgments. Most labor unionists firmly believe that their material standards, their security and even the respect in which they are held are indirectly derived from the right to strike. Their present well-being has been won, they are convinced, by "long and bitter struggles"; and what they have achieved, they have no doubt at all, is capable of being preserved only by retaining the powerful weapons they have forged. Such convictions are, I shall try to show, wrong. *But most of labor's critics today accept the same ideas.* They have grave misgivings and they deplore what they think of as *the abuses* of strike-threat power. But the existence of that power they still regard as a guarantee of justice. It is *this* stereotype which it is my task to demolish.

I wish to express my indebtedness to the following universities and colleges in which I have served as visiting professor or research fellow while the ideas here expressed have been taking shape: the University of Virginia; Rockford College; Wabash College; Texas A & M University; the Hoover Institution on War, Revolution and Peace at Stanford University; California State College at Hayward; and the University of Dallas. I must acknowledge the encouragement and assistance of the Relm Foundation, the Principles of Freedom Committee and the Institute of Humane Studies.

W. H. Hutt

NOTES

[1] I did not then know of Eugen Böhm-Bawerk's important *Control or Economic Law?* which reached conclusions similar to those I reached. It had not then been translated into English. Nor had works by Ludwig von Mises which dealt briefly with the same issue.

[2] I discuss Marshall's contribution on pp. 7-9.

[3] I noticed the important contribution of Professors Johnson and Mieskowski too late to permit a discussion of it in all appropriate contexts. I refer to its findings in an appendix to Chapter 15. I received E. P. Schmidt's splendid study, *Union Power*, on the day I received the page proofs of this book.

[4] W. H. Hutt, "Misgivings and Casuistry on Strikes," *Modern Age,* Fall 1968.

[5] Barbara Wootton, *Freedom under Planning* (Chapel Hill: University of North Carolina Press, 1945), p. 97.

[6] F. A. Hayek, *The Constitution of Liberty* (Chicago: University of Chicago Press, 1960), p. 505.

1
The Crucial Thesis

FOR THE sake of clarity, I shall begin by presenting my case in the simplest terms. In so doing, I run the risk of losing those readers who tend at first to disagree and then are unwilling to suspend judgment. But for the reader prepared to face apparent heresies, disclosure of my position at the outset will be the most fruitful procedure. I shall explain why I believe that coercively imposed wage rates, or more directly enforced restraints on entry to any occupation, cannot redistribute income from "capital" in general to "labor" in general.

A crucial concept must be defined first—"exploitation." *I define "exploitation" as any action taken, whether or not through discernible private coercion (collusion) or governmental coercion, which reduces the value of the property or income of another person, or prevents that value from rising as rapidly as it otherwise would, unless this effect is brought about through: (a) dissolving some privilege; or (b) substituting some cheaper method (labor-saving or capital-saving) of achieving any objective; or (c) expressing a change in consumers' preference; or (d) democratically authorized taxation.*

We shall be concerned almost entirely with the exploitation of workers by investors or of investors by workers. But, as we shall see, every restraint of the price mechanism and every restraint on consumer or entrepreneurial freedom may be held to "exploit" the community as a whole; and any such "exploitation" may be viewed as harming, more or less impartially, both investors in general and workers in general (a) as consumers and (b) as income receivers. For example, if the price of leather is forced up either through collusive action among the suppliers of hides or through a strike on the part of the workers employed in tanneries, the community as consumer will be worse off. Incomes will buy less. Whatever the effects upon the relative shares of workers and investors in the value of leather produced and sold, the economic impact upon the relative value of the shares of workers and investors in all other occupations is *likely* to be neutral, in the sense that both groups will be affected in roughly the same proportion.

The most vital economic decisions are "entrepreneurial" decisions: They are made within an institutional framework of custom, law and knowledge—

the law requiring administration and enforcement by collective action—that is, by government. These decisions, which are being continuously made, are in every case concerned with retaining, replacing, accumulating, or decumulating the physical resources employed in various possible combinations of, in certain specific activities, together with the retaining, recruiting or displacing of labor in accordance with this process. Now, the use of capital equipment, materials and labor in any activity will not occur unless some entrepreneurial remuneration is deemed possible for every increment of resources invested in that activity. Thus a firm will not retain, replace or accumulate additional assets unless the prospective output values of each *increment* exceed the corresponding current and prospective input values by more than the rate of interest.

The size of a firm's inputs—those of its assets and of the labor in which it invests—will be reduced if the predicted residue shrinks through labor costs having been raised by a strike, the threat of a strike, or a wage law. "Exploitable" resources will be neither retained, replaced nor attracted. The only investments which are "exploitable" by the strike or the strike threat, therefore, are those in which entrepreneurs have failed adequately to allow for the probable use of strike power or political action as determinants of labor costs.[1]

Entrepreneurs know and make allowances for the use of the strike threat or similar power to fix wage rates. Hence in general *there can be no "exploitation" of retained, replaced or accumulated capital, except on the assumption of entrepreneurial forecasting errors.*

For parallel reasons, labor is unexploitable. Workers can be said to be "exploited" only if, after investments by them of time, effort and saving in specialized training, unforeseen monopsonistic[2] or oligopsonistic[3] actions (by entrepreneurs) reduce their remuneration.

Hence, in a society where any form of entrepreneurial "exploitation" has been practiced and seems likely to be practiced again, the rate of hiring at *any given wage* by firms or industries will decline, possibly to the disadvantage of the specific investors.

Realistically, the probability of frequent monopsonistic exploitation of labor seems quite remote. For were it not for labor union demarcations and restrictions on entry most laborers (even highly skilled ones) would be almost as versatile as those in "put and carry" services. (There are, of course, some important exceptions.) Let us consider the extreme case of highly specialized, nonversatile labor. If we consider (a) the continuous replacement of personnel who gradually leave through competing employment openings, retirement and death, and (b) (in an expanding industry) the recruitment needed for expansion, we must recognize that the probability of the workers' exploitation is remote. The observable labor turnover between firms suggests indeed that collusive action to reduce the price of labor has virtually never been regarded as profitable.[4] (The necessary—quite *un*important—qualifications of this assertion will be expressed later. See Chapters 8 and 9.) But the principle is based on no inference from empirical evidence (although it does seem to be

4

consistent with observed experience): *The volume of labor which will come forward to be trained for or otherwise become attached to any occupation in which (in the light of past experience) labor appears liable to "exploitation," will be reduced to the level at which the prospective long-term benefits are equated with the prospective benefits from training and employment in other occupations.*

The reader will probably reach the conclusion (after reading Chapters 7 and 8) that where nonversatile plant and equipment are provided, the possibility of *investors* being exploited is greater. But even here we shall see that exploitation forecast is exploitation evaded.

Having stated this broad thesis, it is essential to stress what it does *not* imply: labor costs imposed by duress immediately to change the property rights of individuals or groups. The strike threat works much like a gun threat. In theory it can, therefore, redistribute property as a street robber can, *to the extent to which people carry thievable assets.* I am not questioning anything as obvious as that. Investors who have not foreseen the use of the strike weapon resemble the traveler who carries with him large sums of money. I shall show, in a similar way, that labor can be subject to monopsonistic exploitation by managements if any of the workers allow themselves to be "shut-in," that is, prevented from moving to better remunerated opportunities. When this happens, *the workers' property in themselves* is in some degree seized. What I shall call "the shut-in" is a form of partial slavery, unless it is simply a mutually advantageous contractual commitment, freely entered into and uninfluenced by fraud, to sell certain services for a certain price for a certain period.

The problems to be considered here fall within this theoretical framework. Wage-rate increases enforced through the strike threat benefit those remaining employed at the enhanced labor costs. But, on whom does the burden then fall? On the specific investors? On investors in general? On displaced or excluded workers? On consumers? What is the *incidence* of the burden? This problem is like that which economists discuss under the heading of *the incidence of taxation.* To express the issue in abstract terms (which means in the simplest terms), any one party to the productive process can exploit one or more of the other parties only in a measure determined by the "elasticities of supply"[5] of the different productive services rendered by the people or by the assets employed. In this connection I propose to draw attention to four vital realities: (1) In the absence of man-made barriers to mobility, noticed above (p. 4), there is a wide range of alternative uses for a large proportion of workers and assets,[6] a fact which implies *long-term* elasticities of supply. (2) Assets are often substitutable for labor (a consideration which is usually taken into account under the heading of "elasticity of substitution"). (3) If growing large scale recourse to the strike threat, accompanied by growing hostility to inflation, does not cause a disastrous cumulative decline in real income (depression without deflation), it must eventually force labor somehow to become the residual claimant on the value of the product, in order to make profitable the replacement of the complemen-

5

tary assets labor requires, let alone permit any growth in the stock of such assets in response to society's saving preference.[7] (4) Substitution of the consumption process for the saving process *may* contribute to the elasticity of supply of assets as such. (See p. 145)

Subject to these considerations, property *may* be taken from investors for the benefit of workers, either by way of the strike threat or governmental power. But how effective in practice can such transfer attempts be? Answering this question demands remembering that when everyone expects property transfers of this kind to be attempted, the *long-term* elasticities of supply of complementary factors must be multiplied.

I shall argue that while taxation *can* have limited effects in bringing about property and income transfers from rich to poor, the strike threat cannot. Forcing up the price of labor in different firms, occupations or industries does not effect an income redistribution *from investors in general to workers in general*. Similarly, the forcing down of the price of labor in any field by threats of managements to order a work stoppage is equally bound to fail to enrich investors in general (at the expense of workers in general). The workers' "disadvantage in bargaining," their "inequality of bargaining power," the "perishability" of their labor, and so forth are relevant, I hold, only if we can assume that recruits to a trade can be somehow tricked by falsely represented prospects into specializing in that trade.

The only practically important case of monopsony (to be discussed in Chapter 8) involves some clear "shut-in" power. Yet even the Webbs, in two massive studies[8] (both special pleading for the union movement), have presented no *evidence* of "employers," in collusion or singly, ever deliberately and fraudently enticing employees into specialized occupations, with a view eventually to reducing their remuneration unfairly.

However, insofar as any firm or industry *can* attract and retain more workers by such methods, there will still be no redistribution of income caused *in favor of "employers" as a whole or against the interests of "labor" as a whole*. For *other* "employers" will then be forced to pay more for the labor for which *they* bid. If we assume that one set of occupations engrosses more labor than is just, we must assume that the rest are left with less than is just.

For identical reasons, if the entrepreneurs who have provided specialized resources in any particular field are, through wrong predictions, "exploited" by the use of strike power, other industries will have been robbed of that part of the capital which, given the reduced profits, ought not to have been invested in the "exploited" field. *Ceteris paribus* yields to capital elsewhere must be correspondingly higher.

The effect of wage rates determined under labor union pressure is, I shall insist, to distort society's production structure, while it causes no redistribution whatsoever in favor of the poorer classes as such. The only income transfers that the use of strike power can effect are (1) in favor of those employed in one occupation at the expense of those in others[9], or (2) in favor of workers as such when entrepreneurs generally have failed to forecast

6

the extent to which, as investors, they will be subjected to duress-imposed costs.

When a wage rate is raised so as to price some part of potential output higher than consumers are prepared to pay, the wage gain is partly at the expense of workers who would otherwise have found their most remunerative employment in that trade; partly, of course, it is at the expense of consumers in general; but hardly ever (and I shall be developing this point at some length) is it at the expense of those who provide *complementary resources*—i.e., the assets which, in general, multiply the yield to effort. It is consumers who ultimately pay wages; and when the market value of output of any kind is forced (whether by the right to strike or through legal enactment) above the level which the free market would have determined, the effect is, in general, actually to harm the poorer classes disproportionately. This "regressive"[10] consequence is aggravated because the process keeps (in the long run) a large segment of the work force in low-productivity and low-paying jobs; or (in the short run) forces workers into short-time jobs and (encouraged by unemployment compensation) into idleness. Hence the effect of the strike-threat system upon the distribution of the wages flow is to render it less equitable.

Through the consequences of the strike-threat system upon the composition of the assets-stock, and the nature of the employment outlets available, the flow of output as a whole and hence aggregate real income will be reduced. And, because *all* must admit that it is highly improbable that any *substantial* redistribution of the shrunken real income in favor of labor has ever been thereby effected,[11] obviously *the system has all along been reducing the flow of real wages and the average of real wage rates*.

In the "classical" theory of wages, as it had evolved at Cambridge in the pre-Keynesian era (by which I mean before publication of J. M. Keynes's *General Theory of Employment, Interest and Money* in 1936), the issues which I have discussed in this chapter were *virtually* ignored. On the points which concern society most seriously, exposition was hopelessly contradictory for this reason. An inherent part of Alfred Marshall's imposing synthesis of the "orthodoxy" of his age was the marginal productivity theory of wage-rate determination. This was clear, for instance, when he criticized Cliffe Leslie who (in attempting to justify strike-threat actions)[12] had, Marshall showed, failed to understand why competition tended to establish *equivalence of net advantageousness in labor's earnings*. Yet other passages in Marshall's writings appear to me to have been quite inconsistent with the insight he showed in his reference to Leslie.

This criticism applies, I suggest, particularly to Marshall's discussion of what has been called the "range of indeterminateness" under bilateral monopoly;[13] for the circumstances imagined relate to the problem of income distribution, I maintain, *only under the assumption of wrong predictions*. And I find that his contemporaries and successors who have relied upon similar kinds of reasoning have never stated this assumption—either explicitly or implicitly.

Marshall does recognize, through his notion of "derived demand," that consumers ultimately employ all the resources used. But does not his analysis treat only the particular case? For one thing, it shows that consumers are the more exploitable the greater the inelasticity of demand[14] for the output happens to be. For another, it indicates that the suppliers of fixed and circulating capital *who have failed to anticipate and discount typical trade-union practices* (the vital qualification which Marshall does not specifically make) are more exploitable (a) the fewer the alternative uses there happen to be for the assets they have provided, (b) the smaller the proportion of labor cost to the total cost of the output, and (c) the fewer the opportunities of replacing existing employees by others (for example, strikers by blacklegs) or by labor-economizing machinery or organization.

I contend that Marshall's analysis does not explicitly recognize that the power of the strike threat to raise wage rates (in particular industries) depends also upon the degree to which majorities within unions are indifferent about injustices caused to minorities. Concern for the interests of union members who may be displaced into inferior employments (and possibly forced into temporary unemployment) through duress-imposed costs may curb the extravagance of strike-threat demands. But Marshall does perceive that unions will try not to drive too many firms into insolvency. Yet he does not expressly refer to the condition that *the consumer* will be more exploitable the more effectively the firms supplying any output can act collusively in raising prices to consumers and rely upon the unions to protect them from the competition of nonunion labor.

Hence the possibilities covered by Marshall fail to show how manipulation of the strike threat can influence the division of the value of the product of industry between "employers" and "employed." *For in the economic system as a whole typical strike-threat activities are expected at least to continue, if not to extend, in scope. They are therefore allowed for in every business decision, and this is the overriding consideration in almost every context.*

Marshall's lack of rigor on the labor issue raises a question of great sociological interest. In his *Economics of Industry* he *seems* to imply (without clearly referring to the strike threat) that workers as a whole gain through their unions. He says that their power "to sustain high wages depends chiefly on the influence they exert on the character of the workmen themselves. . . ." If this means that the unions increase personal efficiency so that the market value of the workmen is higher, the question is *how* the unions manage to do so. Exploiting the consumer and excluded workers could, of course, take away, in Marshall's words, "that want and fear of hunger which depressed the physique and moral character of the working class," *on the part of the exploiters*; but as it would further depress those exploited, it is difficult to see how the "working class" as a whole could benefit. He goes on to say, "Unions have been at once a chief product and a chief cause of this constant elevation of the standard of life: where that standard is high, unions have sprung up naturally; where unions have been strong, the standard of life has generally risen."[15] That unions have been *a product*, of which more has in fact been

8

acquired when the standard of living generally has been rising, is beyond question. But overcoats and bicycles and cars and television sets have also been products of which more has been acquired as standards of living have risen. Hence it is quite another matter to claim that living standards generally have risen *because* the unions have been strong, or *because* people generally have more overcoats or bicycles. Marshall refers also to the unions compelling employers to treat the worker "as an equal with something to sell that they (the employers) wanted to buy."[16] Of course union officials who are allowed to use the strike threat will be treated courteously by managements, as will their tax assessors. But will management's fears of a union's powers enable its members to raise their earnings without exploiting people poorer than themselves? Marshall did not face this sort of question with frankness; nor, in my judgment, have most subsequent economists.

To sum up. When the owners of assets or the suppliers of labor anticipate the possibility or likelihood of "exploitation," as they will if society permits attempted "exploitation," they will be unexploitable. Neither the providers of assets nor the providers of effort and skill are *exploitable* by one another (a) unless the former fail to predict and allow for the full cost consequences of future strike threats when they choose their investments, or (b) unless the latter fail to predict the wage-rate consequences of lockout threats or monopsonistic action by the hirers of labor when choosing and preparing for specialized employment. To me it seems unchallengeable that, because during the past half century or more the strike-threat influence has obviously been increasing, *investors* must on the whole have predicted the cost implications and hence have been *virtually* unexploitable. I use the word "virtually" because whether they have overestimated or underestimated the cost effects of strike power is difficult to judge. But if my reasoning is valid, *the major consequences of society's tolerance of the strike-threat system must have been simply a slowing down of the rate of increase in aggregate income, to the disadvantage of both participants, and with no discernible change in the proportion in which income is shared between "capital" and "labor".*[17]

If this argument is acceptable, the policy implications are far-reaching. The strike-threat system must be recognized as intolerable in a civilized age; for it can be observed to be blocking the path to the maximization of the wages flow, the achievement of optimal equality and equity in the distribution of that flow, and the designing of an institutional framework to ensure security of employment without inflation.

I *could* end this book here. The simple argument I have presented *ought* to be sufficient to convince economists and policymakers. Unfortunately, I can anticipate a host of objections, some seriously advanced, other casuistic or obscurantist. Accordingly, the remaining chapters are devoted to meeting such objections as I have been able to find in academic literature devoted to the subject.

9

NOTES

[1] Investors in assets retained *may already have been exploited*. At the reduced value of such assets, their retention implies the prediction of no further exploitation.

[2] "Monopsony" (adjective, "monopsonistic") means "monopolistic buying."

[3] The awful word, "oligopsony" (adjective, "oligopsonistic"), may be defined at this stage as "tacit monopsony" to distinguish it from "collusive monopsony."

[4] Collusive action among firms to resist "the strike in detail" (the "whipsaw") is another matter. I deal with it on p. 47.

[5] "Elasticity of supply" refers to the relative facility with which productive services of men or of assets can transfer to other uses without a material decline in their value. The smaller any such loss of value in alternative uses, the greater will be the elasticity of supply.

[6] Some economists may at first be inclined to challenge this assertion. It will be discussed vigorously in Chapter 10, passim.

[7] That is, as is to be explained later, the workers will be forced to hire or rent the fixed assets they need and to pay interest on the circulating capital because the owners of assets will only make them available on those terms.

[8] Sidney and Beatrice Webb, *The History of Trade Unionism* and *Industrial Democracy* (London: Longmans Green and Co., 1920).

[9] Because, as we are about to see, when duress-imposed labor costs in any activity reduce the number of workers who can be profitably employed in it, the number of workers who must compete for employment in other activities is increased, while as consumers all other workers will be disadvantaged.

[10] A tax is said to be "regressive" when the proportion of the tax to the taxpayer's income is greater the smaller his income. Thus import and excise duties and sales taxes are obviously regressive.

[11] I use the work "substantial" because *in this context* I am relying upon empirical evidence (see chapter 16). In the light of the general case argued in this chapter and the rest of the book, the word "substantial" could be omitted.

[12] Cliffe Leslie was one of a group of writers on wage questions (of whom the others were Thornton, Longe and Fleeming Jenkins) who had tried to show how union initiatives could enable a redistribution of income in labor's favor. They had a considerable influence on John Stuart Mill during the last years of his life, when he was contemplating entry, and after his entry, into politics. I have discussed their contributions in my *Theory of Collective Bargaining* (Glencoe, Ill.: Free Press, 1954).

[13] "Bilateral monopoly" means, in this context, "monopsony" (see above footnotes) among the purchasers of labor and monopoly (a union) among the

suppliers of labor. Under such conditions there is no market determination of the price of labor.

[14] The demand for a thing is said to be "inelastic" when a change in its price will have little influence on the amount of it that will be purchased.

[15] Alfred Marshall, *Economics of Industry* (London: Macmillan, Ltd., 1909), p. 389.

[16] Ibid., pp. 388-9.

[17] *Within* the category "labor" there must have been a consequential *regressive* redistribution (see footnote 10 and below pp. 168, et. seq.).

2

Objections to the Thesis –
Preliminary Discussion

IN THIS and subsequent chapters, I propose to consider whether there are any arguments advanced in the formidable literature of the labor movement which might upset the reasoning briefly submitted in Chapter 1.

The most likely objection can be put as a question. Am I seriously asserting that the unorganized employee needs no protection of any kind over and above the protection of the courts, which can enforce an employment *contract*? Am I suggesting that "unilateral bargaining" can bring about justice in contractual remuneration, even in the presence of the inherent monopsony of a large corporation, oligopsony in bargaining for labor, and the possibility of unprovable collusion between corporations? Am I suggesting that the "bargaining table" is purposeless? Or am I contending that the notions of "labor's disadvantage in bargaining" or of "labor's inequality of bargaining power," which set the tone of current textbook discussion of the issue, have no meaning?

I can at once remove one possible source of misunderstanding by answering the last question first. If the phrase "disadvantage in bargaining" is interpreted to mean "disadvantage in respect of knowledge of alternative employment opportunities," or "disadvantage in respect of knowledge of legal rights," or "disadvantage because an individual (perhaps typically) lacks the necessary resources for enforcing his legal rights," I agree that such disadvantages may exist. But I propose to show that "capital" as a whole cannot benefit at the expense of "labor" as a whole through this possibility.[1] I further agree that a labor union may provide the required knowledge of employment opportunities, supply the expertise and the finance to assist an individual to take advantage of those opportunities, and protect an individual's rights before the law regarding the wage contract as well as facilitate his recourse to the courts when necessary. In Chapter 8, I suggest how such functions may be assumed, discuss the role of the "bargaining table" in that process, and try to deal both rigorously and realistically with the monopsony issue. But I shall try to show that the individual worker can be said to need protection against stockholders (providers of assets) *in no other sense*.

12

This does not mean that I am impervious to the possibility of managerial tyranny. Injustices may, indeed, arise under *all* forms of administration. Executives invested with disciplinary powers under "private enterprise" may abuse their privilege, as may government officials entrusted with similar powers. Hence, I do not dismiss the common and genuine fear that managers can "dictate" to those they manage—with the penalties of dismissal, demotion, or pay deductions at their service. Indeed, I fully understand why workers need some counterforce to insure common justice. Moreover, I appreciate the origin of the claim that labor should have the right to participate in management and appoint some of the managers. In Chapter 6, I discuss the sanctions for managerial authority; the question of managerial tyranny; the settlement of "grievances;" and the demand so often made for "labor's participation in management."

Some critics at this stage may object that my argument seems to be blind to the lessons of history; that it overlooks the distressingly low earnings and the appallingly bad working conditions which existed before unions acquired the powers they wield today; that it ignores the benefits which union pressures have obtained in the way of greater leisure, paid holidays, pension schemes, sickness pay, disability insurance, severance pay, and similar benefits. I expect to be told that the unions had to fight for years for all these things, and only through the eventual capitulation of the "employers," did workers finally win these "fringe benefits." Chapters 3 and 14 are devoted to these questions.

Economists who have not yet discarded the Keynesian yoke will feel that my reasoning has so far ignored the dynamic consequences which follow the lowering of wage rates by market pressures. This process, they contend, exterminates purchasing power, reduces "aggregate demand," and brings developing depression and cumulative unemployment in its train. My reply to this issue can be found in two of my books.[2] It is unnecessary for me to return to the subject. The idea that market-selected price or wage rate adjustments generate recessions and help retard productive activity is fallacious.

But the most fundamental objection I anticipate is that the institutions of the market mechanism are inherently defective. I expect to be told that the "invisible hand" cannot be relied upon to produce industrial peace, just prices, equitable wage rates, or security in respect of earnings and employment. I shall accordingly try to show that *what we call "the market" provides the only conceivable means of achieving either orderliness and the elimination of coercive action in the process of human cooperation, or results which are regarded intuitively as "just" by the overwhelming consensus among free peoples.* And I shall show, for example in Chapter 10, that wage rates, like other prices, perform a crucial coordinative role in any planned and rationally coordinated economy, while determination of prices under the threatened warfare of the strike threat constantly disrupts the economy.

I expect skepticism from business managers, especially those who have been actually engaged in wage negotiation. They are likely to be bewildered by my contention that investors are unexploitable when there is general ac-

13

quiescence in the strike-threat system. They will know only too well that the outcome of negotiations with unions can seriously affect dividends. The apparent paradox is discussed in Chapter 10.

Nevertheless, my suggestion that the strike-threat system is intolerable in an enlightened age will no doubt raise grave misgivings about the full implications in the minds of some sympathetic readers. They will, I know, be asking themselves: If a corporation has the legal right at any time to lay off any number of its personnel—even the whole of its staff—how can a parallel legal right be justly denied for the whole staff to withdraw their labor at any time? As Lord Jeffrey in 1825 aptly put the issue:

> A single master was at liberty at any time to turn off the whole of his workmen at once—100 or 1000 in number—if they would not accept the wages he chose to offer. But it was made an offense for the whole of the workmen to leave the master at once if he refused to give the wages they chose to require.[3]

How inequitable such a law sounds when so described.[4] But if we perceive the significance of the fact that "the master" (or "the employer") is *the residual claimant* on the value of the product, and "the worker" *the contractual claimant,* it can be shown that there is nothing whatsoever unjust in the arrangement envisaged. The distinction is discussed in Chapter 6. But at present its relevance can be briefly indicated as follows.

Had it happened to be a tolerable division of function for the workers (that is, the suppliers of effort and skill) to accept the residual share, they would automatically have had the right, in a "no-strike" regime, to refuse to employ complementary assets except on terms no more costly than the alternatives open to the suppliers of those assets. The workers would have had thereby no power to exploit the other parties to production because it would have been unprofitable for them to offer less for the services of complementary assets needed than those services could command in alternative uses. Similarly, *assuming the absence of collusion or abuse of monopsonistic power*, an "employer" has no power to exploit the workers because *he will always have an incentive to offer sufficiently favorable wage rates and conditions of employment to retain or attract all employees the values of whose inputs are judged likely to fall short of the corresponding output values.*[5]

Under democratic institutions, *the residual claimant* must try to determine the market price of inputs and to offer or accept that price. In the case of his offer for labor, he will have *an interpretative discretion,* exactly as he will in charging output prices. But under our present assumptions, it will be just as much beyond his powers to influence the labor input prices determined by the workers' alternative employment opportunities as it will be for him to influence the prices it will be most profitable for him to charge in the market for outputs. *Failure by labor leaders to comprehend this simple truth has, I believe, resulted in harm to the industrial workers' material well-being the world over.*

14

In part the difficulty labor's friends have had on this point has been because of their belief that the worker has been barred from possible alternatives by ignorance and lack of means. Now just as there is a frustrated incentive for an underpaid worker (who does not have the means) to seek out employments remunerated at what his services are worth to consumers, so is there an effective incentive for entrepreneurs (who have the means) to seek out underpaid labor anywhere in the economy. Let us suppose, then, that a firm employing a large number of workers, knowing that they possess virtually no savings, suddenly requires them all, as a condition for continued employment, to bind themselves to a long-term contract at wage rates much less favorable than the alternatives which they, the workers, would have been able to find had they enjoyed some means of subsistence while seeking those alternatives. Will not "the employers" then have the power to exploit? The essence of the situation imagined rests in the assumed ability of "the employers" to enforce a long-term contract; for otherwise competing entrepreneurs (who *have* the means) would gradually connect the "underpaid" workers with the alternatives we have assumed. Hence the case under consideration is, strictly speaking, excluded by our assumption of the absence of monopsonistic abuse (in the example, exploitation through a "lock-in contract"). Such a possibility is discussed in Chapter 8, on monopsonistic abuse, where the reader will, I think, conclude that the circumstances envisaged are of theoretical interest only. Even so, a simple rule will be suggested to exclude the possibility of any exploitation of the kind we have been discussing (see pp. 101-102). The possibility of exploitation by "employers" in the *absence* of monopsony (or oligopsony) is considered in Chapter 5.

The argument against my thesis which I find most difficult to answer is that which admits the existence of serious abuses associated with the strike-threat system but does not see them as its inevitable concomitant. In practice, it is said, little harm is caused when groups of workers agree in concert on the terms of a labor contract. It is not *the strike* as such which must be condemned but flagrant abuses which characterize the unions through which the striking power is wielded. All that needs to be done, it is suggested, is to withdraw the unions' right (a) to prevent any person who is prepared to accept less than the rest (say, to insure his employment in a post he wants or to improve his prospects) from doing so; or (b) in the event of a concerted withdrawal of labor, to prevent by physical force or threats, or in any way to hinder, the employment of strikebreakers. The critics I am discussing identify the root evils in contemporary labor unionism in the privileged position before the law which labor union leaders have secured, a situation which has enabled them to resort to threats or physical violence to achieve their aims. Critics of this persuasion do not fear the consequences of the use of the price mechanism, via collusion, to substitute private objectives for market objectives. Condemning favors governments have granted to the "labor bosses," they tend to stress (particularly in the United States) the corruption at municipal, county, state and federal resulting from "campaign contributions"—in short, the buying of votes in legislatures in return for union privileges. Such critics cite abuses such as the bribery of juries and annuities to *retired* judges, as though for services rendered. Sometimes they point to (a) the deplorable *quality* of the men who have been attracted into union leadership—the dubious character of many of the so-called "labor bosses"—the Hoffas and the Glimcos; (b) the indefensible methods of achievement and retention of power on which they have relied; (c) the not-uncommon maladministration of pension and other funds for the private benefit of union officials and their friends; (d) the alleged totalitarian form of union government and the tyrannical powers possessed by the labor union hierarchy against their own members, who seem to have no effective remedy; (e) the injustices and general denial of individual freedom under the "closed shop" or the "union shop;" (f) the seeming lack of genuine concern on the part of union leaders for the rights of those persons, classes, and races who are excluded from any effective sharing in the employment opportunities offered in many occupations; (g) and the typical indifference of union leaders to the public interest generally and the interests of those who are not parties to any dispute.

Such critics perceive the wastes of "demarcations," "featherbedding," "make-work" rules generally, "established differentials," etc., which certain unions have imposed upon the economic system. They condemn "unofficial strikes," yet accept the "official" use of strike-threat power as tolerable. But they regard the abuses as eradicable without any assault on the right to strike.

These alleged abuses may well be indicative of something basically wrong in today's labor institutions. But *it is strike-threat activity as such, as it would be in the absence of the practices just mentioned, which I shall be calling in question.* There is no special significance in such methods of seeking sectional objectives. I shall try to show that every maintenance or increase of labor costs resulting from practices enforced through union pressures yield the same sort of economic consequences.

I do not wish, then, to minimize the importance of any of the "abuses" just mentioned. But they *seem* to be the inevitable consequences of an intolerable system. One of the most disturbing aspects of labor unionism *in its present form* is manifested in an apparent lack of sympathy on the part of the movement and its leadership for the welfare and dignity of the workers *as a whole.* No disinterested student can be blind to the truth that the dominating concern of each union is the immediate interests of its own members. In the words of a leading British "Labor" politician (quoted above, p. viii), its aims are "antisocial." The use of the strike threat to enforce "the rate for the job" denies persons of *inferior abilities, or of undeveloped initial abilities,* the right of effective access to the bargaining table and the opportunity of full and free development.[6] Indeed, the worst injustices of the system are borne by minorities, sometimes discernible and sometimes undiscernible minorities, who are occasionally forced (through compulsory membership and the check-off) to finance their own detriment.

I must anticipate also the objection that I ignore the more positive sides of labor union activities. But I have simply chosen to concentrate on the principal purpose of the unions, namely, the use of the strike threat and the strike.

Certainly labor organizations undertake other functions, not all of which are necessary concomitants of the organization of strike power. Their "friendly society" activities, which fall into this class, could be assumed, however, by purely voluntary associations, the members being bound by contract only. However, because the unions exist, it may well be that they are the most appropriate institutions for these purposes.[7]

But unions have become an integral part of a free economy in other ways. They provide essential machinery for the wage-bargaining process, which would probably still need to be carried on by intermediaries in the absence of the strike threat. The role of unions under "no strike bargaining" is discussed on pp. 111-112. Hence because I shall refer only incidentally and occasionally to the beneficial aspects of actual labor union activity, I must make it clear that I do not dismiss the more positive side of union functions. *The union framework has, become an indispensable part of the institutional apparatus of this age. But the private use of coercive power in determining the price of labor is not a necessary concomitant of unionism, although it is its overriding purpose at present.* What I shall call the unions' "noncontroversial" role (apart from their "welfare" activities) is concerned mostly with upholding the "rule of law" or "due process" in the exercise of managerial discipline (discussed in Chapter 6) and with advice, assistance, and finance to union members in their task of seeking out the best employment outlets for the skills and other valuable attributes of union members, discussed in Chapter 8.

NOTES

[1] See pp. 101, et. seq.

[2] W. H. Hutt, *Keynesianism—Retrospect and Prospect* (Chicago: Henry Regnery Co., 1963), passim; W. H. Hutt, *Politically Impossible. . . . ?* (London: Institute of Economic Affairs, 1971), Part V.

[3] Quoted approvingly in Webb, *History of Trade Unionism* (London: Longmans Green and Co., 1920 edition), p. 72.

[4] The ancient common law of Britain which forbade "conspiracy" (reformulated in the 1799 and 1800 "Combination Acts" that Lord Jeffrey was condemning) was, I believe, based upon a remarkable insight into the principle that people as consumers are exploited when the prices of inputs or outputs can be collusively arranged—i.e., in the case of wage rates, fixed at above levels determined in the light of alternative employment opportunities. The same insight *should* have condemned equally collusion by "the masters" to force wage rates below free market levels *through somehow shutting off the alternative employments.* I am aware of no *evidence* that the collusive barring of alternatives ever occurred; but Adam Smith felt it to be unfair that (in the eighteenth century) the law of conspiracy did not condemn agreements among the masters to keep down labor's compensation. Between 1800 and 1824, however, such collusion among "employers" *was* of unquestioned illegality in Britain, as it ought to have been. In fact, the law may not have been effectively

enforced against the masters, through the secrecy of their collusive agreements. (See p. 34.)

[5] Expressed more rigorously, it will pay every "employer" to purchase labor's inputs (and complementary inputs) up to the point at which the marginal prospective yields from the corresponding outputs have fallen to the rate of interest.

[6] For the services of such persons *at their present quality* are priced out of each market protected by the standard rate.

[7] It was partly perception of this kind of usefulness which caused positive encouragement to be given to working-class associations by law and public opinion in Britain as the industrial revolution developed during the 18th century. Laws like the *Friendly Societies Act* of 1793 were intended to foster and facilitate group action on the part of wage-earners. Such laws were (as we shall see, pp. 111-112) seriously abused; but this does not detract from the fact that the organization of mutual support against the hazards of life was (and can still be) an excellent example of "cooperative" response to "needs," that is, a particular form of supply reacting to demand.

3
"Labor's Bitter Struggle"

IN THIS chapter I shall challenge some of the hardier myths that shroud the history of the strike threat.

The gradual increase in average real earnings that has been almost continuously enjoyed by the laboring, artisan, and white-collar classes over the last two centuries has never been the result of *growing* merit on their part. Nor can improvement in the average material condition of the people be attributed to any special changes in governmental power and policy over time (although governments naturally like to claim the credit). Still less can the rise in real working-class income per head be claimed to be the result of successful labor union activity which has redistributed income in favor of "the workers" and at the expense of investors. For one thing, those "unprotected," although often driven by "the standard rate" and union exclusiveness into relatively lower-paid occupations, have *otherwise* benefited more or less proportionately (see pp. 21-22, 245-247).

The improving real income of the wage-earning and salaried classes has been the consequence of (a) what I shall be calling the "economizing displacement" process, namely, managerial, technological and scientific ingenuities which have progressively displaced labor and assets from their existing employments, *thereby releasing effort and resources for providing additional—usually different—outputs,* and (b) thrift—the net *accumulation of output-yielding assets—resources which magnify the real yield to human effort.*

Society has learned how to replace and accumulate assets in an increasingly efficient form, and how to use the services of people in an increasingly efficient manner. The phrase "increasingly efficient" refers to (a) the composition of replacement and accumulation of assets, and (b) the organization of labor, *both occurring increasingly in economizing-displacement forms.* The achievement of given outputs with fewer workers, and with assets of reduced real value, is continuously rendering workers redundant in their existing occupations and specializations, and rendering assets obsolescent or obsolete in their existing form. This process is the most progressive dynamic

19

force in economic activity because, in releasing a proportion of people and assets from their existing occupations, it leaves them available for the production of additional real income. In the absence of governmental or private restraints on the utilization of the displaced productive power, it adds to the source of demands in general and, in turn, *raises the real values at which employment outlets can be profitably offered.* More productive use of labor, with a consequent rise in its real earning power, has resulted since the industrial revolution partly through improved arrangements or incentives for investment in human capital and, more important, through providing people with complementary assets and managerial direction that multiply the yield to the people's innate and developed abilities. This has been possible in most of cases only by overcoming inertias and contrivances that have tended to shut off access to wage-multiplying assets and economizing procedures.

Now unless the almost phenomenal rise of working-class affluence in the western world is recognized as having resulted because of this influence, the material progress experienced can easily lead to the naive inference that it must have been due mainly (or in part) to "a long and bitter struggle" manifested in a growing use of the strike threat. For instance, throughout the last century, the United States experienced a movement of workers from jobs offering relatively low *real* incomes to jobs of greater productivity and hence higher *real* incomes. There has been a movement of wage earners away from agriculture to urban and industrial pursuits; a movement from domestic service, including the domestic service of unpaid housewives, to industrial and commercial employments, a general movement from "unskilled" to "semiskilled" jobs and from "semiskilled" to "skilled" occupations, and so forth. The dynamic forces which have overcome the inertias and barriers to mobility in such adjustments are all consequences of the economizing-displacement process, and that has been due to entrepreneurial enterprise and acumen allied with technological progress and thrift. A rapidly accumulating stock of assets is the chief physical manifestation of the development.

Market forces tending to bring about the just-mentioned upward mobility have succeeded against an organized resistance which intensified as living standards rose. Union exclusiveness generally, featherbedding and other make-work practices, and, the most powerful, enforcement of *the standard rate* have provided the *chief* resistance to the wage-multiplying forces I have been discussing.

The phenomenon has been interpreted rather differently. Tibor Scitovsky sees it as "a changing pattern of *demand* [my italics] for people, with fewer positions available in the higher and more in the lower echelons." "The demand for skilled people," he says, "has declined relative to that of the unskilled, as has the demand for executives relative to that for clerks and for generals relative to privates."[1] Certainly emerging affluence appears to have caused a transfer of preference toward the outputs of labor-intensive occupations. But the egalitarian tendency to which Scitovsky is referring is, I judge, a question of supply rather than of demand. Unskilled workers are becoming relatively scarce and expensive. That is because so many of them (or their children) have succeeded in climbing to wage-rate levels at which, *through developing technologies, their productivities, their real natural scarcity values, are higher*. Equipment in various forms now permits a person without specialized training to do what required long periods of instruction and practice in earlier ages. Normal muscular strength, normal physical and mental health, integrity and trustworthiness—these qualities alone are today very valuable, without any special training and without exceptional talent. If an individual has more than one of these attributes, the value of his services is enhanced accordingly. And if elementary literacy and the ability to do simple calculations can be included in a bundle of such attributes, the value of the possessor's services is multiplied.[2] Many *specialized* skills are in less demand today than in the past (exceptions are largely in the entertainment field), but they have been displaced by demands for other, more general attainments. In the absence of some vertical mobility, the phenomenon that Scitovsky is discussing could not have occurred.

The reason for the rise in "working-class" earning power can be brought home by comparing it with the rise in the aggregate real value of the services of land. This aggregate value—the real income derived simply from ownership of land—tends to increase as the real value of aggregate output increases (that is, as the flow of productive services expands through economizing ingenuities accompanied by population growth and thrift). Early classical economists would have said that, through general progress, *landowners have been able passively to "reap where they have not sowed." But this is equally true of all classes of the community,* not just landowners. Except to the extent to which they have been discoverers, inventors, economizing innovators or savers, all groups, rich or poor, have "reaped where they have not sowed;" and they have not been forced to resort to collusive pricing to do this.

To see the phenomenon in perspective, let the reader consider that every site competes with every other site, every acre of land competes with every other acre; yet incomes from *passive* land ownership have risen as other incomes have risen (I do *not* say in proportion to other incomes). But nothing resembling the strike threat has influenced the value or rent of land. Admittedly, if the owners of sites around a developing town are allowed to act in collusion, they can *exploit* the community by raising the price of land needed for the town's growth. But that *illustrates* my point. If such collusion were effectively prevented, the landowners would not be unjustly treated. They would still benefit from the general progress, although not then to the disadvantage of the rest; and their benefit would be "unearned"! This is equally true of the community as a whole, including "labor."

Now it has seldom been to anyone's interest to draw attention to the real wage-rate increases of those classes which have been excluded from the best remunerated occupations (mainly excluded by standard rates determined under the strike threat). When people enjoy no union protection in the inferior occupations to which they have been relegated, their *real incomes* still tend to

21

rise steadily with the rise in general productivity, just as their *money incomes* tend to rise in accordance with the speed of inflation. As Albert Rees has put it:

> All . . . sources of information are biased . . . Newspapers and broadcasters give prominent coverage to wage increases resulting from strike settlements or from large scale negotiations because they are dramatic, while little attention is paid to the gradual upward creep of non-union wages. Small wonder that the public does not suspect that in this race the tortoise sometimes catches up with the hare.[3]

The evidence establishes, indeed, that the wholly "unprotected" wage earner, with no union to offset his supposedly inferior "bargaining power," gains proportionately as much from general economic progress as the wage earner in a "strong" labor union *unless exclusions enforced through strike-threat pressures* (or other causes) *are currently pushing him further down the scale of relative wage earnings*. That is, in the relatively low-productivity spheres to which the "unprotected" are often confined by the "protected," earnings tend to increase as rapidly as they do in the privileged spheres. Empirical studies disclose no clear correlation between the degree of unionization existing and the speed of wage-rate increases.[4] *The facts suggest that the workers' basic protection against exploitation is market forces*; in other words, the alternatives that are open to any person possessing scarce and valuable attributes—skills, muscles, intelligence, or responsibility. And this protection guarantees nonunion workers the highest possible earnings consistent with the non-exploitation of *others,* that is, of potential competitors and the community in its consumer role.

A curious fact is that at times the unions themselves appear to be pleading that incomes (including fringe benefits) in nonunionized occupations have risen *faster* than they have in unionized ones. The unions argue this casuistically to show the reasonableness of demands for higher wage rates for their members. But it is not without relevance to the claim that the strike threat can alone secure justice in remuneration.

Unfortunately most writing on this topic is emotion-charged. That is hardly surprising. The strike is a form of warfare (see Chapter 4) and the expectation of its use—as a fact or as a threat—has come to condition nearly all private policy in determining wage offers. The strike-threat system has created a species of continuous aggression and resistance to aggression; and as we shall see, union policymakers have felt it essential to keep alive an undamped suspicion of and lurking hostility toward management and investors. And just as exploiters of aggressive nationalism throughout time and space have always relied upon legends of past struggles for "freedom," so have union officials and their apologists found it useful to perpetuate the myths of "labor's bitter history." That these officials are most often deeply sincere in their beliefs is hardly a mitigation.

The genuineness of many of the influential and disinterested leaders of thought and opinion who have faith in the story of "labor's bitter struggle" against oppression is enormously important. For instance in the United States, when the Norris-LaGuardia and the Wagner acts were being passed, the public opinion to which Congress is sensitive reflected the conviction that, in the past, "labor" had been shamefully treated. Time-honored but virtually fictional stories of the inequities and iniquities of former days had been propagated and reiterated with conviction by public-spirited novelists, journalists, jurists, clergymen, and academics, as well as by parties seeking to exploit the myths. And the American labor legislation of the 1930s was endorsed, it seems to me, by people who simply wanted to turn the tables. Whereas until then "labor" had been downtrodden, it was now to be assured that it was to be top dog. All the old injustices, inequalities and exploitation were to be swept away. The power of "the employers" to oppress their workers was to be ended and an age of economic justice to be ushered in. Few economists in the United States who perceived the folly of the legislative steps then being taken could conceive of any effective manner in which to communicate their warnings. The most forthright was Henry Simons; but because his teachings did not conform to those of the opinion-molders, his view was that of a tiny minority.

The Norris-LaGuardia and Wagner acts will, I predict, come to be regarded by future historians as economic blunders of the first magnitude. They were worked for and acquiesced to under motivations of almost unparalleled sordidness and cynicism combined with the highest, misguided idealism. For the American worker had *not* been maltreated and oppressed by managements committed to satisfying the rapacity of stockholders. That was not true of the nineteenth century in either continent; it was not true of the pre-NRA era, and it has not been true since then. "Exploitation" there has certainly been, as we shall see, but hardly at all, *if* at all, of "labor" by "capital." And this is equally true of "labor" in all countries of the western world. Economic injustices have had a wholly different origin.

Among those who have been convinced that in past ages labor had to fight against exploitation and oppression, or who find it expedient to pose as convinced, we find today's "business community" in general. Executives who are wise and expert in the conduct of their functions in markets other than that for labor seldom appear to have any grasp of the economics of wages and no *trustworthy* knowledge of the history of labor relations and income distribution. The typical private entrepreneur, says Arthur Shenfield,[5] generally accepts

> the popular view of early capitalism that it was harsh, cruel and oppressive. Indeed he will often defend the capitalist system by saying that its early defects, and notably that of the exploitation of the worker, have now been removed, so that it is an efficient producer and distributor of wealth and at the same time guiltless of exploitation. He does not realize that there is essentially nothing in the

23

allegation of early capitalist exploitation which cannot be applied to modern capitalism. He thinks that the low wages and long hours of early capitalism bespoke exploitation, while the high wages and short hours of our times bespeak equity and humanity. He thus displays his ignorance of what it is that determines the general level of wages and hours. . . . Of course, the businessman is not to be blamed for accepting this view of early capitalism. It has been propagated by a long line of biased historians and publicists, and it is now common currency in almost all circles.

Unfortunately, in very few business schools or universities is it thought essential to disturb the stereotypes which have been so formed.[6] On the contrary, through most of the "labor economists" the legends are perpetuated.

The following pages are devoted to briefly examining the notions which have been propagated during this century about the oppression of the workers *in Britain* during the emergence of the modern industrial system, and the supposed fight of the unions on their behalf against tyranny, oppression, and injustice in the courts. I use Britain to illustrate because the tendentious writings of British historians such as the Webbs, the Hammonds, Cole, and others have colored the literature of "labor" in many countries.

Since medieval times, the conviction had persisted that it was the will of God that all, except for those in the privileged classes, should work from sunrise to sunset. "In the sweat of thy brow shalt thou eat bread" was unchallenged as a divine precept. The Sabbath was the Lord's provision for rest. It embodied the wisdom of the ages. It was almost unchallenged until industrial capitalism had got under way. Only then did technological inventions plus thrift begin to cause a remarkable magnification of the yield to effort and the emancipation of man from the struggle for physical survival.

The "economizing displacement" process which characterized the new industrialism was gradually able to render possible a quite general enjoyment of leisure, even by the lower income groups, through sacrifices which those groups would have felt were powerful deprivations in earlier times. And as labor-saving developments progressed, especially after 1790, the customary contribution of children to the family income of the poor, and the early education of children in industrial skills under parental discipline, were transferred from the squalor of the domestic system to the relatively satisfactory factory environment. Then, by reason of the very progress which had engendered this transition, the output of children became less necessary for the retention or rise of living standards. Machinery economized labor, competition among the workers in each occupation raised the real earnings of noncompetitors, and because the material well-being of the working class as a whole rose, a potentially more rapid increase in the *physical* welfare of the poorest classes could be sacrificed in return for excluding children from certain kinds of productive work.[7]

Labor's rising average living standard during the industrial revolution was marked less by increases in the *per capita wage rates* of which the records survive than by a rising proportion of workers coming to be employed in occupations offering higher real wage rates (a changed frequency distribution, a gradually increasing proportion of workers finding employment in the more productive and higher-paid kinds of work rather than an increase in wage rates for work of a defined type), the achievement of greater leisure, and the amelioration of working conditions, rural or urban. Such wage statistics relevant to that period as we have are, however, too meager to enable us to estimate *the speed* with which the masses were benefiting. We know that outputs of "wage goods" were increasing rapidly and steadily, e.g., bricks, which were used in building houses for the poor. And we know also that, despite continuous attempts to hinder the economizing displacement process, à la Luddism, the efficiency and the value of the stock of wage-multiplying assets increased. Hence although there must have been some dilution of rising *per capita* outputs and incomes, because of population increases, it appears to be beyond doubt that the workers benefited *absolutely*. Their material well-being probably improved more or less in proportion to that of other classes of the community. But certainly environments of home and workshop which had been inherited from the pre-*laissez-faire,* mercantilist era were steadily being improved. Then, in the light of a rapidly growing ability to produce, the traditional living and working conditions of the wage-earning classes came to be regarded for the first time as deplorable.

This remarkable upward adjustment in standards and hopes, reflecting a new humanitarianism, could well be regarded as emergent capitalism's outstanding attribute. So rapidly did the new (although partial) economic freedom cause people to change their judgments about what was tolerable that, in doing so, *it caused the very forces which were currently eradicating condemned conditions to be blamed for the existence of those conditions.*

It is almost platitudinous to say of any age since the eighteenth century that earnings were lower and working conditions had been less satisfactory in previous ages. We shall reach this conclusion whenever we compare any long historical period (say, a decade) with a later one and use the conventional standards of the latter as our criterion.[8] But that is because thrift, *plus* economizing displacement, *plus* discoveries have been continuously augmenting the yield to human effort. The living conditions of the masses in the 1920s were bad in relation to what they are now; they were even worse in the previous decade; worse still in the last century; and they worsen increasingly the further one moves back in time. Yet this does not allow us to say that there was any *unfairness* in early arrangements for wage determination *against which labor had to fight.* Such *injustices* as existed in previous ages were, as I have suggested, in a different form, but probably neither more common nor more reprehensible than those of today. And they did *not* arise out of the ability of owners of assets, or managements on behalf of investors, to oppress or steal from those who supplied labor inputs.

In the past, general standards of treatment and standards of consideration between different income groups, as well as between different social classes and races, were indisputably such as we should today find intolerable. Precapitalistic attitudes dissolved slowly under the pressures of the free market and competitive institutions. Persons of higher rank would behave arrogantly and peremptorily toward those of a lower rank. The cultured classes would not always cloak their disdain toward groups which lacked refinement of taste, education, bearing and behavior. The upper-middle and middle classes often openly despised "the great unwashed." Such attitudes alone were "institutional barriers" to equality of opportunity, and there were *some* deliberately planned and maintained barriers (more in Europe than in the United States—except for the institution of slavery), intended to preserve a way of life which the privileged and ruling classes thought was basically good. *But the relative economic inequalities of, say, the nineteenth century, were never the result of any power acquired by the owners of assets or by managements to maltreat or tyrannize over "the workers."*

The most persistent and tenacious myth about the origin of the strike-threat system is that it emerged out of a struggle of the poor against subjection by their "employers." The truth is that, with hardly any exceptions, it was relatively affluent artisans (by contemporary standards) who first organized for the collusive pricing of their labor. And their motive was, in every case, to defend their privileges—special rights which were contrary to the interests of the poorer classes (and in multiracial countries, poorer races). On this point, even the Webbs note: "It is often assumed that trade unionism arose as a protest against intolerable oppression. This was not so."[9] Labor unionism emerged indeed in the form of a strongly class-conscious movement, expressing a determination to maintain a class structure. Throughout, this has been an unchallengeable attribute of the union form of organization.[10] The Webbs describe the union system as "strengthening the almost infinite grading of the industrial world into separate classes, each with its own distinctive ends, and each therefore exacting its own 'rent of opportunity' or 'rent of ability.' " *These last terms are skillful euphemisms for "privilege."* The defense of such privilege was, in the Webbs' words, "the common purpose" of nearly all eighteenth-century combinations.[11] Already, in that century, workers' "combinations" in Britain had resisted powerful equalitarian forces that were being released through the emergence of freer markets in most spheres. History records this not only in such evidence as we have of strike-threat action (then technically illegal) but in the evidence of petitions from workers' organizations asking the legislature for protection of their customary position (against unprivileged interlopers). The Webbs write, tendentiously, of the eighteenth-century unions having been forced into demanding protection because the industries in which their members were employed were menaced by "pauper labor." Actually, *the industries* in which union members were employed would have *prospered* had labor been recruited freely from less productive and less well-paid occupations, thereby releasing the "paupers" from their poverty. It was sheer sectional privilege for which the unions were asking protection. The interests of those referred to as "pauper labor" were regarded as of no importance, either by the unions or (in this context) by their famed defenders, the Webbs.

26

Now the method of maintaining the "grading into separate classes" (with the inequalities of opportunity associated with it) has not been *mainly* restrictive apprenticeship rules and such-like devices for discouraging investment in human capital among the underprivileged. Nor has the insistence in the present age upon the maintenance of "established differentials"[12] been relatively important (although this insistence *does* disclose the motivation). The principal method has been a simple insistence upon *the standard rate*.[13] It has been as a defense of the most blatant privilege that the objection has arisen to "pricing labor as though it were a commodity, and buying it in the cheapest market." Yet this objection has been elevated into what has almost become a respected ethical principle. This thesis is examined in Chapter 12.

One very shaky argument is that the emergence of unionism during the late eighteenth century was a reaction against great "monopsonies" (as we now call them) among the masters, with the power to exploit labor. Adam Smith referred to what he believed was a "tacit monopoly" among the masters to keep wage rates down. He noticed that the law did not prohibit masters from combining to lower the price of work although it did prohibit workmen from combining to raise it.[14] Nevertheless, it was the *tacit* combination of masters which he believed was widespread. "Particular combinations" (that is, formal agreements) among masters were, he thought, only "sometimes" entered into.

But Adam Smith's *evidence* of tacit combination was the *unpopularity* of masters who raised wage rates, evidence which suggests rather the normal competitive circumstances of the active world under which competing sellers, hoping that supply conditions are not changing to their disadvantage, regard price cutters with disfavor and reluctantly follow suit.

Regarding the "particular" combinations to keep down wage rates which Adam Smith alleged "sometimes" occurred, although "always conducted with the utmost silence and secrecy,"[15] there is no evidence of any such organization to be found in the secondary sources with which I am familiar or in official reports.[16] I believe that Adam Smith's judgment in dealing with this subject was vitiated by the same defect that George Stigler has held adversely affected Alfred Marshall, "a warm heart."[17]

Even the Webbs' presentation quotes no facts which might suggest the operation of formal monopsonies during the eighteenth and nineteenth centuries. Actually their explanation of the need for the protection of labor relies most often on the fact that "employers" had *not* combined. They refer, for example, to the craft guilds fighting for legislative protection "against the cutting down of their earnings by the *competing* capitalists."[18] This is of course the opposite of the monopsony allegation. If the masters were *competing* in the sale of the product, they were equally competing for the purchase of labor and materials. Hence they would have been tending to bid up the remuneration of the work force (actual or potential) as a whole, not to push it down.

But it is in respect of the history of judicial decisions under the common law and statute law against "conspiracy" or "combination" that the most serious fictions have arisen. Students have been indoctrinated with the belief that laws enacted in the interests of the relatively wealthy were applied over the ages; and that, increasingly as the industrial revolution progressed, these laws were enforced in a dastardly way—to suppress laudable attempts by organized labor to avoid injustices. Partisan textbook accounts of English experience of early strike-threat activities have created this wholly false impression.

We must notice at the outset that, as feudalism and serfdom disappeared during the last two centuries of the Middle Ages, and especially following the Black Death, associations of workers *for peaceful and lawful purposes* had been neither illegal nor discouraged. Nor were they ever illegal or discouraged in subsequent ages.[19] But from the thirteenth century, the conviction clearly emerged that certain antisocial practices *affecting the pricing of products (including the product of labor)* had to be restrained for the common good. Thus, practices known as "forestalling, engrossing and regrating" were forbidden by ordinances and statutes because these were supply and pricing procedures which were perceived to be exploiting the common people through the contriving of scarcities of food and necessities.

Now the common law cases and statutes concerned with the crime of "conspiracy" (dating from the thirteenth century) applied exactly the same principle in more general terms. "Conspiracy" or "combination," *words having an identical connotation until well into the nineteenth century,* were prohibited. Indictments generally read "conspiring, combining, confederating and agreeing." These notions covered any kind of action in concert which aimed at making products (including the product of labor) dearer (for the benefit of those who associated for that purpose) by agreements not to sell below stipulated prices.

The mere fact that the common law on this topic became explicit in statutes suggests that *attempts* fo fix prices in concert must have occurred deep back in history. And there is evidence of this as long ago as 1298, when an organization of coopers in London was prosecuted for having agreed to raise the price of hoops from one halfpenny and three farthings to one penny. And economic conspiracy cases which did *not* directly involve laborers or artisans have been noted as late as the eighteenth century. In 1773, the publicans of Westminster were believed to be conspiring to raise the price of beer. The authorities got word of this somehow, and the publicans were at once warned that if they raised the price collusively they would be prosecuted for *conspiracy*. And there are other examples of steps taken to prosecute for attempts to raise the price of *commodities* (as distinct from labor) by concerted action.

Collusive action to raise the price of labor was, then, regarded as pernicious only in the sense that agreements to raise the price of food or necessities (such as salt) were considered pernicious. The spirit of the law seems never to have been hostile to artisans as such, still less to the laboring masses. Its hostility was directed against what I like to call "the contrived scarcity."

Cases such as those brought against London carpenters in 1339[20] and against shoemakers in 1349 certainly seem to have had the aim of preventing specific commodity prices from being forced up.

One thing which makes the preindustrial revolution era rather difficult to interpret is a blatant inconsistency in this respect. Merchant and craft guilds, constituted by charter, had the explicit right to act in a manner which would have been criminal, under the common law and certain statutes, had it not been for the protection of a charter. Wyclif accused the guilds of conspiring "that no man practicing their craft shall take less payment daily than that they have agreed among themselves," and that "they oppress other men who are in the right" (meaning that these others were prepared to work for less).[21] But the guilds were protected by charter. The anomaly can probably be explained in terms of pre-eighteenth-century conservatism. Unsettling change could be prevented by way of protection of a privileged status quo (and this policy took the form among other things of encouragement of craft and merchant guilds) as well as through the prevention of any *new* privileges which seemed likely to arise. *Revolutionary changes* were feared. By the middle of the eighteenth century, however, the guilds had largely lost their power, and rather different forms of organization—labor unions of the modern type—emerged as "friendly societies."

A supplementary policy, developed following the Black Death, was that embodied in wage-fixing by authority and, following the Elizabethan Statute of Artificers, generally bolstering up the guild system. Important provisions of this statute had, however, the effect of enforcing adherence to contract. An artisan wishing to transfer to another master required a testimonial certifying that he had carried out his obligations to the master he was leaving. In some cases the employee was bound by contract until a specific piece of work had been completed, for example, "any ship, house or mill or any work taken by the gross or piece."[22] If he left before then, his master could claim damages fixed in the statute.

Recourse to special statutes to outlaw "conspiracy" *in particular trades* seems to have been mainly because really effective enforcement of the *common law* (when there was no exoneration through guild privilege) had seemed beyond the administrative machinery of the courts until modern times. Common law cases had to be heard by judges and hence were costly. They were time-consuming. By reason of long delays, artisans charged could often escape trial by moving to other districts where they could seldom be traced. Statute law cases, on the other hand, could be dealt with expeditiously by justices. That is why we found "masters," in the emergent industries of the seventeenth and eighteenth centuries, petitioning Parliament for *explicit statutory protection* against "conspiracy" for their own industries or trades.[23] In Britain, as a whole, some 40 such statutes were repealed in 1824. But before then enforcement of common and statute law in this sphere seems to have been curiously casual. Moreover, as I have already insisted, conspiracy law was *not* aimed primarily at labor.[24]

It is extremely difficult to judge how effective the common law together with general and particular statutes against conspiracy had been before the Industrial Revolution got underway. The domestic system of manufacture, which dominated until well into the nineteenth century, probably meant that members of any trade were *usually* too scattered to be able to act in effective collusion, whether by restrictive agreement or intimidation of nonconformists. Moreover, the distinction between masters and men was often ambiguous. Such conditions, rather than laws against conspiracy, may help explain the apparent rarity of strike action before 1824.

Nevertheless, the problem to which these laws were believed to offer a solution seems to have increased in importance during the late eighteenth century, probably because of the gradual emergence of labor unions in the modern sense in the relatively highly-paid crafts and occupations, and their apparent growing activity.[25] Unions were "friendly societies" concerned with the commendable task of insuring their members against the worst consequences of sickness or unemployment.[26] This was the more conspicuous side of their activities but probably not the most important. Indeed, it seems that their insurance funds were often more in the nature of strike funds. Where apprenticeship had survived, they enforced the rules under some protection from the otherwise virtually moribund Elizabethan Statute of Artificers. Some "friendly societies" were trying to maintain, even at that time, what is today called "the closed shop." In the light of rising sophistication during the eighteenth century, the harm done may well have been becoming more conspicuous. For instance, Adam Smith pointed out that the wool-combers were able, by refusing to take a reasonable number of apprentices, not only to "engross the employment, but reduce the whole manufacture into a sort of slavery to themselves, and raise the price of their labour above what is due to the nature of their work."[27]

Already, throughout the eighteenth century, despite evidence that the demand for leisure as such was tending to fall, some of the unions had perceived that, when artisans were remunerated by time instead of by the piece, to enforce by way of the strike threat a reduction of the hours of labor was an effective method of reducing the supply of effort and raising aggregate remuneration. Other restrictions of output were also imposed. The rules of a society would specify the amount of output to be supplied daily or weekly by the worker. At times, these methods drove industries away from where they had been originally located.

The Webbs suggest, however, that in the *eighteenth century*, the common law was "constrained" to convict striking workers. They present no clear evidence of any such "constraint." The facts suggest (1) that the tradition of no discrimination against labor was maintained, and (2) that there was considerable leniency in the administration of the existing laws when the alleged offense occurred in the form of strikes or strike preparations. This was partly because of lingering guild influences and possibly because the unions did not represent the masses but what the socialist William Thompson later called (in 1827) "bloody aristocracies" of labor.

As evidence of leniency, we can consider the fact that although combinations in the cotton trade had been forbidden *by statute* as early as 1749, cotton spinners were obviously strongly organized in the 1790s and a force with which manufacturers had to reckon. Again, London tailors were prosecuted under the common law in 1765; yet they remained organized and further prosecutions against them had to be instituted in 1770 and 1783.

As evidence that the common law doctrine remained neutral, we can consider the 1783 case against these tailors. It was in these proceedings Lord Mansfield, one of Britain's greatest judges, rendered a famous judgment. The most pertinent passage of the decision reads,

> Persons in possession of any articles of trade may sell them at such prices as they individually may please, but if they confederate and agree not to sell them under certain prices, it is conspiracy; so every man may work at what price he pleases, but a combination not to work under certain prices is an indictable offence.[28]

Obviously this interpretation was aimed against *all* classes of lawbreakers not just striking journeymen. But from the beginning of the nineteenth century, the Webbs maintain, organized workers were subjected to even worse treatment through hostile court interpretations of both common and statute law, and especially of a notorious act of 1799 which had been followed by an amending act of 1800.

Now the actual effect of these two acts was simply to make more explicit what had indeed been the law during four centuries or more. But nearly all writers on this topic, the Webbs being most influential, have represented the "Combination Acts" as the legislative outcome of a sort of conspiracy among "employers" or "capitalists." Actually the reverse is the truth. The 1799 Act came to be passed *almost by accident*. Indeed, so casually were both acts enacted that, in Sir James Fitzjames Stephen's *History of the Criminal Law,* we are told that "there is no account of any debate on these Acts, nor are they referred to in the 'Annual Register' for these years."[29] What actually happened in 1799 was that a bill, more or less in the form of the 40 or so other anticombination statutes already applying to particular trades, was introduced in Parliament. The original aim in 1799 was simply to forbid "conspiracy" on the part of *millwrights*. During the proceedings Wilberforce (the famous antislavery champion) suddenly and unexpectedly moved for an amendment to make the principle apply to *all* industries and occupations. There seemed to be no good reason for opposing this amendment and the bill became law with little opposition. No one spoke against the Act on principle, although some thought that too much power was being given to the lower courts. Some *unimportant* changes were introduced the following year in the amending Act.[30]

The important point to remember is that the new combination laws did not make any activities illegal which had not already been criminal offenses for centuries. They were, writes Donald Dewey, "thought to incorporate no new legal principle but were rather designed to improve the cumbersome enforcement procedure which largely nullified the usefulness of a conspiracy prosecution."[31] Yet they are described as "severe," as inaugurating "a new and momentous departure," "a far-reaching change of policy," an era of "legal persecution" of would-be strikers or strikers. These are descriptions of the acts by Sidney and Beatrice Webb, in a seriously slanted work characterized at times by meticulous scholarship—a work which has had an enormous influence in spreading the myth.[32] The truth is, however, that the "Combination Acts" were just as leniently, almost half-heartedly, enforced as the common law against conspiracy (and the various special statutes forbidding conspiracy or combination in particular industries) had previously been.

Although the costs of proceedings against strikes or against observed preparations for strikes had probably been cheapened by the 1799 Act, the law retained much uncertainty. In the case of convictions by J. P.'s, appeals to the upper courts became almost habitual; and the judges, as is not unknown today, seemed to enjoy showing their authority and superior grasp of the law by upsetting the decisions of their inferiors. The penalties which could be imposed in the lower courts were much lighter than in the upper courts, but whether the likelihood of convictions when the law had been broken was increased (with a consequent rise in respect for the law) is problematical. The Parliamentary agent who drafted the 1824 Act which repealed these laws (who claimed with good reason that this branch of law had been "his particular study for twenty years") maintained that the effects of the combination laws had been "negligible"—a "dead letter."[33] Very few prosecutions had been made under them, he said, but many under the clause of the Statute of Artificers, which forbade any worker to leave his job before the completion of certain specified kinds of work, like a ship or a bridge. Otherwise, such prosecutions of strikers as occurred tended rather to be based on the charge of "conspiracy" under the common law.

The truth seems to be that the masters and the authorities did almost everything within their power to *avoid* prosecutions. A strike of linen weavers in 1823 lasted 28 weeks before the masters drew the attention of the strikers to the provisions of the 1800 Act. We must remember that masters could also be prosecuted under the combination laws, just as they could for conspiracy under the common law; and there was nothing to prevent the workers' leaders from drawing the attention of the magistrates to alleged transgression by the masters.

Some of the facts which point to the leniency in administering the law, both previously and subsequently to the Combination Acts, are *mentioned* by the Webbs.[34] Nevertheless, they manage to leave the impression that an era of unparalleled harshness followed during the first quarter of the nineteenth century. Other "historians" have reinforced this impression. J. L. and Barbara Hammond write that during this age, "the workpeople were at the mercy of their masters."[35] The Webbs' inconsistency on the point is monumental. They admit that the representation of the period 1799-1824 as one of "unmitigated persecution" involving continuous repression of the trade-union movement is a "romantic legend" and "semi-mythical," yet claim at the same time that "the legend is not without a basis of fact."[36] Combinations with the simple aim of insuring enforcement of the law in labor's favor had been tolerated before 1799, they assert, but were suddenly outlawed afterward. The Webbs contend that before the nineteenth century, unions had not always been prosecuted, even if they were "technically within the definitions of combination and conspiracy," but between 1800 and 1824, they were. I find no evidence of this whatsoever in secondary authorities. They allege that from 1800 to 1824 the "combination acts" drove union members "into violence and sedition."[37] The truth is that sabotage, violence and intimidation of nonstrikers, managers and owners had been normal concomitants of such strikes as did occur long before the enactment of the new "Combination Acts," as Adam Smith testified in 1776 (see p. 36). And, after the repeal of these acts in 1824, a year of exceptional disorders accompanied widespread strike activity. It is significant that subsequent history records how, as unions gradually won immunities and privileges before the law, their reliance upon intimidation and violence tended, on the whole, to increase (see Chapter 4). It is not only in the present age that steps taken to achieve peace and protect life and property have been represented as acts of aggression which can thereby themselves be charged with engendering war and violence.

Enforcement of the law against conspiracies seems, then, to have been just as lax, lenient, or reluctant after 1799 as before.[38] And it remained true that when there was no clear evidence of illegal *conspiracy*, associations of workers continued to be looked upon without disfavor. That is, unless they were observed to be arranging in concert not to accept less than an agreed wage rate[39] (which as Mansfield's judgment made clear,[40] alone constituted the ancient crime of "conspiracy" or "combination"), no action against them is recorded, even in the Webbs' great book; and just as had happened in the eighteenth century, "when masters complained, the magistrates were more inclined to seek a reconciliation than inflict penalties."[41]

There is no evidence whatsoever that law enforcement initiatives and judgments in common law or statutory conspiracy cases between 1800-1824 diverged from the long-established principles enunciated with the clarity of simplicity by Mansfield. And discussions by unions with managements about wage rates and conditions of work had never been frowned upon, provided they did not lead to anything resembling the strike threat, or to obvious preparations for a strike (as the Webbs themselves *indirectly* admit.)[42] On occasion, when such discussions appeared likely to be angry, the magistrates would even be invited to be present as conciliators. Apparently, it was regarded as quite legal for a union in one district to correspond with a union in the same trade in another district about wages and conditions of service.

Many cases in the early 1800s concerned organizations of artisans that, faced with the gradual dissolution of their privileges or the competition of labor-economizing machines, fought to preserve their position with every available *legal* means. Generally speaking, they were unsuccessful and often had to admit increasing numbers of poorer workers into their protected trades as interlopers and, according to the Webbs, suffer "the progressive degradation of their wages.''[43] However, the union leaders were free to petition Parliament and use normal channels of propaganda and peaceful agitation. Some asked that their position be protected by restraint on entry through the application of the wage-fixing clauses of the archaic and ineffective Elizabethan Statute of Artificers, or through its restrictive apprenticeship clauses.[44] Even such large-scale collusive activities occurred as the organization of a petition with 300,000 signatures asking for the Statute of Artificers to be made effective, and the organizers were in no danger whatsoever of arrest or prosecution. On exceptional occasions, the unions *were* successful in such requests, presumably because they were *not* regarded as "combinations" in the legal sense of "conspiracies," or because they agreed to abandon such organization machinery as could be used for strike-threat pressures.

From the researches of scholars such as T. S. Ashton (who have dug into the correspondence of industrial firms during the period we are considering), we know today what was not known at the time by the law-enforcement authorities. There were indeed *secret* discussions among industrialists relating to wages. As such, the discussions may have been "conspiracies"—infringements (by "employers") of the 1800 Combination Act. Yet there were "few, if any prosecutions. . . ."[45] It is understandable, therefore, that knowledgeable humanitarians of the day should have felt that gross injustice to the workers was involved. But for reasons to be discussed in Chapters 8 and 9, it is highly doubtful whether the early industrial concerns could ever have wielded effective monopsonistic power. The real purpose of the apparent collusion the researches mentioned have disclosed was, I am inclined to think, defense. We know that many trade unions were being formed during the 1800-1826 period, despite the illegality of "combination." It is scarcely surprising, therefore, that representatives of the investors should have felt it essential to cooperate, not to exploit labor monopsonistically, but in order to resist wage-rate concessions wrung from managements confronted with the strike-threat "in detail." (See p. 47.)

It was, however, the laxity of enforcement of the anticonspiracy law, not any harshness or savagery with which the law was administered, which puzzles the student who is trying to get to the truth. The findings of the Webbs themselves suggest that the police seldom took any initiative unless requested specifically by "employers"; and that "employers" then, as now, would do almost anything in their power to avoid the staff disharmony and the lasting bitterness which, they knew, followed a defeated strike. Far from being billigerent, managements wanted industrial peace, almost at any cost.

It is possible indeed that the widespread tolerance of illegal strike-threat action encouraged the unions to believe that, if they played their cards correctly, particularly their political cards, they were beyond the law. Already members of Parliament whose constituencies included union members had recognized that they constituted a serious voting bloc. For instance, the Webbs themselves mention how both the Whig and Tory members for Liverpool thought it expedient to take up the unions' case against the 1799 Act. Of course, laxity in the law's administration may have created an impression of

34

harshness when prosecutions *were* brought. Prosecutions may have come to be so unexpected and capricious as to be regarded as outrages. But far from enforcement having been carried out in a spirit of repression, the authorities were obviously "reluctant to interfere in such disputes unless the public peace was thought to be endangered,"[46] and even so, in less-dangerous situations, the courts appear to have preferred simply to insist upon the dissolution of the unlawful organizations rather than apply the legislatively authorized sanctions. They tried as far as possible to achieve obedience of the law *without* the imposition of fines or imprisonment.

In part, what seems to have been happening during the first quarter of the nineteenth century was that, because the machinery of enforcement was still inadequate, unions could, by proceeding with careful strategy, often rely upon no action being taken against them. They were advised by such shrewd friends as Francis Place—probably the most successful political intriguer of history[47]—and numerous politicians who had perceived the vote-swinging power of the unions.

As an example of the alleged "repression" which occurred after 1799, we can consider the case of the cotton weavers. They were permitted to organize openly and agitate for legislation which would permit the justices to fix wage rates for them in accordance with the provisions of the outmoded Statute of Artificers. After several years of costly activities, it at last became clear that their efforts had been fruitless. They saw their privileges evaporating as a great increase in the numbers who found their most remunerative outlets in cotton weaving occurred. A huge strike (for those days) was then organized. But no "savage" suppression of these incontrovertibly illegal activities followed. On the contrary, authorities allowed the strike to last for three weeks before calling the police. Then, "the whole strike committee was arrested by the police." They were found guilty and sentenced to from 4 to 18 months imprisonment.[48] There was neither injustice nor savagery in the sentences.

As additional evidence of an almost unbelievable leniency in enforcing the combination laws between 1800 and 1824, we can consider the calico printers. Unable to get any effective protection from the law, a calico manufacturer expressed his grievances in a pamphlet in 1815. Addressing the union, he charged

> We᾿ have by turns conceded what we all ought manfully to have resisted; and you, elated with success, have been led on from one extravagant demand to another, till the burden is become too intolerable to be borne. You fix the number of our apprentices, and often-times even the number of our journeymen. You dismiss certain proportions of our hands, and you will not allow others to come in their stead. You stop all surface machines, and to the length even to destroy the rollers before our face. You restrict the cylinder machine, and even dictate the kind of pattern it is to print. . . . You dismiss our overlookers when they don't suit you; and

35

force obnoxious servants into our employ. Lastly, you set all subordination and good order at defiance, and instead of showing deference and respect to your employers, treat them with personal insult and contempt.[49]

It seems obvious that, in all the cases of which we know brought under the Combination Acts between 1800 and 1824, those charged with breaking the law (1) knew they were doing so, (2) had often organized in secret, and (3) knew the prescribed penalties which they were risking. But action in concert by the unions to insure the enforcement of the law (when it favored their members), seems to have been just as common and uninhibited during this period as it had been during previous centuries.

Nor is there evidence of further changes in judicial interpretation of the common law disadvantageous to labor after 1800, as the Webbs suggest in the phrase, "the common law doctrine . . . , as *subsequently* interpreted by the judges, of itself made illegal all combinations whatsoever of journeymen to regulate the conditions of their work."[50] For "combination" in the sense attached to that word at the time (namely, "conspiracy") had been illegal since the Middle Ages. There was nothing new in that. Are not the Webbs' words, "to regulate the conditions of their work," a euphemism for "unlawful activities deliberately undertaken"?

The objects of the acts of 1799 and 1800 were simply (1) to make more specific (not so much to lawyers as to the community) the illegality of collusion to force up the prices of output (including labor's contribution to output), and (2) (a doubtfully successful object) to render the enforcement of the law less costly and less time-consuming. But what is most surprising is that, despite a certain improvement in the law's explicitness, the apparently quite general acquiescence in collusive action which marked the eighteenth century persisted during the nineteenth. Far from enforcement having become more severe, it seems to have remained disconcertingly mild.

The passing of the generalized Combination Acts may perhaps have been a greater deterrent to strikes. It is rather difficult to judge because, despite the mildness of law enforcement, anything resembling *conspicuous* concerted action by the workers to fix wage rates had been *relatively* rare—although increasing and, before 1799, apparently becoming more and more violent. Adam Smith remarked in 1776, as though it were an unassailable fact, that workmen's combinations "have always recourse to the loudest clamour, and sometimes to the most shocking violence and outrages."[51] In circumstances which so sober an observer as Adam Smith could describe in terms like that, was it really surprising that there should have been occasional recourse to the courts to check the spread of intimidation, disorder, and sabotage? And were not demands for special and general legislation to assist that process wholly reasonable?

The offense of "conspiracy" was *not* in itself, as we have seen, concerned with the use of physical force, although intimidation and bodily violence often *did* in practice supplement the coercive power of "peaceful" concerted action. Nevertheless, the principal purpose of *some* of the special Combination Acts applying to particular trades (for example, one of 1727 applying to weavers, woolcombers, and framework knitters) had been to suppress more effectively *kinds of illegality which were independent of the crime of "conspiracy"* (for example, assaulting or threatening masters, breaking into their houses, destroying work, etc).

The Webbs admit that "some combinations of journeymen were at all times recognized by the law" and that "many others were only spasmodically interfered with"; yet they allege that organizers (or would-be) organizers of strikes were subject to "legal persecution . . . *as rebels and revolutionaries.*"[52] This assertion cannot be substantiated unless the leaders *could* be charged with "conspiracy" or organizing violence.

The case which the books most often cite to show the oppressive nature of subsequent policy in the application of the law against conspiracy is that of the "Tolpuddle martyrs." This case involved farm workers who were trying to form an organization to force up their wage rates. They had established the "Friendly Society of Agricultural Laborers" for their village. Now as a friendly society, such an association was encouraged rather than discouraged by the law.[53] But as a cloak for illegal activities (including "conspiracy"), it was not immune from prosecution. In the Tolpuddle case, however, the alleged crime was not conspiracy, but "unlawful oaths." The society, which had an elaborate ritual and rather frightening paraphernalia—for example, a picture of Death, "painted six feet high"—was demanding loyalty through the administration of oaths. Naturally alarmed, the local farmers pointed out what was happening—preparations for strikes or violence—to the local justices, who were perhaps traditionally sympathetic to farmers (as they were not to the new industrialists). Nevertheless the justices were reluctant to get a prosecution going. They thought it preferable first to warn those concerned of the penalties which had to be imposed under the relevant law—seven years transportation. But apparently the activities of the society continued, and the authorities then felt bound to intervene. It was proved that illegal oaths *had* been administered—in view of the explicit warning, it seems quite recklessly and defiantly. Five ringleaders (the only members charged[54]) were found guilty under the "Unlawful Oaths Offenses Act" of 1797 (an act inspired by the atrocities of the French Revolution), and *not under the combination laws or the common law*. Under the 1797 act, the original sentence had been the death penalty; but this penalty had been reduced to seven years transportation shortly before the Tolpuddle case (a fact which in all probability had encouraged the leaders' defiance). The law (wise or unwise) was clear-cut. The offenses were proven. The court had no option.[55] Yet the Webbs describe the conviction of the Tolpuddle offenders as a "scandalous perversion of the law;"[56] and because the sentence to transportation was confirmed by the Home Secretary, the Webbs refer to his "policy of repression."[57]

The question remains, *were* the judges and J. P.'s (magistrates) *personally* prejudiced against the "working class organizations"? I have found no evidence which might suggest bias in favor of industrialists, although in cases involving farmers, both judges and justices may have tended to feel special sympathy for the classes from which they were mostly drawn—the country gentry—or toward whom they might feel a special sense of obligation, that is, the squires and great landowners. Except for J. P.'s in the newly developed industrial towns who might have known and understood the problems of the factory owners, any bias would almost certainly have been against the industrialists whose wealth and status had been built up mostly by their own thrift and acumen (i.e., not acquired in the honorable way of inheritance); whose culture differed markedly from that of an aristocratic tradition; and whose competition for labor was resented (because it was attracting labor to the urban areas and forcing up agricultural wage rates).

We must remember two things about what the Webbs describe as the "savagery" of law enforcement between 1799 and 1824, as well as later. Firstly, the criminal law at that time imposed what we today would regard as ferocious penalties for offenses *in all spheres*. Secondly, the attitudes of governments and responsible judges were influenced by the shock caused when the murders and other atrocities of the French Revolution became known. No one in England could imagine how the French Government could have been so short-sighted, weak, and ineffective as to allow a group of fanatics to gain control.

But the common law tradition which frowned on "conspiracy" or "restraint of trade" in both Britain and the United States had been throughout protective of the rights of the ordinary man, of the unprivileged, and of the poor. And the destruction of that tradition over the years was a victory for the privileged, not for the exploited or "oppressed."

I have discussed the position of "organized labor" before the law during what is usually believed to have been the blackest period in British social history—the economic dark age of the Industrial Revolution—mainly in order to illustrate how, in studies of industrial relations, the most preposterous myths can gain widespread acceptance and perpetuation. But similarly distorted accounts of experience in this century—new fables relating to "labor's bitter struggle"—are becoming part of supposedly unchallengeable history. They condition public opinion everywhere. *Even the most courageous and independent critics of the strike-threat regime are today apt to refer to the miserable conditions of former times (say, before the Wagner Act in the United States) when workers were intolerably treated*. With such critics, this may perhaps be because of the tactics of exposition; for *the argument typically goes on to suggest that today the position has been reversed. Unions, they say, no longer fight injustices, they inflict them. But this has been true, I suggest, of strike threat activity in all ages*.

NOTES

[1] Tibor Scitovsky, "A Survey of Some Theories of Income Distribution," in National Bureau of Economic Research, *The Behavior of Income Shares: Selected Theoretical and Empirical Issues. Studies in Income and Wealth* (Princeton: Princeton University Press, 1964), 27: 15-16.

[2] An apparent phenomenal decline during the last half century in the efficiency of school teaching in respect of literacy and arithmetic, combined with compulsory prolonged schooling, must have braked this tendency.

[3] Albert Rees, *The Economics of Trade Unions* (Chicago: University of Chicago Press, 1962), p. 80.

[4] For evidence supporting this assertion, see pp. 245-247.

[5] Arthur A. Shenfield, "The Businessman and the Politician," *Modern Age* 15 (1971): 149.

[6] The symposium, *Capitalism and the Historians,* edited by F. A. Hayek (Chicago: University of Chicago Press, 1954) is of the greatest importance in this field. See also W. H. Hutt, "The Poor Who Were With Us," *Encounter*, November 1972; and a most important, recently published symposium, *The Long Debate on Poverty*, ed., A. Seldon (London: Institute of Economic Affairs, 1973).

[7] In Britain, for various reasons, the abolition of child labor in those industries in which their tasks were relatively light, preceded the abandonment of child labor in trades such as dyeing, or in mining, or in agriculture, in which children continued for some time to work under more exacting and even less healthy conditions (on the whole).

[8] Except for wars and revolutions and their aftermaths.

[9] Sidney and Beatrice Webb, *The History of Trade Unionism* (London: Longmans Green and Co., 1956), p. 46.

[10] Where color prejudice has been powerfully present, as in the United States, South Africa and, of recent years, Britain, the unions have been the chief protagonists of the less obvious (and hence the most effective) color bars.

[11] Ibid., p. 45.

[12] Enforced fixed proportions in the remuneration of different "grades" of labor. (See Chapter 8).

[13] Indeed, as I have shown elsewhere, in South Africa the enforcement of "the rate for the job" has throughout created a color bar *in relation to which all other restraints, such as "job reservation," are of almost negligible importance.* See W. H. Hutt, *The Economics of the Colour Bar: A Study of the Economic Origins and Consequences of Racial Segregation in Africa* (London: Andre Deutsch Ltd., 1964), pp. 72-86.

[14] Adam Smith, *The Wealth of Nations,* ed. Edwin Cannan (New York: Random House, The Modern Library, 1937), p. 66. The law *did* prohibit masters from combining to raise prices. (See p. 17, note 4, above and p. 31.)

[15] Ibid., p. 67.

[16] But see p. 34.

¹⁷ George J. Stigler, "The Economist and the State," *American Economic Review* 55 (1965): 14.

¹⁸ S. and B. Webb, op. cit., p. 46 (my italics). On the whole, Parliament sided with the craft guilds until the middle of the eighteenth century (by which time their effectiveness was rapidly weakening); but with the spread of *laissez-faire* ideas in the latter part of the century, Parliament was less inclined to protect craft privileges.

¹⁹ So effectively has the myth I am here exposing been propagated that even in Armen A. Alchiàn and William R. Allen's *University Economics* (2nd ed.; Belmont, Calif.: Wadsworth Publishing Company, 1967), which contains by all odds the most satisfactory elementary discussion of the labor union issue to be found in any currently used textbook, the student is told that the British anticonspiracy laws tried to abolish "the right to form a union—which is a very different thing from a strike." Associations of working people were encouraged rather than frowned upon provided they did not resort to anything resembling the strike. Nor is this textbook quite correct in saying that "the threat of violence via the strike was basically what anticonspiracy laws aimed to stop. . . ." (p. 406). This was true only of certain of the special statutes, referred to on pp. 29-30. The gist of any "conspiracy" offense was concerted action to agree upon a price or wage rate. (See p. 31.) Violence was always a *separate* transgression.

²⁰ The London carpenters were charged with trying to keep "foreigners" (i.e., workmen from outside London) from accepting less than sixpence a day.

²¹ Wyclif was attacking the masons employed in church building. The quotation is A. H. Gardner, *Outline of English Architecture* (New York: Scribners, 1946), p. 24.

²² Quoted in M. D. George, *The Combination Laws Reconsidered*, cited in *Economic Journal History Supplement, 1927*, p. 215.

²³ Important instances were in the woolen, cotton, linen, silk, hemp, fustian, hatters, dyers, pressers and the iron industries.

²⁴ This is surely indicated in the very name of an early *general* statute: *Act of Conspiracies of Victuallers and Craftsmen*, 1549. Consumers' interests were paramount.

²⁵ I say "apparent" because the evidence of growing union activity is mainly indicated in the increasing number of court cases involving unions; and this may have been correlated with rising industrial outputs or due to more vigorous law enforcement.

²⁶ One very defensible practice of those days (which survived into the nineteenth century) was the subsidization of craftsmen in the form of what were called "traveling" or "tramping" benefits if they were prepared to leave an area in which there was unemployment. This could have led to an improved allocation of labor over area—greater geographical mobility.

²⁷ Smith, op. cit., p. 126.

²⁸ *The King* v. *Eccles,* quoted in Donald Dewey, *Monopoly in Economics and Law* (Chicago: Rand McNally and Company, 1959), p. 120n.

²⁹ Quoted in Webb, op. cit., p. 70n.

[30] The amendments concerned provision for arbitration.

[31] Dewey, op. cit., p. 117.

[32] Webb, op. cit., pp. 72 and 81.

[33] George, op. cit., pp. 214-15.

[34] Webb, op. cit., pp. 64-70.

[35] J. L. and Barbara Hammond, *The Town Labourer, 1760-1832: The New Civilisation* (London: Longmans, Green and Co., 1917), p. 129.

[36] S. and B. Webb, *op. cit.*, p. 64.

[37] Ibid., p. 63.

[38] See the *Minutes of Evidence of the Select Committee on Artisans and Machinery* (1824) and George, op. cit. Mrs. George's judgment (which coincides with my own on this issue) is all the more powerful because her obvious bias is against the masters. For instance, one of the examples she gives of the lax enforcement of the law against strikes is of the stocking weavers whose union had organized strikes with impunity in 1817, 1819, and 1821. Only after the third strike was there a prosecution and four members of the workers' committee convicted, but released after successful appeal to the sessions. "The prosecution was a monstrous one," says Mrs. George (op. cit., p. 216). But the strike was unquestionably a criminal act, and Mrs. George (normally an exemplary historian) does not disclose the grounds for her caustic adjective.

[39] Or other conditions of work.

[40] See p. 31.

[41] Dewey, op. cit., p. 188n.

[42] Webb, op. cit., pp. 74-5.

[43] Ibid., p. 59, In the Webbs' account, there is no hint that, at the time, increasing numbers were *raising* their earnings by finding better-paid employment in the spheres in which the supposed "degradation of wages" was occurring.

[44] Whether, on the whole, this statute facilitated the exploitation of labor through monopsony or whether, through response to workers' pressures, it conferred labor privilege is uncertain. It had long been of no clear effect when its wage-fixing clauses were repealed in 1813. The statute as a whole was repealed in 1824.

[45] T. S. Ashton, *The Industrial Revolution* (London: Oxford University Press, 1964), p. 93.

[46] Dewey, op. cit., p. 119.

[47] See Graham Wallas's great and fascinating biography, *The Life of Francis Place, 1771-1854* (London: Longmans, Green and Company, 1898; New York: Knopf, 1918). Wallas was a frank admirer of that extraordinary man.

[48] Webb, op. cit., pp. 58-59.

[49] Quoted in Ibid., pp. 75-6.

[50] Ibid., pp. 58-59. My italics.

[51] Smith, op. cit., p. 67.

[52] Webb, op. cit., p. 64. My italics.

[53] An Act of 1793 was intended to *foster* concerted working-class initiative to establish friendly societies.

[54] Every member of the society *could* have been charged according to the Act.

[55] Those who condemn the Tolpuddle sentences point out that the only evidence given about meetings of the friendly society (which had administered the illegal oaths) was that they had been orderly. At that stage, however, the meetings would naturally have been orderly. But where the authorities had not been so alert, organization of the kind which in this case was anticipated and prevented, had brought arson and murder. In certain other localities, haystacks and farms had been destroyed.

[56] Ibid., p. 146.

[57] Ibid., p. 146. Five years of the seven-year transportation sentences were subsequently remitted, although, through someone's blunder, it was two years later before four of the five returned to Britain. It was quite common to remit sentences or quash convictions in "conspiracy" cases also, once illegal activities had been abandoned.

4

The Nature of the Strike

THE STRIKE, like the boycott, is a coercive or punitive device. It is deliberate disruption of the process of human cooperation by way of the collusive, coordinated withdrawal of labor from an organized activity. Hence "the strike-threat" is essentially a threat *to disrupt* unless (as Henry Simons once put it) "bribed" not to do so. "The strike-threat *system*" is a social order in which the right or effective power exists for those who can apply this method of coercion to seek private objectives by threatening to use it.

Such a system is conventionally described as "the collective bargaining system." In my *Theory of Collective Bargaining* (London: P.S. King, 1930), I referred to the term "collective bargaining" (which had been coined by Beatrice Webb) as "a very useful term." I have since come to perceive that it is a misleading euphemism. We could appropriately describe "collective bargaining" as "a particular procedure for arranging the sale of labor" or as "the cooperative marketing of labor," if there were no question of the strike threat, no such threat of disruption. A union *could* bargain on behalf of *all* its members but, so to speak, individually, warning the management that, if the wage rate offered should be below a certain figure, the union would be in a position gradually to find better jobs (with better remuneration, conditions of service or prospects) for so many of their members. That *would* be "arranging the price of labor through a common agent." But this is *not* what distinguishes *collective bargaining* from entrepreneurial action under the social discipline of the free market. The United States Industrial Commission of 1902 claimed that, under collective bargaining, "the labor contract is precisely similar in nature to the process of bargaining between two parties regarding any other contract."[1] That is a basically false description unless attempted "exploitation" and/or resistance to it are assumed to influence such "other contracts." What *actually* goes under the name of "collective bargaining" nearly always involves the strike threat ("the gun under the table"), in some countries even when the field is one in which strikes are illegal.

The case against the strike-threat system is partly that the strike is an intolerable weapon in a civilized era whatever its objectives. The strike is, of course, *capable* of being used for *ends* of which all could approve. Theoretically, it might be directed against an oppressive government (see p. 49) or against exploitation by other unions in competing or noncompeting occupations. But it is my thesis that strike-threat power is an unacceptable *method* of redressing wrongs in any circumstances, while it is of course doubly objectionable when it is used for indefensible objectives. Even if it could exert an equalitarian influence, we should, I suggest, have to condemn it, just as we should have to condemn the Mafia even if it could be shown that the revenues of racketeering were being used to subsidize opera, cancer research or civil rights movements. But almost meaningless phrases are commonly resorted to in describing present methods of determining wage rates and conditions of service, as though to avoid reference to their essential aggressiveness. For instance, the strike-threat system has recently been described as action to close "the remaining gap between limited means of want-satisfaction on the one hand and desires on the other," and "the need to adapt distribution of income or power in some fashion to changed conditions within the dynamic and complex industrial society."[2] The key word here is "gap." How is it defined? Has *part* of the "gap" already been closed as the words "the remaining gap" suggest? But will there not always be a "gap"? And won't its presence *always* displease some? If moralists fail to condemn such resentments, won't they persist as long as one person's income from property, or one person's ability to earn *without exploitation* exceeds that of another? Suppose the "gap" exists between a poor stockholder and a relatively rich artisan. Does the implied desirability of closing the "gap" still exist? All my life *my* "desires" have exceeded my "limited means of want-satisfaction," and I assume that everyone else is in the same position. How can the "gap" justify strike warfare?

And what is this "need" to "adapt the distribution of income"? Society—the people collectively—may decide that the institutions determining income distribution require refashioning *according to some explicit principle*. But can a civilized social order permit any group with a grievance to be judge and policeman in its own cause and attempt to change income distribution in its own interest?

One of the problems in a good society is greed. An even more important problem is that of curbing the activities of those who seek profit from fostering and battening on human greed. These are problems which grow more acute the more affluent men become. We have been somehow inveigled into apologizing for man's urge to exploit by describing the incentive to get more *at the expense of others* in terms through which envy and cupidity are almost ennobled; while we have been led to condemn individuals who try to get more *by serving others* more efficiently, or more faithfully, or more cheaply.

I shall try to show, however, that the notion that some form of *distributive justice* can emerge when there is reliance upon the strike threat is fallacious. For if the terms of wage "contracts" are dependent on the capitulation of one of the parties in order to avoid warfare, or on the results of actual warfare, the principle of *might is right* must ultimately prevail in each individual

44

"agreement" about how the value of the product of industry is to be divided. Victory in war is to the powerful, not the righteous.

Even if it were possible, therefore, to demonstrate that the right to strike (actually exercised or not) may discourage or prevent exploitation of the poor by the rich, or promote welfare and equality by transferring income from the rich to the poor, we should still be forced back to the question of whether it is a tolerable *method* of achieving such "social benefits." For what guarantee can there be that strike power (or any other form of private coercive power) will be used for the good of the poor or the underprivileged and not to win private or sectional advantages?

In practice, the sheer arbitrariness of any detailed redistribution effected ought to cause misgivings. Let us face this simple question: *How far* is it just to transfer income from those who, in every business, risk providing the assets which multiply the yield to labor? Any such transfer will be for the benefit of those who have already gained from that multiplication in non-competing fields. Hence can *any* transfer of that kind be just? And if it is, what proportion of the investor's earnings ought to be taken for the benefit of the workers? What criteria can be applied in different defined circumstances? Are there any principles at all? What particular investors (assumed to be rich) are to be "soaked"? What particular workers (assumed to be poor) are to receive the transferred income? Surely, the capriciousness of the method ought to condemn it. Why should the beneficiaries be those workers who just happen to contribute to the production of output for which the demand is inelastic or those for whose labor there is no effective substitute? Well, *in the whole voluminous literature dealing with labor unions and collective bargaining, I have been able to trace no attempt at rigorous consideration of the ethical issue involved in attempts to answer such questions.* Have we not tended to rationalize the use of a form of coercive power which it has been politically inexpedient to suppress, and inhibit concern with a glaring problem of ethics?[3]

We can classify arguments that through the strike-threat a more just distribution of a community's income can be effected under two broad headings: (a) that the system serves the purpose of preventing workers from being exploited for the benefit of investors, or (b) that it serves the purpose of enabling investors (assumed to be rich) to be exploited for the good of workers (assumed to be poor). At this stage, however, we are to consider solely the ethical aspect—the question of whether such a system is *a defensible method* of trying to protect the just earnings of the workers from being filched from them to enrich investors or, alternatively, of attempting to serve the community as a sort of Robin Hood device.

If redistribution *is* to be sought on the grounds that income differences, even those determined in a free market, are in some sense "unjust," then the obviously *defensible* way of achieving distributive justice is by transfers via (a) progressive taxation which discriminates solely on grounds of income, and (b) a schedule of handouts which discriminates solely in favor of the smaller incomes. As H. C. Simons pointed out (in 1944), "it is one merit of our pres-

45

ent (past) system that inequality is measured closely by income and can most easily be modified systematically through taxation and spending.''[4]

In any case, the easy assumption that investors are rich and workers poor is rather dubious today. In a country such as the United States millions of relatively poor people are making provision for their old age or retirement, for their children's education, for the future well-being of their family generally, and for the security of all those for whom they are responsible, by investing in common stocks directly or through mutual funds. Inflation has spurred this form of saving. But it makes no difference to the point here at issue whether the "poor investors" are dividend receivers or interest receivers; for if prospective yields in general are reduced, the yield to current and past savings (the rate of interest) will be reduced (thrift being the same). A by no means negligible volume of income from property must be received by people whose incomes from wages *plus* savings are less than the average income—in the United States, say, less than the present wage earnings of New York City garbage collectors! Then if income from property *is* exploitable through the strike threat, why should *this* group, with incomes below the average, be exploited for the benefit of those union members whose incomes are already greater? The "poor investors" are, on the whole, the most independent and worthy of their income class. They exercise foresight; they plan their future; they insure against life's hazards where possible; and, except when they encounter wholly unpredictable misfortune, they seldom make demands on the community. Can we tolerate a system in which their exploitation is *an explicit even if an incidental aim*?[5] I make these points only to underscore the remarkable failure of apologists for the strike-threat system to face the relevant ethics. The blatant arbitrariness of such redistributions as are effected are habitually glossed over in public discussions and in most "labor economics" textbooks.

Other forms of organized disruption may supplement "the strike proper": the "sit-in," "ca canny" (going slow), "working to rule," deliberately spoiling work, "luddism," and various other forms of sabotage, intimidation of nonstrikers, "demonstrations" to impress with the strength of intimidatory power—all these methods of disruption may be threatened or used. They are all forms of the private use of coercive power.

The organization of the power to disrupt can sometimes be effective on a small scale when key workers in an industry are concerned; and in these cases the unions may be quite small.[6] Sometimes the labor monopoly to be protected will be that of a craft, the skills of which can be relatively easily learned by interlopers, in which circumstances the scale of organization likely to be preferred will cover a single craft alone. Under other conditions, disruptive power is maximized when the organization covers an occupation or an industry. In yet other circumstances, a "general" organization covering several occupations and industries will be in a position to inflict the greatest harm. Another way of multiplying the potency of the simple strike threat is cooperation with other unions, with which "strategic alliances" may be formed. This can increase the menace of disruption in breadth and depth. The so-called "sympathetic strike" is an example. We have even had the "super-strike"—the use of disruptive power simultaneously in many fields, sometimes described, euphemistically, as "coordinated bargaining" and represented as the answer to the great corporate conglomerates and mergers. And the unions have never lost sight of the occasional effectiveness of what is today called (in the United States) "the whipsaw," or what the Webbs earlier termed "the strike in detail." This device involves the coercion of one firm after the other, so that the strikers in each case can be supported out of contributions from those still working elsewhere.[7] Or, as was the case with the newspaper industry in the United States, the unions preferred "collective bargaining" on an individual company basis in order to "force a favorable agreement on the most vulnerable employer and then apply the 'pattern' to the other firms."[8] Careful timing also can magnify the harm threatened. For instance, agricultural unions can threaten farmers with the loss of a whole year's income through the withdrawal of their labor just as it becomes essential to harvest a perishable crop. And generally, since the Wagner Act, American unions seem to have been organizing an apparatus for maximizing their power to disrupt a functioning economy when or where the disruption would be most deleterious. One of the most effective forms of exercising privately contrived coercive power in the United States is "the honoring of picket lines" by all unions.[9]

The connection between the use of the strike and *recognized* union organization is not simple. "Unofficial," or "wildcat," strikes sometimes occur and usually appear as challenges to the authority of the elected leaders. But union members who seem to defy their leaders in such circumstances still rely upon the kind of coercive powers of which their leaders claim the monopoly. Moreover, rarely is the machinery of legally established unions used for "strike-breaking" when the elected rulers decide against a strike and their decision is flouted by some part of the membership. For this reason, the suspicion has arisen that, *on occasion,* "wildcat" aggression (supposedly unauthorized strike action) has been quietly encouraged.

Managements in the United States, realistically perceiving that the critical problem in disputes is nearly always protection of the security in office, and hence the financial prospects of the union's elected rulers, have sometimes (I do not suggest often) found it less costly to reward the officials directly in the form of bribes than to satisfy them indirectly through agreeing to terms of capitulation which sufficiently preserve their prestige and authority. But even when no vestiges of corruption exist, it is the interests of the officials which seem to prevail. Realism on this point must color our judgment on the issue.[10] I often think that the only net gainers from the strike-threat system are union officials (as well as union lawyers, consultants, artibrators, mediators, conciliators and the like) who thrive on the union income from membership dues. The interests of this group alone are a powerful bulwark to prevent the rank and file from learning the lesson which John Stuart Mill suggested they would learn[11], namely, that strikes must fail to achieve their claimed objectives.

In using their disruptive power the unions must, at times, recognize the need for some measure of public approval. They must also give due weight to the expediency of satisfying the more critical and observant factions, with divergent interests, within their own organizations. Such considerations *plus* the cost of strikes (in terms of wages sacrificed and funds depleted), *plus* the danger of driving too many existing firms into insolvency (discussed on pp. 70-71, 140-142) have been the chief restraints to which the strike-threat system has been subject.

On occasion, managements try directly to bring public opinion to bear on negotiations via advertisements, but usually only after an actual strike has occurred and managements feel that they must apologize to the public for the breakdown in service. On the whole, although public opinion condones union aggression rather uneasily, the fact that it does not condone *all demands* which unions put forward is a reality with which exploiters of the strike threat must reckon. The terms of settlement in the so-called bargaining field *are* influenced by current ideas about what is equitable.[12] Whether on balance public bias toward approval of what has become customary works as a mitigating factor or the reverse on strike-threat exploitation is difficult to judge.

We can say, then, that the typically "broad-minded" view of well-informed, sensible people about the "right to strike" is that it is obviously legitimate when employed with "moderation." It just happens at times (or often), they think, to be used "irresponsibly," and they feel the only remedy to be that the unions must be persuaded or somehow forced to act responsibly—"not to go too far." I have already suggested that such a view is unacceptable (see pp. 15-16). As Fritz Machlup has put it,

> We frequently hear about some very exceptional trade union leaders who have exhibited an exemplary degree of responsibility and moderation. With all due credit for the wisdom and sincerity of these men, I believe that their moderation was conditioned by the particular circumstances of their trades. The trades in question were characterized by exceptionally high elasticities of demand and of technological, occupational and regional substitution. "Moderation" in these circumstances was in the interests of the members of the union. . . . Full exploitation of a union's bargaining position may appear as "irresponsible highway robbery" or as "responsible statesmanship" depending on whether the union's monopoly power is strong or weak.[13]

Having referred to public opinion's influence on union policies, I must at once confess that, in my judgment, it is *not* very important at present. Until the public generally is better educated about the problems we are discussing, its views on what is proper will seldom exert more than a mildly conservative effect—and probably help to conserve more evil than good.

The strike, and particularly cooperation in strike aggression can be extended to achieve political objectives. The most sensational form in which

48

such action may be taken is that of "the general strike." But unions in cooperation (that is, using "sympathetic strikes") are now often in a position to threaten to create, or actually create, a state of general unrest, disorder or recession; and for that they may be able successfully to blame governments which refuse to legislate as they, the unions, command.

The private use of coercive power to achieve political ends which cannot be won via the democratic voting process occurs in contemporary society in spheres wider than those in which labor unions are concerned. Nondemocratic "dissent"—resort to "peaceful" demonstrations, protests and demonstrations with a view to the incitement of violence, disorder and intimidation of the public, of commercial institutions, and of government (as distinct from their use for publicity purposes)—is now almost accepted in the United States as a fundamental human right (see p. 283). As with other rebellions and mutinies, the objectives sought may be good. Under the "one-man, one-vote" form of representative government, for instance, unless racial or religious minorities are safeguarded by some weighting of the franchise, or some independently enforced "declaration of rights," the revolt of the minorities in one form or other may be the only path to racial or religious justice. But if governments—elected or otherwise—suppress rebellions, their action can hardly be characterized as "oppression." The policies against which the revolt is aimed *might* be so characterized. In this field, as in all others, no government which regards itself as having been legitimately appointed can justify revolt or the infringement of the civil rights of some persons because those who rebel believe (acting as judges in their own cause) that they are the victims of injustice.

The absence of strikes does not mean the absence of private coercion. An armed robber is usually reluctant to assault or slay his victim. And, of course, unions will not *want* to strike if they can get what they ask without the cost and risks of stoppages. When defenders of the present system sometimes stress this *reluctance* of the unions actually to carry out the threat which dominates "negotiations," that is all their argument implies.[14] Attempts to distinguish "militant" unionism from "peaceful" unionism seem never to be expressed in comprehensible terms. To say that we can distinguish "extreme" from "moderate" leaders, and to define as "extreme" those whose demands are most "unreasonable," "irresponsible" or "unrealistic" is not very helpful. The only clear difference as a rule is that the "moderate" leaders think it right or expedient to aim at taking less *by the identical method*. For if the unions led by "moderate" officials fail to secure what they think is just and worth a fight to obtain, they will strike; so that negotiations always take place in the full knowledge that a conflict is possible. The words "reasonable" and "realistic" in this context tacitly assume that there is some criterion of the *expedient* or *just* amount to be taken. (See above, p. 45, and Chapter 15.)

Agreements reached under strike-threat pressure but without an actual stoppage are described at times by propagandists as "mutually agreeable to the parties," as though in some circumstances capitulation under duress is acceptable. Sometimes, indeed, tendentious writings have gone so far as to represent strikes and lockouts as "inherent in free market decision-making." But there is no justification for the use of the word "free" when any worker can be prevented (as he can be today) from improving his income or prospects by accepting *any* offer of remuneration.

Moreover, even when the terms of wage contracts have been uninfluenced by *force majeure*, if they have resulted from industry-wide negotiations, the "peaceful solution" may well embody some measure of what I termed in 1930 "joint monopoly" (see pp. 72-73, 122, 128, 169). There is a possibility that, through many industry-wide collective agreements, the unions (together with the "employers associations" with which they have collaborated) are engaged in exploiting the rest of the community (mainly as consumers) more effectively than could have been achieved by union monopoly alone, and sharing the spoils. But there can be no greater justification for contrived scarcities inflicted on the public under these conditions than those engineered by the most uninhibited cartel action. There is no special problem here. In a regime in which antitrust is effective in all spheres (labor included) and its administration free of political manipulation, there may be little likelihood of abuse of the public.

In negotiations with "employers," union officials typically proceed today with the traditional courtesy of diplomats. Yet they seem to have felt that in economic warfare (as in all warfare) it is essential to keep alive mistrust or even hatred of "the enemy" (see above, p. 22). Managements have found it almost impossible at times to prevent the infiltration of professional troublemakers into the work force. Skilled "agitators" can be planted in a firm with instructions quietly to subvert the efforts of management to create staff harmony and general contentment among these employed (see pp. 87-89). At one time, indeed, some large enterprises in the United States engaged in counterespionage to ferret out those among their employees who were under instructions from outside to sabotage good human relations. Mainly because of the vote-controlling power possessed by the union leaders, the public has been persuaded to regard counterespionage as having invariably involved gross abuses. No one would suggest that there *were* no abuses of the system. It may well be true, for instance, that on occasion "company spies" acted as *agents provocateurs*. Yet counter-espionage was resorted to as a desperate attempt to mitigate the cold war which usually precedes open war.

Faced with the social discipline of the market (exerted often via foreign competition), managements at one time had an effective incentive to resist any collusive imposition of costs; but both the will and the power to resist have been seriously weakened during recent decades. In the large-scale industries of the United States, there were relatively few strikes before the 1930s, largely because managements had succeeded in discouraging effective unionization. Since the New Deal, however, managements have mostly become bewildered and demoralized by their feeling of helplessness when confronted with the growing ruthlessness of union power. Often, only the larger concerns remain in a position to do anything positive to check or prevent strike-threat coercion; and even they are forced to act under tremendous disadvantages.

But why should *managements* be expected to organize resistance? In a really free society, resistance to private force is a function which is properly undertaken by government. When our personal safety or security requires that we all carry guns, it means that government is failing in its functions.

One of the reasons for the appeasement attitude of managements in wage negotiations has been their desire to assuage, as far as possible, the lasting bitterness on the part of the rank and file of their workers which it is so often union tactics to arouse. But long-continued resort to the stratagems through which staff harmony *and* satisfaction of the union rulers have been sought, legitimate though they may be, seems to have created a defeatism on the part of the managers. The feeling that "concessions" must be made has tended to become habitual. And this apparent tendency has been reinforced when, through inflation, continuous upward wage-rate adjustments seem inevitable for the retention of staff.

Because the right to carry the strike weapon means the right to threaten private warfare the actual declaration of a strike has, if we can trust the very earliest accounts of such activities (for example, Adam Smith's), tended throughout history to be accompanied by bodily violence, intimidation and sabotage (see pp. 33-37). The apparent tribute which a successful strike can levy (on the consuming public, on present or potentially competing comrades, and on rash investors) often seems so tempting[15] that unmitigated hatreds are apt to be aroused firstly, at managements which seek to defend the community's interests, and secondly, against nonstrikers or strikebreakers. The bitterness and resentments engendered can be profitably fanned by politicians, in some cases by a cynically subservient press, and by union officials who think it expedient to foster and perpetuate a war psychology. Such is the cupidity of man that, when managements have stood on principle to resist strike pressures, they have at times been in danger of their lives (as have nonstrikers). Even the police have often been compelled to defend themselves against violence when they have tried to protect managers and nonstrikers from physical assault; and when the police have, in self-defense, answered physical force with physical resistance, allegations of "police brutality" have become routinely common.

"Organized economic warfare," wrote Simons, "is like organized banditry and, if allowed to spread, must lead to total revolution."[16] Most readers will probably feel that this dismal forecast exaggerates the consequences. Yet Simons' misgivings should be treated with the greatest respect. He predicted no *inevitable* outcome. But the democratic regimes *have* drifted ominously during the last few decades. Partly because union leaders have shrewdly used the funds and propaganda power at their disposal, the right to inflict civil injury (even on person who are in no sense parties to disputes) without risk of civil suits from those harmed, and the *virtual* right to commit what would be criminal acts unless carried out in the course of wage negotiations, have been conferred by judicial interpretation and statute law in many countries.

These privileges are defended on the grounds that the unions need protection from the possibility of financial ruin through exorbitant damages. But has not the whole purpose of the common law, which traditionally has accorded injured parties the right to sue for damages, been that of suppressing, or at least discouraging, privately-imposed harm on others? Private prosecution has, to some extent, been the servant of prevention.

Siegel claims that strikes today have tended

> to become more rational, predictable and stylized. Sporadic riots, violence, explosive outbursts are replaced by more peaceful varieties of collective bargaining, joint consultations, or political bargaining. Strikes may take place, but if so they are different from those of the past. . . . The new-fashioned strike . . . has become "enlightened, orderly, bureaucratic"—almost chivalrous in its tactics and cold-blooded in its calculatedness.[17]

This sort of writing, which has become almost conventional, expresses wishful thinking, or a semitruth, or perhaps exhortation—the outcome of a desire to lead the union movement to a more "reasonable" or "responsible" use of its powers.

We sometimes hear it said in the United States that public opinion does *not*, as a whole, condone the failure of the authorities to protect basic civil rights in the course of trade disputes. It is argued that the public recognizes, cynically but realistically, the control of political voting-power wielded by the union rulers. This power makes it suicidal for any ambitious mayor, governor, president or other official subject to election to call for effective resistance to strike power or even to crime when the crime is committed under union cover or direction. There is no point, it is believed, in demanding politically unthinkable reforms. I have dealt with this issue specifically elsewhere.[18] In the present context I can simply suggest that the political difficulty exists largely because the public has been conditioned to see the strikebreakers' acts as despicable and the strikers' acts as heroic (see above, p. 44). That is, I believe, a chief explanation of the moral chaos of the present setup. It accounts for the fact that the ethical issue is virtually never discussed frankly or dispassionately.

I have referred to such obviously deplorable methods of coercion because they often form a regular part of the modern labor unions' armaments and *because they illustrate the reality that the strike threat is the private use of coercive power*. But in granting labor organizations what almost amounts to a general indulgence to incite bodily intimidation and physical sabotage during wage disputes, governments have made what, seen in perspective, is merely a concession that aggravates what should already be held to be intolerable. That is, the case which I am making against the strike-threat system does *not*, as I insisted above (pp. 15-16), depend on the indefensibility of coercion permitted through those particular immunities and privileges before the law. *The really vital immunity is that which the unions have won from the ancient common law against "conspiracy in restraint of trade."*

Public opinion, although often flouted, can sometimes temper the ruthlessness of union aggression; and it does tend today to look with disapproval at violence or intimidation. But they are regarded, as I have said, as *abuses* of the strike-threat system. The private use of coercive power as such is not condemned. Yet surely, in a community which does not regard the idea of "the Great Society" as sheer cant, *the right to the private use of coercive power in itself*—the concerted, disruptive withdrawal of labor, however "peacefully" it is carried out—should be recognized as *the* truly deplorable privilege. The suppression of crime committed under labor union cover, connivance or command would *not* eliminate the major evil. Tolerated illegalities merely reinforce an indefensible power. It is the strike weapon as such, however "peaceful" or lawful the negotiations in which a lurking threat to use it may appear to be, which I contend is responsible for the wage injustices and employment insecurities of the present era. For these reasons, I shall seek the reader's support for the proposition that, even when the strike threat does not give rise to fears of physical sabotage, outrage or disorder, but merely to fears of disruption, its use remains objectionable. Properly seen the disruption *is* sabotage in its most serious form; its use remains warfare; and its acceptance as a system implies (as I have already suggested) acquiescence in the principle of might is right.

The ability of the majority employed in any field to compel—by physical intimidation—a reluctant minority to strike certainly does, however, enhance the disruptive power of an enforced stoppage. Hence the protection of the nonstriker or of the strikebreaker against all forms of intimidation (including the threat to deprive the nonstriker of his livelihood) must have a high priority in any move toward a more humane and just system.[19] That is why some statesmen and some economists have felt that, if the "right to strike" ceased to be interpreted as the "right to force others to strike," the worst abuses of the present system would have been eliminated. And such a judgment *could* turn out to be correct. *But our thinking has gone awry if we fail to recognize that the threat of physical harm to person or property is not essential for monopolistic exploitation. The "peaceful strike" can be as reprehensible as the "peaceful boycott."* The threat to disrupt a complex system of social organization by collusive action can intimidate in the same sense that the threat of physical violence to persons or property can intimidate.

To forbid strikes and boycotts would not be to restrain any basic human right. Every person would remain free to refuse to sell his assets, his products, and his services, when the refusal is not a breach of contract. That is, a person would retain his unrestrained right to prefer (a) to be employed by another, (b) to work on his own account, or (c) to enjoy leisure instead of pecuniary remuneration. But this right cannot be appealed to as justification for the *concerted* or the *simultaneous* refusal of a group of persons to continue to work in an industry, in a firm, or in a key position in an industry or firm.

The tragedy of general public acquiescence in the strike-threat system lies, indeed, in the sincerity of many of its defenders and most of its victims. An enormous number of idealistic, middle- and upper-class people (possibly encouraged in their convictions because they suffer from a guilt complex for having inherited differential opportunities and wealth) genuinely believe that—through strike warfare—the workers are fighting for justice; trying to rectify an indefensible sharing of the community's incomes; resisting a sordid and ruthless profit system. And the public shares a stereotype of "profits" which has never fully emancipated itself from the medieval prejudice toward charging interest, or charging for risk-taking, or charging for services performed by the merchant. But the ideas disseminated by the leaders of opinion are seldom the fruit of sophisticated thought, still less of study. When the typical humanitarian devotes some of his mind and much of his heart to the problem, he is almost certain to read of "labor's disadvantage in bargaining," of "labor's bitter struggle" and so forth in the flood of tendentious, and by no means disinterested, academic literature on labor unionism.

John Stuart Mill defended the tolerance of the strike-threat system partly on the grounds that, being allowed the right to strike, would rapidly teach the workers that strikes were futile. "Experience of strikes," he said, "has been the best teacher of the laboring classes. . . . . and it is most important that this course of instruction should not be disturbed."[20] But this case for tolerating the strike-threat system is unacceptable, whether judged by economic analysis or in the light of bitter historical experience. Unions *can* gain sectional advantages for their members or for the majority of their members. They have learned well the opposite lesson from that which Mill suggested.[21]

The argument upon which Mill relied, namely, that general abuse of strike power (presumably to force wage rates above their free market values) would recoil upon the strikers' heads by causing unemployment, is defective for three reasons (each of which is to be rigorously examined later):

1. It emphasizes only the less serious collective detriment which must be borne by the community. *Displacement* or *exclusion* of some workers from unionized occupations does not prevent those diverted from finding *employments* of lower remuneration and earnings (unless *independent causes* like "unemployment compensation" or social security handouts are present).

2. Mill shut his eyes to what was plain to others of his day: namely, that majorities under union protection are notoriously unconcerned about the harm wrought to those excluded, or the reduction caused in the aggregate income of the community.[22]

3. Mill's argument fails to perceive that *displacement* of those employed by a wage rate above the free market level (as distinct from the *exclusion* of those who might otherwise have entered a protected trade) might hardly occur at all where the demand for the product is inelastic.

The deplorable truth is that strikes often *do* pay; and the incredible cost of the "course of instruction" recommended by Mill has failed because the lesson has been diametrically opposed to what his obviously wishful thinking led him to believe.

I do not suggest that many strikes have not turned out to be against the strikers' advantage. I admit that occasionally even when the unions have "won" a drawn-out dispute, they have reduced the *net* income of those of their members who have retained employment for a period of many years following the settlement, because the income foregone during the strike could not be made up by the additional earnings gained until a decade or more later. And I am prepared to go still further and agree that in all probability virtually no group of workers is *absolutely* better off materially than it would have been *in a strike-free economy.*[23] But in a society in which the rules of the game permit a "free for all" at the community's expense, any group which fails to fight for its own interests, without regard for those on whom it tramples, may well come off worst. Moreover, when the majorities in one union observe gains achieved by the majorities in other trades who retain employment at higher labor costs, they are often prepared to take big risks in attempts to win similar gains through the sacrifice of income foregone during the strike period.

This consideration is relevant to labor-pricing which is initially free from obvious duress-imposed influences. Thus, if managements in nonunion firms or industries can rely upon their staff not being inveigled into joining or forming unions at some future time, then investment risks and hence important nonlabor costs of production may be greatly reduced. But under a regime that permits the strike-threat, there is always the possibility of presently ununionized workers, prompted by an awareness of yields to private coercion elsewhere, resorting to similar methods, after investment in nonversatile assets has occurred. For this reason, managements in nonunion undertakings often deem it profitable to discourage unionization by offering wage rates higher than would otherwise have been forced by the free market.[24] Hence the strike-threat system must be regarded as tending to raise labor costs *in this manner* in certain nonunion industries, with consequences similar to those caused by the direct use of union power.

The high cost of warfare *is* one of its chief deterrents. But *the costs of a strike do not fall only or even mainly on willing contestants.* The disruptive effects normally spread injuries over a wide area occupied by noncombatants. When, therefore, the prospective sectional gains seem to exceed the sectional costs, a strike will follow irrespective of the social cost. Is the cost of warfare, then, an adequate deterrent when the detriment to noncombatants may be ignored by the aggressors?

In judging the validity of the arguments submitted in the chapters which follow, readers should be constantly asking themselves whether, unless the strike-threat system is soon effectively checked, it may not turn out to be the major development impelling what were originally democratic and free societies along what F. A. Hayek has called "the road to serfdom." Henry Simons had no doubts in 1944. Democratic government, he wrote, "must guard its powers against great trade-unions, both as pressure groups in government and monopolists outside. . . . Democracy cannot live with tight occupational monopolies; . . . If democratic governments cannot suppress organized extortion . . . they will be superseded by other kinds of government.''[25]

Simons' words, ''if allowed to spread,'' were prophetic.[26] Since he wrote, the strike-threat system *has* spread and has been giving rise to growing concern. Moreover, in Britain widespread misgivings have prompted the first token reversal of policy in this field since 1824, namely, the Industrial Relations Act of 1971. It seems to me, however, that *because the strike threat as such has not yet been recognized as wholly unacceptable in a good society, no thought-out policy to insure simple justice in the wages field has yet emerged.* Public discussions of policy changes are groping, pragmatic, and lack formulated principle. In the United States, for example, we experience pathetic calls to the unions for ''responsibility'' by presidents, governors, mayors of large cities and so forth, addressed to union managements and members. But they amount to abject prayers that the unions shall not actually use the coercive apparatus they have been so carefully fashioning over the years. Have not the unions devised and built this apparatus *with legislative approval and encouragement*? And if, with courageous imagination, we take ''responsibility'' to mean not seizing more than is ''reasonable'' by the use of such weapons, we must be prepared to disclose our criteria of ''reasonable.'' We are here back to the problem we encountered above. Exactly how could a would-be ''reasonable'' union management calculate how much it is ''reasonable'' to squeeze out of ''trapped'' investors (see Chapter 10) through strike threats, or how many actual or potential comrades it is ''reasonable'' to deprive of opportunities via the standard rate? As long as an apparatus designed for the winning of sectionalist gains survives, can we be surprised that, when union leaders happen to feel it expedient to be ''reasonable,'' and refrain from taking all they calculate can be safely taken from others, rank-and-file members are apt to ignore them and resort to ''wildcat'' strikes?

It is rather absurd to expect unions not to play according to the rules of the game. These rules have been deliberately drafted in their favor; they authorize union officials to act against the interests of minorities in, or potential entrants to, the occupations they monopolize; they give scant consideration to the interests of the people as consumers; and they were framed with no apparent concern for the desirability of preserving entrepreneurial inducements to attract the services of assets and labor to where their prospective earnings will be maximized. ''It is one of the popular naïvetés of our time,'' says Machlup, ''to praise the existence of an institution but to condemn it when it carries out its functions.''[27]

Not only have the world's opinion-makers hardly begun to discern the implications of the strike-threat age, they can be observed to have been inhibiting the effort. Certainly they have been growing increasingly apprehensive of the power of the great union rulers, and the influence these people wield on electorates and legislatures. Yet they have not perceived the extent to which the economic ills of present-day society can be traced to an arbitrariness in the valuation of different classes of output. The pricing of labor (and hence products) has been largely shielded from the coordinating pressures of "free market" discipline and determined instead by a process of warfare.

I do not claim that I have here explained adequately the astonishing blindness of judges, congressmen, academicians, school teachers, editors, clergy, and others on this subject. To attempt to answer the question satisfactorily and fully would require a major essay on the genesis of popular opinion. But the fact is that to challenge the virtues of the strike-threat system today is, as H. C. Simons put it, like questioning the virtues of motherhood and the home. To suggest that the system is injurious to the workers, he said, brands one as a reactionary; for "one is either for labor or against it and the test is one's attitude towards unionism."[28] A sentimental public, he thought, regarded the labor movement "as a contest between workers who earn too little and enterprises which earn too much," while they failed generally to perceive "the identity of interest between the whole community and enterprise seeking to keep down costs."[29]

But there is another, not unconnected, reason to which I have already referred. It has been said that in the U. S. Congress every interest is represented except the public interest. It would be felt to be political madness for most congressmen, or most candidates for elective office in any country, to take a lead in educating the community on the great issue we are here studying. Is there then any conceivable method of finding a way out of the moral maze which a long alliance between politicians and the opinion-makers has created?

This is a question I have tried among other things to answer in my book, *Politically Impossible. . . . ?* and I return to the subject in Chapter 19. But I want my present readers to ask themselves whether any solution of the problem of industrial warfare is conceivable unless "the peaceful dispute" is eliminated? *Such a solution would require legislation which placed three objectives above the vested interests of labor union officials and the relatively small numbers of workers*[30] *who are the final beneficiaries of the contemporary "dog-eat-dog" chaos.*

The three paramount objectives are: (1) *the highest possible wages flow, (2) the most equitable distribution of that flow, and (3) the greatest possible measure of employment security*. To achieve these objectives we must, I shall suggest, eliminate "the dispute." We must aim at the creation of institutions which facilitate the free market determination of the value of labor's contribution.

I suggest that if we are ever to achieve peace and justice in the field of wage rate determination, *it will be necessary to insure that no party shall ever gain as a result of the private use of coercive power*. This means that the issues about which economic wars are waged or threatened shall be decided in a different way. And here I categorically challenge my fellow economists. There *is* no other way than the determination of *all* prices by the free, democratic, social process of the market, to the full extent to which human ingenuity can plan the required institutions. And "all prices" covers, of course, the price of labor's contribution to output (the value of the wage rate *plus* fringe benefits). Must this price continue to be the outcome, almost everywhere, of a contest or a threatened contest in which the principle of victory to the most strongly armed is tempered only by the fear of going too far and destroying the source of income?

The frequent direct burden of strikes on third parties has sometimes engendered general misgivings in the public mind. But it would be a mistake to think that the *observable* social detriment in this case is nearly as deleterious from society's angle as is the distortion of the production structure caused, even when there is no actual strike disruption. The source of the burden that the community must carry remains invisible to the masses and their leaders. Consumers are, I shall show, almost universally passive and helpless. They normally bear the brunt. And workers excluded from all hope of entry at the wage rates imposed are usually unaware of the injustices they bear; they are not prompted to any spontaneous protest; and few politicians judge it profitable to champion their cause.

In conclusion I must again refer to the feeling that "the right to strike" is one of the unchallengeable "rights of man" when it is unaccompanied by any threat of *physical* harm to person or property, because its aims are then good and achievable. If we rely on the goodness and achievability of objectives, we must be prepared also to defend the unions' immunities and privileges which make resort to violence and sabotage an ever-menacing reality. Can it not be claimed, equally legitimately, that the right to coerce evil-doers—like nonstrikers and strikebreakers—by the threat of assault, also assists the pursuit of ends which are assumed to be good and achievable?

In this chapter, I have argued simply that the strike-threat system is an intolerable method of *attempting* to prevent the exploitation of labor, or of organizing the exploitation of investors. In Chapters 6 to 10 I shall discuss the possibility of that method *actually achieving* either of these objects.

NOTES

[1] Quoted in N. W. Chamberlain, *Collective Bargaining,* 2nd ed. (New York, McGraw-Hill, 1915), p. 122.

[2] Abraham J. Siegel, "Method and Substance in Theorizing About Worker Protest," *Aspects of Labor Economics: A Conference of the Universities—National Bureau Committee for Economic Research,* Report of the National Bureau of Economic Research (Princeton: Princeton University Press, 1962), p. 42.

[3] In E. R. Phelps Brown's scholarly *Economics of Labor* (New Haven: Yale University Press, 1962), there are several references to "justice," regarding the rights of the worker. I have failed to find a single use of the word in reference to the rights of the investor.

[4] H. C. Simons, *"Some Reflections on Syndicalism,"* in *Economic Policy for a Free Society* (Chicago: University of Chicago Press, 1948), p. 128.

[5] In Chapter 10, I shall show that investors, rich or poor, are inexploitable *in that role* when they foresee exploitation probabilities. But aggregate net interest receipts (after allowance for inflation) will tend to be reduced through strike-threat pressures (as will the aggregate flow of wages) *and affect the less affluent savers regressively.*

[6] On occasion, it has been possible indeed to bring a great range of vertically-integrated operations to a standstill by the withdrawal of a few essential workers in one workshop.

[7] See above, p. 34. My 1930 discussion of the device is relevant. See W. H. Hutt, *The Theory of Collective Bargaining* (P.S. King, 1930), pp. 28, 100.

[8] The phrase (not the illustration) is from Arnold R. Weber, "Stability and Change in the Structure of Collective Bargaining," Lloyd Ulman, ed., *Challenges to Collective Bargaining,* The American Assembly (Englewood Cliffs, N. J.: Prentice Hall, Spectrum Books, 1967), pp. 20-21.

[9] Although the legality of this extraordinarily potent method of disruption is doubtful under certain clauses of the Taft-Hartley and Landrum-Griffin acts, political considerations appear to have prevented prosecutions. However, some "labor economists" have been hinting that the Nixon Administration has been tactfully threatening to enforce the law unless the A.F.L.-C.I.O. refrain from using this weapon, at least during the Administration's attempt to "fight inflation."

[10] The position resembles that which has become common in international relations between the newly independent states where the interests of the inarticulate masses are rarely of any importance, the interests of a very small ruling minority (who may be genuinely seeking the welfare of their subjects) being the paramount consideration in diplomatic dealings. This was recognizably the position in the relations between nations in the Middle Ages. It was largely the ambitions and aims of those who held the royal power which had to be satisfied. The people as a whole were expected, in some cases under the explicit claim of divine right, to accept the objectives set by their rulers without question. That the rulers were usually more enlightened than the ruled does not affect the point I am making.

[11] See pp. 54-55.

[12] Of two jobs demanding comparable skill and energy, the public will tend to regard a wage rate of 20 percent higher for one person than for another as unfair, unless such a differential has become customary. The criterion may be in practice mere job description. If a high rate of remuneration for a crane operator has been established in the past through union pressures, or for some other reason, the man in the street will say, "But that *is* the fair wage for a crane operator." And most people will similarly tend to regard the number who are employable at any such wage rate as an acceptable standard of "an adequate supply" of the labor in question. This point is discussed in Chapter 13.

[13] F. Machlup, "Monopolistic Wage Determination," in *Wage Determination*

and the Economics of Liberalism (Washington, D.C.: Chamber of Commerce of the United States, 1947), pp. 53-54.

[14] For example, consider the quotation from Siegel, quoted above, p. 52.

[15] Although the gains are never as great as they are believed to be. (See pp. 47, 54-56, 248.)

[16] Simons, op. cit., p. 127.

[17] Siegel, op. cit., p. 44.

[18] W. H. Hutt, *Politically Impossible. . . . ?* (London: Institute of Economic Affairs, 1971), especially Part 6. I return to this topic in Chapter 19.

[19] As things are, the political power of the union organizations in the United States has succeeded, in certain states, in getting legislation to make the use of strikebreakers illegal.

[20] John Stuart Mill, *Principles of Political Economy*, ed. W. J. Ashley (London: Longmans, Green and Company, 1909), pp. 936-937.

[21] What they have *not* perceived is the *incidence* of their gains from others. Neither they nor their apologists, recognize that *vigilant investors are unexploitable*, a reality to which Chapter 10 is devoted.

[22] As Machlup has pointed out, what the union members expect their leaders to obtain for them is "the largest wage bill" and "not to sell them down the river in the interests of a fancy 'gross national product' . . ." The unions "will fight for bigger pay envelopes of their members, regardless of the 'unproven' effects upon the economy which academic economists may ascribe to these policies. . . . To expect the union leader to act as a responsible statesman in the interests of the nation is to expect him to do what his followers would consider 'selling out to the bosses.' " (Machlup, op. cit., pp. 52-53).

[23] For justification of this assertion, see p. 248.

[24] But every wage rate raised by duress (or fear of future duress) forces other wage rates down, including some which are still fixed above what the free market would otherwise have determined. See Chapter 7.

[25] Simons, op. cit., pp. 126-7.

[26] Ibid., p. 127.

[27] Machlup, op. cit., p. 54.

[28] Simons, op. cit., p. 121.

[29] Ibid., p. 122.

[30] I say "relatively small numbers" for reasons which are mentioned in Chapter 17.

The "Bargaining Power" Concept

MY *Theory of Collective Bargaining* contains a history and critical discussion of the notion of "labor's disadvantage in bargaining," an idea which, first introduced in Adam Smith's *Wealth of Nations,* remains a powerful influence in popular opinion and has not disappeared from the field of labor economics. In Alchian and Allen's excellent textbook, the concept of "bargaining power" is described categorically as "a vacuous concept of little analytical substance."[1] I hope in this chapter to show that this description is justified. But the term is still widely used. It is treated with such respect by labor economists of high apparent authority that it is at least expedient in a work of this kind to examine the notion.

In a masterly work, Fritz Machlup has collected and classified a wide range of attempts at giving meaning to notions of "inequality of bargaining power."[2] His rigorous examination of these ideas has exposed very effectively the intellectual muddle they have caused. But since his book appeared, the terms and phrases he criticized have continued to be used as though his contribution had never been made.[3] In the following discussion, which is indebted to Machlup's, I shall repeat the challenge in a different approach.

Since I treated the subject in 1930, my interpretation of Adam Smith's famous passage about "labor's disadvantage" has changed slightly. When he referred to "labor's disadvantage in the dispute," I now think he was *not* asserting that labor was at a disadvantage *in the free market*. He visualized two different things.

Firstly, he seems to have had in mind an attempt to force higher wage rates through an actual strike; and he apparently felt that, in the circumstances of his day, efforts to achieve sectional gains in that manner were more likely to fail than succeed (despite the violence which he believed often accompanied strikes). To the extent to which this was his point, there need be no argument. The size of a strike fund can, beyond doubt, influence the chances of the strikers getting better terms *for those of their members who retain employment*[4] at the higher labor costs. And it is true that the individual worker can seldom effectively disrupt the production process,[5] while a few workers among many may have hardly any ability to do so.

Secondly, Adam Smith believed that the masters possessed a *tacit monopoly* in purchasing labor—what we now call "oligopsony." Now if workers who do not act collusively face a monopsonist or effective oligopsony (see Chapters 8 and 9), they may be said to be at a disadvantage. Again, there need be no argument on that point. *But economists who followed Adam Smith began to use the idea of "labor's disadvantage" in contexts in which, by implication, neither a strike situation nor the presence of monopsony is assumed.*

The idea which this century has inherited is that combinations among the workers are needed *to offset* "labor's disadvantage in bargaining" or "labor's inferior bargaining power," because the free market value of labor is depressed *through some disadvantage other than monopsonistic exploitation.* At times, however, monopsony *is* assumed, while at other times the "bargaining disadvantage" implied is the inability of a group of workers to exploit either the other cooperant parties to production or consumers, in the absence of concerted action. Sometimes one or more of these ideas seems to be woven into an argument expressed in terms of a "balance of power" between "employers" and "unions," which collective bargaining somehow brings about. Usually the assumption is that the meaning of all these terms is self-evident. In fact, their use has seriously confused thinking about the wage-determining process.

We can begin by considering the phrase "balance of power." If all this phrase is intended to mean is a situation in which no one can say with certainty which party will succeed in a wage dispute (whatever "success" can imply here),[6] it has at least a modicum of meaning. It suggests that neither strikes nor management-ordered work stoppages will be attempted because, in the presence of this "balance," the outcome is likely to be indecisive and hence resort to aggression too costly (see pp. 54-55). Such a connotation centers attention upon a threatened work stoppage and borrows a perfectly clear notion from political science. War between two powers is, according to the "balance-of-power" theory, unlikely if the armed strength of the two parties is about equal. In those conditions, according to the theory, neither side is certain that it will be victorious, while the costs of war are high. Similarly, the high costs of work stoppages *help* deter attempts to determine labor cost through the imposition of nonmarket values. Hence a "balance of power" will cause the maintenance of the status quo. This is obvious, of course. The burden of any work stoppage on both parties will always be weighed against the prospective gains from it. If both parties think that possible winnings do not justify the stakes, there will be no aggression. "Industrial peace" will prevail.

This is, however, seldom the sort of consideration which is in the minds of economists and others who use terms like "bargaining power," "labor's disadvantage in bargaining," and so forth. To get near to what may be meant when monopoly-monopsony is *not* ruled out, we can, I think, simplify the question by the following approach. In every case the phrases we are examining suggest that, in the conclusion of any wage contract, the party with "strong bargaining power" will get better terms while the party with "weak bargaining power" will get worse ones. *Let us suppose that what is envisaged has reference to whether the wage rates or prices determined are above or below what the free market value would be.* If this is indeed what is meant, then the possibilities *can* be expressed with fair conceptual clarity in terms of monopolistic or monopsonistic influences. A simple diagram can represent the possibilities by representing the wage rates which would be determined under different assumptions.

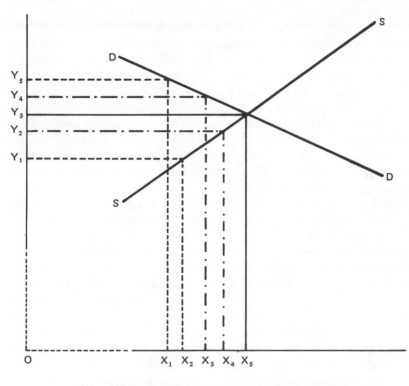

OY_5	Monopolistic Labor against Competing Investors
OY_4	Monopolistic Labor against Monopsonistic Investors
OY_3	Competitive Labor against Competitive Investors
OY_2	Monopolistic Labor against Monopsonistic Investors
OY_1	Competitive Labor against Monopsonistic Investors

On the above diagram, wage-rate possibilities are represented on the vertical axis and numbers employed on the horizontal axis. OY_5 represents the wage-rate that a union would think to be to its members' advantage to enforce (if it could) against uncombined, competing firms. It is described as "monopolistic labor against competing investors." The numbers employed will be OX_1. OY_1 represents the opposite. It is the wage rate which managements (on behalf of investors) possessing the power to purchase labor monop-

63

sonistically might think it profitable to enforce (if they could) where the workers were wholly unorganized. It is described as "competitive labor against monopsonistic investors." The numbers employed will be OX_1. OY_3 represents what the price of labor would be in a free market. It is described as "competitive labor against competing investors." The numbers employed will be OX_5. OY_4 and OY_2 represent what we might *assume* about the extreme possibilities under what used to be called "bilateral monopoly," i.e., with "monopolistic labor against monopsonistic investors." The numbers employed will be OX_3 and OX_4 respectively, or somewhere between.

If by convention we always described wage rates higher than the level OY_3 as due to the "superior bargaining power" of labor (or the "inferior bargaining power" of investors) and those below the level OY_3 as due to the "superior bargaining power" of managements on behalf of investors (or the "inferior bargaining power" of labor), we should at least have intelligible notions. And I think we do find that all attempts at *rigorous* definition on this topic are groping toward a definition of the degree to which the price of labor diverges from the competitive level, OY_3. Thus, the term "bargaining power" *could* be used to refer to the ability of one or other party (a) to force a price or wage rate above or below the free market level, or (b) to neutralize, in whole or in part, an opposed monopsony or monopoly, thereby forcing a price or wage rate toward or across OY_3, in other words, toward or across what the free market level would have been.

Often, however, terms like "bargaining strength" or "labor's disadvantage" are used in a manner which does not enable us to relate them simply to this conceptual framework. For instance, under monopsony, if A has higher-paid alternative employments than B, he may be paid more than B for an identical kind of work. B is then said to have "weaker bargaining power." But A's services are more valuable to society in other uses than B's (although not in the particular job to which A is attracted, where they contribute no more to the value of the product than do B's). If we describe A's greater "opportunity value" as his "greater bargaining power," we must bear in mind the full implications of the facts, *firstly*, that under competition for labor, no individual worker would have any advantage or disadvantage in relation to his competing comrades; and secondly, that even a monopsonist will employ no A's for the job until there are no additional B's available.

Actually, within any competitive labor market, where each worker is free to move to where he believes he can earn most, his "bargaining power" will rise as his services become more valuable through training or experience. The term is then simply a synonym for value! In every case the crucial consideration is the worker's alternatives. Where competitive conditions rule, the refusal of any offer is simply a means of saying, "I have (or I believe I have) a more favorable alternative." Such a communication may result in an improved offer. Where a worker (or his union on his behalf) can say truthfully to management, "I should like to work (or continue to work) for your undertaking but I think I can do better elsewhere," that is, where he refuses an

64

offer because he knows of or expects higher remuneration or better prospects in another firm, we all know what is meant when it is said that his "bargaining power" is strong.[7] But it could then be argued that there is hardly any point in using that term. It only means that his free market value is as high as any other prospective offer. Of course, a person might successfully represent that the market value of his services is higher than it really is. We can then (if we wish) describe his *bargaining bluff* as "bargaining power." It is not a very helpful usage.

Even in a noncompetitive market, we can still say that a worker's "bargaining power" is represented by his "opportunity value," which means the value of his alternatives; but we then mean that this power will be weak (the "opportunity value" low) *when alternative employments can be somehow withheld from him.*[8] In Chapter 7, I shall explain that *exploitation* (whether monopolistic or monopsonistic in origin) occurs through the process of *shutting off alternatives* for those exploited. The important point to remember is that the "weak bargaining power" notion which I have here suggested *might* be used with meaning and consistency *has reference to the individual worker. The notion cannot be simply transferred to labor in general.* We cannot talk of "labor's disadvantage in bargaining," although we can discuss the *individual's.* The remedy for the individual's "bargaining weakness" is to raise the value of his work. His "bargaining power" depends (a) on his having scarce and valuable powers, which simply means that he can provide goods and services which consumers need, and (b) on his effective right to use those powers.

All the workers in an occupation may be exploited under monopsony, however, if managements can tie them under contracts which are not for their benefit, or shut them in in other ways. The remedy in that case is action to remove the barriers to other employments.

But monopoly or monopsony may influence the value of complementary services in the production process *without exploitation,* that is, without the monopolist or monopsonist shutting out any alternatives from any participant. As will become more clear in Chapter 8, discrimination is exploitative *only when the monopsonist himself has in some way held off competing opportunities.* Because the worker who has only lowly-paid alternatives has "weak bargaining power," this does not mean that he is more *exploitable* (under the definition of "exploitation" we are using) than the worker who has relatively well-remunerated alternatives. Thus, a monopsonist may pay the workers he recruits (who have well-paid alternatives) a wage rate just sufficiently above their free market value in their former jobs to compensate for mobility costs, while those he retains (who have poorly-paid alternatives) may be paid just sufficiently to make it not worth their incurring the mobility costs of accepting other alternatives in the free market. As we are about to see, the lower wage rate needed to hold the latter does not mean that they are exploited *under the definition we are using* (see p. 3).

An often-used illustration, assuming (usually tacitly) monopsony, compares the worker who has "reserves" and can "hold out" with the case of the worker who is prepared to accept a lower wage rate than the average because he has no "reserves." The typical example takes an *un*typical case, namely, that of an unemployed person. The argument is that if he has a large fund of savings, he can refuse what he thinks is a poor offer and for the time being purchase leisure, or finance his prospecting for a better opportunity, out of his capital. His less-thrifty colleague, on the other hand, who may have spent his last dollar, will be desperately in need of an immediate material income, so that a monopsonist will be able to discriminate against him.[9]

Now although such discrimination *can* occur if the monopsonist knows the worker's situation, it is not *exploitation* unless the monopsonist himself has been able in some way to withhold employment opportunities from the worker in question. Let us consider a monopsonist who has closed no doors to any other employments, offering annual contracts of employment to individual employees through advertisements, and again assume that he recruits two classes of workers, those we can call As, who have well remunerated alternative employments and those we can call Bs, who have relatively poorly remunerated alternatives. Let us imagine also that the wage rates he offers initially are on the low side, in order to test the market. The first workers to accept the terms offered and to tie themselves for, say, a year (the Bs) will be those who can better their condition most thereby (because they have but poor alternatives, including poor "reserves"). If the monopsonist has been unable to attract all the labor he needs by the first offer (through which he recruits Bs), we can imagine that he will be able to attract some As, by offering *better* terms to them. It is important to notice that the condition of the Bs is improved, not depressed, in relation to their initial condition. The contracts under which the Bs earn less than the As are accepted by the former because they open the way to more highly paid alternatives than society is offering in other ways.

It can indeed be to the Bs' *advantage* that they shall be discriminated against. The principle is particularly clear when economies of scale effect "natural monopsony" (either as the inevitable concomitant of "natural monopoly" or independently.[10] For it is *conceivable* that only under the economies achievable through discrimination against the Bs will it be possible for the new, naturally monopsonistic venture that raises their earning power to be established at all. The general principle here (to be explained in Chapters 8 and 12) is that discrimination is justifiable (in the interests of the "optimization" of the community's "welfare") when the parties discriminated against are nevertheless the beneficiaries of that discrimination.

Hence phrases like "the workers' bargaining strength," in referring to each individual's alternatives, may envisage either (a) alternatives determined in the free market or (b) alternatives influenced by a monopolist or a monopsonist. In the former case, no exploitation is involved. In the latter case, exploitation *may* be a factor. But labor's "bargaining power" *in a different sense* will be influenced by the elasticity of demand for the end product (which will determine the exploitability of consumers) and by the elasticity of supply of complementary factors (which will determine the exploitability of suppliers of raw materials and/or investors in fixed capital). "Exploitative power" would be more apt.

When "bargaining strength" is sought by the unions by way of the strike threat, that itself involves what in practice is the most important shutting off from alternatives for the less-fortunate workers. Any duress-imposed wage rate in excess of the free market level denies access for some to jobs of higher productivity and remuneration. It may be held therefore to *reduce* their "bargaining power." At the same time, it means that the "bargaining power" of a privileged group is strengthened. The principle is, then, that any individual denied access to any bargaining table is usually left with curtailed "bargaining power" in the employment outlets for which he is allowed to bargain. The depleted earnings he must accept in order to get immediate or early alternatives to the job he has lost, and his weakened security of employment, are *consequences* of restraints enforced through the strike threat.

In a competitive labor market, a temporarily displaced worker is confronted with a wide range of "take-it-or-leave-it" choices, just as is a shopper regarding a range of competing commodities and competing shops. Under such conditions, managements buy labor through wage-rate offers and shops sell goods through price offers which those who want employment (or better paid employment) or goods accept. It is said, however, that the worker is "at a disadvantage" compared to the shopper because he has no "waiting power." But as we have seen, the lack of "reserves" is no disadvantage in a competitive market. Shoppers equally have no "waiting power" regarding certain of their purchases. They must buy food for the immediate future or starve.

The word "monopoly" is conventionally used to describe what Ludwig von Mises has argued cogently ought to be called the union's "supply restriction." Mises's case is that "monopolistic action" is advantageous to a monopolist only if total proceeds at a monopoly price exceed total net proceeds at the potential competitive price.[11] That is, the monopolist must allow for the loss in respect of the capacity he withholds; whereas the organizers of supply restrictions, like unions, "are not concerned with what may happen to the part of the supply they bar from access to the market. The fate of the people who own this part does not matter to them."[12] The important but generally overlooked difference in principle to which Mises is here referring is one which I tried to get round in 1935 by introducing the term "contrived scarcity" (contrasted with "natural scarcity").[13] In Chapter 7, I shall use this and related concepts in an attempt to clarify the issue further. But when I use the term "monopolistic *restriction*" or "monopsonistic *restriction*" I shall have in mind the *shutting out* or *shutting in* of those who believe they could otherwise improve their earning power or profits by moving their labor or their capital to another occupation, industry, firm, or area. And every such "restriction" (or "shutting out" or "shutting in") involves "exploitation."

I propose now to draw the reader's attention to some typical uses of the term "bargaining power" in contexts in which the market alternatives available to the bargainer are obviously *not* what the writer has in mind. Suppose we consider the situation which arises when unionized workers, acting in concert, are in a position to say to management, in the *friendliest* way, "We have the power to ruin your stockholders. We don't want to do that. A fight will involve some costs to us; but we shall feel forced to use this power unless you agree to our very reasonable terms. If you refuse to make the consumer pay a modest extra sum on our behalf, you will have to transfer some of your investors' income to us. What we ask won't actually *ruin* your undertaking. We know what your profits are. If you want what is good for your stockholders, you will agree to our terms."

This coercive power *may,* if we wish, be termed "bargaining power." But it is then an exact parallel to the "bargaining power" of the salesman of jukeboxes, gambling machines, and vending machines, who (in the United States) sometimes tells his prospective customers, with the greatest politeness, "If you know what is good for you, you will sign this agreement for the installation of one of these machines." Every customer then knows that failure to agree will bring costly damage to his shop or personal violence against himself.

"Bargaining power" in *that* sense bears no resemblance to the ability to command a certain wage rate because of the existence of actual or potential competing offers. Hence although we might say that that party's bargaining power is greatest which can convince the opposing party that it is in a position to do that party the greater harm, ought we not to convey our meaning by a simple descriptive term and say that the "stronger" party is that which has the greater "coercive power"? If I am stopped by a hijacker who has a gun while I have only fists, isn't it just a misleading euphemism to refer to his superior "bargaining power"?

However, if the term *is* defined to mean "power to disrupt and hence to coerce," it is both realistic and understandable, but it cannot then be used in the other connotations! Presumably managements rely upon a similar power if they themselves order a work stoppage with coercive intentions. But the literature of the labor movement leaves the impression that the actual use of a parallel power by management is *virtually* unknown and the threat almost as rare. Mere refusal to accept union conditions is *not* a work stoppage. As we have seen, there is a continuous offer of employment from management's side, at stipulated wage rates, just as there is a continuous offer of goods, at stipulated prices, in a shop.[14]

Moreover, the downward adjustment of wage-rate offers when a wage contract is renewed, where necessary to price some current output within reach of the community's income (that is, following reduced entrepreneurial bidding for the available labor supply), is not coercive. It is a means of avoiding (a) the displacement of labor and (b) (from society's angle) the depletion of the wages flow. It is no more *disruptive* than is inflation which, since the Keynesian era, has been a crude alternative way of reducing real wage rates (as a means of mitigating the depletion of the wages flow caused through strike-threat action). The step taken by managements is not evidence of their superior "bargaining strength" but a consequence of their subordination to consumers' sovereignty, as representatives of the residual claimants on the value of the product.

I know of no recorded case in which general wage-rate reduction has been used as *a threat* by managements, or punitively. But the workers in an undertaking have often been warned about the impossibility of continuing the employment of former numbers in the event of a forced wage-rate increase. It is easy enough to describe such warnings as "threats"; but they are no more *coercive* than warnings that smoking is liable to cause lung cancer. Admittedly, in the course of negotiations conducted in the shadow of the strike threat, managements are likely to paint the consequences of enhanced labor costs in unduly somber colors. Hence there *may* sometimes be a "threat" element present.[15] In fact, I believe, the threat of disruption as a "bargaining weapon" (in the sense of a means of coercion) is used almost entirely by the unions. But no matter what party may actually be guilty of using it, either the threat of or the use of private coercion in the "bargaining process" is intolerable.

N. W. Chamberlain brings in such factors as "the pressure of immigration, the cityward movement of farm population, the speed of mechanization and mass production techniques" among the circumstances which create "labor's disadvantage," because they "place employment at a premium."[16] But all this means is that one's "bargaining power" is raised or lowered by anything which causes demand for what one has to sell to rise or fall or its competing supply to fall or rise! Chamberlain may possibly intend, however, that these are circumstances which limit the exploitative power of the strike threat. He regards labor's "bargaining weakness" as overcome when "by common action workers could prevent themselves from being played off one against the other."[17] But the "playing-off" of one would-be seller or buyer against another is the only way in which any party entering into a contract can protect himself *against* exploitation; and the collusive action which is here represented as rectifying the "bargaining disadvantage" turns out merely to be a particular method of contriving a scarcity. In other words, "labor is at a disadvantage in bargaining" comes to mean, "labor finds it difficult to exploit displaced or excluded workers, consumers, risk-takers and the providers of complementary assets in production."

Most discussions of this issue view the parties to negotiations over a wage contract, under the strike-threat shadow, in a most unrealistic way. They portray the workers (or the union) on the one side and the "employer" (presumably management representing investors) on the other side. But the reality that successful wage negotiations require the expression of agreements or settlements in a form which maintains the prestige (and hence maintenance in office) of the union officials is seldom mentioned (see above, p. 47).

In practice this is often (if not most often) the vital consideration. As skilled negotiators, managements understand the expediency of allowing the union officials to receive the whole credit for every improvement in wage contracts. When managements make concessions, they must do so in such a way that the union rulers will be able to show *a capitulation* on the part of the enemy—"the employer." Indeed, managements normally permit every intermittent restoration, full or partial, of real remuneration in the course of an inflation to be claimed as a union triumph. And more generally, when the maximum concessions managements can contemplate are small, it is at times good strategy for them to stage a fight against certain fringe ·benefits demanded, which cost little. After thus making an effective show of opposition, their (the managements') eventual retreat will preserve the illusion of successful strike-threat pressures, and hence make it possible or expedient for the leaders of the unions to recommend acceptance of the terms. Occasionally, by such tactics, managements can get away with relatively small concessions. In some cases indeed, the prestige of the union officials can be protected by the acceptance of conditions of which the burden may fall wholly on the union membership itself.[18]

Moreover, what actually happens in almost every case when both parties have become accustomed to, and experts in, the "bargaining process" is that managements begin negotiations with a fairly clear idea of the limits to which they are prepared to go in concessions (in order to avoid an *actual* stoppage). They will declare at the outset their determination not to concede more than a very small part of what they expect to concede; while unions will begin by asking for more than they believe managements will concede (with or without actual recourse to the strike). For instance, managements which, in a free labor market, would have found it profitable to offer, say, $400 per month in order to retain (from alternative employments available) the most profitable number of workers may think it good tactics to begin by offering, say, $350. They know that, in the market circumstances ruling, such remuneration offered would be disadvantageous (or even ruinous) to them because it would mean their losing too many of their most valued personnel; but they regard their initial offer, maintained for a time, as serving the practical purpose of enabling an apparent *capitulation*; for such a capitulation is above all essential in order to satisfy the union leaders.[19] If we are realistic, then, we must perceive that there are three parties involved in "collective bargaining" over wage contracts. It is not the conflicting interests of the workers in relation to the interests of the investors which constitute the really crucial issue in the struggle, but the interests of the elected rulers of the union.

In thus insisting that the essential condition is the satisfaction of the union rulers, I am envisaging as realistically as I can the internal democracy which is characteristic of the majority (but by no means all) unions. In general it is true that, in B. C. Roberts's words, "while there is little direct check upon leaders during the course of negotiations, they must be able to . . . secure the votes of members in referendums and elections for office."[20] But it is just this concern of the leaders with reelection that is the critical issue with which managements are confronted during wage negotiations. Union officials are faced with the dilemma that they do not wish to kill the goose; and sometimes they clearly do not wish to harm the general economic conditions which provide sustenance for the goose (see pp. 140-142). Yet most union members ex-

70

pect immediate results, while rivals for power are prepared to claim that *they* could win more. Indeed, there will often be competitors for office who are as unscrupulous and irresponsible in promise-making as the typical politician during election campaigns!

We sometimes hear it said that it is the *duty* of unions *and* of managements to bargain in good faith, not merely to demand. Does this mean that it is their duty not to dig their heels in and refuse to make concessions? If so, it implies that *it is the duty of both sides* to begin by asking more favorable terms than they are prepared eventually to accept. What else can it mean? Because the strike-threat system exists, it may well be good tactics—even inevitable tactics—for managements to carry on more or less continuous discussions with union officials. But recognition of this practical reality must not blind us to the basic principle that it is *managements'* task to offer such wage rates as they predict will justify the purchase of labor services for investment into work in progress; and this must be seen as a facet of the continuous process of investment of stockholders' capital into the retention, replacement, or accumulation of inventories of materials and fixed capital.

This does not mean that under nonstrike negotiations the wage rates set can be said to have been determined "unilaterally," "without negotiation," "dictatorially," and therefore unjustly. The word "unilateral" which has been used in this connection is a red herring. Collective bargaining is not an alternative to unilateral decision-making. Every offer accepted *must* be bilateral. Prices are marked for goods offered in shops but this does not prevent every purchase from being a bilateral transaction. Would a system of haggling over every retail transaction result in greater consumer freedom, security, or justice? Similarly, no employee is *forced* to retain or accept any employment at the remuneration set by any management in a free labor market. On the termination of any wage contract he may leave, as he *will,* if he can get better terms or prospects elsewhere. It is that which, as we have seen, constitutes his "bargaining power" (in the least unsatisfactory use of that term). And a management may be just as helpless in respect of the wage rate at which it forecasts that the most profitable number of workers can be retained by or attracted to the enterprise as is a shopkeeper in fixing prices which he predicts will retain or attract the most profitable number of customers (when he is not in a position to act monopolistically). (See p. 14.)

Where no unions exist, one management makes offers for different types and grades of workers on behalf of many stockholders, while an individual decision to accept an offer must occur before any person becomes an employee or continues as an employee. On the other hand, at the bargaining table, a union may accept or reject offers not specifically on behalf of individuals but on behalf of large groups of those it represents. That is not a *necessary* arrangement, however, whereas it *is* impossible for each individual stockholder to make a separate contract with every worker; for the plant and the firm constitute a unity. The only parallel to this unity on the labor side is when several persons form a partnership, like a cooperative theatrical group, and offer their services *as a whole* to the highest bidder. But then they have

71

usually already arranged among themselves for their *relative* individual remuneration. And dealing in that case with the executive of the group, or with the union executive, does not cause the decision-making to be more (or less) bilateral.

Ideally, collective bargaining involves the union officials negotiating, so to speak, bulk contracts for groups of individuals. In some circumstances, we can regard all the workers employed as having agreed, in advance, to accept whatever terms the officials accept on their behalf, subject to their retaining employment under those terms. But if union officials are seen as servants and not the masters of union members, each member should be free, if he should so wish, to make an independent contract with management, especially those who might otherwise be laid off.

As every worker knows if he participates in sports, human abilities in different directions vary considerably. Hence *bargaining freedom* requires that those who contribute differentially to the satisfaction of consumers' demands should be allowed to make available their services for remuneration in proportion to what they believe the value of their contribution to be. And that value may be *higher than* or (when the alternative is displacement) *less than* the wage rate which a union might have negotiated. "Bargaining justice" requires therefore that while a union should retain the right to *advise* an individual against what is thought to be his wrong judgment of the value of his services, that word *advise* should not be allowed to be interpreted in the way in which the words "persuade" or "induce" have come to be so often interpreted, namely, as synonyms for "intimidate" or "coerce." The individual's "bargaining power" means, indeed, his "bargaining freedom."

Let us consider in this context the case of a worker whose way of life faces the prospect of disruption through his threatened displacement following a change in consumer preference. The right of such a person to offer his services at a reduced wage rate in order to avoid displacement (which consumers would otherwise enforce) ought to be recognized as the source of a basic security—a fundamental freedom. Even if he is confronted with the dilemma of accepting or rejecting a wage rate set below what he believes will ultimately be his free market value, he can still retain an income by temporarily accepting a wage cut, and live on the curtailed income while he (or his union) is looking for an opening remunerated at what would perhaps be the present value of his services in a better-coordinated society.

When industry-wide bargaining is enforced (as it is for instance in the steel, coal, automobile, tire, trucking and other industries in the United States) *a monopsonistic structure representing the managers of the producing units is almost necessarily created*. But in the absence of agreements not to "poach" labor (and assuming that antitrust is effective) individual managements will be competing for such labor supply as the standard rate leaves profitably employable by the industry as a whole. The *real* danger in these circumstances is not of exploitation of labor but of the public; for with the support of unions, corporations with which the wage contract is made have the power to create "joint monopolies" with labor,[21] or to encourage unions to bring under their wing the employees of concerns (perhaps of a different type) which, by reason of some greater technical efficiency or superior price policy, appear to be taking business from them.[22]

Unions are fully conscious of their exemption from antitrust or similar penalties, and whenever competition from substitutes appears, they may recognize a solidarity of interest with stockholders. What, then, becomes of the notion of labor's supposedly inferior "bargaining power?" A divergence of interest about the division of the spoils of joint monopoly will remain, and the "just" sharing of gains at consumers' expense will be as indeterminate as the "just" sharing of stolen booty always is. This is one of the cases in which the "bargaining power" notion seems to be concerned with who will get the biggest share of ill-gotten gains; that is, the case in which the superior "bargaining power" will reside in the party which is apparently in a position to harm the most. When unions and managements resort to such collusion, unions will, naturally enough, express concern for justice toward their competitors in the expanding enterprises which are offering substitutes that are better value for money. They will want the interlopers to be brought into one "bargaining unit" for the protection, they will say, of their competitors as well as of themselves.[23] The merging of the steel and the aluminum workers in the United States, as technical progress caused formerly complementary products to become competing products, is a case in point. But the "protection" achieved is essentially of the power to exploit.

Let us now return to the question of the actual determination of a wage agreement when the strike threat is an influence. If an offer by the management of a corporation is at first refused by a union, there is very little that the economist can *usefully* say about the terms which are likely to be eventually accepted. That is, the determinants of the wage agreement (wage rates *plus* fringe benefits for work during a certain period) can then be subjected to purposeful economic analysis only in the sense that the use of resources in the course of warfare can be studied.[24]

Now in warfare, the *ultimate and overriding objective,* namely, victory, is a product to one party and a negative product (namely, a deprivation) to the other, and there seems to be little purpose in showing that, if we have sufficient data, we may be able to forecast the probable result of any resort to the strike threat (or to an actual strike). The result is certainly not relevant to the vital question that concerns society today: Can we tolerate economic warfare unless we have satisfactory grounds for believing (a) that it is inevitable, or (b) that it is likely to result in victory for the good and defeat for the wicked? Obviously, analysis of strikes and the strike threat can throw no light on the relevance of their outcome to the *socially desirable* division of the value of output. Yet it is just this relevance with which many writings on collective bargaining have *ostensibly* been chiefly concerned.

Attempts have been made nevertheless to study rigorously the factors which are likely to lead one or the other party to victory in the clash between the unions and the "employers." Studies in this field may be said to have begun with J. R. Hicks's *Theory of Wages* (London, 1932), although

Edgeworth, Marshall, Bowley and others had previously discussed the indeterminateness of value under bilateral monopoly.[25] But in my judgment, Hicks' discussion and all subsequent explorations in this field, down to recent contributions by N. W. Chamberlain,[26] C. Stevens,[27] B. D. Mabry[28] and others have done little more than elaborate the truism that, in warfare of the kind analyzed, and looking at the issue from the standpoint of one of the parties, (a) the greater the resources in supplies and weapons of aggression possessed by that party, and (b) the less onerous the terms of surrender it offers to the other side, the more likely it will be that that party will be able to force the capitulation of its opponent, with or without an *actual* strike or management-imposed work stoppage; and that, in the event of a party meeting more stubborn resistance than it had expected, it may have an incentive to soften the terms of surrender it demands.

I conclude that "labor's inferior bargaining power," which is said to be strengthened by agreements in concert to refuse a particular employment at less than a certain wage rate, refers most often to monopolistic power to exploit three groups, namely, and in order of importance: *firstly,* displaced or excluded comrades; *secondly,* consumers; and *thirdly,* the suppliers of complementary productive services, including those investors in fixed resources who have not adequately allowed for the risks arising from the strike threat when they have invested. Only when monopsonistic power can be wielded by managements to maintain or reduce wage rates below the free market level, by somehow excluding access to alternative employments, can it be claimed that phrases like "labor's disadvantage in bargaining" are anything more than unintended euphemisms.

NOTES

[1] Armen A. Alchian and William R. Allen, *University Economics* (2nd ed.: Belmont, Calif.: Wadsworth Publishing Company, 1967), p. 420.

[2] Fritz Machlup, *The Political Economy of Monopoly* (Baltimore: Johns Hopkins Press, 1952), pp. 333-58.

[3] To the best of my knowledge there has been no attempt at refutation of the chapter in question.

[4] The terms of a so-called wage contract, "agreed to" under coercion, seldom binds any firm to provide so much employment at the stipulated wage rate. The firm merely binds itself *not to employ* any person who might find that he can better his condition by working for less than the "agreed" figure.

[5] I say "seldom" because, as we have seen, a single key worker *may*, at a crucial point of time, be in a position to disrupt operations by the withdrawal of his services.

[6] The use of the strike threat or the strike may be said to be "successful" from the standpoint of those who retain employment at a higher real wage rate. Those who are laid-off in consequence, or whose prospects are damaged, will (if they perceive how they are affected) regard it differently.

[7] "What bargaining power may mean . . . is simply the highest salary one can get from other jobs" (Alchian and Allen, op. cit., p. 402).

[8] His remuneration could then be represented as OY_1, in the diagram on p. 63.

[9] Actually, as Alchian and Allen point out, "the employee does not lose his entire source of income; he loses the premium he was getting in his former job over the next best alternative adjusted for moving and job-exploration costs," (p. 402).

[10] The adjective "natural" describes monopolies or monopsonies which emerge without collusion. (See pp. 103, et seq.)

[11] Ludwig von Mises, *Human Action* (New Haven: Yale University Press, 1949), p. 374.

[12] Ibid., p. 373.

[13] W. H. Hutt, "Natural and Contrived Scarcities," *South African Journal of Economics*, 1935.

[14] I return shortly to the suggestion that for managements simply to make wage offers would be for them to determine labor's remuneration "unilaterally," that is, without bargaining (see p. 71).

[15] The real danger today, however, is that managers who explain *objectively* the market factors through which social discipline could replace economic warfare, and who, in so doing, point to the probable immediate labor displacement consequences when labor costs are determined under the strike threat, may be accused and even convicted, in the United States, of "unfair labor practices." I have been assured that, if a negotiator points out that the number of workers employable in an undertaking will increase more slowly, cease to grow, or even decline as a result of consumers being forced to pay more for output, his assertion might be ruled by the NLRB as in the nature of a threat to rob the workers of their livelihood!

[16] N. W. Chamberlain, *Collective Bargaining*, 2nd ed. (New York: McGraw-Hill, 1965), p. 123.

[17] Ibid., p. 124.

[18] As one shrewd commentator has put it, "the novel feature in the compulsory (pension) plans promoted by most union leaderships does not lie in what the unions take from the companies but rather from what they take from their own members, namely, the power to decide freely on how to dispose of each member's income." Philip D. Bradley, *Involuntary Participation in Unionism, in Labor Unions and Public Policy* (Washington: American Enterprise Association, 1958), pp. 57-58.

[19] Hence it is *theoretically* possible that, through *bargaining tactics*, the settlement will determine wage rates no higher than the free market would have guaranteed. Through such a stratagem, managements may be said to have performed their duty to the community as well as to stockholders.

[20] B. C. Roberts, in John Dunlop, *Theory of Wage Determination* (London: Macmillan, Ltd., 1957), p. 109.

[21] See the next paragraph and pp. 50, 122, 128.

[22] For example, some of the self-service stores in the United States, con-

fronted with the more effective economies of the discount houses, *seem* once to have followed this (probably short-sighted) policy.

[23] The reader should be reminded that the expanding enterprises of which the progress is thus curbed had been attracting labor from less productive to more productive and more highly remunerated work.

[24] The concept of "economic" is not irrelevant in war operations. In rationally conducted warfare, although forecasts in detail, and hence proximate objectives, are in process of constant revision, or even fundamental change (as the pattern of events confirms or negates forecasts), each proximate objective can still be pursued in a manner calculated to minimize detriment to other proximate objectives.

[25] If there is a corporation with monopsonistic powers facing a labor union with monopolistic powers there will be, for a certain range, nothing resembling a market price to determine the wage rate (e.g., on the diagram on p. 63, the range will be between OY_2 and OY_4). The position will be similar to that which exists under "pure barter." Marshall illustrated the situation by the exchange of nuts and apples between two persons in isolation. (See above pp. 62-63.)

[26] N. W. Chamberlain, *Collective Bargaining*, 2nd ed. (New York: McGraw-Hill, 1965).

[27] C. Stevens, "On the Theory of Negotiation," *Quarterly Journal of Economics*, February 1958; *Strategy and Collective Bargaining Negotiations* (New York: McGraw-Hill, 1963).

[28] B. D. Mabry, *Labor Relations and Collective Bargaining* (New York: Ronald Press, 1966). Mabry's book contains a short bibliography covering this topic (pp. 239-240).

6

The "Employer" Stereotype

IN AN age in which semantics is an academic discipline, it sounds almost platitudinous to refer to the misleading images which mere words often evoke. Yet I feel compelled to stress the adverse effects which one such image has had upon the quality of our thinking. There is an innocent, apparently neutral, nonemotive, word which, through the deceptive picture it conjures up, has caused greater intellectual havoc in the social sciences than any other misleading stereotype. I refer to the concept of "the employer." Although this term has legal recognition and definition in many countries, it has been and still is largely responsible, I am convinced, for incalculable intellectual harm. The reader may have observed that I myself have so far avoided the use of the word in the present book, except in quotation marks.

I am *not* thinking of the word sometimes bringing to mind the conventional caricature of "the capitalist"—a bloated bully with an enormous belly emphasized by a heavy watch and chain. I am thinking simply of the notion of "the employer" as one party in wage-bargaining and wage settlements, as the owner of the capital employed, and as he who wields the authority to manage—to give orders and direct the processes of manufacture and marketing. The concept of "the employer" is confusing because, in reality, *employment is not offered and wages are not paid by investors*—normally the residual claimants on the value of output—*except as intermediaries*. Nor can we say that employment is offered and wages are paid by the *managements* responsible to investors. Employment is offered and wages are paid by the consumers of the product; while physical equipment and "circulating capital" are equally *employed by* and their services remunerated by the people in their consumer role. The undertakings which offer wage contracts are essentially intermediaries or agents, not "employers." The resources they own and their entrepreneurial skills are *employed,* just as is the labor required.

It is true that the owner of a business may be said *to invest* in its inputs, labor's inputs included. But these inputs become assets, namely, inventories of "work in progress" and inventories of end-products *acquired on consumers' behalf.* The residual claimants are even more directly under the command of prospective customers than are the contractual claimants. The dominating reality which needs explaining is that "producers," in which category I include both investors (represented by management) and wage earners, are essentially employees while people in their consumers' role are *employers*. And consumers are ruthless employers! They dismiss without compunction "producers" whose output, in relation to quality and price demanded, and alternative output available (of the same or a different kind), is overpriced. "Producers" are "laid off," "sacked," "fired," "discharged"—by the simple process of not buying their output. There is, however, an enormously important difference between the two parties who make up the category I have called the "producers." By accepting the *residual claim,* investors normally bear almost the full burden of the democratic social discipline that consumers exercise—buying or refraining from buying in the market. Poor or unlucky judgment in forecasting and bad management in economizing are drastically punished. But good luck or judgment in prediction and wisdom in effecting economies are voluntarily and liberally rewarded by consumers. On the other hand, all wage-paid employees are provided, via their employment contract, with what, dispassionately viewed, is *the most important form of social security that has ever been devised.*

Naturally, this security does not shield artisans and laborers from *all* social discipline—for instance, from the consequences of any pricing of their services so that their full employment in their existing occupation is beyond what consumers can afford. Thus, if they force output prices to a higher level than the public can meet, they must expect the displacement of some of their number into lower-paid occupations (or into short-time, or unemployment) unless inflation rectifies the position. Nor can the wage contract protect the workers from the insecurity created when, faced with declining demand for any one kind of output, those displaced are prevented by some labor union demarcation or "closed-shop" rule from accepting other, possibly equally well-paid jobs. Nevertheless, in itself, the wage contract is a device by means of which investors bear the chief risks, with the result that artisans and laborers may enjoy the greatest possible continuity of income and employment.

It is equally important to see that because investors accept these risks, they must have the right (through their managerial representatives) of determining the use to be made of the resources they provide. It is by reason of the fact that investors are those whose incomes are least protected from market discipline that the sanctions for managerial authority are derived. It is often claimed that labor has "a right to participate in *management*." A typical claim is that workingmen have the right to "a stronger and collective voice in determining the conditions of and reward for their work."[1]

Whenever a firm is selling to a large number of people and/or buying from a large number, its pricing of what it has to sell and its bidding for what it has to buy constitute, perhaps, its most important administrative and coordinative acts. For prices determine rates of flow of services or materials into, and rates of flow of products out of, that focusing of entrepreneurial responsibility that we call "the firm." Now whenever a wage-rate offer ceases to be the decision of managers representing the residual claimants, legitimate managerial authority has already been partly usurped. Small wonder, then, that when this has occurred demands arise that the usurpation shall be carried a little further, and labor allowed "a voice in management," or even participation "coequal with management." In some industries, managements have already relinquished many of the powers which the rational evolution of the economic system accorded them. Even in such things as the selection of key personnel, product pricing policy and plant location, the unions have, on occasion, used strike-threat coercion to override managerial discretion. All these encroachments on the managers' sphere tend to hamper the ability of the managers to economize resources and thereby maximize the community's income.

Then let us return to the question: Why should not the workers be allowed to "participate" in the making, changing and enforcing of the rules to which they are subject in the industrial and commercial world? The answer is that that right exists! The workers do not have to *fight* for it. They can, if they wish, make and themselves enforce *all* the rules. It is not necessary that they shall own the assets with which they work in order to delegate to managers of their own election the authority to direct the process of production (which is what Marxists would assume). They can do so by hiring the assets. That they never actually do this in practice is because the incidence of risk-taking under the present system of entrepreneurial direction is so much better. That is, the workers benefit enormously from contracts under which they agree to accept the commands of others. But there is no *legal* obstacle to their setting up businesses controlled by themselves, and there never has been. Nor, I think, has there ever been any private opposition or any contrived obstacle to their undertaking the whole of the planning and direction of industrial or other enterprises if they think that that would be to their advantage. If they wish to shoulder a major part of the entrepreneurial function, the workers have simply *to accept responsibility* for the decisions of the managers to whom they delegate decision-making powers. This means that, in a free society, they must *accept the consequences of those decisions* in the sense of meeting contractual obligations, taking the residue (that is, the profits) and *bearing the losses.* All that is necessary is that they shall rent or hire the fixed assets with which they work and borrow capital for self-liquidating assets like materials and work in progress and for the drawings they make (as wages) in prospect of profit. If they are prepared to accept the residue and *to pledge future earnings to cover possible losses* (hence accepting the risk), paying a contractual income—rent or interest—to the providers of capital, it will be their legal right to appoint and direct the managers—the decision-makers. In assuming the right to manage, they will of course have to contract to pay interest to those who (by refraining from consuming the capital they have saved or inherited) provide the "other resources" needed for production. But then they can then share the whole of the residue as their remuneration, which will be wages *plus* profits or *minus* losses.[2]

The issue can be put this way. In a "democratic," "free enterprise" community, both the formulation of the complex of rules which govern the activi-

79

ties carried on within a workplace *and* the administration of these rules are functions which may be assumed *either* by officials appointed by the workers (for example, chosen by artisans, laborers, and clerks) *or* by officials representing those who finance provision of the other resources needed (the site, the buildings, the machinery and equipment, materials, power, and finance). Whichever group elects to accept the residual claim (positive or negative) on the value of the product acquires automatically the right to draw up the rules (or to appoint those who do so) as well as the right to select and appoint the managerial hierarchy.

Hence, if the workers (or their representatives) so choose, they can be completely free to *make* and *enforce* all the rules, with no interference whatsoever from the other parties to production. The sole condition is that they are prepared to bear all the losses and share (among themselves) all the profits. Their incomes will then depend upon the wisdom of the rules made by their appointed managers, the wise administration of those rules, and the general shrewdness of managerial predictions.

A much less unlikely arrangement, however, is one in which the workers in a corporation contract *to share in* profits and in management *in proportion to that value of their inputs which they put at risk*. For instance, if they are prepared to risk, say, a sum equal to a fifth of their current aggregate annual earnings, by pledging future wage receipts, they can do so by a sort of installment purchase of the corporation's stock. They can borrow this capital sum through their union or through the corporation for which they work. With the borrowed funds they can acquire a special issue of the corporation's ordinary stock. Their commitment can then be to repay capital at, say, an annual rate of 10 percent of the sum borrowed *plus* interest on the balance, the amount due being deducted from every wage payment. The deduction from each man's wages at the outset could then be one-fiftieth of the gross wage rate at the outset *plus* a small proportion to cover interest. If the business is successful, the workers will receive more than their interest payment in the first year, either as a dividend check or indirectly in the form of capital appreciation. In subsequent years, of course, the deductions needed to pay *interest* on the loan will fall progressively. On the other hand, if the business is unsuccessful the workers may have to pay more in interest than they receive in dividends. Moreover, if losses are incurred and dividends have to be passed, the workers will still be committed to paying off the debt and interest on any outstanding balance.

Each worker will have to pledge wages yet to be earned for his share of any outstanding debt; and this will be possible only if he binds himself by an iron-clad lock-in contract or offers some other form of security. Perhaps each worker's loss of his rights in the stock, if he left before complete settlement, would serve as an effective lock-in. But the corporation or the union could act as his agent and sell his share of the stock, with its obligations, to a newcomer. Hence the "lock-in" disadvantage may perhaps be held not to be too serious.[3]

But compulsory loss-sharing (with profit-sharing) in the form envisaged still seems to be objectionable. If the undertaking has to close down, the worker will lose his job just as he loses what may have become an important portion of his savings. Alternatively, should things go badly with the undertaking, he may have to accept a wage cut to retain his employment at the very time that his dividends cease and the value of his capital in the corporation falls, while the value of the outstanding part of his debt is unaffected. Nevertheless, an experiment with such a method of sharing entrepreneurial power with the wage earners *could* have important educative effects. As stockholders, the workers would certainly gain some insight into the sanctions for managerial authority. Moreover, with all its defects, some such system may eventually come to be recognized as a better method of mitigating strike-threat chaos than inflation. It may be forced on any community which is determined to avoid union-enforced contractions of the prospective wages flow without relying (as at present) upon the progressive debasement of a nation's currency as a corrective.

Should this alternative ever be sought, we are, I think, likely to find two kinds of corporations emerging, one owning plant and equipment, which it offers for rent, and another which hires labor, rents plant and equipment (from the other kind of corporation) and borrows to finance inventories. Under *this* scheme, labor does not rent the resources needed directly, but through a corporation in which it holds part of the equity. Such a corporation can take the initiative by recruiting labor solely on the loss-sharing and profit-sharing terms discussed above. Firms of that type will need relatively little capital, and if all workers are committed to contribute, say, merely one-fiftieth of their annual earnings to finance the loan through which part of the corporation's stock is acquired, the workers can gradually build up a substantial representation on the board and a substantial voice regarding management. "Workers' control" will be in direct proportion to the financial responsibility (or risk) they assume.

The reader should notice that, under this highly imaginary scheme, the intermediary corporations with which wage contracts are made do not invest in the fixed capital used but merely in the services it provides, together with the services of the workers *plus* materials and work in progress. The purchased services of men and of assets are invested in inventories of products for sale. The workers participate in the process partly through the skill and effort they contribute but partly through actual membership in the corporation which invests in this manner. They can be said to be partially but collectively self-employed. The corporations owning the *fixed* resources (plant and equipment) will employ labor only to *service*, not to *use*, its assets.

I have sketched possible arrangements of this kind, *not* because I believe that they offer an advisable or practical solution, but because I want to show that there is no legal obstacle to labor playing a part—even a major one—in the direction of an undertaking, including the appointment of managers, the determination of the rules under which work must take place, and procedures for dealing with grievances of all kinds. To be defensible, some sharing in the fortunes and misfortunes of the undertaking would be essential. But *I can think of no reason for supposing that under such arrangements the rules would differ one iota from what they typically are today or that the exercise of the necessary discipline would be any more (or less) just.*

It appears to me that the only reason why obviously *possible* arrangements of this kind have never been advocated by those who have discussed such things as "profit sharing" or co-partnership" is that mentioned earlier. It seems to involve a sociologically inappropriate division of function. The most important attribute of the present system is that it is harsh on investors and the managers but soft on workers. The system is a good one precisely because it loads the risk-bearing function almost wholly on those who have the facilities for risk-spreading. But in return for assuming the risk burden, investors may rightly expect the workers to accept a contract under which they submit to the direction of managers whom investors appoint.

Unfortunately, advisers of the labor movement have almost entirely encouraged unions (with grave irresponsibility) to demand the right to share in direction without sharing responsibility and risk. Influential "labor economists" such as John Dunlop, Clark Kerr, Frederick Harbison, and Charles Myers (as summarized by Elliott J. Berg[4] allege that the workers "live in a state of perennial latent protest arising from the frustrations implicit in being governed by a web of rules they usually have little to do with making." But there is nothing to protest about. The right to make "the web of rules" is not *withheld* from the workers. They have simply not chosen to use that right because they have not been in a position to accept the responsibility for so doing, in whole or in part, without an unwise assumption of risk.

It is typical of the lack of consistent principle among apologists for union claims to management's prerogatives that the representatives of the movement seem always to contradict themselves on the topic. Lindblom's excellent chapter, "Management's Shrinking Domain,"[5] contains several exasperating examples. In the National Management Labor Conference of 1945, the labor members of a committee reported (perhaps unguardedly, thinking that it would be a mere meaningless gesture) that "the function and responsibilities of management must be preserved if business and industry is [sic] to be efficient, progressive, and provide more jobs." But when the management representatives took this admission seriously and "drew up a list of some thirty-odd specific acts . . . which [they thought] it seemed clear . . . must be reserved to management . . . labor refused to accept a single one."[6]

Claims by labor unions to "a voice in control" can now be seen to be essentially *undemocratic* unless the suggestion is that labor wishes, to a degree commensurate with the measure of control claimed, to share in any losses incurred. For the industrial and commercial system can be said to be "democratic" when it is controlled ultimately by the people in their consumer role; and when, in accordance with that control, the rules under which production and marketing activities are directed, and the appointment of the managers to administer these rules is made by the residual claimants on the value of the product. And when this is recognized in policy, *the right to make the rules and to direct a productive undertaking is assured to that party which protects*

*the other parties from the defensible ruthlessness of the consuming proletariat
and the market generally.*

To recapitulate, the economic arrangements of the western world have always *permitted* the providers of skill and effort, as a group, legally to determine the rules which govern the general conditions under which they work, and the administration of those rules. The fact that the workers have hardly ever made any use of this right is (a) because it entails the workers *investing* their services in the replacement and maintenance of the resources they must hire and preserve intact;[7] (b) because it would, in general, be a disadvantageous form of division of function; and (c) because although loss-sharing and profit-sharing arrangements with labor are conceivable, the risks associated with acceptance of any part of the residual claim are incomparably more wisely borne by independent investors who can spread the risks in the capital market.

In the contemporary world, the rules—typically codified into "operations manuals," "standing orders," and so forth—are often inevitably intricate and technical. They form part of the institutional framework needed for direction and coordination under social discipline. But when wisely designed, this discipline does not mean constraint. On the contrary, it secures that freedom which is created when one man can act in confidence because he knows that another will act in an agreed manner. The rules must cover, of course, the actual giving of orders (see p. 84). But if the deliberate creation of hostility to and suspicion of those who must issue the commands, which has become so common today, could be eradicated, the whole process of command could occur in an atmosphere of good fellowship and mutual understanding.

Whether investors or workers take the risk (and hence assume the managerial function) *managements* must obey society's commands. Because the prospective yields which determine rational entrepreneurial action are forecasts of the public's preferences, the consumers' sovereignty to which both managements and, through them, all employees, are subject represents a basic *social* discipline. It has been the use of the misleading term "private enterprise" to describe this relationship which has left the wholly false impression that managerial power is arbitrary power.

The "personal power" of managers, to which apologists for the unions so often object is, in fact, purely *an interpretative power*. Their authority is not autocratic. They are, as we have seen, continuously deciding whether to incur the labor costs (market-determined or influenced by the strike threat) and other costs of retaining, replacing or adding to the resources which it is their duty to direct. Their judgment must involve countless imponderables, but they are helpless to control the factors which determine the relations between objective input values and prospective output values—relations on which all their decisions must be based. There is no "governing class exacting implicit obedience from inferiors," as they were being described a century ago. Nor does subordinacy mean inferiority. If A accepts commands from B, *who is responsible for A's performance,* he is subordinate but not inferior. When the traffic policeman finds it necessary to divert my car in an emergency, I obey him without feeling inferior. And yet it is the tactics of labor propagandists habitually to confuse subordinacy with inferiority.

Propagandists in this field often refer scathingly to the "employer's" insistence that his servants shall "submit to his authority as master." But market commands being those of society, managerial authority is a legitimate and democratic interpretative authority; and the managers' commands, unless against the interests of the investors, *ought* to be obeyed. I do not say "obeyed without question." For instance, I have no right to give illegal orders. But when I engage a gardener, I expect him to carry out any specific tasks to which I direct him—planting, pruning, spraying, weeding, mowing, as the case may be. He may, of course, suggest to me that it is too early for pruning or spraying, without questioning my authority. When it is said that his conformance to my instructions means his "submission" to "authority" (and that is what the modern textbooks mostly say[8]), it creates an impression of *intolerable* subservience. And that is not all. The hackneyed suggestion that managements and workers should "meet as equals" is meaningless unless all it means is (as it has never in fact meant!) that the workers want arrangements under which they can share according to some equitable formula the profits and losses accruing, pledging future earnings against possible losses.

It is sometimes said that the workers want a share in management in order to win a sense of recognition and self-expression.[9] But when we try to find what is meant by such phrases, we discover that all the notions are distressingly woolly. There may be something to be said for allowing schoolchildren to pretend to run schools or undergraduates to pretend to run universities; and there is a similar case for pretending to allow the workers a voice through "works committees" and that kind of managerial gimmickry. There is evidence that it can be educative. But if there is one clear-cut principle which emerges from the literature of management above all others, it is that power without responsibility leads always to inefficiency, to waste, sometimes to chaos, and all too easily to injustices. And you cannot have responsible decision-making without accountability and penalty.

In a totalitarian system, the worker can hardly have true freedom in selling his services. In a competitive labor market, however, he sells the product of his labor, either directly, as when he is "self-employed," or indirectly, as when he takes advantage of the social security and enormously widened contact with customers that is afforded by the wage system. In the latter case, he sells his contribution to the product, his "input" (as economists call it). *Perhaps the greatest virtue of a free market, strike-free wage system would be that it would clarify what the union obscures, namely, that the worker is a free being, not a commodity; that he is free to contract, through any firm with which he accepts employment, for protection from most of the inescapable risks of a progressive age, and at wage rates which managements are unable profitably to influence* (any more than they are able to influence the prices of the materials they purchase or the interest rates on the funds they find it profitable to borrow).

The moral sanctions for managerial disciplinary authority are, as I have been reiterating, derived from society in its consumer role. This authority is enhanced by the fact that the command-obedience relationship is based on a contract in which the worker's inducement is his judgment that he will be better off in the undertaking he enters than he is likely to be in the next best alternative known or available to him. The strongest penalty any management can apply is the lay-off, and that simply means refusal to renew a contract. All other penalties are subsidiary—demotions, loss of increments, pay deductions. I shall shortly refer to safeguards against the arbitrary use of these penalties; but the existence of the market is the *chief* safeguard against injustice. Any apparent harshness seems always to vary more or less in proportion to the extent to which a person's remuneration tends to be above his market value. In nonunion firms, for instance, case studies suggest that punctuality, regularity, and general efficiency are easier to achieve when conditions of service, prospects and wage rates are favorable in relation to the outside market. But that may be due to recruitment of specially cooperative staff having occurred. If allowance is made for quality, what appears as a policy of paying more than the market may not be that at all. It is said, for instance, that a South African businessman of the last generation, I. W. Schlesinger, used to pay his executives well above what they could earn outside his organization because in that way he could command meticulous obedience, loyalty, and alertness. He had the reputation of being an exceptionally strict and exacting disciplinarian. Of course, fear of poor performance (including fear of disobedience) cannot be eliminated in any system in which consumers' rights are honored. Bad workmanship is automatically penalized where it is recognizable. Yet the social discipline exerted is for the greatest good of those subject to it when it *is* "ruthless" *in the sense of always to be expected*—inexorable.

In suggesting that the market is the most powerful safeguard against the exercise of managerial tyranny (which is not to claim that it is an all-sufficient safeguard), I must stress the corollary that anything which might leave a flavor of injustice is contrary to the interests of stockholders. For it is to the advantage of those who take the risk of financing production that all available labor which offers a prospective yield greater than its cost shall be engaged. And if any available labor fails to be purchased by reason of, say, personal spite or prejudice on the part of managers, the prospective profits of the enterprise will be sacrificed for the private ends of the managers. The danger to the organization is that it will lose, possibly to its rivals, the valuable services of those employees who perceive that they have been unfairly dealt with. Unrestrained market activity not only releases motivations which are indifferent to color or race, it constitutes the most powerful safeguard (I repeat, not an all-sufficient safeguard) against injustices which might be encountered in the course of the exercise of managerial authority.

Perception of the validity of command by the residual claimants does not permit us to ignore the problem of justice in relation to command. A command is unjust when it harms the person commanded in some measure which is inconsistent with the achievement of the socially-determined objectives of the organization he is directly serving. A command which is discourteously given may, for instance, harm the respect of the person commanded.[10] But admonishments, reprimands, and penalties are unavoidable if command is to have meaning; although the certainty of their just use in cases of trespass or poor performance always minimizes the need for actual recourse to them.

On the other hand, in every conceivable kind of organization of society, persons entrusted with authority may abuse their power through a reprehensible act or decision, whether by reason of incompetence, ill-will or prejudice. For instance, the head of a department may report falsely on the competence or loyalty of a subordinate—perhaps of one whose advancement in the firm he fears. But because this possibility and similar abuses are known to exist, promotion plans as well as job evaluation and merit-rating programs have been explicitly designed to minimize their likelihood.

The loss-avoidance, profit-seeking incentive is the best safeguard against unfair treatment that has ever evolved in the sphere of human relations. And the wage contract, in addition to conferring on the worker the most all-embracing form of social security that has been contrived in response to human needs, enormously magnifies his freedom. For in agreeing to submit to managerial discipline, he becomes part of a complex system of cooperation which permits one man to act in a certain way under the assurance that another will act, simultaneously, or at an agreed time, in some stipulated complementary manner. It is a method under which the intermediary (the firm, with whom the worker concludes a contract of employment) can play off on his behalf an enormous number of individual *employers*—that is, consumers or clients. Instead of being able to serve, say, a few dozen or hundred customers as a "self-employed" person, the corporation which assumes responsibility for his wages may serve hundreds of thousands or even millions.

It is almost universally accepted by writers in this field, however, that it is a legitimate union function to assist in drawing up and occasionally revising the rules of the business organizations in which their members are employed, and to play a part in the administration of those rules. There can be no controversy on the point that there may be a case for sometimes bringing in union officials as expert advisers during the drafting of operating manuals or the standing rules and orders of business concerns, just as industrial consultants can be brought in. Indeed, it may be good sense to submit proposed revisions of the rules to the staff generally before their adoption. Comments and criticisms could be valuable. But there is not the slightest reason why it should be regarded as a *duty* of managements to do this. How can the managers accept full responsibility for their stewardship (to the residual claimants) if outsiders are allowed to have any right to veto or amend their plans?

We have had a mass of what may be quite fairly called "managerial gimmicks'' aimed at meeting the workers' ''psychological needs.'' We find suggestions which imply that ''participation'' can in some way generate ''respect.'' Even schemes for relaxing discipline are sometimes claimed to have worked wonders in morale improvement. We are told for instance that the great British firm, Imperial Chemical Industries, has achieved better personnel relations by just such methods. ''Supervisors do not check the quality of our work,'' a shop steward is reported to have remarked. ''We do it ourselves, and it is as good or more often better now. . . . If we feel like a tea break or lunch, we take it at the time best for us. . . . The foreman used to be called 'a white-coated bastard', now he is more a father confessor.'' A union secretary remarked of the same experiment, ''You can now feel a relaxed, sensitive mood in this plant. . . . No one is looking over your shoulder.'' The shop steward just quoted left an impression of greater honesty when he went on to say, ''Control by the worker is inevitable. We are capable of running and controlling this plant. Obviously the next step for us is to have more involvement in the broader decision-making.''[11] But how nauseatingly false it all sounds. The critical attribute of good discipline, like efficient law enforcement, is that hardly anyone fears it; everyone knows of it; but virtually no one is currently reminded of it; for the penalties being known to be severe and certain, only a negligible proportion of those subject to it ever dream of transgressions, and they are a very small and nearly always stupid, pathological minority.

The source of sound morale in industrial relations is to be found primarily in an understanding of the sanctions for managerial authority on the part of all affected—the legitimacy of command by those executives to whom responsibility has been delegated. All need to be taught that the decision-making function is exercised on behalf of the residual claimants on the value of outputs. And this is true whether the workers or the providers of the capital happen to be the residual claimants.

Because I insist on the right of the managers to make untrammeled decisions, I am not, I repeat, suggesting anything so foolish as blind obedience. Are not the managers themselves employees? And do they not habitually delegate the discretion entrusted to them (namely, authority together with responsibility) right down through the administrative pyramid to the overseers and foremen? Indeed, in the business world, commands are communicated in the course of a process of continuous consultation at all levels. And this process could have been not only *more obvious,* but *much more effective* in today's world had the atmosphere created not been almost universally influenced by the lurking strike threat. For the fostering of warlike attitudes is the almost inevitable concomitant of the labor union system in its present form (see above, pp. 22-23, 50-51, 73-74).

Moreover, attempts by managements to attract and retain labor by means such as developing the atmosphere of a club, maintaining a strict insistence upon courtesy to subordinates, and striving to create friendliness toward and from those whose input is purchased by wages and salaries (similar to the friendliness which every salesman habitually displays) tend to be described by union leaders in terms of the scornful epithet, "paternalism"! The use of that epithet is effective propaganda. But the tragedy is that efforts on the part of managements (and in small businesses, endeavors by the actual owners), as leaders prompted by humanity, or perhaps prompted by the moral teachings of the age, to concern themselves with the welfare of those who have accepted wage contracts, and to treat them as free cooperators in the process of production, have been continuously sabotaged. And the incentive for the sabotage has been the interests of the union leaders in perpetuating that hostility toward and suspicion of investors and managements ("the employers") which seems to fortify the *raison d'être* of their profession.

There is no really satisfactory authority for the settlement of grievances (for example, over work rules, product standards, output measurement under piece rates, and so forth) other than management; for it is in the interests of those who direct great enterprises that agreements shall be meticulously carried out and that *they shall be seen to be carried out*. Good morale can ultimately be based on trust alone, and the cooperative endeavors within a firm require faith in the justice of decision-making at every level of the administrative hierarchy.

This does not mean that some form of independent representation of the rank and file is incapable of assisting the achievement of harmonious relations, especially during the determination and interpretation of employment contracts. It ought to be an offense, however, for any worker (whether a union member or otherwise), an offense for which he should be liable at least to dismissal, to attempt to cause unrest and distrust of management, let alone intimidate any employee. If grievance procedures are laid down in wage agreements and alleged to be working unsatisfactorily, every wage earner should of course have an effective right to complain to top management, with no fear of victimization, of what he regards as injustices. This he could do either personally or through his union representatives. But managements ought to be envisaged as having been vested by society—that is, by the people—with the right to watch over the community's interests in *least-cost production*.[12] For instance, it is their duty to resist adamantly all suggestions that they will be courting trouble if they do not acquiesce in color or race discrimination. And the overriding democratic responsibility of business managements needs protection from inflammatory and subversive talk and action. In the good society, it will be recognized as just as intolerable that known troublemakers should be allowed free rein as that, in an active army, a hostile infiltrator should be allowed deliberately to undermine morale.

From the very beginnings of the free enterprise system, the right of managements to accept market discipline and, in turn, to use the interpretative discretion which society (in its consumer role) delegates to them has been resisted. Such resistance has been mostly blatantly manifest, I think, in action taken at times to restrain managements which have tried to perform their difficult and dismal duty to root out the instigators of dissension and unrest. I have already referred to the forced abandonment of "company spies" (see pp. 50-51). But it has been the obvious obligation of managements to discharge employees whom they know are tending to wreck the process of orderly cooperation. The presence in industrial firms of implanted troublemakers created one of the circumstances in which, in the United States, fights arose this century between the Supreme Court (which *originally* had tended to protect the interests of the unprivileged) and the Federal Government (which was under political pressure from the privileged—that is, the unions). This ominous phenomenon was observable in federal legislation as early as 1898[13] in the United States, when railroad managements were forbidden to end contracts with employees whom they perceived were trying to destroy good personnel relations. In 1908, the upsetting of this legislation as unconstitutional meant the temporary restoration of the right of every person to better his position, if he believed he could, by bargaining for employment on the railroads.[14]

It was not difficult, of course, to persuade the public that the unions were fighting for one of the common rights of man, and that the "blacklist" (used cooperatively among firms to warn managements of persons who were expert in disseminating unrest with a view to ultimate strike-threat disruption) was reprehensible. But the public had been hoodwinked. Since then, by several acts, of which the Norris-LaGuardia Act and the Wagner Act have been most important, the right of managements to exercise the disciplinary power which society delegates to them has been seriously curtailed. They can no longer keep open the channels through which the least privileged may bargain for employment opportunities. And this has gravely restrained society's power to foil, by way of managerial authority, the deliberate fostering of bad morale.

We must never lose sight of the reality that the *actual* "employers"—the consumers—are mainly those who enjoy relatively small incomes. The great bulk of consumption-demand is expressed by persons who fall into the lower income groups. When this is recognized, the notion of an "employing class" vanishes. Stockholders, through the managements responsible to them, are completely powerless (and properly powerless) against the commands which the market expresses;[15] while through wage contracts the residual claimants shield the workers from the otherwise inescapable consequences of unpredictable forms of economic change, coordination to which is ordered via market pressures.

In conclusion, I must return the reader's attention to the crucial point made at the beginning of this chapter. If governments are performing their role in the free market, the interests of investors and of workers are not opposed; for the services of assets and the efforts and skills of the workers are both purchased by the ultimate consumers. Admittedly, in *every* transaction, although both parties gain, their interests are opposed. But the "other party" concerned in the remuneration of labor is not that abstraction which is sometimes called "capital" or, at other times, "the employer." The "other party" is primarily consumers. True, the worker is hired through managers who represent investors; but the firm which offers the wage contract is essentially an intermediary, and the investors' resources (including the labor purchased) which the managers direct, are "employed" by those who eventually buy the output. Whatever one's opinions may be about the defensibility of accumulated or inherited wealth, there are no grounds for accepting the Marxist notion that the income flow to private savers and inheritors represents the proceeds of their exploitation of the workers or that it has conferred the power to maltreat or tyrannize.

NOTES

[1] E. Wight Bakke, Clark Kerr and Charles W. Anrod, *Unions, Management and the Public,* 3d ed. (New York: Harcourt, Brace and World, 1967), p. 19.

[2] Only one economist has, as far as I have noticed, referred *specifically* to this possibility. I. B. Kravis remarked, in a well-known article of 1959, ". . . when the entrepreneur commits his labor and his capital to an enterprise, he is taking the risk that he will get less than the market rates of return on both the labor and the capital in the hope, of course, that he will get much more. Since the two types of input are jointly committed, there is a case for allowing both to share in the ups and downs of entrepreneurial income." I. B. Kravis, "Relative Income Shares in Fact and Theory," *American Economic Review,* December 1959, p. 925.

[3] To prevent unwieldly stockholders' meetings, attendance could be limited to shareholders with a minimum holding, personal or through proxies. Each small stockholder among the workers could be represented through a limited number of proxies, voting power being of course according to the value of holding (that is, in proportion to the risk being taken).

[4] Elliott J. Berg, "Comment," *Aspects of Labor Economics: A Conference of the Universities—National Bureau Committee for Economic Research,* A Report of the National Bureau of Economic Research (Princeton: Princeton University Press, 1962), pp. 52-53.

[5] Charles E. Lindblom, *Unions and Capitalism* (New Haven: Yale University Press, 1949), Chapter XII.

[6] Ibid., p. 156.

[7] They could, of course, add to those resources by a ploughback as well as by further borrowing.

[8] Thus one of the most influential textbooks (Bakke, Kerr, and Anrod, op. cit., p. 18) says: "Employers attempted to justify their control over the workers by invoking religious sanctions for . . . submission by the 'servant' to the authority of his 'master.' "

[9] Actually, as I shall be showing, in holding back progress in material well-being on the part of the "working class" as a whole, and especially in slowing down the advance of the least fortunate classes and races, the strike-threat system must have hampered their acquisition of greater dignity, self-respect, and sense of self-expression.

[10] One must beware of exaggerating this point. The technique of some very

successful football coaches is to disparage what they regard as poor performance (by the team or by individuals) in the most abusive and even blasphemous terms! The players love it (at least in some instances).

[11] *Business Week,* 7 October 1970, p. 59.

[12] As well as with the corresponding right to serve the community's interests in determining the *form of production.*

[13] The Erdman Act, 1898.

[14] *Adair* v. *United States,* 1908.

[15] They may of course try to condition those commands through advertising, and restrain them through collusive price or output determination.

7

"Exploitation" – By Shutting In or Shutting Out

IN THIS chapter I explain that, when antitrust does not stand in the way, it is relatively easy to exploit actual or potential competing parties (competing workers or owners of competing assets) by *shutting them out* from an occupation, industry, or area, but extremely difficult (and, in general, impossible) to exploit complementary parties (capital by labor, or labor by capital) by *shutting in* workers or assets, that is, confining them to a particular occupation, industry, or area.

The term "exploitation" (defined on p. 3) is intended to have a completely neutral, nonemotive connotation. But let us assume at present that "exploitation" is justified if investors or the rich are exploited, and unjustified if the workers or the poor are exploited.

I shall here make use of certain simple concepts, the meaning of which I intend to be self-evident. I originally suggested the first five of these concepts in 1935.[1] Few economists have made use of them. Yet I still feel that, if more generally used, they could greatly simplify our attempts to understand *most* of the problems we meet in studying the phenomena of economic conflict. The concepts are:

1. *"Natural scarcity."* This is an attribute of the value of assets, and of the value of *the services* of people and of assets, when people in their role of entrepreneur (choosing means to ends) are completely free to choose the least-cost means (according to their judgment), while in their consumers' role (choosing ends) they are free to substitute preferred ends and the preferred (including the cheapest) source of supply. Under such "competitive" circumstances, I shall regard the values of assets, the values of their services, and the values of the services of people as "natural scarcity values" (equivalent to "free market values").

2, 3. *"Contrived scarcity"* and *"contrived plenitude."* These terms refer to the values which emerge when persons acting in collusion, or relying upon such monopolistic or monopsonistic power as is inherent in largeness of scale of operations, can fix a price or wage rate higher or lower than the natural scarcity value respectively, or alternatively, when they can "control" the amount supplied or demanded of anything so as to cause its price to diverge from the "natural scarcity value." I shall then refer to a "contrived scarcity value" if the price so determined exceeds the "natural scarcity value," and "contrived plenitude value" if the price is lower than the "natural scarcity value." I prefer the term "contrived" to "artificial" because there is nothing *unnatural* about deliberate scarcity contrivance where "the rules of the game" permit it.[2] Did not Josiah Tucker rightly remark in the eighteenth century, "Every man would be a monopolist if he could"?

4, 5. *"Incidental contrived plenitude"* and *"incidental contrived scarcity."* Every contrived scarcity, in *diverting certain assets or people away from* one field, must cause the services of such diverted resources to be valued *below* their natural scarcity in the less productive uses into which they are forced. I call such values *"incidental* contrived plenitude values."[3] Similarly, when the use of monopsonistic power can create a "contrived plenitude" *by preventing certain assets or people from moving away from* one area, activity, occupation or firm to another, so as to reduce the value of their services where they are retained *below* the natural scarcity level, the value of like productive services (and the corresponding assets) outside the area, occupation or firm must be *above* the natural scarcity level. We can describe the values so caused as *"incidental* contrived scarcity values."

6, 7. The *"shut-in"* and the *"shut-out."*[4] (a) *The "shut-in"* refers to a *man-made barrier* which creates or maintains a "contrived plenitude," that is, which prevents resources (labor or assets) from *moving away from* an area, activity, occupation or firm to other areas, activities, occupations or firms which offer more productive and better remunerated employment outlets. The "shut-in" prevents advantage being taken of offers that outside entrepreneurs would otherwise make. *The "contrived plenitude" is the consequence, and the "shut-in" is the means.* (b) *The "shut-out"* refers to a man-made barrier which creates or maintains a "contrived scarcity." It "shuts out" resources (including labor) from moving into an area, activity, occupation or firm which offers more productive and better-paying opportunities than are available outside. *The "contrived scarcity" is the consequence, and the "shut-out" is the means.* Both the "shut-in" and the "shut-out" are methods of holding off such offers as pure entrepreneurial incentives (profit-seeking, loss-avoidance incentives) would otherwise allow to be made.

All serious "exploitation" must rely upon either the "shut-in" or the "shut-out." A wage rate materially less than the "natural scarcity" level in an area, occupation of firm can persist only if the exploited labor is "shut in," that is, only if certain entrepreneurs' bidding for this labor can be held off. A wage rate materially above the free market level can persist only if labor is "shut out," that is, only if interlopers—potential competitors—can be kept out. Apparent exceptions to this categorical assertion are to be considered shortly.

Whenever a "shut-out" contrives a scarcity in a field, some assets and/or labor are *cheapened for other purposes.*[5] The effect of each such scarcity contrivance is usually to cause the initiator (the "exploiter") to gain (a) (through the contrived scarcity) ultimately at the community's expense in its consumer role; (b) at the expense of competing parties—those investors whose property and those workers whose efforts are diverted to, or kept in, less remunerative and less productive activities; and (c) *(for a quite different reason)* at the expense of a complementary party (for example, labor exploited by investors or vice versa).

What complicates the matter is that the exploitation of a *complementary* party can occur only *through a "shut-in" which accompanies the "shut-out."* For instance, a "shut-in" of capital must accompany the displacement or exclusion of workers due to the raising of a wage rate by duress, if the maneuver is to be successful. That is, if the "shut-out" is to be effective, owners of assets in the exploited field must be somehow debarred from offering employment in that field to displaced or excluded workers at wage rates which would make their inputs profitable. *Managements, on behalf of the investors who have provided assets, will be denied access to certain workers the actual or prospective availability of whose services had induced the provision of the assets.*

Hence, already provided assets will have been "shut in" in exactly the same way that labor will have been "shut in" under the opposite case of monopsonistic exploitation of labor. When labor is exploited, managements must somehow hold captive the workers employed, paying them less than they could, if free to move, command outside. In both cases, if the assets or labor *could* break out and join forces with complementary labor or assets outside, they would find better remunerated employments.

Exploitation of *competing parties* can occur only through the "shut-out," as for example when apprenticeship restraints limit recruitment to a privileged trade; while exploitation of *complementary parties* can occur only through the "shut-in," as when monopsonistic exploitation of labor occurs for investors' benefit.

An important principle can now be enunciated. To the extent to which *exploitation in "shut-in" forms can occur, it can effectively redistribute income as between labor and capital (in the short run). It is incapable of doing this in "shut-out" forms, except to the extent to which assets compete with labor.* Otherwise, through the "shut-out," one group of workers can exploit other workers (and consumers) only, and investors can exploit other investors (and consumers) only.

The importance of the above stated principle is enhanced when it is considered in relation to the hardly disputable fact that it is much easier to exploit by *"shutting out" competing assets or labor* (i.e., substitutable resources) from a field of production (and this has *no* redistributive tendency as between investors and labor) than it is to exploit by *"shutting in" complementary* (i.e., nonsubstitutable) assets or labor, through which a redistributive effect *is* achievable. This is another way of saying that the contrivance of scarcity (with an incidental plenitude elsewhere) is much easier than the contrivance of plenitude (with an incidental scarcity elsewhere).

If permitted by law to do so, however, either managements on behalf of investors, or unions on behalf of labor, are able (by collusion) to resort to the "shut-out," that is, to enter into arrangements under which capital or labor respectively are excluded from kinds of productive activity which it is wanted to protect. But the "shut-in" is another matter. Consider the workers trying to exploit the investors who supply the assets with which they work. Such exploitation is possible, as we have seen, only when the investors have allowed themselves to be vulnerable to the "shut-in," through immobilizing capital in nonversatile forms; and this must have been simply *because they have failed to foresee their vulnerability* (Chapters 10 and 11 discuss possible objections).

However, short of some fraudulent (and easily discernible) device, managements are unable to lure apprentices or other recruits into "shutting themselves in," that is, into specializing their skills in a particular field so as to permit managements, relying on the workers' lack of versatility, to reduce wage-rate offers. That is, managements have no means of forcing labor to seek employment in activities in which the workers feel there is a chance that they will be exploited monopsonistically. But, if workers do not foresee their vulnerability, they may acquire vulnerable skills without anything resembling managerial misrepresentation, yet render themselves liable to later exploitation. If they do foresee such vulnerability, they can cover themselves through contractural "tenure." (In a strike-free regime, the offer of contractural tenure as a recruitment inducement would, I think, become rather more common.)

To recapitulate: While a contrived scarcity (achieved through the "shut-out") is easily accomplished and indeed widespread, the contrived plenitude (achieved through the "shut-in") is difficult and rare. For in the latter case, *it is essential to entice resources or people into a trap, or to rely upon investors or workers walking into a trap;* and in general ordinary foresight can eliminate the latter risk.

The difference is fundamental, and in a study like the present it needs the strongest emphasis. If the *direct* contrivance of scarcity (when permitted by law) is easy, while the *direct* contrivance of plenitude is both difficult and avoidable, it means that *the burdens of the strike-threat system fall mainly with an incidence that involves no redistribution for the benefit of labor* at the expense of investors. The beneficiaries from the fixing of the price of labor through the private use of coercive power achieve their gains: *firstly,* from consumers; *secondly,* to the detriment of displaced or excluded competing labor; and *thirdly,* at the expense of the providers of complementary resources, due to the incidental "shut-in" which accompanies an effective "shut-out," while this last possibility is of little long-run importance. (Objections are considered in Chapter 10.)

For logical completeness it is necessary to refer again to the exception referred to above (p. 94). Investors who have inadequately allowed for the strike-threat may be exploited via a shutting-out of capital resources which *compete* with the labor employed. Managements have at times been effectively called upon to abandon labor-economizing machinery or to refrain from installing it. Or, a variant of the same situation, the unions have allowed resort to labor-economizing machinery but enforced featherbedding.[6] The exclusion of such labor-economizing assets illustrates aptly the principle I wish to stress. It is certainly *possible* for organized workers, by threatening to strike, to "shut out" *competing* forms of assets. But the workers will never purposely "shut out" assets which they recognize to be *complementary*. On the contrary, it will always be to their advantage to encourage their provision; for *ceteris paribus,* the greater investment is in such assets the greater will be the demand for the labor with which the assets cooperate.

Moreover, it must seldom be practicable to employ private coercive power to compel the provision or replacement of complementary assets (except as amenities which may become the chosen form of labor's remuneration).[7] Theoretically, the strike threat *could* be used in this manner where the alternatives would be even more burdensome on investors. We can *imagine* a firm getting into a position in which it resembles a person blackmailed—forced to pay more and more in order to retain what it has left. But actual cases in which the strike threat has forced investment in any assets must be difficult to find.

Later on, we shall notice the puzzlement of a dozen or more distinguished statistician-economists at the tenacious constancy of the empirically-determined ratio between the shares of labor and property in aggregate income (see Chapters 15 and 16), despite all the efforts, via the coercive power wielded by union organization and government, to change those shares. The argument I have advanced provides, I believe, if not a full and adequate explanation, at least an important link in the causation chain. *Strike-threat gains are entirely, or almost entirely, at the expense of competing resources "shut out," and not at the expense of complementary resources "shut in."*

Nevertheless, I do not propose to allow my whole thesis to stand or fall according to the acceptability of the broad thesis of this chapter. For the benefit of skeptics, I shall examine in detail the chief arguments which have implied that it is possible to exploit a complementary factor as well as a competing factor—that is, that union aggression is capable of wresting from investors some part of the ill-earned gains which the free market would otherwise have yielded them, or alternatively that it is able to win back from investors some or all of the spoils of monopsonistic extortion (due to the price of labor having been forced below its free market value). These possibilities are discussed in Chapters 8 and 10.

This distinction between the *"shut-in"* (with the consequential *contrived plenitude*) and the *"shut-out"* (with the consequential *contrived scarcity*) does *not* coincide with the more common distinction between monopoly and monopsony in the currently accepted connotation of those terms. To the extent to which exploitation of investors for labor's benefit occurs, the case falls, as I have just shown, into the *"shut-in"* category. Such exploitation would at once *appear* as monopsonistic if the workers happened to act as entrepreneurs (as imagined above, pp. 79 *et seq*), that is, agreeing to accept the residual share of the value of output, paying rent for the services of plant and machinery, interest on circulating capital needed, and salaries to managements responsible to them for entrepreneurial decision-making. The organized workers would then appear as *buyers* of the services of assets, materials and so forth; and any exploitation by them of the owners of plant and machinery used would clearly be monopsonistic.

For these reasons, when planning the present chapter and the three following ones, I considered the desirability of discussing both the exploitation of labor and the exploitation of investors simply as different examples of monopsonistic power. I decided against doing so because I thought possible confusion from such an unusual use of terms could not be wholly offset by the greater conceptual clarity won. Accordingly, I shall deal with the exploitation of labor on behalf of investors under the heading of "monopsony," and discuss the exploitation of investors by the strike threat without again reminding the reader that it represents a perfect parallel to the exploitation of labor.[8]

In conclusion I must refer to a situation in which the validity of some of the above assertions or conclusions may not be obvious. What is often *called* "taking advantage" of workers who provide services which are relatively cheap for any firm, activity, occupation or area is not "exploitation" by the entrepreneurs making wage offers if they are not themselves responsible in any way for that cheapness. Consider, for example, what is often called "sweated labor." The firms which find it profitable to offer employment because there happens to be an "incidental contrived plenitude" of such labor are not themselves exercising any exploitative power unless they themselves are using some "shut-in" device. I shall return to a consideration of such circumstances.

NOTES

[1] W. H. Hutt, "Natural and Contrived Scarcities," *South African Journal of Economics,* 1935.

[2] I defended this usage originally in the article referred to in the previous footnote.

[3] In the extreme case of completely nonversatile assets, *"incidental* contrived plenitude values" may be *nil.*

[4] I originally thought of using the terms "lock-in" and "lock-out." But because the latter already has a conventional meaning—a management ordered work stoppage—it could puzzle some readers.

[5] "Shut-out" labor may be (a) "displaced," the case in which the contrivance of a labor scarcity in a field causes a layoff of some currently employed, or (b) "excluded," the case in which the labor would have been recruited for employment in a field but for the scarcity contrivance. Category (b) seems to be far more important in practice. (See p. 54.)

[6] See pp. 133-134.

[7] See Chapter 14.

[8] Nevertheless, I have found it helpful to return to this point on pages 223-224.

8
"Exploitation" of Labor –
"Monopsony"

Is THE argument for the tolerance of the strike threat that the free market price of labor is "unfair"? Or is it alleged that the market price would otherwise be forced below the free market value? It is often difficult to tell. However, it is the second allegation that we are to consider in this chapter. Can the threat or use of the strike prevent the workers' *exploitation*? Can it somehow achieve the results that a competitive labor market would bring about?

We can get the issues into focus, I think, if we envisage all labor union bargaining in which the threat of a lockout or a strike is a factor as falling into three categories: (1) a struggle over the division of the spoils of monopolistic exploitation, consumers being the exploited party, with investors and the union protecting one another in this process but quarreling about the reward (see pp. 50 and 128); or (2) as an attempt by management to neutralize exploitation of consumers, when such exploitation via the strike threat happens to harm investors also; or (3) as an attempt by managements to exploit labor for the benefit of investors by the use of monopsonistic power, while that attempt is resisted via the strike threat. It is category (3) alone which is now under consideration.

"Exploitation" of the workers *means,* under the rigorous definition discussed in the previous chapter, forcing the terms of wage contracts below the "natural scarcity values" which the unhindered free market would have determined, thereby creating a "contrived plenitude" of labor. Is it possible, then, for the strike threat to assist the conclusion of such wage contracts as are likely to be offered when managements are seeking to maximize profits (which means "minimize losses") in the absence of any effective power on their part to "shut in" and hence "exploit" labor? *If managements are somehow able to suppress competing demands for the services of workers to whom wage offers are made, can strike power effectively countervail such subterfuges as are used?*

If a strike threat or strike has had the effect of raising the wage rate in a particular occupation from below the free market level *to* that level (that is, to the natural scarcity level), the situation will be characterized by the condition that no worker can be found prepared to accept less than the wage rate established for the occupation concerned. If a union insists, in these circumstances, that no interlopers shall be *allowed* to work for less, that is proof that, in the union's judgment, their forcing up the wage rate was *not* a countervailing of monopsonistic exploitation. *The test of whether any wage rate is at or below its natural scarcity level is whether any other persons are prepared to perform identical work for that or a lower wage rate.* As long as any such persons exist, the price of labor is above the free market level, and if a strike threat has enforced it, the effect must have been not to nullify attempted exploitation of the workers, but the exploitation of others—investors, or displaced workers, or excluded workers, or consumers.

I have never recognized in practice the existence of the conditions here specified *as tests for the antimonopsonistic effects of strike-threat pressures.* No case studies that I have seen have ever left an impression of the required conditions having been fulfilled. Hence for some readers the remainder of this chapter, as well as Chapter 9, will appear redundant. They may feel that in pages 99-123 I am discussing a chimera—a merely notional circumstance which cannot be found in the real world. Such readers can usefully jump to Chapter 10. But I am trying to reach readers who will be extremely loath to accept the convictions to which I myself have been led. I propose therefore to examine contrary arguments with care. The well-entrenched idea that union power is essential to correct monopsony or oligopsony needs patient examination.

We need not discuss at length the case of monopsonistic exploitation of wage earners which occurs *incidentally,* through monopolistic output restraints superimposed upon a previous condition of competitive supply. If the monopolist has no power to restrict his employees' mobility, any "exploitation" is likely in practice to be negligible; and although the situation imagined is one which needs rectification in the collective interest, the defensible remedy is "antitrust," not recourse to private duress.

Monopsonistic exploitative power directed effectively against labor would, as we have seen, be derived from the ability of managements (independently or in collusion) to use some device or stratagem in order to retain workers under their direction although they are remunerated at less than they *could* otherwise command elsewhere (which means at less than the "natural scarcity" value of their services). Expressed in the terminology of the previous chapter, exploitation would require that managements could "shut in" their employees and thereby create a "contrived labor plenitude." Such a situation implies that the labor provided is so specialized that the workers have no alternatives of comparable value *and* that they have been somehow *tricked* (a) into training themselves for that particular specialization, or to become *attached to* the operation in question, or (b) into chaining themselves to it by agreeing to a "lock-in" contract.[1] The crucial point is that the workers concerned would have avoided that specialization or refused, say, "lock-in" terms of remuneration if they had foreseen the possibility of the exploitation.

Any effective organization to shut in labor in this way would, I feel, always be at least discernible if not conspicuous.

The theoretical possibility of monopsonistic exploitation occurring cannot be challenged of course; and evidences of actual monopsonistic influences are not lacking. Nevertheless, I am inclined to accept H. C. Simons' 1944 judgment that "monopsony in the labor market is . . . very unsubstantial or transitory."[2] His conclusion was, I think, based on realistic observation and perception. The only *convincing* example of continuous "pure" labor-purchasing monopsony which I have found (apart from explicit and formal "lock-in contracts," discussed on pp. 101-102) is that of the recruitment of Africans for the South African mines, which is organized through a centralized agency.[3]

If monopsonistic exploitation of labor exercised on behalf of investors were *practically* important, however, it would almost certainly manifest itself in the form of discrimination in wage rates offered according to management's judgment of each individual worker's alternatives.[4] Some workers have a wider range of skills or other valuable attributes than others and under monopsony some might be paid more or less, not in relation to their special competence in their actual employment but in relation to what they are believed to be able to command elsewhere (see pp. 65-67, 163-166).

This is the one sense in which *ceteris paribus* the standard rate ("the rate for the job") principle *might* be held to be defensible. A nondiscrimination rule could weaken or destroy the profitableness of monopsonistic discrimination where it might otherwise occur (in theory at least). The difficulty in practice, however, would be to distinguish the case in which any rule of uniformity would discriminate against a worker who has not only poorly paid alternatives but is *also* handicapped in other ways, for example, by being more expensive to employ, or by reason of being *initially* less efficient for the work offered.[5]

Among the other kinds of possibly exploitative action which fall under the monopsony heading and certainly do occur, are agreements or understandings not to "poach" labor—particularly labor of a special type—in order to keep down wage rates or salaries. But unless action of this type is organized openly and is accepted as desirable by all parties *as a method* of achieving some other agreed collective objective,[6] it can, I guess, *seldom* have much success. It seems to me that as soon as any agreement to maintain a wage-rate ceiling, or otherwise to limit demand for any kind of labor, begins to have any effectiveness, all the phenomena of "labor shortage" must emerge. It will then be to the interests of both managements and individual workers, who can hardly long remain unaware of the "shortage," to find subterfuges for getting around the agreement. I do not suggest, however, that we must necessarily leave the matter here. Some economists have alleged that collusive monopsonies to forego "pirating" have at times existed in named districts of the United States.[7] They have charged that certain managements have agreed to recruit no worker unless the firm which last employed him has given its approval, and that "gentlemen's agreements" not to steal one another's employees have been arranged. But if the facts were as these economists allege, and as discernible to government authorities as they were to the economists, one wonders why antitrust officials did not at once step in. The allegations, which refer to a period of vigorous general antitrust enforcement, concern conduct of patent illegality by the "employers," yet the supposed offenders were not prosecuted; and as their managements would presumably have denied the accusations, the *evidence* of the monopsony is, to say the least, far from convincing.

In so far as monopsony in the labor field does occur, however, the unfairly low wage rates due to contrived plenitude will be accompanied by wage rates in other labor markets which are set at "incidental contrived scarcity values," that is, *higher* than they would otherwise have been, because some of the *captive* labor (which the theory assumes) is withheld from those markets. Hence although monopsonistic power may, theoretically, enable certain investors to benefit directly at the workers' expense, we must not overlook the countervailing advantage to the workers in the markets in which labor is rendered relatively scarce, i.e., endowed with an "incidental contrived scarcity" value. Labor's strongest case against such monopsony (if it has any importance at all) may be more its injustices to the "shut-in" workers, and its regressive consequences for workers generally as consumers, than any general redistribution of income which can be effected through it in investors' favor.

The form of pure monopsony which is most likely to be occurring today is that due to "lock-in contracts." A corporation may, as part of the remuneration it offers to attract and retain labor, include "employer's contributions" to, say, a staff pension fund; or it may issue employee bonus shares, or other forms of conditionally owned capital to "loyal" personnel. Those who remain in the service of the corporation until normal retirement age (or for some other specified period) will retain these rights; but should they take up other employment before, they may stand to lose a large capital sum in accumulated benefits.

To see the problem in due perspective, let us remember that no person is *forced* to commit himself to such a contract. He may be held to have accepted, willingly and without duress, a condition which means that, for him to change jobs profitably in the future, the remuneration and prospects offered him elsewhere will have to be greater than his existing earnings by a sum at least equal to the accrued value of "the employer's contribution." If the system *is* abused, then the issue resembles that encountered in installment selling. The suggestion is that people can be *tricked* into tying themselves by contract because they do not realize the implications of their commitment. The remedy then requires careful specification of the conditions under which such contracts may be legally entered into. It seems to me that, *as part of a wider plan for eliminating the strike-threat influence,* there would be no harm in legislation to render void or unenforceable all "lock-in contracts" unless (a) they are genuinely providing an incentive for investment in human capital; or (b) they are an agreed means of reimbursing removal expenses advanced; or (c) they are necessary for the completion of a specific piece of work (that is, a bridge, or a round trip on an ocean vessel). Of these three (a) appears to be the most important. A contractual lock-in can be a *bona fide* device for conferring a "reasonable" measure of property on the investment a firm makes in imparting special skills and trade secrets to its personnel. In the absence of such a contract, those whose services have been rendered more valuable through expensive training could otherwise be "poached" by firms which have made no contribution to their training costs.

I am prepared to go further and concede that even when the "lock-in" contract possesses one or more of these attributes which render it beneficial, its duration should be limited—the limitation being no more and no less arbitrary than the limited period over which a patent monopoly is allowed to run. And it ought, I suggest, to be laid down that all "employers' contributions" to pension funds and the like should, subject to the exceptions just mentioned, belong unconditionally to the wage earner (or salary earner). This will mean that if the worker accepts other employment, he may take with him the surrender value of any "employers' contributions" (to pension funds or similar retirement savings plans).

In most cases firms seem to resort to these "lock-in" devices innocently enough, and often obviously beneficially for both parties as well as for the community. The aim is solely to attract and retain the workers whom managements find it profitable to hire, by what seems to them to be a simple and wholly legitimate type of offer. Nevertheless, the "lock-in contract" does differ in principle from other nonwage methods of retaining staff.[8]

A wholly different suggestion is that labor is monopsonistically exploitable, not by reason of its being locked in, or tricked into an exploitable specialization through some managerial stratagem, but by reason of some inherent immobility of labor. To judge this idea we must begin by recognizing that labor market freedom is not *limited, restricted, or rendered imperfect* because labor movement is not costless. Through the existence of obstacles to mobility (including man-made barriers), switching from one occupation to another, or moving from one district to another, involves costs; but only if these costs are man-made—the consequence of deliberate action by governments, by unions or by managements—can we say that *the market is restrained*. It may, of course, be *profitable* for the community, collectively or privately, to invest in the steps needed to reduce spatial mobility costs when they have a natural origin, as when a tunnel is cut through a mountain range; and any such reduction of costs in expanding, say, the area of competition, is widening the spatial range of coordination.[9] But that process is not removing *restraints*. For instance, if the workers' immobility over space is the result of his lack of capital to finance movement, relatively cheap labor in a district (whether the "plenitude" is contrived by lock-in or otherwise) will create an incentive for entrepreneurs outside the sheltered area to advance removal expenses in the form of loans or in return for appropriate "lock-in contracts" (under which an agreed minimum period of service is deemed to wipe off the debt).

However, because the labor employed in a particular area or in a particular trade *would* be more valuable if it were not for (a) the pecuniary cost of movement to other areas, or (b) the workers' own inertias or preferences, or (c) the impossibility of circumventing union-imposed demarcations or like restraints, that does not imply that it *ought* to be remunerated at what it *would* be worth in the absence of those conditions; or that if it is not so remunerated, it is being "exploited;" or that the strike threat can nullify the "exploitation." Labor is only being "exploited" when the lock-in barriers are man-made; and in practice, unless fraudulent enticement is present, *the only clearly discernible man-made barriers which restrict labor mobility in this manner are created by labor unions themselves or imposed in response to their political pressures*. This is a glaring truth which ought not to be a matter of controversy among scholars. It is confirmed by any dispassionate observation of the institutions of the modern industrial system. In offering jobs in any area in which certain labor happens to be plentiful and cheap, and certain occupations therefore profitable, *yet no managerial restraints on mobility exist,* it is absurd to suspect or accuse managements of *aggravating* the cheapness. On the contrary, the initiatives (which lead to offers of employment to workers displaced or excluded by contrived labor scarcity) mitigate the injustices. Indeed, they raise the incomes of those employed in the cheap labor areas.[10]

To get our logic into perspective, it is useful to enunciate a general principle about the determinants of the wages flow and its distribution. Within any area sheltered by economic distance, by human enertias and by union-imposed restraints, *in the absence of any "shut-in" of labor contrived on behalf of investors, the flow of wages will be highest and the distribution of the flow will be most equitable, when every wage rate is fixed at the lowest level necessary to retain or attract labor for each activity judged to be profitable*. I stress that word "profitable."[11] The ideal will be most closely approached (a) the more successfully any labor which may have been "underpaid" for any reason can break through natural or man-made barriers to an occupation in which its remuneration is higher, and (b) the more successfully such transfers can dissolve privileges, that is, eliminate such "overpayment" of some as may be causing others to be "underpaid."

The term "overpayment" in this context can be defined as "remunerated higher than is compatible with ideal resource use, maximization of the wages flow and distributive justice." Under this definition, labor will be "overpaid" when it is benefiting from some removable obstacle to equality of opportunity. The *test* of whether labor is "overpaid" in any undertaking is whether additional workers, *technically qualified to do the work (or potentially qualified) in the judgment of managements, would find it profitable to accept employment in the undertaking at less than the wage rates ruling,*[12] in the absence of legally imposed barriers, or barriers enforced through unions. *Within* any sheltered area there might be no "underpaid" or "overpaid" labor *in relation to that area*. But in relation to a wider area, *if the shelter were the consequence of deliberate restrictive action,* labor could be "underpaid" or "overpaid" respectively according to whether the restraints imposed were confining labor to the sheltered area or keeping the competition of interlopers out.

In the absence of deliberate restraints, wage rates will tend to rise in any expanding industry or firm by reason of inelasticity of labor supply.[13] There is no exploitation of investors involved in such a case. Similarly, there is no exploitation of labor when, because there happens to be inelasticity of labor supply in a declining industry or occupation, the wage rates at which such workers as choose to remain in the industry[14] can escape displacement are forced down. The downward wage-rate adjustments they must accept to retain employment are in no sense a consequence of any monopsonistic power. They are the kind of pricing needed to soothe the pains of recoordination.[15]

Consider, for instance, the rapid decline of laundry work through the competition of washing machines and laundromats. This may well have meant that many laundry employees found themselves caught in that occupation. The owners of the laundries were unable to prevent their more versatile and enterprising workers from leaving, in spite of laundrymen's unions having been unable to force money wage-rate increases similar to those which inflation was permitting elsewhere. It seems almost absurd to suppose that monopsonistic exploitation was a factor assisting the survival of laundries in these circumstances. But lack of mobility on the part of some of their employees, especially the older ones—victims of their own inertia—*may* well have helped the survival of laundries. In doing so, it would have contributed to an orderly transition to a new division of labor, with a minimum disturbance of established expectations. Hence we must be careful not to attribute to abuse of monopsony the consequences of lack of enterprise on the part of many of the older laundrymen; and we must remember that the *relative* fall in rates of remuneration in the laundry industry did not aggravate but rather softened the harsh effects due to change confronted with very human inertias.

It is now possible to enunciate a corollary of the general principle stated above (see p. 103), a corollary which may have seemed outrageous to many readers if it had been put forward earlier. *If labor is cheap partly because it is unable to move from a firm, activity, occupation or area except at prohibitive costs of movements, but entrepreneurs are in no way to blame for these costs, the susceptibility of labor to monopsonistic exploitation is not enhanced by the immobility.* Let us consider the possibility under "*natural* monopsony," that is, in the case in which there is no collusion and hence no *visible* intention to exploit, which is the usual signal for antitrust to intervene. Can it be argued that, because antitrust protection is ruled out, labor is forced to rely on strike-threat defense?

A distinction must be made between "natural monopoly" and "natural monopsony." We get "natural monopoly" when economies of scale are so important that only one firm can operate economically in a particular activity in a particular area. Now such a concentration of economic power *vis-à-vis* consumers does not automatically create monopsony *vis-à-vis* labor and suppliers of complementary resources;[16] and if it does, it does not necessarily confer the ability to exploit. "Natural monopsony" requires that there shall be one firm only that offers a particular type of employment in a sheltered area. And under such monopsony, *exploitation* of labor still requires some device which either lures workers into locking-in themselves to employment in that undertaking or locks them in directly.

It is useful to consider the case in which the product of the monopsonistic undertaking, which we can assume constitutes the only output of the district, is sold competitively and mainly outside the sheltered area (for example, in world markets). Under our assumptions, *if the demand schedule for the end-product rises, the price of this product will rise but the "natural scarcity level" of wage rates will not rise until the demand schedule has risen sufficiently to make it profitable to recruit labor from outside the area.*

When such recruitment occurs for the first time it will, of course, make it essential to meet the higher wage costs ruling in competitive labor markets outside (as well as any costs of movement inwards). If, when that situation is reached, *the rule of nondiscrimination is enforced* (see pp. 164 *et seq*), it will suddenly become necessary to raise wage rates in the sheltered industry by a large jump, to bring the remuneration of the original workers in the sheltered area into equivalence with the remuneration needed to attract the newcomers. The original workers will then experience a sudden great increase in the value of their services. This big windfall gain to labor would *not* mean the ending of previous exploitation. It would represent either the consequence of a switch of consumer preference toward the product, or the consequence of the growth of outputs in noncompeting fields generally (through which *real* demands for products as a whole would be rising). These two factors together could build up a condition at which, owing to a rise in demand for the product in question, consumers (the ultimate "employers") are all at once offering a large addition to the wage rates of labor in the area.

It is important to notice that, up to the time when recruitment from outside has become profitable, all increased revenues due to rising demand for the output will (in the absence of the strike threat or wage fixing by law) accrue to the owners of the undertaking. *This is not because of some special attribute of services rendered by assets, but because the owners of assets are the residual claimants on the value of the product.* If it had been a wise division of risk-taking for labor to have accepted the residual claim (renting the site, building and machinery and paying interest needed to finance inventories and work in progress—the possibility discussed in Chapter 6) the whole of the additional revenues would have accrued to labor; for in such a case the workers are entrepreneurs.

But suppose that, irrespective of any change in demand for the product, one or more other entrepreneurs perceived that the cheap labor of the sheltered area could be still more profitably used in producing commodities or services which did not compete in markets for the monopsonists' product but did compete for labor and locally provided materials.[17] Their intervention would bid up labor's remuneration there and reduce the original monopsonist's yield. *Exploitation* would occur if the original monopsonist could insert an obstacle between the workers in the sheltered area and any potential new investors who might wish to bid for their services. In other words, if some law-conferred privilege or some tolerated abuse of the pricing system conferred power on the monopsonist to block freedom of access between factors of production, exploitation *could* certainly happen.

Let us ask ourselves why labor in the sheltered area might happen to be initially cheap (in relation to the earning power of similar workers in other areas). One possibility is that the workers there had agreed, quite freely, to accept employment under what amounted to lock-in conditions under a long-term contract. (We are here excluding the possibility that they were fraudulently lured into accepting such a contract.) Whenever workers conclude a long-term contract of that kind, they are acting as entrepreneurs. They may gain or lose from the commitment they enter into. Should it subsequently turn out that their contract is unfavorable, that no more implies their exploitation than the opposite would imply exploitation of investors. But the workers in the area might have been cheap for quite different reasons, such as a differential birth rate in the past which has left an exceptionally large number of persons of conventional working age in relation to the resources of the district. Or the reason might have been a decline in demand for the output of a former industry. Through all such possibilities, workers in a sheltered area might have poor employment alternatives.

Let us now assume for simplicity that the exceptional cheapness of labor in that sheltered area happened to be *the* critical factor in causing investors, in what was to become a natural monopsony, to risk locating their plant there. In doing so the investors in the new enterprise (or rather the managers on their behalf) closed no existing employment outlets *except by offering the workers better terms*. They must have *raised* the natural scarcity value of those employed. Moreover, an expectation that countervailing increases in labor costs would *not* have to follow forecast increases in demand (and rising end-product prices) may well have created an additional investors' incentive. Indeed, that very expectation *could* have been mainly responsible for the enterprise being located where it was—in the sheltered, cheap labor district.[18]

But suppose there had been several different groups of investors competing for the cheap labor stock postulated, instead of one monopsonistic corporation, would not the remuneration offered then have had to be higher? The answer is, no—not unless we can *assume* (a) that prospective yields in the area were then somehow greater in the aggregate so that entrepreneurs found it profitable to bid more against one another for labor in the sheltered market; or (b) that prospective yields in the aggregate being assumed the same, one or more competitors decided to attempt "predatory buying" (see p. 122) with a view to rendering the field unprofitable for the rest, that is, by bidding up wage rates so as to corner the labor supply in order then to *exploit consumers*.

The natural scarcity value of local labor is determined by its alternatives, but these alternatives are at once improved if entrepreneurial interlopers, who judge prospective yields from employing the local labor to be favorable, intervene with better offers. But because the district is sheltered by economic distance, it is possible that the wage rates which the new, monopsonistic undertaking can initially offer are lower than wage rates for similar work elsewhere by an amount equal to the costs of movement. Since, however, the wage rates originally offered represent natural scarcity values, the monopsonist will only be *exploiting* labor if by some stratagem he can pay less than this. And to do so he must devise some shut-in arrangement which renders the alternative still less favorable to the workers.

It must be borne in mind, however, that the specially cheap labor available for the "naturally monopsonistic" undertaking (specially cheap to the extent of labor mobility costs) is initially equally available for *all* potential investors to bid for, before the enterprise is established. Hence the actual wage rates it is found necessary to offer (in order to attract the workers from their previous occupations) are determined, so to speak, in an environment of *potential* competition. Stockholders in the corporation can hardly be imagined as the only capital owners whose managements realize that there are profit advantages in bringing more productive work to any cheap labor region. If other investors—at least within the same country—refrain from intervening, it must be because they feel that the lowly paid labor of the region is not cheap enough, presumably because they cannot envisage equally productive ways (or still more productive ways) of using that labor. It follows that the "natural monopsony" we are considering arises simply because whoever gets in first with one big dominating plant, excludes others from a *possible* big profit gain. The actual promoters are those who happen to perceive before others that, at the estimated labor costs necessary to persuade the required number of workers to accept the new jobs, their proposition justifies the risk. Therefore, if no actual additional[19] bidding for labor against the monopsonist occurs, that will be due to the fact that at the new wage rates established, further investment in the area is rendered unprofitable (possibly through the additional costs of overcoming the workers' inertia).

In a free labor market, the services of workers everywhere are, so to speak, continuously up for auction as their existing contracts of employment (which may often be by the week or even by the day) expire. Only if some potential investors are prevented from engaging in unhampered competitive recruitment of labor in an area is there monopsonistic exploitation.

Once the monopsonistic undertaking has been established and is operating, and on the assumption that the demand schedule for the product remains unchanged, only potential or actual competition from other entrepreneurs, either offering employment outside the sheltered area (in which case their offers would have to be sufficient to compensate for the high migration costs) or inside (which would mean that new productive potentialities inside the area had come to light) can raise the natural scarcity value of the given labor stock. But there is no exploitation simply because, until that happens, the labor is relatively cheap in comparison with, say, other areas of the country concerned.

Monopsonistic *exploitation* cannot occur, then, unless the monopsonist can contrive a "shut-in" of the complementary services he purchases. Any measure of monopsony which may exist in the absence of some deliberately contrived "*shut-in*" is nonexploitative. Admittedly, the imaginary "naturally monopsonistic" condition we have considered constitutes one of the situations in which the strike threat can be used to seize income at investors' expense without direct harm to consumers or to displaced or excluded workers. But as will be further explained in Chapter 10, *the prospect of costs being raised in that manner,* even when monopsony is present, must deter some investment in those forms of assets which most successfully multiply the flow of wages and income.

Strike-threat action might of course be used to lessen the costs of labor mobility. Some interunion fights may have had this effect. But unless the unions can use their organization somehow to lower or demolish man-made barriers to the better utilization of labor and of the tools with which labor cooperates, they are powerless in this respect. As I insisted above (see p. 103), in practice these barriers, and the economic injustices and wastes they cause, are created almost entirely by the very union policies which purport to be fighting for justice in distribution; and the power of the unions to erect the barriers is dependent ultimately upon their use of the strike threat. Local discrepancies in real wage rates must exist *for "natural" reasons* as long as areas are insulated by economic distance from other areas. But the more burdensome discrepancies are caused when spheres of employment are hedged in by the standard rate, demarcations, occupational licensing, apprenticeship rules, color bars, and the like.

As an example we can consider a type of labor "shut-out" which exists in the United States where the unions have been strong enough to secure occupational licensing. When this has happened, we find the unions opposing reciprocity in respect of qualifications (determined for the different states individually). This is quite rational, given the sheer selfishness which is regarded as ethically acceptable in labor unions because, as Rottenberg points out, "If reciprocity prevailed, people would enter through the widest door."[20] But from the standpoint of the workers in any state, they are denied access to opportunities, not by any management-contrived arrangements, but by union-contrived arrangements. I have found no parallel in the whole literature of the labor movement of a man-made barrier to mobility of labor which is *equally obvious*;[21] and this barrier is imposed, not in the interests of rapacious capitalists, but in the interests of labor and professional organizations.

The reader must be reminded that the circumstances I postulated on page 105 in order to illustrate "natural monopsony" were highly abstract and notional. Nothing resembling that model of one firm producing a particular product in a sheltered district and selling it almost entirely outside is, I believe, to be found anywhere in practice. True "natural *monopolies*" are in practice almost always undertakings in which the output cannot be rendered apart from the plant; they essentially serve therefore the areas in which they are physically situated, and this fact means that there are people in other occupations in their district earning through the production of noncompeting things,[22] whom it is their (the "natural monopolies") purpose to serve. In every realistic example of "natural monopoly" undertakings of which I can imagine, there will be highly competitive *natural* markets for the materials and the labor they employ. The adjective "natural" here means that competitive conditions would exist in the absence of legal or collusive restraints imposed in those markets. Normally we may expect a wide range of occupations to be competing for nearly all kinds of labor—firstly, for juveniles to choose from on entering the labor market, and secondly, for labor of different degrees of versatility which may be attracted from other firms, activities, occupations or areas at appropriate wage rates, even if the costs of labor movement to and from other areas happen to be high.

We must be careful, then, not to exaggerate the importance in the real world of some of the circumstances we have been imagining (for purely expositional purposes). Thus it is doubtful whether even the largest cartels can often, say, *profitably* force down the price of the materials they use. They may certainly benefit from purchasing economies which are sometimes achievable through large, or guaranteed continuous orders, or through shrewd investment in a developing supply source. That is something quite different. But not only does a monster corporation or a great cartel usually express a very small part of the total demand for any raw materials, but it is to its advantage that a *continuing supply* shall be forthcoming. In a rather different way the same is true *vis-à-vis* labor.

Even the most careful empirical studies throw little certain light on the problem. For instance, J. W. Garbarino[23] and H. M. Levinson[24] have found that what they call "noncompetitive" industries (*assuming* that the concentration of output into relatively few firms implies less than normal competitiveness) have raised wage-rates by *more* than the average. Unfortunately, the data they present are no proof of the absence of monopsony; for the differential rate of wage-rate increases may obviously have been the consequence of strike-threat pressures possibly facilitated by joint monopoly. M. W. Reder, who has criticized these contributions on other grounds, suggests that "large firms are more dilatory about correcting overpayment . . . ." (when wage rates get out of line) "than correcting underpayment"; and he finds that "large and profitable firms do tend to pay more at any one time than could be explained by the competitive hypothesis." He finds further that "high concentration ratios . . . measured by (say) the percentage of the industry's employment concentrated in the four or eight largest firms" are associated with "high wages at a *given moment of time*."[25] Such findings tend, superficially at any rate, to contradict the notion that monopsonistic exploitation of the workers is correlated with scale of operations or ownership. But using data presented by G. Warren Nutter, for the extent of monopoly, Reder shows that the figures indicate "a slight (negligible) tendency for a decrease in monopoly to accompany an increase in wages. . . ,"[26] and he refers to similar conclusions reached for the Canadian economy by D. Schwartzman. This is exactly what we should expect in the light of the analysis presented in this and the previous chapter. When exploitation of consumers by, say, manufacturers is weakened, their demand schedules for labor and other productive services will rise and, except under the wholly unrealistic assumptions we made on the preceding pages, the increased bidding for labor will raise wage rates in the industry.

To assess the practical importance of the monopsony argument for acquiescence in the strike-threat system, we should remind ourselves that in the United States and Britain this system originally emerged in spheres in which the entrepreneurial undertakings were small, and where the relations between separate undertakings could only be described as highly competitive. Obviously, then, at that epoch, resort to the private use of coercive power by the unions can hardly have been a countervailing response to monopsony. Moreover, even today a very large area of union operation is in fields in which the typical undertaking is small relative to the market, and where competition in the sale of output is not subject to any *obvious* restraints. Consider, for instance, building, printing, textiles, footwear, transport and mining in the United States. Antitrust has kept these industries competitive (superficially considered at any rate); and certainly one finds nothing resembling cartels or explicit price agreements, for output agreements and any other apparatus of collusion are illegal. Hence in such instances there can hardly be any question of the unions, through the use of the strike threat, having been able to act as an antidote to monopsony. Yet unions are powerful in these industries (for instance, the Teamsters). It follows that any valid argument for permitting the strike-threat influence in wage determination has to be developed so as to cover circumstances in which neither monopsony nor joint monopoly (to which I refer in the following paragraph) can be alleged. "Countervailing power" is clearly irrelevant.

Empirical evidence suggests that it is to the advantage, not the disadvantage, of a union that the undertaking with which it is "bargaining" shall be organized monopolistically. This is because its *power* to exploit the consumer can be magnified through joint monopoly (see pp. 72-73). But it is true also that strike-threat action on a union's part is essential for any actual exercise of this joint power. For example, if a union is confronted with an association of undertakings which arranges the pricing of output, only the use of strike-threat power can insure its members a share in the spoils. There is no reason why this should occur automatically unless the associated managements regard collusion with the union as a means of perpetuating their ability to exploit consumers. Managements have, on occasion, taken the initiative and offered "sweetheart contracts" to raise the remuneration of their workers in return for union protection against interlopers. And there are other possibilities. For instance, a union's initiative might force what had been competing undertakings to adopt collusion in order themselves to share some part of the

110

spoils; or, as it would probably appear to the managements, in order the better to off-load increased costs on the public. *In all of these cases, it is the public which is exploited; yet it is a form of exploitation which would be impossible if the strike-threat power were absent.*

There is one further possibility. *Given the legality of strike-threat pressures,* managements may have found an incentive to rely upon "reasonableness" (so-called) in competition for labor; for increased reliance upon an "oligopsonistic" situation may be expected to appear in that light. It *seems* as though union pressures cause competing undertakings to act less competitively (that is, having a reduced incentive to substitute the least-cost method of achieving outputs for the community's benefit). And in the extreme case the effect may be, as Albert A. Rees has pointed out, "to create effective cartels in the product market."[27] Rees suggests that this may be the position in the building trades and the local service industries in the United States, but I feel that he is thinking rather of the cases discussed in the paragraph above.

In a strike-free system, an incentive to oligopsonistic "understandings" about wage rates might well arise among managements; but a strong counterincentive to bid against the rest for underpriced labor would remain. Competition could hardly be effectively restrained, one feels, *except under some explicit agreement.* Managers are like the rest of us, reluctant to pay more or to accept less. But that will not prevent some from anticipating future labor scarcity and, possibly through the offer of fringe benefits and stress on superior prospects, outbidding the rest. The withheld bidding of firms which hold off vigorous recruitment (via the offer of higher wage rates) until their managements feel certain that a real labor scarcity *is* developing, is likely to become active bidding through the fear that rivals may get in first. And this likelihood will be increased if the unions begin to act as entrepreneurs, which I am about to suggest should be their chief function when the strike-threat system is abandoned. The oligopsony possibility will be discussed in the next chapter. I shall try to show that it is unimportant.

I have been stressing the apparently rare occurrence, the inherent instability, and the ephemeral nature of labor-purchasing monopsony in the absence of conspicious "shut-in" power. I have shown the *improbability* of more than negligible abuse, but I cannot deny the *possibility* of serious exploitation in particular cases. Where managements are in a position to restrain labor mobility, "shut-in" arrangements may be discernible. There are, however, three general methods of insuring that such theoretically conceivable abuse from monopsonistic exploitation shall be avoided. Among these methods, the use of the strike threat is not included.

(1) To bring collusive monopsonistic exploitation of labor *explicitly* within the scope of antitrust (or other legislation aimed at eliminating socially indefensible use of private power to contrive scarcities and plenitudes);

(2) To forbid "lock-in" contracts with labor except under the conditions specified above (101-102):

(3) To encourage labor unions to take up cases of monopsonistic abuse in the purchasing of labor and:

> (a) to act entrepreneurially on their members' behalf, firstly, as an employment agency, and secondly to finance or otherwise assist the transfer of "underpaid" workers to *the better-paid jobs available, the potential existence of which alone can justify the term "underpaid"*;
> (b) to initiate antitrust (or similar) action against what they believe to be deliberate collusive monopsonies, or "shut-in" devices, including nonpoaching agreements;
> (c) to initiate similar proceedings against firms which are held to be exploiting consumers, and thereby *incidentally* acting against the interests of the union's members as wage earners;[28]
> (d) to initiate private proceedings against firms alleged to be using *unjustified* "lock-in" devices.

But in cases (b) and (d) the unions surely would have to establish initially the absence of potential interlopers. That is, they would have to demonstrate that no outside workers were prepared to accept less than the existing, allegedly monopsonistically determined wage rates being paid in the firm or firms challenged. (See pp. 98-99 above.)

The typical laborer or artisan is said to be badly informed about alternatives. It is contended that he usually begins to try to become informed about the market only when he is laid off. There seems to be considerable scope, therefore, for the sort of expert guidance recommended under 3 (a); and if the unions can play on the divergences of interest which exist under monopsony or oligopsony, and are also able to disclose employment opportunities outside of the area, they can reduce or wipe out the prospective profitableness of any attempt at monopsonistic exploitation.

I have treated respectfully the notion of managements using monopsonistic power to force down wage rates only because I do not expect all readers to share my judgment that such a possibility is of negligible practical importance. But I have shown also that in so far as evidence of monopsonistic abuse *is* forthcoming, recourse to the courts and not recourse to strike-threat power is the defensible remedy. "Antitrust" or its equivalent is the answer, *not private coercion*. Admittedly, if justice is not effectively *and promptly* obtainable through the courts in labor disputes, men may be expected to take private steps to protect themselves against invasion of their rights. In the sort of issues with which we are here concerned, it is exceptionally desirable that "the law's delays" should be minimized. But the cost of achieving reform in this direction—possibly the establishment of special courts—would be negligible in comparison to the benefits of eliminating the injustices which are inevitable when wage rates are determined through any form of warfare.

To sum up. Demonstrable monopsonistic exploitation seems to be remarkably rare; yet the remedy we are asked to tolerate is a *general and universal* right to strike. Moreover, if the right to strike is defended because it *can* be used defensively, the fact remains that it can equally well be used aggressively. "Those who understand the economic, social and political implications of monopoly power," says Fritz Machlup, "must deplore the lack of imagination and intelligence of a society which in the name of 'equalization' embarked on a policy of combatting occasional monopsony by creating more monopolies. The hope that they may neatly offset one another is plainly naive."[29]

There remains one aspect of the topic which requires mention. I am convinced that neither managements nor sole proprietors do typically act in the rapacious spirit which nearly all the textbooks in the labor economics field manage to imply. This is a conclusion reached after a long academic life devoted to the study of business administration in which I have relied on the recorded experience that constitutes the literature of this subject. The late Sumner Slichter (on the whole an apologist for the strike-threat system) admitted that managements tend to appear generous when it is at all possible and to resist demands for wage-rate increases or to call for cuts, only when things are going badly.[30] But when an undertaking is prospering in the sense that the business is expanding, *managements are often forced to pay a wage premium to get the additional labor they require,* even in what is regarded as a competitive labor market. And when they have had to accept a union-demanded standard rate, there still seems to have been a tendency toward what has been called "wage drift," that is, payment of more than the standard rate when there is "excess demand."[31] What Slichter may really have been observing was managerial appeasement—the unwillingness to fight on consumers' behalf, especially when confronted with expanding demands or when inflation is relied upon to validate any concessions.

Of course, salaried managements, as distinct from proprietors, have no *right* to be generous at stockholders' expense. When they *appear* generous in wage negotiations, I judge it to be due to their trying to show that the offers they make (on behalf of the residual claimants) are highly favorable to the workers they wish to attract or to those they want to persuade not to strike. But the popular and propaganda-perpetuated stereotypes of avaricious investors and unscrupulous managements anxious to carve out careers by exploiting the workers, and held in check only by union power, are grotesque caricatures.

"I think the robbery of labor by capital is a humbug," concluded Mr. Justice Oliver Wendell Holmes as he approached the end of his famous career.[32] This chapter has tried to show that, even it it is not "humbug," it *is* a delusion.

NOTES

[1] A "lock-in contract" is one in which the employee binds himself for a period, or under the terms of which he is subject to some penalty if he leaves before the expiry of a stipulated period, for example, the confiscation of deferred pay, profit-sharing rights or pension rights.

[2] H. C. Simons, *Economic Policy for a Free Society* (Chicago: University of Chicago Press, 1948), p. 129.

[3] Whether there is indeed any effective monopsonistic *exploitation* in this case is, however, far from certain; for it is difficult to see anything resembling a "shut-in." The number of South African workers in the mines has been declining (because better-paid or more attractive work is available elsewhere in the Republic) and more and more foreign Africans (migrants) are being employed.

[4] Similar discrimination by monopolists against consumers, based on estimates of the urgency of their need for the product, is normally impracticable, although sometimes contracts can be entered into prior to investment in fixed resources under which some consumers or users of products agree to discrimination against them under long-term contracts—*but in their own interests* (see pp. 163-166).

[5] Such a worker would be harmed by the enforcement of so-called "equal pay for equal work;" for it would disallow him the effective right of bargaining. Any acceptable nondiscrimination rule would have to guard against all the possibilities which, in practice, make "the rate for the job" the most effective discriminatory device that has ever been invented (as I shall be explaining in Chapter 12).

[6] For example, in British professional football, maximum wage rates were (until recently) enforced as a means of ensuring that the wealthier clubs did not attract all the best players and thereby destroy spectator interest in the game by reason of contests becoming too one-sided. This is an interesting example of a general problem known as "externalities."

[7] For example, see A. Myers and W. R. Mac Laurin, *The Movement of Factory Workers* (1943), quoted by Fritz Machlup, *The Political Economy of Monopoly* (Baltimore: Johns Hopkins Press, 1952), pp. 353-4.

[8] For instance, offering better terms than competitors in respect of provision of special "fringe benefits," an attractive place of work, playing fields, sports clubs, and other "extramural" facilities and amenities.

[9] In practice, when such natural barriers are broken down, the unions tend to substitute man-made barriers for them. For example, Phelps Brown, referring to "the improvement of communications exposing once sheltered local markets to the vicissitudes of wider competition, . . ." says that this phenomenon "heightened the need felt for a union." E. H. Phelps Brown, *The Economics of Labor* (New Haven: Yale University Press, 1962), pp. 40-41.

114

[10] Incidentally, we cannot assume that undertakings which are viable because labor is plentiful and cheap where they are located, are able to earn a larger proportion of the value of output for investors than can be gained for them in similar activities in other parts.

[11] The word "profitable" is justified here only because monopsonistic exploitation on the part of managements is assumed (in this paragraph) not to exist.

[12] In other words, wage rates raised by any sort of compulsion other than the social discipline of the market, cause the labor they remunerate to be "overpaid" in the light of the definition given.

[13] An apparent exception is discussed on p. 106.

[14] The workers' lack of versatility, ignorance, lack of enterprise, or simple preference—or the pecuniary costs of mobility—may determine such a choice.

[15] If demand for the product is declining, *ceteris paribus* it will be to the interests of both investors and employed that wage rates shall fall relatively to wage rates in general until the more versatile of the workers have found better openings elsewhere, which may happen rapidly or slowly. In that way, not only may the burden of lay-off be mitigated, but the contribution of the industry to the source of demands in general will be maximized (although it will be declining).

[16] The labor market in question may be *sheltered* (in that all entrepreneurs enjoy exceptionally plentiful and cheap labor) but *competitive* (in that there is a wide range of employments).

[17] The entry of competing capital to supply the same kind of product is of course ruled out by the assumption of natural monopsony.

[18] Actually, under the simplified situation I have envisaged for exposition purposes, it *could* be to the advantage of the workers in a sheltered area *to be discriminated against* by the monopsonist during a transitional period. Such discrimination might cause expansion of profitable outputs to occur sooner, as demand for the product was rising. Recruitment from outside at wage rates considerably higher than those ruling internally *could* make it possible thereby to raise the remuneration of existing employees, although not to the point at which equivalence of remuneration with the lucky newcomers had been established. If, however, anything distantly resembling this situation ever came into being (which I myself can hardly imagine) in a nonstrike regime, it could be a union function to agree to the suspension of any antidiscriminatory rule and allow its existing members, *for their own benefit,* to be paid less than newcomers (see pp. 163-167).

[19] "Additional" to the bidding offered in the previous employments from which the recruits are attracted.

[20] Simon Rottenberg, "The Economics of Occupational Licensing," *Aspects of Labor Economics: A Conference of the Universities*— National Bureau Committee for Economic Research (Princeton: Princeton University Press, 1962), p. 19.

[21] I do not say "equally burdensome." The most effective barrier to spatial

or occupational labor mobility is enforcement of "the rate for the job" (see Chapter 12, passim).

[22] "Noncompeting" in respect of outputs, not in respect of resources used in production.

[23] J. W. Garbarino, *Quarterly Journal of Economics*, May 1950, pp. 299-300.

[24] H. M. Levinson, Study Paper 4, Joint Economic Committee, U. S. Congress 1960, pp. 2-5.

[25] M. W. Reder, op. cit., pp. 285-6. Actually, there is some reason to believe that large firms shrewdly recognize the advantages of outbidding competitors and purchasing the cream of the labor supply. They may obtain thereby what Reder has called a "richer skill mix." It is a way of purchasing labor's inputs more cheaply, and a particular economy of scale. Another suggestion mentioned by Reder is that large undertakings "over-pay" for prestige reasons. But prestige contributes to "goodwill"; and "goodwill" is an item in a firm's stock of assets.

[26] Ibid., pp. 286-287.

[27] Albert A. Rees, *The Economics of Trade Unions* (Chicago: University of Chicago Press, 1962), p. 84.

[28] If a union can prove that the consumer is being compelled to pay too much for a certain output, for the very reasons which are keeping the earnings of those who make it unjustly low, it will have an iron-clad case; and, incidentally, it will be fighting the case also for better remunerated opportunities for diverted capital resources.

[29] Fritz Machlup, *Wage Determination and the Economics of Liberalism* (Washington: U. S. Chamber of Commerce, 1947), p. 56.

[30] Sumner H. Slichter, "Notes on the Structure of Wages," *Review of Economics and Statistics*, February 1950, pp. 81-91.

[31] The term "excess demand" is a misleading way of describing the situation when there are more vacancies than unemployed in any field at current wage rates.

[32] In a letter to Harold Laski, quoted by Helmut Schoeck, *Envy—A Theory of Social Behavior* (New York: Harcourt, Brace and World, 1970).

9

"Exploitation" of Labor
—"Oligopsony"

IT WAS argued in the previous chapter that, if monopsonistic exploitation of labor is feared, the obvious defensible remedy is dissolution of collusive practices, not the encouragement of a supposedly countervailing monopoly. It is, I think, because academic defenders of the strike-threat system recognize the possible force of such an argument that they often suggest that the problem arises not because of formal collusion between firms, or by reason of any natural monopsony, but through an inevitable tacit monopsony or "oligopsony" as it is called. *But every consideration we have noticed in discussing monopsonistic exploitation is relevant to an understanding of oligopsonistic exploitation; for oligopsony is simply a weaker form of monopsony.* If cases of undoubted exploitation of labor through the abuse of *monopsonistic* power are difficult to find, even in the form of quite open and explicit lock-in contracts, how much more unlikely it is that we shall be able to find genuine cases of *oligopsonistic* abuse.[1] Nevertheless, for the sake of readers who are disinclined to accept what is merely apparent, I propose to examine the notion that it is possible for an oligopsonistic situation to arise and operate against the workers' interests (as indeed Adam Smith believed it did).

We can best approach the possibilities by first envisaging oligopolistic and oligopsonistic incentives together; for the question here at issue is ultimately whether informal understandings, as distinct from open or secret *agreements*, can "shut-in" or "shut-out" resources, preventing them from entering or leaving any firm, activity, occupation or area (which means holding off bidding for the services of one productive factor by the owners of complementary productive factors). It is, I suggest, entirely a matter of the effectiveness of restrictive *understandings* as against the effectiveness of restrictive *agreements*.

Entrepreneurs usually realize that, in fixing product prices *too high* (which means selling *too little*) they are likely to induce their rivals to devote additional resources (possibly machinery sunk in concrete!) to the production of what they have overpriced. Similarly, in bidding for materials and labor, entrepreneurs usually know that if they offer too little (which means taking too little off the market) they will again run the risk of causing their rival's operations to expand rather than their own. They normally perceive also that, in keeping their own product prices down, they are applying pressure on their competitors to do the same; and that, in offering more for materials and labor when prospects seem favorable, they are applying similar pressure on their competitors to follow suit. Such perceptions influence pricing conduct.

The terms "oligopoly" and "oligopsony" describe hypothetical situations in which entrepreneurs can reckon on their rivals not acting *as* rivals but in the opposite way. Each feels bound and able, without collusion, but through some sort of tacit understanding, to raise prices when any other entrepreneur (giving a lead) does so, or to refrain from cutting prices unless some other entrepreneur does, because each can rely upon all the others in the same field judging it to be profitable to follow his restraint. In particular, no entrepreneur will try to undercut another in selling the product, or try to outbid him in purchasing materials and labor, through reluctance to spoil a good buying or selling market. The assumption is that *with no collusion*, they will all act *as though* they were in formal collusion.

How important can such a situation be, especially in relation to the exploitation of labor in a society in which the strike threat is banned? Is it possible for an oligopsonistic set-up to bring about a "shut-in" of labor? The answer is, I think, that it is inconceivable. Tacit collusion must be ineffective collusion. There are two broad reasons.

Firstly, the circumstances of different firms, even those engaged in the production of *the same kind* of commodity, are normally so different from one another in respect of methods, detailed range of products, and in other ways, that it seems to be stretching the limits of common sense to suppose that in the real world they will refrain from any opportunity of cutting prices (a) when larger outputs promise economies of scale, or much larger sales, or (b) when reduced prices are thought profitable as a response to declining sales (to maintain normal or nearer normal outputs). And this is equally true in respect to the bidding up of costs under free market conditions.[2] Thus, an undertaking which so interprets prospective yields that it would judge it to be profitable to offer, say, a 5-percent increase in the wage rate so as to attract an additional 10 percent of employees, would not be put off by the fear that these employees might then be "poached" by its competitors, through the offer of still higher wage rates. If expectations of that kind *did* exist, they would surely include the expectation that, prospective yields being high, the undertaking which was first in the field would be in a position to expand to an extent which would make it *unprofitable* for its rivals to follow suit.

Secondly, competition for labor is not confined to those in a particular industry. The suppliers of assets in all industries and occupations are bidding for the complementary labor and materials needed. Can we, then, entertain the idea that entrepreneurs generally will refrain from making effective offers for marginal and relatively versatile workers from other firms, occupations or areas whom they forecast can be profitably employed by them? Would the knowledge that their bidding will contribute to a general rise in the free

118

market ("natural scarcity") value of labor (or, in an inflation, contributing to a rise in the money value of labor) be a sufficient deterrent?

The most typical expectations of an entrepreneur who decides to expand his sales by improving quality or reducing price, and to increase his productive capacity in order to do so, are that if he expands, it will be thought less profitable for others to expand. He may in part rely upon others thinking that his judgment of elasticity of demand or of rising demand, has been unjustifiably optimistic. But he may rely on *similar* projected growth on the part of others being postponed, curtailed or abandoned simply through his having gotten there first. Less often, I think, he may expect some of his rivals to share his explicitly demonstrated faith in general prospects and follow his example.[3] Unless he supplies a small part of the market, however, he will in most cases expect market prices to fall because it will be to his rivals' advantage to match his price adjustments (possibly in order to minimize any detriment to them due to his growth), while *ceteris paribus* costs of materials and labor will be somewhat higher. *All these possibilities will induce caution in investment risk-taking. But there is no reason why they should induce oligopolistic restraint concerning prices or oligopsonistic restraint concerning bids for materials and labor,* even if the number of legally independent firms is small.

All business decision-makers must, then, in every decision, take into account the possible reactions of their competitors, of their suppliers of materials, of labor, and of their customers; *and it is easy for their calculated caution to be wrongly interpreted as oligopolistic or oligopsonistic in nature.* But they are simply allowing for the fact that, if they do attempt to get a larger share of a given market,[4] or a larger proportion of an expanding market, their competitors are unlikely to remain passive. When they cut prices and/or begin outbidding other entrepreneurs in the same field for materials and labor, perhaps investing in additional fixed assets, they *expect* reactions from their rivals. Any such initiative in the first place is likely, however, to have been due to the conclusion of one entrepreneur that his competitors have not as yet (as he himself has) perceived the extent to which the demand schedule for the product is elastic or rising. But he knows also that, if he discloses his judgment of the profitability of his own expansion so explicitly, he will almost certainly cause rival producers to reappraise prospects. Thus by continuously making allowances for his competitors' forecast reactions, he is not cooperating oligopsonistically. And as far as his bidding for labor is concerned, it will usually be folly for him to hold off unless he can rely on *a tight agreement* that his rivals will do the same.

Among the risks that every investor in a competitive industry must take is that, partly because one entrepreneur does not know what decisions other entrepreneurs have made or are currently making, there may be overinvestment in specific assets. That is, every investor knows that either he or one of his competitors may prove to have provided more resources to produce a thing than will turn out to have been profitable in the long run,[5] and that this will adversely affect his realized yields and those of one or more (perhaps all) other investors in that field. Such a situation creates, it is sometimes felt, a strong incentive for oligopsonistic restraint.[6] The urge to oligopsonistic "reasonableness" is believed to be particularly powerful when the high-cost firms in the overinvested field remain in production. Theoretically, these less-efficient competitors may contribute the outputs which they originally planned to supply. That would mean, however, at a yield which would have induced them to invest very much less, or make no investment at all in that form, had it been forecast.

But an increased *incentive* to consider restraint in these circumstances does not mean an increased *power* to restrain profitably; and the entrepreneur who relies on the forbearance of others for his protection must know that he is taking a great risk. If there *is* indeed a possible increased group advantage to be gained from oligopsonistic restraint in the presence of underutilized capacity in the industry, there will be a concomitant risk of increased loss to any participant who should discover that his failure to compete for labor and materials has allowed one or more of his rivals to get ahead of him.

A quite different situation which superficially resembles that just discussed and has been *treated* as *oligopolistic* arises as a result of misconceived forms of antitrust control. Because high profitableness rather than scarcity contrivance has all too often tended to become the sin for which managements and the investors to whom they are responsible may be expected to be punished, especially when the high profits are gained through economies of scale, it seems often to have become expedient for low-cost firms to be careful not to allow their efficiency to affect high-cost rivals too adversely. There is profit in maintaining the solvency of some of their competitors because that reduces the risk of a misconceived antitrust case. The estimation of this risk enters prospective profit calculation in exactly the same manner that predictions of output and price decisions on the part of others enter that calculation. Certainly in these circumstances the output of the industry will be less than the social optimum; but that will have been due to an imposed cost factor (caused in turn by a misconceived form of antitrust policy) and not to oligopolistic exploitation.

The truth seems to be that *effective* tacit collusion cannot be imagined as having more than a negligible effect. Collusive exploitation requires quotas, with sanctions for their enforcement; or else sufficiently attractive prospects of a certain share of the market will have to be assured for every voluntary participant. But can we conceive of *any* substitute for the quota or the prospective market share inducement under simple tacit abstention from competition? Just think of what we must postulate. The low-cost firms (probably the most efficient) must judge it to be profitable to sacrifice prospects of a growing share of the market and spontaneously protect the high-cost firms (probably the less efficient). While this is conceivable when the risk of misconceived antitrust proceedings is the alternative, or under ironclad cartel *contracts,* it is hardly conceivable in their absence. In general, the advantage to the low-cost entrepreneurs of passing on to consumers the economies of their relative efficiency will outweigh all other considerations.

Experience seems to teach that the effectiveness of collusive restrictionism has required not only reliance on quotas, but the ability to discipline participants; and a system of policing has often been felt to be essential for successful exploitation. Those who collude may be few, but in the absence of any acceptable criteria for the "just" sharing of the spoils, the fear of various forms of nonprice competition working "unfairly" for some in the ring; the probability that some at least of the low-cost producers will feel that they can gain more through expansion than through the higher margins assessed; the eagerness of rival producers to get in first in times of real growth; or fear of losing sales in a declining market—all these and other factors seriously weaken the power to exploit, except through mergers and enforceable agreements.[7] How then can the consequences on pricing of those who merely *refrain from* competition (price or otherwise) in the hope that their rivals will do the same be more than a niggling factor? In my judgment, most appearances of tacit collusion are illusory. *Apparent inhibitions* toward competition in the absence of definite restraint of trade are to be explained quite differently.

We can now turn from tacit restraint in general to oligopsony and consider the case of exploitation of labor. As we have seen, those who buy labor do so *in the whole market for labor,* except where very specialized skills are involved; while the ability even of a *natural* monopsony to exploit workers whose developed powers are unversatile depends upon the monopsonist's ability to trick such workers into shutting themselves into a specialized undertaking. An oligopsony can hardly do that!

For instance, in the idle capacity case, where decline in demand for the product has been followed by a long-delayed failure to adjust product prices sufficiently, the situation is much more likely to be explained as a consequence of the maintenance of labor costs, especially when this occurs during recession. The idleness of many workers is then not due to managerial understandings that hold off bidding for idle labor (which, from the standpoint of an individual entrepreneur, could be employed profitably) but to wage rates tending to be more rigid downward than prices. If incentives for downward wage rate adjustments to protect the wages flow in depressed industries were as effective as incentives for downward price adjustment on the part of producers and merchants in most industrial materials, any *appearance* of oligopsony would probably vanish.

Again what may seem superficially to be lack of competition for labor, of oligopsonistic origin, among corporations in an industry may well be, ironically enough, evidence of the very perfection with which the free market is working (that is, in markets which are relatively unencumbered by strike-threat restraints or legally enacted restraints). When managements have created good relations with their staff, labor turnover is likely often to be very slow (under general economic stability). It may then *look* as though managements are not competing in the labor market. Yet even when the number of workers each firm is employing changes very slowly, there may be continuous competition, each firm retaining its valued employees by insuring that earnings and working conditions are at least as favorable in their service as any compensation likely to be offered elsewhere. Moreover, in these circumstances they will recruit juveniles by making offers, quietly communicated to parents and schools by letter or by advertisements, in a manner which entails bidding against rivals for a limited supply.

The fear of competition breaking out *where an infectious optimism has created an unstable price or cost situation, or where formal collusion exists* is sometimes wrongly identified with fear of "predatory selling"—the attempt by one producer, or more than one acting in collusion, to ruin one or more competitors, drive their operations out of the industry, and so leave the aggressors a monopoly. But that is to confound pressures toward the survival of the least cost methods of using resources with a wholly different phenomenon. The former situation is brought about by a process which causes the withdrawal (through nonreplacement) or the writing off of resources which are being inefficiently utilized (which *may* mean the insolvency or winding-up of a firm). But "predatory selling," as I define it, is the use of the pricing mechanism to render unprofitable the continued operation of one or more competitors. The essence of the situation is that, in the absence of such abuse of the pricing system, the firms eliminated would be quite capable of continuing to supply output, whether they were relatively efficient or relatively inefficient.[8] The possibility of "predatory selling" can be a serious deterrent to investment in a field—a case of the private use of coercive power which can be classified with the strike threat.

When some competitors have been caused to fear that, if they act in their own self-interst by cutting prices and/or bidding up costs, predatory *selling* to drive them out will follow, *we have one of the clearest examples of how antitrust law (wisely and disinterestedly administered) is the required remedy*. The type of "predatory selling" which I judge to make up at least ninety percent of all such selling in practice takes the form of price-cutting in certain districts only or in respect of some special range of products; it is likely to be deliberately punitive in intention, in order to discourage others; it can be prevented by the enforcement of a simple rule—nondiscrimination in price[9]— a rule which will provide a kind of collective security; *but it is not a phenomenon of oligopoly-oligopsony*. Hence, in discussions of this topic, if it is said that *fear of retaliation* prevents price cutting or prevents the bidding up of material prices or wage rates, it may be either of the two conceptually distinct possibilities we have just noticed which may be envisaged. But I do not think that fear of "predatory *buying*" of labor[10] has ever been an important factor limiting investment in any field. It *has* been used, however, to create "joint monopoly."[11]

The conclusion seems to me to be unchallengeable. Because the exploitation of labor requires a clear and rigorously enforced monopsonistic agreement among the purchasers of labor and cannot exist *effectively* in oligopsonistic form, even though managements may sometimes be *reluctant* to raise wage rates voluntarily at the first signs of labor scarcity, the needed protection for labor lies in the prevention of collusion. Laws which can most effectively prevent or restrain the *formal contrivance of scarcity or plenitude* (that is, which can weaken the private profitableness of the restrictive determination of outputs, prices and sales territories) as successfully as is achievable in the imperfectly governed world in which we live, can at the same time be equally successful in rendering impotent or trivial such oligopsonistic exploitation as might otherwise occur. Antitrust can, I think, prevent the private contrivance of scarcities or plenitudes (a) through collusion, or (b) through the scope for exploitation inherent in corporations which are large in relation to the scale of markets. It can effectively forbid pricing practices that use the value mechanism as a subtle means of private coercion for exploitative purposes. It can supplement the common law against fraud and misrepresentation by enforcing truthfulness in descriptions of the quality, content or weight of products (to protect the honest manufacturer or dealer from damage due to less-scrupulous competitors). And in so doing it can automatically cause such imperfections in the free market system as might be due to oligopolistic or oligopsonistic tendencies to be of niggling practical consequence.

I insist that it is no criticism of my argument that the content of antitrust law and its administration must necessarily have defects. All human institutions, however wisely thought out, are capable of constructive criticism. All too often they are immune from improvement only owing to the intellectual and moral shortcomings of opinion-makers.

I am not suggesting, it should be clear, that labor can be passive and ignore its own entrepreneurial function: firstly, in investing in skill acquisition and secondly, in discovering employment outlets. The latter is indeed *the* important function which the unions could undertake on behalf of their members in a strike-free system—playing on the divergencies of interest among producers and thereby breaking through any signs of oligopsonistic tendencies. But the survival of the right to strike would hinder, not assist, the performance of that function. For virtually all man-made obstacles to labor mobility, and hence to the advantages of widely spread labor markets, have been erected through strike-threat pressures.

One final but *unimportant* point. I have not discussed the possibility of oligopolistic exploitation of investors by labor. An official wage commission in South Africa suggested in 1925 that the Africans in that country were in a "tacit combination" not to accept less than a certain wage rate. But as I pointed out in 1930, all that that really meant was that they all knew what the market rate was—that is, what they could get.[12] It illustrates my contention that the very perfection of some markets may leave an impression of oligopoly.[13]

NOTES

[1] That *oligopolistic* abuse tends (like monopolistic or monopsonistic abuse) to rest essentially upon what I have termed "shut-out" or "shut-in" power respectively is partially recognized in Franco Modigliani's well-known article, "New Developments on the Oligopoly Front," *Journal of Political Economy* (1958), p. 216. He says, "undoubtedly the impossibility of entry is frequently at least implicit in the treatment of oligopoly;" and "oligopoly could also be defined to exclude entry . . . the impossibility of firms not now in the group, of producing the commodity—whether for physical or legal reasons."

[2] Faced with a monopoly or oligopoly of labor (say, in the form of the maintenance of a union-enforced or a tacitly-enforced "standard rate," when demand for the product has fallen off), entrepreneurial incentives would be to offer the fullest employment profitable at the contrived labor scarcity value expressed in the standard rate.

[3] This is more likely to be the position, however, when the initiating entrepreneur's decision to bring in additional resources is interpreted as his judgment, not that demand for the product is elastic, but that the demand schedule has risen or will rise.

[4] "Given market" means that the demand schedule for the product is judged not to be changing.

[5] "Profitable" means yielding more than the rate of interest on all increments of capital invested in the long run. The qualification, "in the long run," is necessary to cover the case in which assets in the form of equipment are provided in the expectation that demand for their output will only gradually develop to justify the venture (see p. 152).

[6] If overinvestment *has* occurred for this reason, the ideal reaction *from society's angle* will be a cutting of the price of the end product, and perhaps an outbidding of competitors for materials and labor so that the least cost firms come to supply a relatively large part of the cheapened output. The cheapness of the additional output provided in such circumstances is, so to speak, *society's partial compensation* for the social detriment caused by the specific overinvestment—that is, *society's loss of additional output in other forms;* for one overinvestment *means* another underinvestment.

[7] The enforcement may be through private coercion, of course.

[8] In an early article, I tried to draw attention to this important distinction. I used the term "aggressive selling" for what has subsequently become known, more appropriately, as "predatory selling." See my "The Nature of Aggressive Selling," *Economica* (1934).

[9] Unless the parties discriminated against freely accept the discrimination because they are the beneficiaries therefrom. I have explained this point in the *Economica* article, "The Nature of Aggressive Selling," referred to above and more specifically in "Discriminating Monopoly and the Consumer," *Economic Journal* (1935). See also pp. 163-164.

[10] The cornering of labor supply in order to raise its price, thereby to ruin certain competitors, to monopolize the production and sale of a product, and then to raise its price and reduce the price of labor.

[11] See pp. 8, 50, 72, 98, 110-111, 128, 169.

[12] W. H. Hutt, *The Theory of Collective Bargaining* (Glencoe, Ill.: Free Press, 1954), p. 34.

[13] Curiously enough the shoe was on the other foot in South Africa. A highly organized, collusive monopsony existed (and still exists) for the centralized purchase of African mine labor. I do not suggest that there has been monopsonistic abuse. See footnote 3, p. 114.

10
"Exploitation" of Investors

LET US now ask whether the strike threat *permits exploitation* of investors (assumed to be wealthy) for the benefit of workers (assumed to be poor). As we have seen, the private use of coercion is, in this case, regarded as a permissible way of "soaking the rich." The crucial general proposition has already been stated in Chapter 1. Our task at this stage is to consider certain arguments which seem to conflict with it.

Remember what has already been shown. When the price of labor in an activity is raised above its free market value, not only will the real value of labor inputs which can continue to be profitably absorbed in that activity be reduced, but the real value of utilizable complementary resources in the activity—and particularly the fixed assets needed—will also be reduced (or maintained below what would otherwise have resulted) when their renewal has to be considered. Managements (on behalf of stockholders) will not retain, or replace, let alone add to assets for labor to work with if their retention or provision offers a prospective loss. Hence vigilant investors are unexploitable except through a breach of some agreement, or as a consequence of some other wrong prediction about the use of strike-threat power. But *if this power is used in a manner which the investor failed to forecast, he may (in the extreme case) lose the whole value of his investment*. In that case, we can say that the investment ought never to have been made at all.[1] On the other hand, if entrepreneurial decisions are the outcome of realistic forecasting, we have the phenomenon of *labor exploiting labor*, as consumers and as displaced or excluded workers, with investors being exploited only in the same manner (and roughly in the same degree) through being denied the most profitable outlets and as consumers.

To generalize, it can be said that the inexploitability thesis regarding forward-looking entrepreneurs depends upon the observed fact that the prices of different productive services determine, immediately or ultimately, the magnitudes and the proportions of the different inputs acquired. In the economists' useful jargon, different elasticities of substitution between "capital" and "labor," different elasticities of demand for end-products, and different entrepreneurial interpretations of these elasticities, will influence the size and composition of the stock of assets in various productive activities. The most important relevant substitutions are: (a) of less exploitable *forms of assets* (generally the more versatile, and in some circumstances the more liquid[2]) for more exploitable forms (generally the more unversatile or "specific"[3]); (b) of assets for labor; and (c) of *contracts* which do not permit the exploitation of owners (for example, when assets are provided only for renting or leasing) for conventional wage agreements (see pp. 79, *et seq*).

When any kinds of costs rise through duress, then substitutions will still be made in attempts to equate marginal *prospective* yields with the rate of interest. This will *always* happen if we can assume all entrepreneurial action to be rational, in spite of *previous* action having turned out to have been based on wrong predictions of strike-threat use. And it *is* realistic to regard entrepreneurs as continuously vigilant—often engaged in research and experiment—in their efforts to observe and interpret *the facts* about current changes in the composition of consumer preferences and the availability of different kinds of means for their satisfaction. These facts, which are the data of business prediction, are frequently in the form of probabilities. They are used to determine both the prospectively profitable prices for outputs and the costs which it is prospectively profitable to incur. A business executive who makes the relevant decisions will in practice often say that he seeks an "adequate" yield and avoids an "unreasonably low" yield or a loss. He may mean by this that he is taking possible future competitive reactions into account, or that he is not trying to enhance returns via collusive price or output determination. But his thinking on such issues falls always into the category of what may be termed the "maximizing" type, *despite the imponderables*. And that means that he is groping toward the points at which marginal yields (to what he decides shall be invested in various input-mixes) shall reach but not fall short of interest.

In referring to "imponderables," I have in mind a host of factors, some of which would have to be classified under the category described by the unsatisfactory but often used term, "degree of monopoly," which influence forecast prices, sales and yields, and hence the input costs that entrepreneurs will incur. Because of inertias, rigidities and errors of prediction, changes in costs (including duress-imposed costs) and current prices do not always *immediately* affect sales out of inventories of end products, or purchases of equipment, materials and labor. Costs may rise while prices and sales are, for the time being, unaffected. But all this means is that sporadic rather than day-to-day investment decisions will be made. Even so, the exercise of foresight will be continuous. Indeed, while negotiations about a wage contract are in progress, managements will often be preparing and studying a range of different production and pricing programs ready for immediate adoption according to the outcome. Even before the labor costs which will have to be conceded have been arrived at, the appropriate reactions concerning the

127

retention, replacement, or net accumulation of inventories and equipment will have been planned in detail.

Obviously the incentive for the owners of an undertaking to withdraw resources (that is, not to retain or replace them) will be very great if that undertaking is singled out for exploitation *in a competitive industry* (that is, where the product is sold, and the materials and complementary services are purchased in effectively competitive markets). That is why in practice unions seldom act against particular firms faced with competition. They bargain rather on an industry-wide scale.[4] This usually recognized unprofitableness of the strike threat when it is exercised against a firm which operates in competitive markets is, properly interpreted, proof that the fixing of wage rates under duress can normally win gains for union members, not so much through exploitation of the investors against whom the strike threat is ostensibly aimed, but only against those who are most often considered the *incidental victims*: (a) the consumers and (b) investors and workers whose assets and efforts are diverted to less productive and less profitable fields. As a rule, it is only if industry-wide protection can be provided for investors (against the competition of firms which might otherwise offer employment at nonexploitative wage rates) that the strike threat can be used effectively.[5] When managements capitulate to strike-threat demands because they recognize their competitors are to be burdened in like manner and degree, they have become agents (if unwilling agents)[6] for union exploitation of the "incidental victims." And managements are similarly motivated, and consumers (or suppliers of materials) similarly exploited, when wage demands are conceded because unions have successfully lobbied for tariff protection (or for restraints on the export of materials). In both circumstances, *the investors against whom the strikes are threatened may not be exploited at all.*

The protection of investors as a means of exploiting nonparties to wage "agreements" occurs in its least conspicuous form through the industry-wide enforcement of "the rate for the job." In a rather blatant form, which is now and again evident, it occurs through "joint monopoly."[7] Managements and unions collaborate to exploit consumers and share the spoils through the mutual protection from competition they give one another.

An argument which, in various guises, has been used to suggest ways in which capital might be exploitable via union aggression depends on the assumption that entrepreneurial decision-makers do not think and act rationally in response to the above-mentioned imponderables. Particular instances of this sort of reasoning are to be noticed later; but at this stage it seems desirable to face the general issue. Unless the allegation of irrationality merely refers to unduly optimistic expectations of yields because of the clumsiness of some managerial procedures in predicting profitability, it has, I hold, no substance. For instance, it has been suggested that once labor costs have been determined, managements simply add a conventional gross profit margin over direct costs in order to get end-product prices, while these prices in turn determine saleable outputs. Well, managers who behaved like that, assuming that such a formula was as good as any other which might be used for setting the price of a particular product (and hence its prospective sales) at the *outset,* would know that their assumption might soon prove to have been wrong.

An industrial firm's production budget will typically specify in detail the various outputs the production managers are called upon to put through the assembly lines month by month during the following year, just as the sales budgets will specify expected monthly sales for the same period. But actual realized sales as the year goes on, salesmen's reports, cost changes, interest rate changes and so forth will bring about *immediate* changes in the budgeted outputs (increases, curtailments or abandonments). And in respect of the operations of a particular plant owned by a firm, or the operations of a firm as a whole, the question of whether to expand, maintain or curtail operations (that is, whether to scrap or sell assets, replace an equal value or add to them), the vigilance is continuous. And in every case the notion of marginal prospective yield, however vaguely envisaged, *must* be the determining decision-making factor. No entrepreneur will replace or add to the assets used by an enterprise unless he expects a yield in excess of interest on all input increments.[8]

But the argument presented here does not depend on any assumption that entrepreneurs do, on the whole, act with such thought, prudence and initiative as most students of business administration believe them to act. The validity of my claim that wage rates and prices are but one factor in the determination of income shares is not upset by the possibility that time lags in the adjustment of input and output magnitudes to market values may be experienced. And whether those values are determined under competitive pressures (the free market case) or whether they reflect deliberately contrived scarcities, or managerial sloth, or other phenomena leading to "market imperfections" is irrelevant to the point here at issue. Only if purchases of inputs and sales of outputs were independent of costs and prices (which they are not) could the strike threat, "degree of monopoly," and the whole gamut of inertias, rigidities and irrationalities, directly determine income distribution. Yet all the attempts I have found to imply that the imposition of wage rates under duress can be used to exploit investors depend ultimately upon such an assumption; and they all seem to me to obscure the reality that capital will avoid exploitable fields.

In envisaging entrepreneurs predicting yields, I have made no use of the often-used but clumsy notions of (a) "the rate of return to capital," meaning the rate of interest *plus* the rate of profit or *minus* the rate of loss; and (b) "normal profit," meaning the volume of profit at which the value of assets retained and replaced in an activity remains constant. In groping at profit maxization and loss minimization during the course of ordering different input-mixes of different magnitudes, entrepreneurs cannot avoid *aiming at* (however wide of the mark their achievement may fall) the point at which further increments of inputs of a particular kind will bring lower yields than could be obtained if the resources needed to produce those further increments were used in some other way. There is *inevitably* an element of hit and miss in their predictions; but if the contemplated output of a certain commodity at a provisionally envisaged price is 500, the sole reason why the figure is not 550 or 450 is that the responsible decision-maker *guesses* that 500 is *more likely* to be the most profitable. As I have insisted, however, judgments on such matters are under continuous vigilance and continuous or spasmodic revision.

Entrepreneurial forecasts are, then, *continuously* operative, even when at times much productive capacity is judged to be temporarily incapable of profitable utilization. Curiously enough, this is not generally recognized. Thus, we find an economist as rigorous as Scitovsky saying that "it is difficult to imagine the forces of demand and supply in factor markets influencing prices at times when the labor force, existing plant capacity, and the potential supply of savings are all under-utilized." It is not difficult for me to imagine it. Scitovsky does "not deny that market forces operate in factor markets," but thinks "they may be much weaker and much more sluggish than is generally supposed; and . . . they may, in some respects, operate quite differently from those that operate in the market for bread."[9] I myself have difficulty in imagining in what sense "demand and supply" forces *can* be thought of as failing to operate simply because entrepreneurs are frequently slow to react to "market signals," so that some services or assets come to be priced beyond what consumers are judged to be able to afford (or inconsistently with price expectations). These forces continue to work when the services of some assets are temporarily valueless, exactly as they work when prices are so flexibly adjustable under market pressures that all resources are optimally employed. However drawn out the period of adjustment, the pricing process determines the values of the services of labor and assets just as it does with bread, or leisure, or annuities. Services which are priced out of the market represent "withheld capacity"—withheld supply—that is all. Hence, to anticipate an objection I expect, the thesis here presented does *not* assume "full employment." Entrepreneurial expectations still determine *the form* of such replacement and *the form* of such net accumulation of assets as continues when much existing capacity and the labor it uses are priced into wasteful idleness.

But the adverse effect of wasteful pricing decisions upon the aggregate flow of income to be divided will be magnified if the displaced resources remain idle instead of finding other (less productive) uses. This is equally true whether the antisocial pricing is the result of deliberate monopolistic decisions to contrive scarcities or of mere price inertia. But in the absence of inflation, there will be a tendency created by every contrived scarcity to set in operation a *cumulative displacement* of other resources into less productive activities or into idleness. A contraction in the output of any industry means a reduced contribution to the source of demands in general, while price and cost rigidities will hold back attempts to adjust. On the other hand, in such circumstances, there will be a tendency toward a cumulative acceleration of aggregate income in the event of a cut in the price of any productive services (through the avoidance of any particular restraint on the utilization of labor or assets) in the broad direction of the prices consonant with optimal resources utilization.

A separate substitution reaction to prospective yields judged to be temporarily low *through price and wage-rate rigidities judged to be of an unstable nature* is that certain kinds of replacement are likely to be postponed. Not only will investment in inventories and work in progress decline, but entrepreneurs may be expected to replace scrapped equipment by relatively liquid assets until the costs of maintaining or adding to former capacity have reached their forecast reduced ultimate values. This will happen even when managements do not contemplate any important change in the eventual form of assets. Thus, if entrepreneurs can rely upon a governmental promise that, whatever happens, the inflationary solution can be ruled out, we can expect them to be waiting for greater "reasonableness" on the part of the unions, as well as for costs other than labor to fall. In more general terms, the prospective yield from money or near money in such conditions becomes greater than the yield to non-money. *That is one of the substitutions through which the exploitation of investors is avoided.*

I must now deal with a predictable objection. I may be asked: If your argument holds, what point is there in resistance to strike-threat demands? Do you maintain that managements' reluctance or refusal to surrender to the strike threat is pure public spirit—the protection of consumers' interests, or concern with the welfare of workers who may be laid-off and robbed of their present employment, or altruistic resistance on behalf of potential workers who are denied access to the bargaining table?

My answer is that, in each individual case in which the strike threat is an issue, it *is* invariably to the advantage of investors that the threat (or the strike) shall fail, and it *is* a disadvantage to them when the threat (or the strike) has some success. The advantage gained by the defeat of duress-backed demands is in the nature of a *windfall,* the *possibility* of which was one of the incentives to such investment as has occurred. Similarly, capitulation to strike-threat demands will mean a *detriment* to investors, the *possibility* of which will already have limited the volume of investment and influenced the composition of assets in the enterprise. Both possibilities are of some consequence, but managements are expected to (and are relied upon to) resist duress-imposed costs. Hence the prospective yields to assets which are retained, replaced or added to in particular undertakings are envisaged as *a range of probabilities* based (among other things) on strike-threat predictions. Resources of reduced aggregate value will stay in or be directed into activities in which prospective costs are thought likely to be forced up through the private use of coercive power, *in spite of the hope that skillful "negotiations" will brake that power.* Obviously, then, *marginal* prospective yields from fields in which a strong probability exists of successive capitulations to union demands will be no lower than they are in spheres in which no duress-imposed costs are forecast. Some resources will be diverted to other activities.

This argument must not be interpreted as meaning that forms of production involving a very high strike-threat risk cost will not be undertaken at all. It means that the profitable outputs in these cases will be smaller and hence much more expensive for the consumer. For when this risk is high, investing is like backing a horse at long odds. The investor, like the punter, will expect an exceptionally large yield in the event of his winning; and the investor "wins" when, through skillful bargaining techniques or strategies, he can evade coercively imposed labor costs, wholly or partially, and enjoy a fabulous return for having surmounted high strike-threat hurdles. Such exceptionally high yields, it must be recognized, are the consequence of the strike-threat system, not returns to the exploitation of labor which that system is presumably intended to resist.

To recapitulate on the point at issue. Investors know that the depleted *prospective* yields which constitute their incentive may be enhanced by *windfall gains* if managements are successful in dissuading the unions from pressing their claims as far as they (the investors) have forecast as probable, or further depleted by *windfall losses* if the unions are more successfully aggressive than seemed likely. But *prospective* marginal yields, and in the long run realized yields, will be equated to the rate of interest in both unionized and nonunionized activities. *The vulnerability of investments in specific, non-versatile assets, in heavily unionized sectors of the economy simply reduces the rate of growth of those sectors—to negative growth in some cases.* Unionized industries may expand, but the rate of growth where much exploitable fixed capital is needed will have been substantially curtailed.

Among the ways in which the avoidance of strike-threat consequences causes the emergence of a capital structure in which the risk of exploitation of investors is minimized or evaded is by the substitution of capital for labor. Quite apart from resort to labor-economizing machinery and methods, more highly mechanized methods of production generally (that is, capital-intensive methods), in which the ratio of labor costs to total costs is low, will tend to become relatively efficient as duress-imposed labor costs rise. Such growth as occurs is then more likely to be in these forms, while types of production in which the ratio of labor costs to total costs is high (that is, labor-intensive methods) will tend to contract, or even to cease operations except in nonunionized activities. Developments of this kind are more likely to reduce than raise labor's relative share in the value of the product affected.

But the reactions we may expect are far from simple. *Investors in the production of outputs in capital-intensive activities happen to be exceptionally exploitable by strike-threat action.* Unless the substitutability of assets for labor in such operations can be used strategically by managements to make "reasonableness" in strike-threat duress expedient, the advantages of non-union organization will be very large indeed. Wage rates profitable under "yellow-dog" contracts (enjoining employees not to join a union) will be much higher than wage rates under union agreements (where, of course, "yellow-dog" contracts are not prohibited by law).

Labor-economizing developments in technology or management may be *autonomous* (that is, unaffected by prior changes in cost conditions) or *induced* (that is, brought about by a rise—or expected rise—in labor costs); and the rise in labor costs (actual or expected) in any case may be caused (a)

132

by increasing competition for the labor in question or (b) by duress-imposed wage rates.

Autonomous economization of labor in any industry reduces the relative claim of wages *in that industry,* and *ceteris paribus* tends to reduce labor's percentage share in aggregate income. But it releases labor for the production of other things and adds to the source of demands for all noncompeting outputs. The products toward which the increased demands are directed may well be those of labor-intensive activities, and there are indeed reasons why this might be expected (see p. 229). Hence when the qualification *ceteris paribus* is relaxed, we have no certain way of telling how *relative* demands for labor and for the services of assets in the whole economy will be affected. We do know, however, that *the most conspicuous* inventions which have multiplied the yield to labor since the beginnings of the industrial revolution have been labor-saving rather than capital-saving. That such inventions have not tended to reduce labor's relative share is probably due to the benefits having been largely consumed in the form of greater leisure.

Induced labor economization may be regarded as having a similar effect in one set of circumstances, namely, when the rise in labor cost in the firm or industry in question has been due to enhanced demand for labor services in other industries. In these circumstances, a tendency for labor's share of income to increase in these other industries will be more or less offset by any substitution of machinery for labor in the industry which economizes. But the dynamic consequences of the economization—the factors mentioned in the paragraph above—will still be operative.

On the other hand, *induced* labor economization due to costs imposed through the strike threat does *not* seem so likely to have the broadly neutral consequence we have noticed. The technical developments called forth are labor-economizing in a manner which mitigates the burden on consumers and investors, yet *in this case the economy achieved seems to be contrary to labor's advantage* and specially against the interests of the less well-paid wage earners. For under the circumstances we are considering, *the community's resources are not increased, as they are when the economy is autonomous.* The displaced workers are available to produce *different* things, not *additional* things (as they are when they are released by autonomous economization). The laid-off workers can typically enter only occupations of inferior productivity and remuneration (and they may perhaps be forced into temporary unemployment). The distribution of the aggregate wages flow will tend to be more unequal. Moreover, the diversion of capital into labor-saving assets will have robbed the community of assets in other forms—presumably *relatively* capital-economizing—developments which one would expect to raise the proportion of labor's share in the value of the product of industry as a whole.

Circumstances sometimes exist in which unions are in a position to insure that there shall be no displacement of labor following duress-raised labor costs, and that redundant workers shall be paid an income although they provide no services (as in the case of various "feather-bedding" conditions). But that extreme possibility is simply one of the situations in which investors in already existing assets can be exploited when the possibilities of future exploitation had not been foreseen. Under feather-bedding, the spoils of exploitation are divided either among the whole body of previous workers in the industry or among certain favored individuals.

Consideration of *the immediate effect,* then, forces us back for a moment to contemplation of an issue which is not *directly* under examination at this stage. The community in its consumer aspect is doubly exploited: *firstly,* in being denied the most fruitful utilization of labor and assets in the industry in question; *secondly* in being denied the alternative product which the "feather-bedded" workers could have been providing. But *the long-run effect,* which *is* relevant in the present context, is even more burdensome. As we have seen, the rate of growth of an industry or firm which is so exploitable will be slowed down or reversed. Investors as such will no longer be exploited, but the community may suffer a grievous detriment.

An empirical study by Paul H. Douglas of the period 1890 to 1926 suggested that a union can win large gains for its members when they first organize, but "thereafter the rate of gain enjoyed . . . tends to slow down to a speed which does not appreciably exceed that of the non-union industries."[10] Other investigators have reached similar conclusions. In 1962, Melvin Reder, relying also on the empirical researches of Paul Douglas, A. M. Ross, and William Goldner, referred to "the well-known conclusion. . . . that new unionism is associated with differential percentage wage gains to an industry, but long-established unionism is not."[11]

This is exactly what one *would* expect, for two main reasons. Firstly, we have the factor already mentioned, that elasticities of demand for end-products tend to be much greater in the long run than in the short run. But secondly, and this is the point which is relevant in the present context, the elasticities of supply of complementary assets also become greater as time passes. When a new union first uses its powers of aggression, it can exploit not only consumers and displaced or excluded workers[12] but (a) those investors who had not fully allowed for strike-threat possibilities, and (b) those investors who, *hoping* (rather than *expecting*[13]) that skilled management could prevent the formation of a union or defeat attempts to strike effectively, are disappointed in their hopes. "Profits" can be exploited only when the exploitation was not in prospect when the entrepreneurial decision was made. Thereafter, the explanation of experience may be that strike-threat policy tends to be "reasonable," in the sense of calculated to keep the undertaking going or even expanding. If it *is,* then it is in the light of the expectations created by *that* "reasonablensss" that future investment will occur. Thereafter there will be no further gains at the expense of "profits" except to the accompaniment of a *further* slowing down or reversal of any rate of growth in the accumulation of assets in the field affected.

What is essentially the same line of reasoning is to be found in Eugen von Böhm-Bawerk's *Control or Economic Law.* He perceived, as clearly as we can today, that yields in the loan market or from real estate, etc., limit the extent to which "capital" is exploitable.[14] He said "there would be little inducement to replace *used up* capital funds, if the investment should promise a smaller return to its owners than the same capital could produce in other kinds of investments"[15] (my italics). And in exposing the "hallucination," as he called it, that labor can increase its share at the expense of capital,[16] he reiterated several times the point that, *in the short run,* strike-threat coercion might sometimes be able to confiscate a large proportion of the prospective yield which had induced an investment.

But I would go even further than this. It is *theoretically* possible for a union, faced with an undertaking which has made a large investment in non-versatile equipment, to force up wage rates to a carefully calculated extent *so that the undertaking is exterminated gradually,* thereby permitting the continued employment of all surviving union members as their numbers decline through retirement and death. In other words, it is possible to envisage a model of strike-threat action in which the imposed costs are meticulously adjusted to ensure that it is *just profitable* for the undertaking to retain and replace as much of the capital as is needed for the continued employment of the declining labor force which the union allows to be available.[17] But it is precisely because of such possibilities (illustrated by a wholly imaginary extreme case) that *an enormous volume of specific assets which would otherwise be provided for the community's benefit must fail to materialize.* Both replacement and development take on less exploitable, but almost certainly less productive forms. For instance, the value of already provided non-versatile equipment may decline in value through *unanticipated* strike threats over the period of the economic life of the equipment[18] (which life will be reduced); but thereafter the equipment may not be replaced at all or not replaced up to the same value (unless, of course, demand has subsequently risen).[19] At the time of the investment, admittedly, entrepreneurs *knew* that the technical form of that piece of plant might commit them for years to the purchase of materials and labor, possibly in hardly changeable proportions. Wrong forecasts about union coercion can be disastrous in these circumstances, and investors know this only too well. On the other hand, *some* complementary inputs (for example, those devoted to the replenishment of inventories of materials) may shrink *immediately* the cost of labor's contribution to the input-mix is forcibly raised. That is, the providers of "circulating capital" may be hardly exploitable at all via unforecast strike-threat pressures.

At this stage, it is necessary to draw the students' attention to a very simple but important aspect of "collective bargaining" which, to the best of my knowledge, has not been stressed by any contributor to this subject. It concerns the *nature* of any temporary, short-term transfers in favor of union members (and union officials) which are achieved when investors have underrated the degree to which strike-threat exploitation will be tolerated and practiced. What has actually happened when investors have been forced to accept yields below those the probability of which had induced the investment is that *capital* (that is, *property*) has been transferred, not in terms of legal definition but in terms of economic realities.

The point can be very simply illustrated by consideration of the circumstances in which, theoretically, the power to exploit investors who are trapped is greatest. Let us make the following assumptions. (1) A corporation's assets have been provided by stockholders who initially expected no strike-threat action. (2) The assets are of very long physical life and highly specific. (3) The demand schedule for the output is highly elastic and does not change. (4) All other complementary services needed are purchased in competitive markets and their supply schedules do not change. (5) Duress-imposed labor costs are then forced on the firm. (6) The situation is not countered by a management-imposed work stoppage, that is, the laying-off a large number of workers solely in order "to teach the union a lesson." Under these assumptions it will be profitable for managements to discharge very few workers, if any, and unprofitable to raise the price of the product. Hence labor's gain can be said to wholly (or virtually wholly) achieved at the expense of capital. The value of the corporation's shares will fall because the entrepreneurial residue will fall, while the earnings of the workers will rise by a more or less equal value. The aggregate loss of value in the corporation's shares will tend to equal the present capitalized value of the increase in the aggregate earnings of the workers. *The identical physical assets will be contributing services of about the same value to the productive process, but part of the capital value of those assets will have been seized by labor.*

The issue is as simple as this. The threat of a strike, like the threat of a gun, *can be used to seize the property of others,* defensibly of course in the eyes of moralists who hold that Robin Hood objectives justify the means. I suggest that it is solely when *capital* can be transferred in this manner that investors *are directly exploitable* (that is, damageable otherwise than as consumers and beneficiaries from general prosperity). The principle is clear. The strike threat can be employed to expropriate certain kinds of assets when they have already been provided, but it cannot be used to enforce their continued provision as they are depleted or as they depreciate.[20]

In the hypothetical example through which the argument has just been illustrated, the gains enjoyed by union members are *assumed* to have hurt neither excluded comrades nor consumers. But in practice fellow workers and customers bear virtually the whole burden. For this reason we must be careful not to confuse the capital confiscable from investors under the circumstances imagined (in other words, the capitalized value of the increased labor earnings *from this cause*) with the capital value of *new union privileges,* that is, sectional increases in income enjoyed because certain workers are priced out of the market and customers are disadvantaged. For gains at the expense of these last parties may *also* be expressed as the pecuniary value of a privilege—a capital value of which the yield is the union's wage gains; and although such a privilege is in practice normally involved in some measure in all "collective bargaining" agreements it is conceptually distinct from the seizure of investors' capital. It may sometimes have an objective pecuniary

136

price; for example, it may be expressed in the form of union entrance dues. (It then resembles the market price of a transferable import permit.)

It is necessary now to bring our minds back to the realistic principle that, once trapped, investors will be twice shy. The assets which cooperate with labor will not be replenished by the original investors, except in the sense and in the circumstances discussed above. A *possibility*—although scarcely imaginable—is that the beneficiaries of the property transfer will themselves become new investors and find it profitable somehow to provide complementary assets for replacement or growth in the undertaking in which they are employed. If we conjure up the idea of union members saving (out of the yield to capital seized) a sum equal to what they have taken by force, we can *imagine* them offering to subscribe to a new capital issue or buying debentures in order to maintain intact the fixed capital they need to work with. But the *rational* investment of their future savings would mean choosing investment outlets offering the relatively highest yields; and this would hardly be in any undertaking which they intended to exploit later on.

In any case, there is no evidence to suggest that the thrift of union members compensates by replacing confiscated capital by way of investments anywhere in the economy, either out of real net savings on the part of members, or through the unions stepping up their investment of accumulated funds. In other words, the capital transferred tends in practice to be squandered. I do not question the probability that union members in any group save about as large a proportion of their incomes as nonunion workers of the same income group, and perhaps a somewhat larger proportion for an indefinite period immediately after their real earnings have been first forced up. But as their wages in such cases include an important element of capital, it seems certain that *material capital squandering is the inevitable concomitant of unforeseen strike-threat action.*

In the extreme case, assuming now (quite absurdly) (a) highly *elastic* demands for all products, (b) high *inelastic* supplies of all complementary resources, and (c) the failure of investors to foresee the possibility of the strike-threat system being used in the manner which is about to be described, we can imagine the workers as a whole, operating through a central agency, being able to seize all fixed assets through the use of the whipsaw or strike in detail. We can envisage, for instance, the AFL-CIO borrowing big sums from its members and using the funds to support strikers against one firm at a time, in each case forcing up wage costs to the point at which, while no business is driven into insolvency, the price of each one's shares is driven down in turn to near zero. When that has happened, each undertaking's workers will already *virtually* own the fixed assets, whether or not they subsequently purchase the shares. But we can imagine them using their funds to do this because they can acquire the shares at a negligible price. Eventually, by this stratagem all previously provided *fixed* assets will be owned by existing workers. The new worker-capitalists will have no incentive to *share* the capital so obtained with future workers allowed in. They can protect their property by insisting upon "yellow dog" contracts with any new entrants who can be offered wage rates below those paid prior to the strike which seized the capital, or by insistence upon entrance fees equal to a proportionate part of the capital at what its value had been prior to the strike. The worker-capitalists will then find it advantageous to retain, replace or add to the assets they own in accordance with *their* forecasts of the yields. In such circumstances, there will be no reason why the relative shares of income accruing to owners and workers should have been changed one iota; but there will have been a large redistribution *among individuals* of income from the services of assets.

Alternatively, centrally directed strike power is capable of being used to permit the nationalization of one firm after the other at negligible stock market prices. All firms can become owned by "the people" at niggling costs, while "full compensation" can be claimed to have been paid! That is, the burden of nationalization on the taxpayer *qua* taxpayer can be infinitesimal.

But let us now drop the unrealistic assumption (c) and assume instead that investors do foresee the possibility of exploitation via centralized whipsaw tactics. The fear of losing any return from the assets they have provided will lead to no further resources being provided in exploitable forms or under conditions which permit exploitation. *Investors in fixed assets will refuse to offer them under contracts which yield a residual claim on the value of the output, or they will do so only under iron-clad "yellow dog" agreements.*

But when the owners of capital begin generally to refuse to accept entrepreneurial responsibility by insisting upon contractual instead of residual yields, an enormously important division of labor is being abandoned. The functions of (a) saving (financing the replacement or net accumulation of assets in general), and (b) investment (choosing the most productive, and hence most profitable, form in which assets are to be replaced or accumulated) are usefully linked in the entrepreneur who takes the residue after all the other parties to production have been paid at previously agreed prices. The merits of the specialization which would be upset are derived from the ability of investors to own assets in many different undertakings and so to spread their risks. If the workers must take the residual claim, they are subject to risks which cannot be spread, as we saw in Chapter 6. The circumstances envisaged show how harmful to the workers themselves—as a class—general attempts to exploit investors (such as we have been considering) would be. Owners of assets would escape exploitation because they would allow their property to be used only in return for rent or interest; but that would mean an enormous sacrifice of the social security provided by the free market. The function of risk-taking would be forced on the classes least able to spread risks.

But let us now drop assumptions (a) and (b). In practice, the forcing up of labor costs under duress would mean the forcing up of product prices and the immediate diversion of complementary resources from any field against which the centrally planned whipsaw was directed. In the absence of inflation, the raising of prices by any firm expresses a shrinking of its contribution to the source of demands for the products of all noncompeting activities.

Dynamic factors would therefore engender catastrophic depression with the cumulative falling off of outputs in general, to which reference was made above (p. 130). The recovery or counterforce would then be the strong incentives which I have just stressed, to offer the use of assets only in return for contractural rent or hire.

In the light of the insights gained so far in this chapter, we can turn now to an objection which has at times been expressed to me verbally. The questioner has in mind, not the extreme form of strike-threat coercion strategically directed according to whipsaw principles, which we have considered above, but an extension of the kind of situation which already exists in western communities. I am asked: If virtually *all* investors who accept the residual claim on the value of output are subject to exploitation via the strike threat, can my reasoning still be accepted? Surely, it is asserted, in a regime in which most (or a large proportion) of the workers do rely upon union coercion (instead of, as today, a small proportion in all industrial countries), even if all investment decisions take full account of the probable consequences, entrepreneurs as a class will have no alternatives. Hence (I am asked) if *no* unexploitable investment outlets are left anywhere in the economy, must not *some* redistribution of profits be achievable for labor's benefit?

To consider the truism which this last question implies, we must begin by recognizing that as long as investors do, on the whole, correctly forecast the cost consequences of duress-imposed wage rates, their realized yields on the value of all input increments in the investment channels they choose will still *tend* not to fall below the rate of interest. The outlets chosen as *relatively* most favorable will continue to be those in which *ceteris paribus* the probability of exploitation—valued as a cost—is *relatively* low, while this cost (that is, the value of the probability) will be least when savings and disinvested funds seek contractual yields as distinct from residual yields.[21]

I have explained above how the extreme use of strike-threat power would cause the owners of assets to force "labor" to assume the greater part of the entrepreneurial function. It seems to me that this is what would be bound to happen under the circumstances imagined. Let us assume that all prospective residues (profits) in all sectors of the economy are *regarded as equally likely to be exploited*, in the sense that the same proportion of what would otherwise be residues are forecast as destined to be lost through strike-threat concessions. Because all prospective yields are assumed to be reduced by the same predicted percentage, the higher this percentage, the smaller the proportion of investment that will be devoted to equities (with prospective *residual* remuneration), and the greater the proportion which will be devoted to loans, debentures, bonds, mortgages, etc., or to the provision of assets to be leased or rented. The extent to which prospective losses will be avoided via the sacrifice of prospective profits (under the highly unrealistic assumption we have accepted) will depend upon this valuation of the liability to exploitation. We can, if we wish, envisage the extreme case in which the degree of forecast exploitation is such that entrepreneurs calculate it will confiscate a value equal to or exceeding profits.[22] In such a situation all *new* assets[23] not operated by their owners, or by the owners' families, or by partners would be leased or rented. But in practice, long before prospects of exploitation had created anything approaching such a state of affairs, the contraction of the flow of wages and of income so caused would have forced governments either to take effective action against the strike-threat system, or to fall back on the inflationary palliative, or to resort to the political determination of wage rates.

At this stage, however, the relevant issue is that even under the most extreme assumptions favorable to the notions which I am refuting, direct exploitation of investors would be avoided. Investors would suffer from the absurdities of the system (that is, be exploited) in the same way that the workers would. Demands for the services of assets would fall, but so would demands for the services of labor. All broad categories of income would be reduced *more or less* in the same proportions (the consequences being therefore regressive).

This argument applies fully to the category "profits." There is no reason why, in the circumstances imagined, society's valuation of entrepreneurial services should be reduced *more than in proportion to aggregate income*. There are no grounds, that is, for assuming that there will be a decline in the *relative* natural scarcity value of the function performed by those who *finance production at risk* and direct productive operations. Stockholders who anticipate strike-threat pressure will either choose outlets with the prospect of huge windfall gains (see pp. 131-132) or accept risk in the less sensitive and less productive way of a contractual yield; but they will never be able to avoid the risk-bearing function altogether. In the extreme case, they will assume risk in deciding what kinds of assets are likely to be most profitably offered for renting or leasing, leaving to labor the greater part of the risk-taking (and relinquishing to labor, of course, the greater part of remuneration for risk-taking). The category "investors" will then overlap, including both "stockholders" and "labor." But when stockholders' investment decisions correctly allow for exploitation probabilities, contractual yields to investment will be as unexploitable as residual yields.

In practice, the unions seem to follow the principle of forcing wage rates upward according to "what a firm or industry can afford to pay." Sometimes the phrase is "ability to pay." Presumably, duress-imposed burdens are in each case calculated with a view not to destroying the source of employment or not reducing the rate of growth of the firm or industry by more than is judged to be expedient. The expediency in this case is concerned with the support of members who may be threatened with displacement.[24] Accepting this interpretation of the phrase "ability to pay," limits to the exploitability of a firm or industry by strike-threat power can be said to be set by the inadvisability of causing too many lay-offs of union members. Even where governments (that is, taxpayers) in some form foot the wages bill, the unions know that the fertility of the goose that lays the golden eggs may be reduced by trying to squeeze too much more out of her than she normally delivers. Hence they must always weigh up the question, *How many* additional eggs will it be wise to require? The caution shown is usually described as "union reasonableness." The expectation of such "reasonableness" in any activity is, as we have seen, a determinant of the amount and composition of investment in that activity; and it is that which is of vital importance in the present context.

While there is little awareness of the long-term consequences of strike-threat action, the unions do, then, recognize the short-term dangers. They can see for instance that, while they are in a position to exclude (or even displace) workers from industries which are responding mainly to domestic demands, it will be against their interests to try to do this in industries which are subject to foreign competition, or which produce largely to satisfy export demand. In the words of B. C. Roberts, "while under full employment unions are little concerned with the effect of wage increases on the level of employment in industries engaged in supplying goods to the home market, they are conscious of the relationship between wages, costs, and prices and do take some account of it in the export industries."[25] It happens also, and not infrequently, that in expanding industries, especially when *earnings* are high in relation to the basic wage rates stipulated in wage agreements (because incentive bonuses are earned, or various forms of overtime), suggestions that the basic wage rates shall be pushed up under strike-threat pressure are rejected by union ballot.

Again, when *the standard rate* is enforced on a national scale, the local unions in areas of relatively high nonlabor costs will often press for the right to accept a scale below the national standard; and if the national union is threatened with a break-away, the members will agree, probably to the great relief of the officials. Should the position then be that the industry neither grows nor declines in any area (whether high cost or low cost), we can say that exploitation is maintained in just such intensity in different places as to permit a positive yield to all increments of assets *retained or replaced* but not to any increments of assets *accumulated*. Each area is forced to pay what "it can afford" because it is thought dangerous to displace any present union members, or inexpedient to cause a reduction of the employment outlets available as present union members leave, retire, or die. There is no merit in such a situation (which is sometimes defended on grounds to be later examined—that increased wage rates for some are "absorbed by the profits" of the efficient—see pp. 153, *et seq*). It is just as indefensible to destroy the profitability of *growth* in any field as it is to destroy the profitability of *maintaining currently used capital intact*.

Recognition of possible backlash from "unreasonable" strike-threat demands *in particular cases* is frequently clearer in the minds of the union rulers than it is among the members. As we have seen, union officials perceive at times that it is to the interests of those they represent that an industry or firm should be allowed to grow. They will then warn the membership not to expect "unrealistic" wage improvements. Yet it is precisely because of the "democratic" control exercised by the rank and file that, when elected union rulers try to protect, say, the interests of a minority likely to be jeopardized by "irresponsible" demands, they are all too apt to be overruled. Moreover, as with so many democracies, there are often "extremist" rivals for power, while the majority of union members are typically ill-informed—so much so that they sometimes insist on policies through which even their short-term interests are harmed.[26]

Although on occasion managements can rely in some measure upon the "responsibility" or "reasonableness" of union officials, these officials seem prepared all too often to capitulate to cupidity and shortsightedness, rather than risk loss of power and income. Shrewd managements are under no illusion on this point. The risk of unions being forced to act contrary to the interests of their whole membership is felt as *an aggravation* of the process under which incentives to growth in the relevant industry are weakened, or accepted as yet another factor hastening its relative or absolute decline. But, as we have seen, managements typically realize the need to think up capitulation formulas which will allow the hierarchies who govern the unions to satisfy their membership that they are just as successfully aggressive as other union rulers. (See pp. 69-70.)

There have been periods in the past during which the great majority of investors in unionized or potentially unionized occupations may be assumed to have failed to forecast the intensity of the future use of the strike threat. In particular, the growing political power of the union organizers has probably been insufficiently allowed for at certain times. Transfers of capital (regarded as income) in favor of labor *could* have occurred, I think, if other reactions had not offset the possibilities we are here considering. Before the New Deal, entrepreneurs expected neither the disastrous price-cost policy of 1929 to 1933, which unnecessarily transformed unparalleled prosperity into unparalleled depression, nor the extent to which politicians (successfully seeking profit from the distress, fears, and disappointed hopes due to price discoordination) would find it expedient to capitulate to the labor lobby and bestow privileges and immunities on the unions. Even after the Wagner Act, the quiet ruthlessness with which sectionalist aims would come to be pursued seems to have been generally underestimated. Hence some considerable exploitation of the providers of assets almost certainly did occur *at first;* and we should expect to find evidence of short-term union gains (observable in the shape of a larger percentage of aggregate "income" being received as "wages"). Empirical studies do *not,* curiously enough, support this inference. But for reasons to be discussed in Chapter 15 and 16 this does not permit us summarily to reject the inference.

The consequences of entrepreneurial reaction to exploitation expectations during this period have been far-reaching, even if hardly noticed. They are to be discerned in a changing composition of the assets stock, gradually assumed over the years. Directly or indirectly, a growing (although undistinguishable) proportion of the equipment and tools which are used by labor has come to compete with labor rather than to act as a source of demand for labor. The bias toward assembly-line, mass-production and automated plants, machinery and operation patterns, which strike-threat anticipations have induced, has been a powerful force even in nonunionized activities (for the possibility of later resort to economic duress can nowhere be dismissed). The development is one which has squeezed out much of the meaning from empirical studies of changes in "labor's relative share" of income (see Chapter 15). Its significance from the standpoint of the *quality* of the response of the productive system to consumers' sovereignty may one day be recognized as having been profound.

It is not uncommon for "labor economists" to refer obliquely to the vital issue of the avoidance of imposed burdens following input-output value comparisons. I say "obliquely" because they typically do so in the vaguest of language. Occasionally they refer to the "harshness of the market" or to "budgetary restraints;" they sometimes hint that the existence of foreign competition could "aggravate" the "harshness;" and at other times they admit that the productive system may "adapt itself" to strike-threat pressures in some usually unspecified way. But passages of this kind are never, as far as my reading has gone, followed up by careful definition of concepts or rigorous analysis. I have sought in vain in the "labor economists' " contributions for any systematic consideration of the change in the composition of the stock of assets (and hence in the form of output) which is the consequence.

The blindness of organized labor to the consequences of the strike-threat system upon the *wage-multiplying* structure of assets, and this concerns the long-term benefit of the wage earners, is quite remarkable. For instance, managerial techniques of an economizing nature which do *not* displace labor (for example, capital-saving technological innovations which might greatly decrease the nonlabor cost per unit of product) are far more likely to be adopted in a free labor market than when the arbitrariness and uncertainty of the strike or the strike threat are present. For capital-economizing innovations usually require formidable investments in specific, nonversatile forms (perhaps of what the Austrian economists called the "roundabout" kind) and they are normally more exploitable than labor-economizing innovations. Investments of that type are never lightly undertaken; they will certainly be deterred if the very fact that they have been made increases the risk of future strikes; the possibility of recourse to them cannot reduce the incentive actually to use the strike weapon, as can recourse to labor-economizing inventions; yet they are the investments most likely to accelerate the wage-multiplying process.

At the other extreme, we have assets which possess no wage-multiplying power and of which the yield consists wholly in gratifications for the owner. For instance, a wealthy investor may put much of what he disinvests or saves into assets like private parks, big estates, mansions, yachts, luxury cars, valuable paintings, diamonds, pearls and consumers' capital goods generally. It is obvious that capital held in that form has no wage-multiplying power. That is, it does not contribute to the production of wage goods nor cooperate with the labor required to replace or add to the assets used and consumed in the production of wage goods.

I draw attention to these two extreme cases in order to stress the broad nature of the generalization that I have enunciated, namely, that entre-preneurial avoidance of strike-threat exploitation seriously reduces the wage-multiplying attributes of the stock of assets. The disturbing reality seems to be that *those assets which can most effectively enhance the flow of wages are those of which the replacement and provision are most seriously deterred by strike-threat restraints.* In most countries of the western world, the unionized sector covers industries which are *key factors* in general material progress and prosperity. The conclusion is surely incontrovertible. *Attempts to transfer income from investors to labor must have destroyed income-creating and wage-multiplying possibilities on a formidable scale.* All contrary notions can be seen to ignore the reality of investors' freedom. Prospective exploitation is avoidable exploitation.

The hardy notion of investors being effectively "soaked" via duress-imposed wage rates depends hardly at all, I think, on experience of the cir-cumstances in which, because investors have not yet come fully to anticipate strike-threat consequences, income transfers *have* been forced. The "hallucination" (as Böhm Bawerk called it) can be traced, I suggest, rather to (a) misinterpretation of the "economizing-displacement" process (which is the phrase I have used to stress the economic significance of technological progress (see pp. 19-20) and (b) a failure to perceive the dynamic consequences (via the operation of Say's law) of labor-economizing and capital-economizing innovations. Progress in the form of "economizing displace-ment" happens to have accompanied the emergence and growth of the strike-threat era, and this progress has been continuously making tolerable labor costs raised by union pressures. Yet these pressures themselves have actually been curbing the process of adding to the stock of assets in the most ef-fectively wage-multiplying form. As we have seen, the strike-threat system has, among other things, caused productive operations within the unionized sector to take on capital-intensive rather than labor-intensive characteristics, and it has forced the process of replacing assets, and the deployment of labor, into fields of lower productivity and remuneration. The almost paradoxical truth is that the "validation" of labor costs by managerial and technological in-genuities (building often on developments in science) seems to have given rise to the firm conviction that rising standards of wage remuneration, including fringe benefits, are the *results* of gains achieved through labor's fight for just wages.[27] Ultimately, as Böhm-Bawerk put it in 1914, the belief that "during the last decades countless strikes have led to an improvement in the workers' economic status"[28] must be attributed to a general unawareness of "outside influences . . . which have increased the marginal productivity of labor, and therewith increased the possible permanent higher wage level. . . ."[29] The enhanced wage rates could survive, he added, because of "the stupendous progress of our times . . . great technological improvements, im-proved methods of utilizing human labor. . . ."[30]

The "hallucination" has been intensified through misinterpretation of inflationary experience. The rise in money wage rates, which is one of the consequences of inflation, happens to occur within the unionized sector

144

through negotiations conducted by the unions. It *appears* therefore as though only lurking strike power has achieved the periodic increases in nominal wage rates which characterize an inflationary era.

One further source of the "hallucination" should be mentioned. We find also misinterpretation of the sort of experience which is encountered when rising real wage costs in a particular productive activity do not bring reduced outputs because demand for the output in question happens to be growing. In such circumstances, a rising output of, say, 20 percent in the course of a decade could, perhaps, have been 50 percent in a free labor market, and have resulted in a much cheaper product. It would therefore have exerted a greater incentive for an expansion of the outputs of noncompeting goods and services. Let us consider, for instance, the price of steel in the United States. It seems to me beyond question that a free labor market in this industry would have achieved a very much lower price of steel with appropriately larger outputs. It would have served therefore as a contribution toward lower production costs and higher wage rates in almost every American industry.

I shall return to this important example (see below, pp. 147-148). The spread of the unionized sector has largely been toward those productive activities which have been *tending* to grow most rapidly, so that *the general detriment caused by duress-imposed costs in curbing their rate of growth has been obscured.* That is, strike-threat pressures have been most successfully parasitic (and hence most rewarding from the sectionalist angle) in those industries and occupations which could otherwise have made the greatest contributions toward real income and the well-being of the community as a whole. The unionized occupations have been mutually harming one another, while diverting much capital investment into assets which cooperate with labor in the less productive, nonunionized occupations.

At this stage, it is essential to refer briefly to a point already mentioned, namely, the possibility of reaction to the strike threat by the substitution of the consumption process for the saving process. A very large (although unidentifiable) proportion of the flow of savings is altruistically or prestige motivated, being based on the desire to bequeath capital to those of the savers' dependents or others who are dear to them, or to those causes they favor, such as universities, favorite charities, etc.; while many savers are influenced by the prestige which attaches to persons who are successful in amassing capital (a success which, in the absence of exploitation, theft or fraud, must be broadly correlated with the degree to which they have served the community[31]). The expectation that a considerable part of their savings which is not destined for consumption during their lifetime (for example, which is not invested in annuities) is going to be seized and used or squandered by others, is likely to reduce individual saving preference. But I refer to this possibility solely for the sake of completeness. It is, I think, of no great importance because (as we have seen) investments in nonexploitable forms will still be available to the prudent saver. Redistributive taxation *can,* however, induce a decline in saving preference (although whether it *must* do so is a matter of controversy).

The reactions of exploitation-avoidance upon the production structure are sometimes far-reaching in their effects upon the *spatial spread* of investment. Development tends to be diverted toward *areas* in which the prospects of exploitation are least. Countries or districts in which the "unreasonable" use of the strike threat is judged to be particularly likely will attract less capital—just as they would had they been burdened with a discriminatory tax. Thus, during the interwar period, a large proportion of British savings was driven abroad for precisely this reason. Such *international* capital movements can be curbed by "controls" and taxes (like the American "interest equalization tax"), but only at the expense of assisting the exploitation process. Fiscal restraints have (not very consciously) originated in part from attempts to prolong the period in which home investors have been exploitable.[32] The locking-in of capital by exchange control certainly *may* facilitate its exploitation—an almost exact parallel to the locking-in of labor by restraints on emigration. But restrictions on capital exports will tend to reduce the domestic rate of interest[33] rather than profit residues. Otherwise the argument of this chapter needs no modification.

Within a country, evaluations of the strike-threat burden can be seen to have driven the net accumulation of assets or the replacement of disinvested assets from districts thought prone to strike-threat activity to relatively strike-free areas. There is, for instance, little doubt that in the United States the individual states which have made use of the provisions of 14 (b) of the Taft Hartley Act and passed "right to work" laws have attracted development, because these laws reduce the risks of the strike-threat (although in some states minimum wage enactments, under the Fair Labor Standards Act or otherwise, have possibly more than countervailed any advantage).

Again, within Britain during the interwar period, virtually all development of new industries (such as artificial fibers, plastics, foam rubber, electrical equipment, and so forth) took place southeast of a line drawn between Bristol and Hull. This southeastern part of Britain was relatively nonunionized, having about only a fifth of total union membership after World War I. And one region to the northwest of the line, the South Wales district, which had become a depressed area,[34] was unable to attract investment in a new stock of assets, in spite of a plentiful supply of idle potential labor (masses of ablebodied unemployed) and the presence of rich natural resources capable of development. In this case, it was largely the fear of relatively *militant* unionism which deterred investment there and caused South Wales to remain chronically depressed.

The spatial distortion of the production structure is, however, simply one manifestation of the general tendency we have noticed for exploitation-avoidance to cause the composition of the stock of assets to be less productive and less conducive to maximization of the wage flow.

Having considered the fundamental factors *of the composition and spatial distribution of the stock of assets,* we must turn our attention to the conceptually distinct factor of *the labor cost of assets.* We have seen that the strike-threat system amounts to a form of economic warfare under which labor is mainly exploiting labor (through regressive, imposed burdens on consumers and displaced or excluded workers.) We can now observe that "labor exploits labor" in yet a third way, namely, *in raising the cost of replacing or adding to the stock of assets which cooperate with labor*. This burden is imposed *irrespective of the composition of the stock*. The capital resources which the workers must use have had the services of previously existing capital resources as well as the services of labor incorporated into them. But except for that relatively small element in the value of those resources which is the result of scarce *natural* assets, these capital resources have themselves been the product of labor. It follows that any forced enhancement of the labor cost element in their value must harm the workers as a whole not only as consumers but as wage earners. (Of course, nonlabor incomes in general must also be adversely affected.) A fuller explanation of this important point is given below (pp. 223-224).

The adverse effects of the strike-threat system upon the composition of the assets stock which has been explained in this chapter can be illustrated by examples from recent American experience. It has become evident that the United States is unable to compete advantageously with foreign fishing vessels outside her monopoly defined by the 12-mile limit. American investors dare not risk capital in great factory ships with attendant fleets of subsidiary vessels such as are operated close to the United States' shores by Russian, Japanese, and German vessels. This is simply because of the virtual certainty that *force majeure* would later, subsequent to the investment, push up labor costs above the level which would have justified the risk. The situation is currently depriving large numbers of relatively poor Americans of opportunities of better-paid employment, as well as robbing consumers in the United States of cheap fish.

Again, if American merchant vessels could have been protected against strikes, the United States could today have been one of the world's leading mercantile marine powers if not the world's leading power; and if her shipbuilding industry could have operated under similar protection from the strike-threat, the technological genius of her intellectual élite would, it is not unreasonable to assume, have led her to dominate international developments in marine engineering. Certainly, protected from duress-imposed costs, vessels flying the United States flag could have offered relatively well-paid jobs to large numbers of presently underprivileged American nationals—especially those in the minority groups.

Finally—an example which, it is felt, ought to have been causing the gravest misgivings—we have the American steel industry, to which I have already referred. Costs imposed by the strike threat have brought about ageing plants and hence high nonlabor costs. Moreover, in plant replacements, the urge to "economizing-displacement" and modernization has been dampened. In a key industry, the unions have been allowed to destroy the incentive for large-scale experiments in capital costly yet capital-economizing methods. All American manufacturing activities have shouldered the burden. The fact that the British and German steel industries have been similarly handicapped has softened the blow to American investors in steel, although 1971 seems (from the profit angle) to have been one of the worst years those investors have ever experienced. Small wonder, then, that the Japanese and Soviet steel industries boomed as the American languished. Although "the Soviet system is ridden with waste and inefficiency,"[35] the Soviet Union's steel output for 1971 exceeded America's for the first time in history. But American steel output would have been incomparably greater under market freedom, and it would then have been cheapening the costs of wage-multiplying assets in all noncompeting activities (and so benefiting the whole community in its consumer role).

The reader must now be reminded that, in this chapter, only occasional and incidental account has been taken of the fact that in each case the consequences of *attempts* to exploit investors (or of actual exploitation when investors' predictions are at fault) are regressive in their systematic closing of potentially higher-paid employment outlets for unprivileged workers (quite apart from their consumer impact). Gains won by the private use of coercive power are *not* achieved at the expense of "rich" investors. Indeed, were it not for the fact that unions certainly *can* gain at the expense of (a) comrades confined to or driven to less well-paid work, (b) consumers, and (c) (in government employments) the taxpayers, they would be forced to consider more explicitly and more often whether attempts to get *any* additional eggs from the goose at all would not bring adverse repercussions on too many of their members (in the long run if not immediately).[36]

The sacrifice in material well-being which the system must have caused would have been even more serious had it not been for a collective (although essentially ephemeral) method of evading the consequences. The manner in which money wage rates in the unionized sectors have been forced up in the great industrial countries of the western world during the last three decades *could* have brought disaster—a general running-down of the economy—had the situation not been crudely rectified through chronic inflation. Thus, in the United States, it has been, perhaps, the very skillfully planned and executed destruction of the real value of the dollar which has prevented the unions from forcing down the flow of wages catastrophically. Inflation seems to have been the only alternative to (a) governmental restraint of the strike threat, or (b) "incomes policies"—the authoritarian imposition of maximum wage rates as a politically acceptable means of maintaining the flow of wages and the prospective yields needed to call forth sufficient replacement and growth. In 1949, Lindblom expressed grave forebodings about the ultimate consequences of unionism as it then appeared to be developing.[37] He had not foreseen, I think, the success which inflation could achieve as long as people generally could be misled about its intended speed and duration (see Chapter 17). But are not his dismal predictions likely yet to be justified unless a wiser policy toward the private use of coercive power is not soon adopted? For do we not all still expect inflation to continue?

It is important to notice that this discussion of what is achievable through the private application of coercive power has been concerned only with its effectiveness when it operates directly through the price system—either through imposing wage rates and prices, permitting supply and demand factors to react to these duress-fixed values, or by restraining the expression of supply and demand factors and allowing wage rates and prices to react to the restraints. But of course strike-threat power *could* be used via the general strike or otherwise,[38] in order to gain control of government. By such methods all capital *could* be seized on behalf of the proletariat (or for the private benefit of those who organized the disruption, if they could keep control in their hands). That could well be a more effective strategy for revolution than the centralized use of the whipsaw because the responsibility of the unions would be less obvious to an electorate. But our interest in this chapter has been confined to the consequences of attempting to redistribute income, not by way of taxes and capital levies, even when these are a response to strike-threat coercion, but by the fixing of wage-rates and prices under duress.

NOTES

[1] We must be careful not to exaggerate the extent to which, in practice, assets already provided in a given physical form are exploitable for such reasons. If only a tenth of the aggregate stock of assets has to be replaced on the average in each year, it still allows some considerable scope for modifications in the composition of the stock of assets over the course of, say, a decade.

[2] See p. 131.

[3] The substituted forms of assets may be of types which produce different kinds of output, that is, goods or services for which the required productive arrangements are less exploitable although the product stands lower on consumers' scales of preference than those which would be preferred in a strike-free economy but for which the productive arrangements are relatively exploitable. *Leisure* may be one of the outputs.

[4] There *are* exceptional circumstances. Sometimes the use of "the strike in detail" ("whipsaw") appears to be good tactics (see p. 47), and on occasion discrimination against the more efficient firms is deemed advantageous (see pp. 153-155).

[5] Curiously enough, Phelps-Brown and Hart (*Economic Journal*, 1952, pp. 269-73) have argued that, where prices of end products cannot be raised (or cannot be raised "proportionally"), the forcing up of labor costs means that unions can "squeeze profits" and hence cause redistribution in labor's favor. But that is true only if the dynamic factors, to which the whole of this chapter is devoted, are ignored. I deal specifically with a model based on that assumption on pp. 136-137.

[6] The word "unwilling" (in the sense of "coerced") is justified when investors do not themselves benefit from the "joint monopoly." But (as we are about to see) both *may* benefit and share the spoils.

[7] W. H. Hutt, *The Theory of Collective Bargaining* (Glencoe, Ill.: Free

Press, 1954), pp. 96-104. Such joint monopoly has, at times, had the express support of legal enactment. In the United States wage agreements in this category are often called "sweetheart contracts."

[8] In stressing the importance of *prospective* yields, it is important to perceive that *current realized* yields are most misleading at times—and business decision-makers have learned this truth through bitter experience. There can be no simple extrapolation of current yields to get prospective yields. Still less are the sales of one month simple evidence on which to forecast sales of subsequent months.

[9] Tibor Scitovsky, "A Survey of Some Theories of Income Distribution," National Bureau of Economic Research, *The Behavior of Income Shares: Selected Theoretical and Empirical Issues. Studies in Income and Wealth* (Princeton: Princeton University Press, 1964), p. 25.

[10] Paul H. Douglas, *Real Wage Rates in the United States, 1890-1926* (Boston: Houghton Mifflin Co., 1930), p. 567.

[11] Melvin W. Reder, "Wage Structure Theory and Measurement," *Aspects of Labor Economics: A Conference of the Universities—National Bureau Committee for Economic Research,* A Report of the National Bureau of Economic Research (Princeton: Princeton University Press, 1962), pp. 297-298.

[12] The reader is reminded that by "excluded workers," I refer to those who could have improved their incomes and prospects in the absence of duress-imposed labor costs, as well as those actually "displaced"—"laid-off."

[13] See pp. 131-132.

[14] Eugen von Böhm-Bawerk, *The Shorter Classics of Bohm-Bawerk,* ed. Hans F. Sennholz (South Holland, Ill.: Libertarian Press, 1969), p. 181.

[15] Ibid., p. 182.

[16] Ibid., p. 192.

[17] Simons has used this illustration of the point at issue, *Economic Policy for a Free Society* (Chicago: University of Chicago Press, 1948), p. 132.

[18] Because the capital value of the equipment will fall as its prospective earning power falls.

[19] It may, however, cost less to replace a piece of equipment than it cost originally to install it (for example, the renewal of a railroad track).

[20] Some part of the value confiscated may be that of natural (as distinct from man-made) assets, which are not subject to depreciation and replacement. Owners of such assets are extremely exploitable. But in an economic system which tolerates the strike threat this fact will hold back investment in their development, for example, of mines. In other cases natural resources are highly versatile. Land is a case in point, although a nationwide union of farm workers would have formidable strike-threat power.

[21] The *ceteris paribus* qualification here is meant to remind the reader that this particular cost has to be reckoned together with all other costs in entrepreneurial decisions.

[22] I say "exceeding profits" because investors in debentures and bonds are also exploitable—although of course to a much smaller degree—when insol-

150

vencies on the part of the borrowers are caused by unexpected strike pressures.

[23] I am making abstraction here of those replaced assets which may be needed to minimize losses due to previous exploitation.

[24] And whose subscriptions could be lost to the union in the event of their lay-off.

[25] B. C. Roberts, in J. T. Dunlop, ed., *Theory of Wage Determination* (London: Macmillan, Ltd., 1957), p. 117.

[26] "The process of decision-making based on the economic knowledge of the leaders is . . . sometimes frustrated by the attitude of the membership." (Ibid., p. 118.)

[27] This conviction is shared by judges, superficial sociologists, journalists, school teachers, clergy and other opinion-makers, as well as by politicians, labor consultants, labor lawyers, and so forth, for many of whom it is (to use the phrase of a shrewd observer in this field, a century ago) a "paying opinion."

[28] Böhm-Bawerk, op. cit., p. 192.

[29] Ibid., p. 189.

[30] Ibid., p. 196.

[31] I say "broadly correlated" because sheer good luck, although often indistinguishable in practice from good investment judgement, is in itself hardly meritorious. The winner of a bet or of a sweep has not served the community.

[32] I feel that Kaldor's plan for a consumption tax was intended more as an attempt to prevent exploitation avoidance (in this and other ways) than as a means of discouraging ostentation. See Kaldor's *The Expenditure Tax* (New York: Macmillan Company, 1956).

[33] Unless fear of being caught in that way drives away capital imports, that is, foreign capital which would otherwise have provided wage-multiplying assets in the country concerned.

[34] After a Labor Government had forced a cartel on the coal industry in order to insure the raising of wage rates for those miners who were not to be displaced when the price of coal was raised.

[35] S. Pejovich, "Economic Reforms in the Soviet Union," *Modern Age*, 16 (1972): 68.

[36] It is not irrelevant to point out that the fields in which gains from union pressures are *popularly* regarded as most "unreasonable" or "outrageous" concern occupations in which the possibility of exploiting investors in fixed equipment is least or wholly absent, for example, among plumbers, medical practitioners, barbers, lawyers, and so forth.

[37] Charles E. Lindblom, *Unions and Capitalism* (New Haven: Yale University Press, 1949).

[38] E.g., via pressures calculated and planned to create unemployment, insecurity, discontent, racism, disorder and generally deplorable conditions which can be blamed on existing governments (or on "the capitalist system" or "the profit system").

11

Some Special Cases of Investors' "Exploitability"

IN THIS chapter, a number of special cases of apparent investors' exploitability must be considered. *At first sight*, the cases we are about to examine may all seem to constitute exceptions to the principle that forward-looking entrepreneurs who expect the strike threat to operate are unexploitable, except as third parties subject to the detriment of restrained productivity in general. In fact, I hope to show, the principle is universal.

One such case arises where fixed, durable, specific equipment has been provided in the expectation that it will have to be used for some time at below its full technical capacity. It may be planned to employ relatively few workers at the outset, but under the prediction that a gradual growth of demand (perhaps through subsequent prospecting for new markets) will eventuate, thus justifying ultimately the investment and bringing an increasing demand for labor. Such a situation will create one of the circumstances in which, if labor costs are levered up following the investment, it *may* prove unprofitable to economize labor. No lay-offs, or very few, may follow the rise in labor costs for some considerable period. Thus, while the abandonment of the venture may follow when renewal time arrives for the key equipment, the combined workers (it may be thought) will be able to command substantial gains in the interim. Such a situation creates no exception, for *it is the very possibility of such circumstances occurring which, given the community's acquiescence in the strike-threat regime, must be currently preventing much investment in the kinds of fixed equipment here envisaged*; and these are forms of investment which could often magnify the yield to labor as a whole far more effectively than the forms of investment which are assumed by the capital diverted.

A rather similar case is that in which the enterprise confronted with a strike threat has entered into a contract to supply output at an agreed price, without including a strike clause. In such circumstances, the undertaking can be forced to pay almost *any* price for the labor required up to the point at which it has to dishonor the contract through its insolvency. But here again, contracts of that kind will no longer be made when the risks of strike action are generally predicted; and so one of the most fruitful forms of cooperation from the standpoint of society, that based on long-term agreements between independent undertakings, will be shackled if not completely eliminated from the pattern of fruitful cooperation. *Exploitation of investors is avoided; but society's gains from entrepreneurial planning (in which all parties share) are greatly depleted.*

Another special case which we should notice is that of a wage-rate increase *forced on an exceptionally efficient undertaking or industry.* This will not, the argument goes, cause a decline in output, nor reduce the volume of employment offered at the higher labor cost; for the exceptional efficiency must be earning exceptionally high profits which *can* "absorb" the cost burden. An interesting tacit implication in this case is an abandonment of the usual labor union principle of the standard rate. The thesis assumes that firms or industries can be discriminated against for the advantage of labor. It is thought, for instance, that if the high profits of a relatively efficient firm are caused by an exceptionally low capital cost per unit of output, resulting from managerial ingenuities exercised subsequent to the original investment in the plant, then the undertaking can "afford" or can "bear" higher labor costs per unit of output without the original profitable output declining. The less efficient firms can be treated more gently. But *ceteris paribus* new efficiencies of the kind envisaged would, in the absence of exploitation of the efficient undertakings, *raise* the number of workers who could be profitably employed in plants with relatively low nonlabor costs. Hence, an enhancement of the wage flow through increased recruitment by such firms will be frustrated by strike-threat concessions. It is obviously impossible, I suggest, for labor as a whole to gain from any policy which means levying a sort of discriminatory private tax on capital-economizing developments, or on undertakings in which labor already receives a greater than average proportion of the value of the product.[1]

In the parallel case in which the special efficiency is derived from some innovation (managerial or technological) of a labor-economizing type, it might seem at first as though we have circumstances in which *theoretically* a relatively efficient firm will be exploitable—up to the point at which the full yield to its differential efficiency can be seized—without any curtailment of employment, and even with no consumer detriment. As we have seen (pp. 133-134), the unions can demand featherbedding or work-sharing to the point which simply prevents labor costs from falling below what they would otherwise have been. The implication is, just as in the capital-economizing example, that investors are robbed of possible profits which they did not expect when they invested and hence could hardly have influenced their investment decision.

Now this is merely a particular case of the confiscation of property through the strike threat. It does not affect the principle that the volume of investment in assets which are perceived to be vulnerable to exploitation will be reduced in every case in proportion to estimates of the vulnerability. And, moreover, the prospect of *future* economies due to managerial perspicuity *is* equally one of the incentives to the retention, replacement and accumulation of resources in any undertaking.

A variant of the argument suggests that certain forms of managerial efficiency are contrary to the workers' advantage unless part of, or the whole of, the fruits can be seized for their benefit. Thus, it is thought that labor-economizing developments which actually cause some workers to be laid-off *must* contribute to the disadvantage of labor as a whole unless the innovators can be forced fully to compensate the persons displaced. Now if the idea of labor's disadvantage refers here to the workers' *relative share* in aggregate income, it is true that *ceteris paribus* the tendency of labor-saving economies must be to reduce labor's *percentage* in the activity immediately affected. But as we have seen, all human progress in the material sense has been a consequence of the economizing-displacement process, achieved through scientific, technological and managerial insights which, since the inventions of the wheel and the lever, have permitted the attainment of given objectives with fewer resources in men, man-made assets, or natural assets. The release of resources thereby for the pursuit of *additional objectives* (or more of the same objective) has been the ultimate source of every physical advancement in the well-being of mankind. It has been the consequence also of every *acquisition* of knowledge relevant to man's material well-being. *Machinery and equipment which economize labor are wage-multiplying, not in the occupations in which they are used, but in contributing to the source of demands for labor and for the services of assets in all noncompeting occupations*; and there is no reason why the rise in such demands should favor rewards to capital more than rewards to labor.

The differential profits which it is thought may be taxed, so to speak, for labor's benefit may be due to factors like a firm's lucky choice of an advantageous location or its chance possession of specialized equipment which has unexpectedly become valuable through a transfer of demand—factors unrelated to managerial efficiency. But to permit that part of a firm's earnings which is due to some special advantage, *including a windfall advantage*, to be seized by way of strike-threat pressures is still open to the same objections. The prospect of exploitation, even if these circumstances should arise, will discourage development.

Differential high profits are, moreover, in nearly all cases, an indication to managements that, if they do not attract additional resources (including usually additional labor) to supply additional output, *competitors* will do so. *The normal reaction to the growing profitableness of an undertaking is expansion*. And this reaction, which imposed costs can prevent or restrain, is always to the consumers' advantage, and always in the interests of the additional workers attracted to the undertaking, who will typically be provided with an opportunity of increasing their incomes.

The trouble is that if costs *are* imposed on an exceptionally prosperous undertaking *which had failed to predict the strike-threat demands* (or on an industry or area in which entrepreneurs had similarly predicted wrongly) on the grounds that it can "afford" the imposition, it is not an unreasonable use of

154

words to say that the additional costs have been "absorbed by profits;" for theoretically dividends can be reduced and wage receipts increased through the property transfer effected. But such phrases are disastrously misleading, partly because the enhanced wage receipts include elements of capital seized (see p. 136) and partly because the dynamics of the real world are ignored. The important consequence will, I repeat, be a reduction of the rate of increase in the contribution of the exploited undertaking (or the exploited industry or area) to the flow of income (and to wages as part of income), while some consumer detriment is *likely* to be immediate.

A wholly different argument about the possibility of efficiency being tapped via the strike threat concerns the raising of *the standard rate* throughout an industry by union pressures, i.e., *without* discrimination against firms, industries and areas which are exceptionally prosperous (or discrimination in favor of the less prosperous). It is suggested that exploitation in this form need cause no unemployment, nor bring any disadvantage to consumers, because the *concentration of output into the more efficient undertakings will be brought about*.[2] But such a process must still drive out competing enterprises which, in spite of some differential disadvantage (*which need not be inferior managerial efficiency*), can make their greatest contribution to aggregate income by relying upon the availability of labor which is cheap for them because their better-placed competitors are not offering to employ it. Undertakings in that position can at times survive in their present operations only because union-imposed or government-imposed obstructions are closing more profitable openings for the workers they employ. Hence *the firms to be penalized are those which are rescuing excluded workers from relative poverty*.[3] If this low-paid labor is *bid away* by the more efficient firms, that is a quite different matter.

Under truly competitive conditions, some firms appear at times to be paying higher wage rates than others. Then, presumably, they are doing so because it has been their policy to attract the more efficient labor. It does not necessarily mean that they are purchasing labor's output at a higher price than their competitors, or that they are more efficient. Firms which employ the less efficient workers may be using different methods for which different grades of skill are appropriate. Hence any extermination of the competition of undertakings which are organized for offering employment outlets to workers of below the average in productivity must have an inequalitarian effect. We shall discuss this issue again in Chapter 12, but it should be pointed out here that to force enterprises which offer employment to the less well-endowed workers to remunerate such workers as though they *were* highly endowed, is to impose higher labor costs upon those enterprises than upon their competitors. When the standard rate has the effect called "concentrating production in the more efficient plants," it must be reducing demand for labor in the relevant industry.

The relevant general principle is, I suggest, that there is never any justification for allowing those firms which find it, say, *just profitable* to replace their assets rather than disinvest them, to be driven into decline or out of operation

155

by *imposed* labor costs so that more advantageously situated firms can take over their contribution. "Inefficient" firms may be *legitimately* driven out only by the process of *bidding away* the resources they are using, including the labor (through the offer of better remuneration or prospects). Moreover, the suggestion that, because of the concentration of production in relatively efficient undertakings, *consumers* will not be harmed is unacceptable. For to the extent to which there is *really* an economy to be gained by such a concentration, it will be profitable for the entrepreneurs to act just as was suggested above and *attract*, through their wage offers, all the resources required to achieve the economies.

When it happens that the reduced outputs caused by coercively imposed labor costs do come to be concentrated in fewer undertakings, these undertakings may be in a position to cease recruiting workers who are not worth the additional costs, and even to displace some of their less gifted workers. They can then replace those laid off by workers of relatively high efficiency, possibly taken from the very undertakings which have been compelled to close or curtail operations. It is then possible that *the surviving undertakings* will not be disadvantaged from the standpoint of profits. That does not mean, however, that managements have been encouraged to be *more efficient* in achieving labor- or capital-economizing improvements in manufacturing or marketing.[4] There has simply been a rational adjustment to a changed situation which *mitigates* the detriment that the community is forced to accept. More than that cannot be claimed. And even so, the process must rob workers who are below the average in natural endowment or developed powers of *relatively* highly remunerated avenues of employment (possibly with training opportunities) for which they would otherwise have been regarded as competent. For instance, virtually no workers of the unskilled class are today employed in the United States steel and automobile industries, although large numbers of them were once so employed. The effects seem to have been strongly regressive.[5]

A quite different (although related) point is that there is likely to be greater anxiety among the retained workers to demonstrate their efficiency in these circumstances. When they perceive that there are excluded competitors who would jump at the opportunity of doing their job for less, they are likely to view the threat of displacement very seriously. For if they are laid off, they face a bigger prospective loss than confronts workers in a relatively competitive environment. The social discipline of the market is held off, but when it breaks through the dikes erected, it punishes with greater ferocity.[6] Fear of market punishments may, therefore, to some extent mitigate the situation, through greater efficiency on the part of the workers retained. But again, all that can be claimed is that labor costs have been pushed up to a lesser extent than they would have been in the absence of this reaction. The other implications are undisturbed.

It is sometimes said that, when "industry-wide" or "national" bargaining occurs, wage rates tend to be demanded which are calculated to keep undertakings of "average profitability" in operation, although the phrase more commonly used to describe the position of such an enterprise is "what the average firm *can afford.*" The suggestion can be regarded as a special case of the contention that enforcement of the rate for the job concentrates output among the relatively efficient producers. It clearly means that *some* undertakings which might well be in a position to continue to provide, say, their *current* outputs for an indefinite period, and at least maintain their real capital intact, will be pushed out of operation, or forced to contract. Hence the relevant principle which we must apply is that stated above. If the contribution to outputs by firms of below-average profitability is rendered unprofitable by duress-backed wage demands (as distinct from the case in which their workers are attracted away from them through the offer of higher wage rates by their competitors), it means that the strike threat has been used to destroy not only a source of demand for the labor employed by the ousted enterprise but, and more important, to destroy a contribution to the source of demands in general.

What I take to be a quite different claim is that the tolerance of strike-threat pressures causes "competition in wage rates to be replaced by competition in efficiency," or forces "employers" to "compete on a basis of efficiency instead by depressing the price of labor" (or some similar phrase). But what does this mean? The critical reader will notice that the words "compete" and "competition" are used in two opposite meanings in the sentences quoted. In the one case, actual competition is apparently implied while "monopsony" ("depressing the price of labor") is implied in the other. But *the seeking out of underutilized labor* (buying it in the cheapest market) does not conflict with any inducement to efficiency. Indeed, the discernment of such under-utilization elsewhere (the availability of cheap labor) is an important form of efficiency in itself.

In its least objectionable form (which has become known as the "jolt theory" or the "shock effect") the argument is that, through imposing burdens on business undertakings, the managers can be *jolted* or *shocked* into acting with more enterprise and imagination in their profit-seeking. Thus, Sumner Slichter claimed that "the strong pressure of unions for higher wages . . . has undoubtedly helped to raise the standards of living because this pressure has forced management to work harder to keep down labor cost and has thereby accelerated technical progress."[7] "Wage increases," write Reynolds and Taft (less dogmatically, "may force management to take remedial action"[8] and, as labor costs are raised, to reduce nonlabor costs. This sophism was expressed quite often by labor union apologists during the nineteenth century; it was ultimately given respectability by Walker, Marshall, and Pigou; and it has been repeated again and again during the present century.[9] Despite the intellectual caliber of the three famous economists just mentioned, I maintain that the argument is wholly indefensible. Pigou's treatment was rather subtle. He relied upon the "jolt theory" to explain how it was possible for labor to rectify a monopsonistic situation (in other words, one in which, in his terminology, labor was paid less than the value of its marginal net product).[10] But there is no clear reason why the ability to exploit labor

157

monopsonistically should be accompanied by some rectifiable *inefficiency*. Hence the notion is just as indefensible in this form as it is in its most usual form, that is, as an explanation of the ability of duress-imposed labor costs to create their own justification in the form of countervailing output increases. It is true, as we have seen, that *the forms* of technological progress and managerial ingenuity will be affected by the need to adjust when increased labor costs are imposed through the strike threat. For instance, there will be an enhanced incentive (which we have noticed) to displace labor by the substitution of machinery.[11] But it is just not true that prospects of adversity stimulate managerial and technological imagination, enterprise, and effort more than the prospects of prosperity. *If it were true, it would be wise for governments to impose burdens on any sector of the economy they wished to foster—taxing an industry to give it a jolt and thereby to cause it to flourish!*

In the case of a sole proprietor, a reduced demand for leisure might well result from a diminution of his income, however caused. A shopkeeper faced, say, with an increase in the minimum wage, may substitute his own labor for that of an employee. But that is hardly a case of increased efficiency and hardly to the advantage of the laid-off worker.

All market changes, *general* (growing or declining total profitability of a firm) or *particular* (growing or declining profitability of any set of activities in the firm), are a spur to managerial *action*. It is very doubtful whether any one type of change acts as a *special* spur to greater efficiency, acumen or effort. Most students of business administration would hold, I think, that the enthusiasms aroused under growing profits, and not the anxieties aroused under adversity, are *most likely* to stimulate imagination and the will to experiment. But the exercise of managerial ingenuity in the search for least-cost methods is continuous. When managers introduce labor-saving machinery, or product designs of a kind which require less labor, because profits have dwindled through strike-threat influences, their responses represent normal managerial reactions, not exceptional originality, efficiency or initiative. "Economic pressure" is the persistent call to action; and the reactions which the "jolt" theorists have been observing are simply the process of economizing innovation[12] as it has been *affected, not stimulated*, by imposed labor costs. In the absence of the strike threat, technological progress would admittedly have been *different in form*. And in Chapter 15 I shall give reasons for believing that it would have been incomparably more fruitful.

The most plausible argument for the "jolt" theory is found in the circumstances of regulated monopolies, or of unregulated monopolies wishing to avoid regulation, or of large, supposedly monopolistic corporations wishing to avoid antitrust proceedings against them. Mainly, I think, because of the pressure of politics on what, properly conceived, are quasi-judicial functions—namely, the regulation of natural monopoly charges and restraint of or dissolution of monopoly by way of antitrust—the payment of high dividends instead of the contrivance of scarcity has come to be the private sin which government agencies condemn. It seems that, for this reason, a tendency has developed for investors to acquiesce in managements making extravagant concessions to strike-threat pressures. Stockholders cannot be paid more, so why should not managements be liberal in wages and salaries? For the same reasons, managerial and executive compensation is likely to be generous when the yield to entrepreneurial wisdom or luck is high, especially in the form of large pensions, extravagant expense accounts and so forth. It will then be true, in a sense, that the prospect of imposed burdens has made wage-rate and salary increases acceptable. Moreover, in the conditions we are considering, as Alchian and Kessel have pointed out,[13] managers and executives are likely to gain in the form of nonpecuniary benefits: lavish offices, imposing buildings and factory gardens, sumptuous board rooms with paintings by famous artists, other amenities calculated to enhance prestige, long vacations, leave for "civic duties," large contributions to "charity," pretty secretaries, discrimination in hiring, buying from congenial salesmen and "conspicuous expenditure" generally. When these conditions exist, duress-imposed labor costs in the narrow sense are not only more likely to be conceded, but they are likely to be achieved for wages (in the narrow sense of remuneration for artisans and laborers) at the direct expense of the share of profits which would otherwise have gone in high salaries, liberal expense accounts, and the nonpecuniary amenities enjoyed by executives and managements referred to earlier. But what happens here is not an increase in efficiency which gives rise to a new source of income out of which labor can be paid more. It is (in the words of Alchian and Kessel) simply a revised "pattern of distribution of benefits." Hence the grounds for my rejection of the "jolt" theory of redistribution via the strike threat do not have to be qualified. All that happens is an arbitrary redistribution of income in favor of a particular lucky group of workers; and the redistribution is ultimately made possible by the use or threatened use of governmental power against those investors whose managers have been more successful than the average in satisfying (or exploiting) consumers. But the flow of resources into fields in which profitableness (as distinct from the proved contrivance of scarcity) is penalized must act precisely as tolerance of the strike threat does in diverting investment into relatively less productive and less wage-multiplying activities.

Lloyd Ulman says that the academic economists "rejected the notion that, by leaning on costs, unions could force even monopolistic employers to be more efficient" because "they assumed *a priori* that all businessmen maximize profits and therefore minimize costs in any event."[14] No such assumption is needed to show the weakness of the claim that imposed burdens act as a stimulus. What disinterested economists *have* shown is that all rational entrepreneurial action is loss-avoiding and profit-seeking through the continuous comparison of objective and prospective input values with prospective output values.[15] Entrepreneurs simply have *every incentive* to predict wisely. That is all that any economist, thinking rigorously, has ever assumed about the nature of business action under market discipline. Lloyd Ulman has destroyed a straw man.

Parallel to the view that burdening the investor by duress-imposed labor

159

costs forces managements to be more efficient is the view that paying workers more increases the workers' efficiency and therefore justifies the forcing up of costs. That theory appears to me to be equally unacceptable. If it were really true that the entrepreneur who paid more than the market wage rate would enjoy reduced labor costs, that would surely have been discovered by at least some entrepreneurs originally and thereby have forced competitors to follow suit.[16] Even slaveholders knew that it was to their benefit to maintain their human property in good condition for the type of work required from it; and for all beasts of burden there is a certain expenditure on food and shelter which maximizes their efficiency. But while incentive wage-payment systems may raise the workers' inputs and increase their remuneration, there are no grounds for believing that the simple payment of higher wage rates will act as an incentive for larger inputs.

It has been suggested that imposed labor costs can be "absorbed out of profits" because in practice managements do not really know the prices they can most profitably demand for output. It might well be, the implication is, that higher end-product prices *could* have been set for the investors' advantage, even in competitive markets. When costs are forced up, managements are surprised to discover that raising prices enables them to make up the enhanced wages bill. Such a notion is, I feel, an outcome of experience, not of pricing under conditions of competition, but under inflation.

It is true, however, that there will often be a range of possible product prices which can be asked without demand for the output being felt likely to fall away *immediately*, or *entirely*, or *disastrously*. But the interpretative discretion so created does not alter the fact that there can be only one product price for management to fix which will ultimately *turn out to be* to the investors' maximum advantage. As we have seen (pp. 128-129), *it is expected that judgment about what this price is* (and the appropriate inputs for that price) *will change over any "budgetary" period*, as buying and selling markets are observed; and adjustments from time to time in prices and inputs, in the light of the observations, will tend to reduce but not eliminate the inevitable risks. Hence while "entrepreneurs' discretion in pricing" remains, that word "discretion" simply covers all the imponderables which have to be taken into account. The truth remains that, when costs rise, it will not be profitable to retain, replace or add to the resources used in any type of production to the former extent.

The special arguments noticed in this chapter disclose, then, no reasons for modifying the thesis developed in Chapter 10, namely, that labor costs imposed by duress are not an effective device for exploiting investors. The loaded costs cannot be said to be absorbable out of profits except in the sense that entrepreneurs who fail to forecast exploitation may be its victims.

Moreover, the argument of this and the previous chapter is relevant to the belief that strike-threat pressures can at least insure a prompt or just sharing with the workers of the results of increased productivity. Such a belief is wholly wrong. Every increase in aggregate income (that is, every growth in productivity generally) tends, through market reactions, to raise all real in-

160

comes subject to recontract in roughly the same proportion, just as inflation tends to raise all money incomes subject to recontract in roughly the same proportion. But this occurs, not because capital- or labor-economizing developments in any firm or in any industry justify or bring about increased real yields to labor and capital respectively *in that firm or industry*, but because the benefits are reaped in noncompeting activities.

Labor-economizing developments in any activity tend to raise the wages flow in all *other* operations. Moreover, to the extent to which improvements in productive methods in one sphere are offset entirely or partially by imposed labor costs, the tendency for the wages flow as a whole to rise is slowed or stopped, not accelerated. Contemporary policy in this respect is self-defeating. When it is said that rising productivity can validate real wage-rate increases, and that labor costs may be legitimately imposed by force when productivity is judged to be rising, it is important to insist that this is true only when, in every case, the increases are such as the free market itself is tending to enforce. Moreover, while market forces raise real wage rates as a whole as productivity in general rises, this does *not* mean that increased productivity in any industry or firm necessarily justifies higher wage rates *in that industry or firm*. As I have explained, it tends to bring about (and hence may be said to "justify") increased remuneration for labor and for other factors *in noncompeting activities*.

NOTES

[1] It is "obviously impossible" in this case. But although less self-evident, *all* action which discourages the supply or raises the costs of providing the tools which multiply the yield to human effort is to the *absolute* disadvantage of labor in general (see pp. 146-147, 222-224).

[2] In this paragraph, I ignore the possibility of the "more efficient" firms taking over the more efficient workers and dismissing the less efficient. *This* possibility is discussed on p. 156.

[3] As will be explained in a different context, a policy of sterilizing land which, although productive, is of low productivity (e.g., having a rent of less than so much per acre), is exactly similar to a policy which forbids or otherwise prevents the employment of labor for any purpose when its marginal productivity is low (see pp. 172-173).

[4] The general argument that labor costs enhanced by the strike-threat *stimulate* greater efficiency is about to be examined.

[5] My conclusion expressed in this paragraph is identical to that reached by Henry Simons in 1944 (*Economic Policy for a Free Society,* [Chicago: University of Chicago Press, 1948], pp. 139-40), although mainly reached from consideration of events since that time.

[6] Competition is like gravity. If you don't resist it, you cannot fall and hurt yourselves.

[7] Quoted by J. T. Dunlop, *Theory of Wage Determination* (London: Macmillan, Ltd., 1957), p. 13.

[8] L. G. Reynolds and C. H. Taft, "The Evolution of Wage Structure," E. Wight Bakke, Clark Kerr, and Charles W. Anrod, *Unions, Management and the Public*, 3rd ed. (New York: Harcourt, Brace and World, 1967), p. 597.

[9] One interesting variant of the notion—equally fallacious—is that managements become more efficient *in depression* because they have "received a nasty jolt." Roy F. Harrod, *The Trade Cycle* (London: Oxford University Press, 1936),

[10] Pigou, *Economies of Welfare*, 3rd Edition (New York: Macmillan Company, 1929), p. 592.

[11] It must be remembered that such a substitution may be expected to accompany *an independent* displacement of labor due to a prior cause—the general rise in costs to which the labor-economizing machinery or managerial arrangements may be a *subsequent* response.

[12] I use the word "innovation" here, although at times economizing techniques and machinery substituted are already recognized and well known. It had previously not been profitable to utilize them.

[13] Alchian and Kessel, *Aspects of Labor Economics* (N.B.E.R., 1960), pp. 161 *et seq.*

[14] Lloyd Ulman, "Introduction: The Problems in Historic Context," Lloyd Ulman, ed., *Challenges to Collective Bargaining*, The American Assembly (Englewood Cliffs, N. J.: Prentice-Hall, Spectrum Books, 1967), p. 2.

[15] In popular language, this means that entrepreneurs "seek profits." It does *not* mean that they do in fact maximize profits! Their forecasts of yields to different "input-mixes," although usually shrewd extrapolations, are fallible; and while their forecasts are in process of continuous modification—as achievements are compared with expectations (for example, through budgetary controls), budgeted sales and outputs are normally far from being realized *in detail*.

[16] This argument does not hold under the assumption of monopsony of course. But see Chapter 8.

12
The Standard Rate

My purpose in this chapter is to show that the enforcement of "the standard rate," also called "the rate for the job" or often, misleadingly, "equal pay for equal work," operates as a powerful factor not only in reducing the flow of wages and income, but in creating or perpetuating inequality of opportunity, and hence avoidable inequalities of income. Yet insistence on the standard rate (more and more on a nationwide scale of recent years[1]) has come to be the cornerstone of strike-threat policy.[2] It is the principle on which resort to legal enactment in the labor market has relied. It is represented—sometimes sincerely—as a means of entrenchment of equality of treatment for all persons. It has a powerful psychological attractiveness. Through the slogan of "equal pay for equal work," it can be presented as a precept of transparent fairness. It appears superficially as a straightforward way of insuring protection against caprice or favoritism in remuneration.

Now it is true that equal remuneration for work inputs of equal content in respect of quantity and quality is, with one practically *unimportant* exception (mentioned below), the consequence of freedom in the labor market. *But the imposition by legal enactment or private duress of what is intended to be equal pay for equal work operates as an extraordinarily effective method of shutting off access to the bargaining table for the least privileged or least well-endowed members of the community.* Whether intentionally or unintentionally, *the uniformity imposed constitutes the most formidable device ever invented for enforcing discrimination against what H. Demsetz calls* (in a courageously rigorous analysis of some of the issues[3]) *(a) "nonpreferred" groups, and (b) "relatively unproductive" groups.* It is, I shall argue, far more powerful than *obvious* forms of exclusiveness, or entrenched privilege, or *overt* discrimination against "nonpreferred" groups.

To explain this contention, it is essential to stress at the outset that by "the standard rate" I do not have in mind *all* forms of wage-rate standardization.

For instance, we have seen that, when monopsonistic power exists, managements can maximize the residual yield by remunerating each worker in relation to the value of his alternatives (see p. 100). Now although such discrimination is not necessarily *exploitation* (see p. 114, note 4), and may in some circumstances be to the advantage of the particular workers discriminated against, one may have every sympathy with the desire to prevent discrimination of this type. Uniformity of remuneration *in respect of inputs of equal quantity and quality* seems on the face of it to be so unquestionably *just*, that some readers may well feel that discussion of the topic is superfluous. That it is a desirable *outcome* is indeed hardly a matter of controversy; but any attempted imposition of such uniformity is another matter. *Our attachment to the notion of the inherent justice of nondiscrimination of this type seems to have its origin in our familiarity with free market influences in the determination of wage rates, which tend always to bring about the equality envisaged!* And our intuitions derived from perception of the nondiscrimination enforced under competitive conditions lead us, on the whole, to sound ethical judgments. Nevertheless, we must try to avoid a simplicist trap.

To get to the root of the matter we have to begin by recognizing that there is a certain arbitrariness about the price or wage-rate uniformity which is enforced by the social pressures found in competitive markets. An awareness of this arbitrariness prompted Mrs. Joan Robinson, in 1935, to argue against the *laissez-faire* system precisely on the grounds that it tends to make the discrimination we are considering impossible.[4] I attempted at the time to answer Mrs. Robinson's criticisms and to defend the responsible planning and coordination of the economic system under *laissez faire*. But I could not question at all her demonstration of a possible inherent arbitrariness in competitively determined price uniformity. I expressed the problem as follows:

> Because discrimination is prevented where there is free exchange, and because it happens to maximise a monopolist's return, does not prove that it is opposed to consumers' advantage. On the contrary, it may be beneficial. The uniformity which is the product of the purchaser's right to resell may, on occasions, conceal some important elements of arbitrariness. This is possible because successive increments of a particular kind of commodity may be regarded as having a different "urgency" to a particular buyer—as occupying a different place on his scale of preferences; and as between different buyers, we may regard the increments that are purchased at a uniform price at any moment as being wanted with different degrees of urgency—as occupying different *relative* positions on the individuals' scales of preference. Now it has been suggested that the ideal production and exchange system, if planned by a divine hand—by one completely conscious of every individual's scales of preference (that is, of his aspirations and strivings, and his powers and resources), would lead to a set of prices for each commodity which in certain circumstances also varied for each individual. In so far as this could be so, it follows that a social loss might be incurred as a result of the uniformity imposed by competitive conditions. A set of prices other than the uniform prices enforced by the

consumers' right to re-sell *could* serve their "real desires" more effectively.[5]

But having explained why discrimination may, under theoretically conceivable circumstances, be socially beneficial (that is, tending to bring about the optimal use of human powers and resources), I went on to explain why, in practice, accepting the ideals of a democratic consumers' sovereignty, there is a case for a rule which, under nearly all circumstances, forbids discrimination. In my plea for this general nondiscrimination rule I had to insist, however, upon a *theoretically* important exception, namely, when the discrimination is "the fulfillment of an expected condition essential for the specific investment to take place."[6] The required condition for tolerable discrimination is that *the parties discriminated against benefit thereby*. In the case of a commodity or service, the parties who are forced to pay more than the others may nevertheless get it cheaper in consequence; or they may benefit because they can afford to buy some of it whereas otherwise they could afford to buy none of it. And in the case of a worker selling his services, the condition is that through accepting lower wage rates than others, he is a beneficiary, that is, he can find better-paid employment than he could if entrepreneurs were forced to pay all workers equally for identical contributions to the value of the product (at identical employment costs).

However improbable, such a possibility *could* arise where there are economies of scale (in production and marketing) of such a magnitude that the condition known as "natural monopoly" and "natural monopsony" are present in any degree. It *may* then be to the advantage of those workers employed by the "natural monopsonist" who have the poorest alternatives, that they accept long-term contracts under which they are remunerated according to their "opportunity values," that is, according to the value of their services in the occupations from which it is necessary to attract or (on the contract's expiration) to retain them. I explained above how (in abstractly conceivable circumstances) workers with lowly-valued alternatives could gain by entrepreneurial action which, although discriminating against them, (a) removed no existing employments and (b) improved their earning power, because the economies (low costs) so secured made the venture that employed them worth risking. (See pp. 105-106.)

I am not, it should be noticed, pleading here for a general tolerance of discrimination. On the contrary, I am adhering to my argument put forward in 1936 and advocating legally enforced nondiscrimination *when this objective can be proved to be unachievable sufficiently successfully through the safeguarding of the competitive process*. The aim of direct legal enforcement of nondiscrimination is to insure that every worker shall be remunerated *as though* he were selling his contribution to output in a competitive market. Thus, the required rule could provide that, if he is paid by the piece, he shall receive the same wage payment as another worker (with better alternatives) whose contribution to output is identical. But to be able to advocate such a rule, without misunderstanding, I am obliged to make it clear beyond any possible doubt that, unless any discrimination is due to what I have termed "exploitation" (the deliberate withholding of alternatives from the lower-paid groups), there is nothing *unjust* about it. Moreover, the application of any defensible nondiscrimination rule ought to be (a) contingent upon positive proof of *"natural* monopsony"[7] and (b) subject to the exception that no worker (or group of workers) exists who believes he can raise the value of his contribution to the common pool of output by accepting less than would be needed to retain or attract the services of others doing the same kind of work. *The nondiscrimination rule should be inapplicable when it stands in the way of the economic advancement of any person or group with poorer alternatives.* Equity in such circumstances requires that a worker whom it is just profitable to employ at, say $500, and who can improve his earnings and prospects if his offer to work at that figure is accepted, shall not be turned away because *the market* requires that other profitably employable workers have to be paid $600. In other words, no potential employee in any occupation who thinks he will benefit by undercutting, whether or not because he happens to have had less valuable alternatives than the average worker (although this *might* be his position), shall be denied this elemental human right. If the employment he wishes to get (at the wage rate he is prepared to accept) represents the best employment outlet available to him, the refusal of permission for him to accept that alternative is essentially exploitative.

We must remember that the kind of discrimination we are discussing is possible only in the presence of monopsony. In a free competitive labor market it could not occur. Should it be due to *collusive* monopsony, then *antidiscrimination policy should aim rather at eliminating the collusion than at the pricing consequences of the collusion.* Hence, if true discrimination in remuneration[8] does seem to be found in an *apparently* free market, the likely explanation is that it is a consequence of that very small degree of short-term natural monopoly and monopsony which, we know, inevitably characterizes almost every firm in practice.[9] Any such discrimination will be short-lived if antitrust is performing its function. But what can possibly be very important is that, in the meantime, it may be assisting a relatively poor worker to overcome the costs of getting a permanent entry into better and more productive employment outlets. The importance of the exception (which could be phrased so as not to constitute a loophole) is that it can insure that no avenue toward material advancement on the part of the poorer workers shall be closed.

The obvious danger in permitting any exception to the rule of nondiscrimination in remuneration is that it *might* become a loophole. But there is a very much greater danger that attempts of lowly-paid workers to break into well-paid but entrenched employment preserves for which they are competent or for which they can be trained will be prevented by any unqualified nondiscrimination rule. Hence conditions necessary for the imposition of the rule (as distinct from the achievement of nondiscrimination via the market) must be, as I have already shown: (1) proven *natural* monopsony; (2) the effective right of persons whose alternative opportunities are of low value[10] to dis-

166

count this disadvantage; and (3) unrestrained managerial power to employ any workers willing to undercut at a discriminatory rate even if (a) existing wage contracts, or (b) other forms of union resistance, or (c) present market alternatives for existing and essential employees, prevent a reduction in the standard rate sufficient to permit the profitable employment at that rate of the would-be newcomers.

We turn now to quite different reasons why a degree of standardization in wage rates, *in a quite independent sense*, is at times acceptable and, indeed, unavoidable. In some circumstances the value of individual outputs cannot be measured or estimated with adequate accuracy. In this case the standardization involves equality of remuneration for workers the value of whose contributions to output differs within a moderately narrow range. When payment by the piece is out of the question owing to the difficulty of defining the unit of work done, there is often a situation in which, while the really unsatisfactory worker is discernible, it is impossible to recognize *measurable* differences of efficiency over the narrow range mentioned. By "efficiency" here is meant the value of an individual worker's output in relation to its cost. Sometimes managements do not know with any certainty how the one individual's contribution to the undertaking (in the group accepted as "satisfactory") differs from that of another. When this is the position, a common time rate *for the grade in question* is the only answer. A standard rate for these reasons is equitable and nonrestrictive, but it implies that managements may establish many grades when that happens to be practicable.

In other cases, however, although actual *measurement* of efficiency is more or less ruled out, managements can rely upon less simply described evidences of the value of individual labor inputs, and differentiate accordingly. To avoid or minimize suspicion of arbitrariness, caprice or discrimination in such valuations, resort has been had to various forms of "job evaluation" or "merit rating" (see p. 197). In the ideal, however, managements ought to have untrammeled discretion in offering specially high wages to those whose services they particularly wish to retain or attract. The question of "quality" as a determinant of worth to the undertaking is influenced by such things as the worker's versatility, his trainability, his cooperativeness, his reliability, his integrity, his experience, and other definable, clearly recognizable, but often unmeasurable attributes. When estimates of the usefulness of combinations of such qualities are possible and relevant, managers can act at least as rationally (which does not mean infallibly) as the selectors of, say, a professional football or baseball team when they offer different terms to different players, or the director of a ballet when he offers different terms to different ballerinas. There are always imponderables, but the differentiations are normally profitable and accepted as just.

Let us now turn to the case in which differences in individual worth are observable and *measurable*. When this is the position, payment by the piece may be possible; for there can then be an objective measure of the number of units of output contributed by each worker. Moreover, where it is possible to define adequately a general "work unit," a common measure of the contribution of workers in quite different kinds of work may be available. And allowances for measurable differences in quality of work can be made where tests are practicable and spoilage is definable. One of the chief advantages of payment by the piece (apart from the incentive created by the almost self-evident justice of the principle) is that, even when there is a *standard piece rate* imposed by union duress, greater numbers of the less efficient workers can be profitably employed than is possible with *standard time rates*. This is still more the situation when a general formula is possible by means of which allowance can be made for the economizing of time by the faster workers—that is for those who use the plant *more intensively*. Under such a formula, that is, when for this last reason the slower worker has the right to be paid less per unit of output than the faster workers, *there will be no discrimination against him as there necessarily must be under rigid standard piece rates*.

It should be noticed that, even when a piece rate system permits the slower worker to escape injustice because the rates are arrived at by a formula which amounts to a lower rate per piece (in order to compensate for his less intensive use of the plant), the rate fixed may still be exploitative. That is, a high standard piece rate may yet be creating a privilege. The privilege in this case will be shared by a group which includes *some* of the slower workers. The underprivileged then consist of all who could improve their earnings if the standard piece rate did not exclude them from the protected employment field. Thus a standard piece rate adjusted for the slower worker *can* still operate as a subtle exclusive device. Like the standard rate in other forms, it can suppress free bargaining—deny the initially less valuable workers the right of access to employment outlets.

The forcing of a standard rate by strike-threat duress or legal enactment on any group of workers merely imposes a minimum. It does not *normally* prevent differentiation in the form of higher wage rates offered to exceptionally valuable individuals. The effect is (a) to displace or exclude[11] the least valuable workers (the least well-qualified or those whose employment involves the highest special costs) *and* (b) to reduce the earnings or prospects of those workers who were earning more than the standard rate before it was imposed (because enhanced costs reduce the profitableness of the productive activity as a whole).[12]

Through reactions under (b) a certain leveling tendency is exerted within the protected occupation. This does not mean that an egalitarian pressure is thereby applied on the distribution of the community's aggregate wages flow.[13] When all workers are brought into the reckoning, including those displaced into lower-paid employments (possibly into temporary unemployment), or forced to remain in lower-paid employments, the effect is to cause the distribution of the national income to be less equal as well as less equitable. In this connection, we should notice that the imposition of a higher standard wage rate, or the raising of a minimum wage rate, can have the effect of slowing down the *subsequent* rate of progress in earning power which

168

an existing employee or a recruit (supposedly benefiting from the increase) would otherwise have enjoyed following the acquisition of experience over the next few years. For *ceteris paribus* duress-imposed costs reduce an undertaking's demand for the services of *all* labor and not merely for the services of grades subject to the minimum;[14] and because a firm's competitors will presumably find the profitability of purchasing labor adversely affected more or less in the same proportion, the wage rates needed to retain or attract experienced employees will be lower than they would have been had the minimum not been imposed or raised. Such a reaction may therefore *partially* offset the effect on labor costs of the imposed or raised minimum.

Again, when the condition I have called "joint monopoly" (see pp. 72-73, 128) is present, it sometimes creates a monopsonistic power which managements can use to ease the aggregate burden. They can on occasion practice discrimination against the more efficient, causing the latter to be paid (in the extreme case) the same wage rate as the average or the substandard worker who retains employment.[15] The enforcement of time rates where piece rates are practicable is one stratagem for discrimination against the better workers. If the employees of above-average efficiency have highly specialized skills which they acquired not expecting discrimination against them (in standard rate form, or otherwise) they will be exploitable (in this case jointly by the workers of average or substandard efficiency and by managements on behalf of investors). And in the case in which the exceptionally efficient can be shut in they will be exploitable even if their skills are versatile.

It is, however, the use of a supposed nondiscrimination principle to effect discrimination that I wish now to stress. Demsetz has put the gist of the problem so clearly that I cannot do better at this stage than to quote briefly from his contribution. He is dealing mainly not with "the standard rate" enforced through the strike threat, but with wage-rate uniformity imposed under legal enactment. But the implications are the same whenever nonmarket values are imposed, regardless of whether they are enforced by governmental power, the strike threat or the boycott.

"Minimum wage law," says Demsetz, "concentrates the criterion for employability on the personal characteristics of workers, a criterion under which the nonpreferred will suffer."[16] "Wage uniformity at levels above the minimum. . . . works to the disadvantage of even the very productive nonpreferred workers."[17] "The nonpreferred either will not be hired or they will be hired in lesser jobs in which they are more productive than their preferred counterparts."[18] Nonpreferred persons are prohibited "from compensating discriminating employers by offering wealth compensation"[19] although "an employer who does not discriminate according to personal characteristics will, *ceteris paribus*, be the most profitable competitor in the market place."[20]

The "equal pay principle," continues Demsetz, is equally "disadvantageous to those workers who are relatively unproductive,"[21] and in practice, because there is "a strong positive correlation between persons discriminated against for reasons of personal characteristics and persons who are relatively unproductive,'' the adverse effect on the ''nonpreferred'' of enforced wage-rate uniformity is doubled.

Many ''nonpreferred'' or ''relatively unproductive'' persons are in practice to be found distributed irrespective of race or sex groupings. Nevertheless, in the western world the injustices of the standard rate system can be observed to fall most heavily on those who make up *two great unprotesting groups, namely, nonwhites and women*; and I shall be dealing mainly with the consequences upon these two categories. I say ''unprotesting'' because although nonwhites, for instance, certainly protest about many real or imaginary grievances, the extraordinary thing about the injustices suffered by the ''nonpreferred'' is the almost universal innocent acquiescence by their ''leaders'' in the causes of the injustices.

Gary Becker, an eminent economic theorist, seems to me correctly to describe what the *disinterested parties* who approve of minimum wage legislation believe the aims to be. For them, the purpose of the ''equal pay for equal work'' principle is ''to prevent various minorities, especially working women, from receiving lower wages than other apparently equally productive workers, that is, the aim is to reduce discrimination against them.'' But the actual lobbyists and politicians responsible have recognized quite cynically, I believe, that, as Becker puts it:

> The direct effect is quite different, for by preventing disadvantaged groups from offsetting the prejudice against them, the legislation tends to increase rather than decrease the observable discrimination. Legislation is not the only source of a direct restriction on the incomes of minorities. . . . The important point is that, whatever the *intent* of the legislation, unions, or other institutions, the *effect* may well be to increase the observable discrimination. . . .''[22]

The effect of the standard rate principle, he says, is ''directly [to] reduce the cost of discrimination and encourage discrimination.'' Controls ''placed on the money incomes that can be received by discriminators . . . reduce the cost of discrimination . . . and thus encourage discrimination.''[23]

The *device of the standard rate must be recognized as the most damnably successful means of unjust discrimination that has ever been invented*, largely because it almost universally commands the support of its victims—the more unfortunate members of any group against which the discrimination is exerted. In the United States, for instance, the provisions of the Fair Labor Standards Act of 1938, which declared it illegal in production for interstate trade to discriminate in the terms on which workers are hired (on the basis of color, race, etc.), have acted as viciously effective measures of discrimination—measures through which the more fortunate areas or races have had their privileges very powerfully protected.

There are various *more obvious* forms of economic injustice which survive or are imposed through law, custom, personal prejudice and collusive action against "nonpreferred" groups. But these, including such blatant exclusions as are effected *through explicit color bars* and the like, are of *relatively* little importance anywhere. Enactments like the South African "job reservations" may be said to proclaim *the spirit* of color exclusiveness; but even in South Africa, protections in that honest form are minor obstacles to racial equality of opportunity when compared with "the rate for the job" (enforced in that country by the unions and by the Industrial Conciliation and Wage acts).

As we have seen, equal remuneration for work of equal value would always be the *consequence* of any truly free market process. Entrepreneurial incentives to seek out and offer better-paid opportunities to any presently underpaid labor would bring about equality of opportunity and a distribution of earning opportunities in accordance with the distribution of developed and valuable abilities. When we buy a commodity, we do not ask, "What was the color, race, ancestry, social class, religion, language or sex of the person who made it?" We ask, "Is it good value for money?" *The free market is color-blind.*[24] It is tending constantly to bring about "equal pay for equal work" in the special sense that I have explained. If the market fails to achieve this result, and "natural monopsony" is not the explanation, successful resistance to the operation of the market and not its own inherent tendencies will be to blame. It will not then be a *free* market. (See p. 100.)

Noneconomists are often nonplussed by this argument. They have no answer; yet its implications are irreconcilable with their firm convictions. They feel almost instinctively that there is something basically misleading about it. They often ask this sort of question, "Why do you object to the imposition of the standard rate, as a condition always to be observed on an otherwise free market, when you claim that the free market itself always tends to achieve something resembling this condition?" The question is genuine and pertinent.

What the unions *call* "equal pay for equal work" is usually not that at all. What they are really insisting upon is equal pay for persons whose contributions to the productive process differ in value. That is why, as I have explained, the standard rate locks out from the bargaining process those workers whose labor is worth less than the rate fixed. The people so excluded are *kept in lower-paid kinds of work* because they are denied any opportunity of discounting their initial or innate inferiority, or discounting *any extra cost of employing them* due, perhaps, to threatened unrest among existing staff for reasons of caste or race or sex prejudice, etc. (see below, pp. 182-183).

To illustrate how *legally imposed* standard rates (a special case) not only *maintain* less qualified and nonpreferred classes in lower-paid occupations, but sometimes *force them into* such occupations or into unemployment, we can consider evidence presented by Yale Brozen. Discussing the position which existed immediately subsequently to 1949, when private household work was a principal occupation *not covered* under the Fair Labor Standards Act, Brozen showed that "in each instance in which the minimum rate rose, the number of persons employed as household workers rose," although "there was also a rise in the percentage of household workers unemployed in each instance."[25]

The standard rate, which may be enforced in the form of a uniform rate for each occupation or for each defined grade within an occupation, resembles a law which forbids the working of any land to produce a certain crop of which the rent is, say, less than $100 per acre. And a statutory minimum wage rate applying to *all* occupations is similar to a law which prohibits the use of land for any purpose whatsoever unless the rent is at least, say, $25 per acre.[26] But why should the less productive land be forced to be treated as though it were completely barren? And why should those persons who are below a certain efficiency (present or permanent) be forced to forego the full remuneration of such efficiency as they do possess? Why should a person who, let us assume, could maximize his income by working in an occupation in which he can produce only four-fifths of the average output per worker, be refused the right to accept four-fifths of the time rate which his faster competitors can command?

Ought we not to encourage the less well-endowed (the relatively inefficient or substandard workers) to seek that independence which is conferred by the right to contribute the maximum to the common pool of output? It is irrelevant to this right whether a worker's inferiority is due to an illness, an accident, war service, an innate inability to acquire valuable skills, the lack of exceptional muscular power or some fault of character. And ought we not to recognize also the rights of the "nonpreferred" classes, whose presence arouses the resentment of "preferred" workers at having to work side by side with them?

If we are to do so, we must rid ourselves of any illusion about the consequences and, in the majority of cases, the purpose of "the rate for the job." *Most often its whole claimed object, although obscured by tendentious terminology, is to insulate the high grade and more fortunate workers from the competition of the low grade, "nonpreferred" and generally less fortunate workers. It does so by forbidding the latter the right to compete by pricing themselves into the most remunerative employment outlets available to them.* I shall have to reiterate this truth in several contexts.

I am pleading here, among other things, firstly, for the rights of the low-grade worker who has to be classified as such by reason of his inborn qualities, even in the occupation in which his productivity is highest; and secondly, for the rights of the worker who must be classified as low-grade solely by reason of lack of opportunity. The incentive to invest in human capital through "on the job training" can often be destroyed if persons who are in a position to benefit from the training cannot be employed *at what they are initially worth*, while the value of their efforts is being built up. In many undertakings it requires a good deal of time to habituate a recruit, including an adult recruit, for the task he is to perform. And it may take even more time to inculcate in him the skills which are essential.[27] During an inevitable tran-

172

sitional or adjustment period, "the rate for the job" can close the door to the most hopeful prospects available to many.

Moreover, as Henry Simons pointed out, "The old-established firms have skimmed off the cream of the labor supply and have trained their workers to a substantial superiority over the inexperienced. If potential competitors must pay the same wages as old firms, the established enterprises will be immune to new competition, just as high grade workers are immune to the competition of poorer grades."[28]

In the case of a statutory minimum, as under the U. S. Fair Labor Standards Act, it is juveniles who appear to be immediately and particularly harmed. Statistics presented and explained by Yale Brozen show that the trend in the proportion of teen-age unemployment to general unemployment has risen continuously since 1938, in spite of a growing proportion of juveniles being held off the labor market by prolonged compulsory schooling. Since 1964, teen-age unemployment has remained continuously nearly 3-1/2 times as high as general unemployment. And with juveniles belonging to a "nonpreferred group," the detriment is multiplied. Thus, the proportion of nonwhite teen-age unemployment to white teen-age unemployment increased from the ratio 1.3 in 1949 to 2.3 in 1968.[29] Why did this burden thus fall so heavily and unjustly on nonwhite juveniles? Again to quote Brozen, "without a minimum wage floor, the nonwhite teen-ager could offset this disadvantage by working for less than the white teen-ager."[30] The statutory minimum had shut the door.

All juveniles have been adversely affected, then, by the minimum wage laws, while *Negro and other "nonpreferred" juveniles have been harmed differentially*. Now as I have already insisted, a minority of workers in *all* protected wage groups (including both white and nonwhite juveniles) may well have benefited in the short run. But money wage rates of low-paid workers generally had risen (following 1938) with a trend of about 4 percent per annum, so that (in Brozen's words) the increase "would have come anyway, in most cases, within two to five years."[31] Brozen concludes:

> If all that happened as a result of the minimum wage statute was a change in the timing of wage-rate increases, there could be little to concern us. However, in the interval between the time that the minimum wage is raised and the time that productivity and inflation catch up with the increase, thousands of people are jobless, many businesses fail which are never revived, people are forced to migrate who would prefer not to, cities find their slums deteriorating and becoming over-populated, teen-agers are barred from obtaining the opportunity to learn skills which would make them more productive, and permanent harm is done to their attitudes and their ambitions. This is a very large price to pay for impatience.[32]

If the *aim* of policy had been not to fix wage rates below which no employment could be legally offered or given, but *to raise the free market value of the poorest races or classes toward or above a stipulated target* the objective could have been wisely sought via the removal of discernible barriers to equality of opportunity. But of these barriers, wage-rate minima appear to be the most effective and harmful.

The oppressive incidence of nonmarket wage rates upon the poorest classes can be discerned to be even more serious than Brozen's grave conclusions suggest when the *private* imposition of standard rates (via strike-threat duress) is taken into the reckoning.

Not only can the standard wage rate, whether the result of legal enactment or the strike threat, have the effect of forcing down the earnings and prospects (possibly affecting adversely thereby the health, efficiency and ambitions) of the least well-endowed or least well-trained, it can harm the workers of *whole districts* which are less "developed" than others. And in a country as large as the United States, the injustices so wrought are greater than they are in smaller countries. It would be very difficult for the British unions to persuade French, Belgian, or Italian workers to price their labor so as to protect workers in British industries; but it has not been difficult for unions of workers in established industries in the northern areas of the United States to achieve a similar result within their own country. Bolstered by the Fair Labor Standards enactments, labor unions' pressures have effectively retarded the relatively young industries in the South.

What would be the attitude of the Latin American countries if the United States, lobbied by the AFL-CIO, tried to get the International Labor Organization to sponsor an international convention enacting minimum wage rates to insure that the outputs of those areas could not compete with American products in the world? But the wage-rate standardizations the unions have imposed (directly and through political pressures for the minimum wage) have, within national areas, blocked the path toward the maximization of earnings through the most productive geographical deployment of the labor force and, in particular, workers whose labor happens to be relatively plentiful and naturally cheap in certain districts have been denied the right to price their efforts in their own interests.[33]

The unions' demands are almost invariably for a standard *money* wage rate; and in practice this means insistence on *a higher real wage rate for areas of relatively plentiful labor*; for such areas have virtually always relatively low living costs. But it is obviously to the advantage of workers *as a whole* in areas of plentiful labor supply that their real wage rates shall at least not be higher than those in areas in which labor is scarce. Hence the standard real wage rate is doubly harmful. Refusal to allow for geographical differences in determining the wage rates imposed (on industries which serve interstate markets) can be, indeed, a most effective means of holding back the competition of any initially cheap labor district. Its effectiveness depends upon its power to prevent or slow down the development of the people of a region without arousing their opposition. The unions are very seldom willing, in industry-wide bargaining, to agree to allowances for area differences in living costs. Occasional reluctant exceptions seem to occur only where the secession of locals would otherwise be threatened, or in areas where the standard national money rate would clearly cause too many unpopular lay-offs. Similarly, legally enacted minimum wage rates seldom allow for area differences in the real value of the money unit. The reader should keep this important point in mind as the subsequent argument is developed. When I expose the deleterious consequences of standard *real wage rates*, the fact that standard *money rates* are normally imposed means that the social detriment is aggravated.

Even so, a minimum wage-rate adjusted for local living costs which in, say, New York State, merely condemned a relatively small proportion of the less well-qualified to low, but not disastrously low incomes, could cause dire distress in Mississippi, Louisiana, Georgia, or Tennessee, by reason of the numbers affected.[34]

Let us return to the supposed "unfairness" of the poorer workers toward the better paid, and consider the case of the lowest-paid American industrial workers. After World War II, unskilled labor costs (in real terms) *for industrial workers of comparable efficiency* in the least affluent areas of the United States seem to have been materially higher than those in any other part of the world apart from the *developed* areas of Canada. In the light of what criterion, then, could labor costs in the South, as they then were, be held to have been unfairly low *in relation to competitors abroad*? Practically all foreign unskilled labor would have had to be regarded as even more unfairly cheap in the light of American unskilled labor earnings. Had all costs been equalized over all geographical areas by an "international fair standards convention" (possibly covering "fair profits" also), all interarea trade would have been brought to an end! To what absurdities, then, does *this* notion of "fairness" in competition lead? (See pp. 180-181.)

In the United States the mitigation of poverty in the South has long required the attraction of wage-multiplying assets to that area. The attractive force needed has been there all the time—a huge mass of labor in the southern regions, priced below its potential earning power. Because the specialized assets and cooperant skills needed for modern industry were initially scarce, unskilled labor was relatively cheap. Hence new corporations could, in the absence of "fair labor standards" restraint, have invested the capital needed and raised earning power in the low-wage districts. They could have offered new employment outlets without closing any other such outlets except through the bidding away of labor by higher wage offers. Moreover, they would have found it profitable to invest in the training of the initially low-paid southern workers for better remunerated, semiskilled or skilled operations, although at the outset, many of the trainees would have been worth relatively little.[35] But through the "fair labor standards" policy, the profitableness of business investment to prepare the South for skilled industrial employments was materially weakened,[36] and the entry of low-productivity farm labor (often easily replaceable by mechanization when labor cost rises) into much better-paid and more productive work (which would have been available in industry at market-determined labor cost) was slowed down.[37]

It seems that if the relative incomes of unskilled and semiskilled southern workers are to be more rapidly (if gradually) raised, the South must continue for some time to be a capital-importing region; and because the savings of the South are as yet inadequate to finance the provision of a growing stock of industrial assets, the interest element in yields to investments there will have to be high (a) to attract savings from outside and (b) to retain local savings. Moreover, and quite separate, a material risk premium in prospective yields will be unavoidable. The crucial point here is that areas of high nonlabor costs need low labor costs if the real earning power of their people is to be maximized. And if essential skilled labor, executive ability and "know-how" are initially scarce in an area, and hence expensive (in relation to developed industrial areas), that similarly makes *relatively* low unskilled wage rates necessary if the progress of the region is to be set going.

Cheap and plentiful unskilled labor, provided it is cooperative and reliable, is, in other words, a source of attraction (a) for capital, (b) for entrepreneurial enterprise, and (c) for complementary skills. If this cheapness is forbidden, a fructifying redeployment of a nation's productive assets is frustrated; the workers in the less-developed areas are prevented from, so to speak, *bidding* for the complementary assets and services they can use; and because they are denied the right to contract for a smaller claim on the value of output, the profitability of further investment in wage-multiplying assets there is reduced.

Yet another important consideration is that workers in areas of relatively low free-market wage rates "need" cheap products, in the sense that (as consumers) they are more severely harmed by any contrived scarcity than are the less needy. For example, they "need" cheap local transportation and that is hardly possible if their bus and local truck drivers have to be paid the wage rates which are ruling in developed areas. Similarly, they need cheap retailing. And initially poor people need cheap clothing, cheap footwear, cheap housing, cheap amusements; and these things may be in some measure denied to them if the price of any labor is forced above *its natural scarcity value in its own area*.

Legislative moves to restrain the progress of less affluent areas may be said to have begun in the United States with the Walsh-Healy Act of 1935, which prevented Government contracts from being awarded to firms which did not pay "a fair wage." But if those who lobbied for this act had been deliberately and rationally seeking a humane objective, at a recognized collective cost for the community, they would have proposed that tenders submitted by firms which were mitigating inequalities of income by employing labor that was available at lower rates than the average *should be given preference. The greater the percentage below the national average a firm's wage rates were, the greater the preference they should have been conceded*. The act was intended, of course, to have exactly the reverse effect. Moreover, it was left to an official to apply arbitrary and meaningless criteria. In practice, all that

176

"unfair" came to mean was *harmful to privileged labor*. Some blame the Davis-Bacon Act (1931) for having initiated the policy.

The Fair Labor Standards Act has, as we have seen, worked in the same manner. It might be said that just as the major aim of the Wagner Act was to legalize the application of the standard rate on a national basis via industry-wide use of the strike threat, so the aim of the Fair Labor Standards Act, three years later (1938), was the application of a national standard rate (in the form of a minimum wage rate) to all labor employed in producing goods or services entering into interstate trade (agriculture being excluded). The standard rate imposed by strike-threat duress on an industry-wide scale, and minimum wage rates imposed by legal enactment, can be observed to have had similar effects on one another. Both have restrained the coordinative mechanism of the pricing system over space; for if allowed to work, this mechanism allocates assets to where human powers are prospectively capable of being used most productively and profitably developed, while attracting labor from where, through history and policy, it is presently employed relatively unproductively.

Almost universally, the claim has been that the purpose of resort to the standard rate principle through legal enactment is that of raising the material well-being (including the health and efficiency) of those destined to become its victims. But as we have seen, it nearly invariably harms such individuals as suffer from some defect of nature or nurture, or those broad groups of persons against whose employment in certain capacities there is a prejudice; and such less efficient or nonpreferred persons are morally harmed also if some character-destroying handout is resorted to by way of mitigation. Patently sincere humanitarians have been tricked into believing that the minimum wage can rescue the poor from poverty, that it can help them to lift themselves. Yet the absence of more tangible progress in many backward areas or among unprivileged races is due, in my own judgement, chiefly to the standard rate barrier.

As I have already suggested, the less disguisable means to the perpetuation of inequality of opportunity between races (union control of entry, apprenticeship subterfuges, "job reservations" and the like) are *relatively* unimportant. But the actual initiators of minimum wage legislation—the lobbyists and the politicians responsible—seem always to have inhibited concern about the consequences upon those people who might be disadvantaged. I find it difficult to quarrel with Demsetz's judgment that laws restraining the free labor market which have been *actually designed* to affect "nonpreferred" persons (such as Negroes) beneficially "are not generally found in our legal framework and we shall need some imagination to conjure them onto its pages."[38] The beneficiaries—indeed I must reiterate the *intended beneficiaries*—have almost universally been the workers in high wage-rate, privileged areas.

Insofar as the South *has* progressed industrially during the last half century, as H. C. Simons warned in 1944, it has been "in spite of the intentions of the northern unions and the Massachusetts Senators."[39] The Fair Labor

Standards Act, asserted Simons, "was designed . . . to retard migration of textile production and textile capital into southern states, . . . [It was] legislation which protected . . . northern workers and employers . . . against the South as tariffs and subsidies had earlier protected them against foreigners."[40]

We must remember that attracting assets to areas like Louisiana and Mississippi would "naturally" be less costly in money and "psychic costs" than moving poor families and their possessions from, say, those areas to Illinois. It is indeed, as John Van Sickle insisted long ago, incomparably more humane. As things are, the poor Negroes of the South have all too often found their best opportunities or prospects not in the southern environment in which they are psychologically and sociologically best adjusted, in contact with their parents, friends, and familiar ways of life, but in distant parts. In these strange areas, they usually earn well and welfare benefits are generous, but they often feel deracinated. Then, the failure to solve the problems created by rising affluence in an unfamiliar environment appears to have created some of the most intractable sociological disturbances of this generation. In spite of a policy of unparalleled enlightment aimed at the achievement of equality of respect and consideration for persons of all races and colors, and the attempted dissemination of goodwill and racial acceptance, the vested interests in disorder have had everything in their favor. It has been easy for troublemakers to exacerbate the stupid yet typically human prejudices and animosities which plague us all, whether we are white or black.

The effect of a competitive market for labor will be gradually to eliminate geographical differences of remuneration. The fewer the restraints on competition, the more rapidly will equality of that kind be established. "Putting a floor under competition" (as an apologist for the standard rate has described it) is simply to deny the lower remunerated areas the right to bring the "net advantageousness" of occupations in different parts into ultimate equality (allowance made for pecuniary and "psychic" costs of movement). For *firstly* (as we have seen), it prevents those who live in the less well-paid regions from raising their earning power through attracting capital via the offer of free-market determined labor costs, and guaranteeing the future determination of labor costs through the free market; and *secondly* (although less effectively, I think), it *discourages* profitable migration from low- to high-wage regions.

But the "labor economists" are teaching that a duress-imposed "floor to competition" can actually bring about this equality. This is, for instance, the position of L. R. Reynolds and Charles P. Taft,[41] who argue that geographical differences of wage rates in the United States are "more a reflection of union weakness than of union intentions." They admit, it must be stressed, that equalization of money wage rates over area will reduce the differences "by more than is desirable," because this will mean higher real wage rates in the South than in the North. They admit also that differences in money wage rates may be desirable "in order to encourage location of new industrial investment in the Southern states and small towns." They are here referring, of course, to the advantages for the workers in underdeveloped areas of offering lower real wage rates to attract capital, although they refrain

178

from pointing out the general principle. Nevertheless, they maintain that "the imposition of a standard wage scale throughout an industry would appear, prima facie, to bring the industry closer to the situation which would prevail under perfect competition."[42] "The change produced by unionism is in the direction of competitive norms. . . ."[43] These fantastic assertions are backed by the plea: "The less profitable firms cannot, because of their unprofitability, pay less for bank loans, machinery or raw materials. Why should they be permitted to pay less for labor?"[44] The answer is that their illustration is wholly inapplicable. Interest rates on bank loans are *not* standardized throughout a large country; the amount and the terms on which a firm can borrow depend on its creditworthiness, while risk premiums will differ; raw material prices do differ from area to area, and attempts to enforce uniform prices for them at all points of sale are subject to the very vice which is alleged against standard wage rates.

The difficulty with most "labor economists" on this issue is their extraordinary inconsistency. For instance, Reynolds and Taft typically admit from time to time that competitive forces tend to bring about the greatest conceivable measure of equality, but they say that "to the extent that trade unionism has accelerated this development" (competition) "its influence has been beneficial."[45] They remark also that "high wage companies are . . . likely to favor industry-wide standardization on competitive grounds."[46] Such phrases almost suggest irony or equivocation. The union influence has throughout obviously been intended, in almost every way, to restrain the achievement of equality of opportunity and earning power. And their words "on competitive grounds" *mean*, of course, "as a method of restraining competition"! Only to the extent that the voting power of the lower-income groups ("the unskilled" or "semiskilled") within industry-wide unions, or in organizations like the AFL-CIO or the TUC, has somehow caused barriers to skill acquisition and utilization to be lowered, has any equalitarian effect (a narrowing of the range of differentials) been brought about through the labor union organization. Yet common sense suggests that any such influence has been of no very great importance. (See pp. 201-202.) And in so far as those organizations *have* indeed worked to break down restraints on equality of opportunity, it has been through their mitigating the effects of strike-threat action, not through their employing it. It has been suggested that the Swedish Federation of Labor has indeed acted to facilitate mobility upward. If so, the Federation has been carrying out what is more appropriately a function of government.[47] In general, the whole force of the labor union movement has been used *to suppress* competitive pressures toward the "leveling up" of the poorer groups with some "leveling down" of the more affluent (that is, privileged) groups. Enforcement of the standard rate has been an almost infallible method of suppressing the necessary competition.

Yet Reynolds and Taft seem to condemn policies which permit enterprises to raise the earnings of the relatively poorly-paid workers. Offering the poorer classes or races wage rates which are higher than they are presently earning, yet less than the privileged rates currently ruling in other undertakings, can, they say, "become a threat to the entire wage and price structure of the industry."[48] But must that structure be regarded as sacrosanct? Where the power to uplift the underprivileged by undercutting exists, a threat to the whole exploitative set-up is indeed created. The "threat" may certainly have the effect of forcing competing firms to reduce their prices. But this is adding to the source of demands for all noncompeting output, and raising therefore the aggregate flow of real wages.[49]

"Labor economists" are sometimes masters in the use of language that clouds this disturbing aspect of contemporary reality. With elegant phrases, they befuddle their own minds and those of their readers. For instance, Clark Kerr, who always writes in dignified prose, with academic detachment and seldom an emotive adjective, illustrates the powerful appeal which the standard rate has in union circles by referring to "workers in low wage plants thinking they are worth as much as those in high wage plants and the workers in high wage plants feeling uneasy about unfair competition possibly threatening their jobs." But instead of going on to expose the preposterousness of the situation in which enforcement of the standard rate denies the lower-paid group the right to increase their earnings by bargaining against the higher-paid group, he remarks: "Considerations of equity for one group and security for the other move hand in hand."[50] Let us ask ourselves: *Is it not the very "security" of the well-paid group which constitutes the "inequity" from which the poorer group suffers?*

Clark Kerr's comment illustrates admirably the blindness of learned and influential teachers of labor economics to the reality that, as Arthur A. Shenfield put it recently, "the system is one which is approved by its victims." Perhaps Clark Kerr intends the passage merely to reflect how typical workers think. But that hardly seems possible; for the reference to "unfair competition" exposes a failure to recognize that *while competition can injure the privileged, it can never harm the unprivileged.*

Returning now to the case of areas in which the "unprivileged" dominate—the low-wage districts—if policy concerned with helping the workers in such areas were built on explicit recognition of their right to price their inputs according to their natural scarcity value, then *the dynamic* consequences of the accumulation of industrial assets which would be attracted could be multiplied. (By "dynamic" here is meant that the increase of any one kind of output would contribute to the source of demands expressed in the area for all noncompeting outputs, including "the service industries"). Free-market wage rates would rise automatically.[51]

I anticipate here the objection that less-affluent areas like the South have no right to compete "unfairly." But all that would mean is that the process of selling the output of such areas in competition with the output of more affluent areas is "unfair" if entrepreneurs offer wage rates which make due allowance for other cost disadvantages of their district. And as we have seen, demands for industrial labor in the South could have made their greatest contribution to wage income in that region if labor cost there had fully compensated for the high-cost factors mentioned on page 176. The southern industries are still often *infant* industries, like many of those in, say, Latin America. They can play their full part in raising the material well-being of the workers they employ only if their labor costs are freed from control in the interest of their competitors. (See p. 175.)

Investors are (as we noticed in Chapters 8 and 9) sometimes said to "take advantage" of the initial cheapness of labor in underdeveloped areas, although in doing so their investments tend to raise the earnings of those to whom they offer additional employment and training opportunities. As I have already insisted, new enterprises set up in such regions shut no doors to any income sources which had previously been available; hence they can hardly be rationally accused of "sweating" or "exploiting" the workers to whom they make wage offers, simply because it is "cheap labor."

Under the U. S. Constitution all states are guaranteed freedom of trade in the sense that tariff and similar barriers may not be erected between them. But the federal government has not been constitutionally restrained from itself erecting barriers to the free deployment of investment over area, when the barriers take the form of legally enacted minimum wage rates. Nor has the Constitution forbidden the erection of privately imposed barriers of the same kind. Yet enhanced labor costs enforced in the less-affluent areas to enrich politically powerful union members in the more affluent areas are restraints exactly similar in aim and content to import tariffs framed on the principle of the "equalization of costs of production" to insure "fair trade."[52] Had the fathers of the Constitution been able to forecast developments in the form of federal wage-rate enactments or the use of industry-wide strike-threat duress in the pricing of labor, they would both have been explicitly prohibited. Because the required prescience did not exist, the provisions of the Fair Labor Standards Act and the Wagner Act have been operating so as to permit a veiled exploitative colonization of the relatively underdeveloped states for the benefit of the developed states.

I have been illustrating the injustices of the standard rate mainly by reference to disadvantaged *areas*. But that has been merely to highlight the general exploitation phenomenon. Through custom, unquestioned habit, their own social heritage, the color prejudice and the vested interests of the whites, we find that in the United States the Negroes, the Puerto Ricans, the Chinese, the Japanese, the Indians, and Spanish-Americans generally are still, on the whole, restricted to low-paid occupations and hence relatively poor living standards and less favorable environments. *Their original inferiority (of status, condition and opportunity) was bequeathed to this generation by history.* For over a century this racial relationship had been sociologically stable although not rigid. *The urge for minimum wage enactments emerged only as the traditional relationship began to be seriously disturbed by free market forces.* As soon as entrepreneurial incentives became powerful enough to threaten the demolition of historically determined inequalities, a "floor to competition" was demanded. That is, as soon as the restraints of custom, habit and prejudice were beginning to be overcome, the unions and the politicians erected standard wage and minimum wage restraints to perpetuate an inherited income structure. The motives of the white Americans were human enough. They saw that technological progress was creating, through the color-blind free market, a motive for and the possibility of investment in the industrial training, and employment in semiskilled or skilled work, of races traditionally confined to agricultural work or "put and carry" jobs. Both artisans and laborers of the privileged race then began to fear that the competition of the nonwhite races would affect their *relative* economic level, that is, in relation to the underprivileged groups. For reasons which we can all understand, it appeared to be outrageous that time-honored, mutually accepted or acquiesced-in relationships between the races should be changed, and "the rate for the job," enforced by the strike threat or minimum wage laws, came to be tacitly recognized as a highly effective stratagem for protecting the status quo while nominally conceding equality of civil rights.

One possibility is that the southern Negroes and other unprivileged races simply lacked sufficiently disinterested or sufficiently enlightened leadership to perceive what had been happening. They have certainly often allowed representatives of labor unions from the North to persuade them to organize for the achievement of their own collective retardation, and to acquiesce in laws with the same objective. Of course, *some* of the southern workers—including some blacks—benefited relatively as the rate of investment in the South was slowed down. But such are the powers of persuasion possessed by the vested interests, and the self-perpetuating nature of inculcated stereotypes, that the injustices are *acquiesced in* by electors in the areas which particularly suffer, and often even *approved of* by them (partly because many really *do* benefit in the short run while others think that their turn is, perhaps, yet to come).

A device which has served to confuse the issue (if not purposely used for that purpose) has been treating color or race discrimination as though it originates from the prejudices of "employers" or managements. Admittedly, white managers *as persons* may be reasonably held often to share the race attitudes of the white proletariat. But any discrimination against "non-preferred" races is damaging to the pecuniary interests of managements or the pecuniary interests of the stockholders to whom they are responsible. Thus, a sole proprietor may be said to have the right to be generous to those he favors; for although obvious favoritism on his part might lead to ill-feeling, no one would wish to deny any person an unrestrained discretion in making making gifts. But as soon as a firm has become a corporation, this right ceases. Managements have no right to be *generous* at their stockholders' expense (see p. 113). If they discriminate in respect of employees whose efficiency and worth to the undertaking are the same, they *are* being generous to the individuals favored, and foregoing thereby their ability to maximize *pecuniary* profits.[53] It is *a breach of duty* if corporation managements refuse to permit the underprivileged to price themselves into higher-paid employments (when society allows this).[54] As we have seen, because society, in its consumer role, is generally indifferent to the color or race of the labor employed in making a product, but critical about price in relation to alternatives, *managements would be unable to afford to respect racial bars if they were not concerned also about adverse staff reactions*. Had they no worries about labor troubles, American executives could hardly ignore the prospective yield to investment in human capital through the training of all the disadvantaged races in the qualities essential for *efficient* semiskilled or unskilled work (regularity, punctuality, responsibility, submission to discipline, etc.), as well as in actual skilled operations. When managements in the United States fail to take advantage of these possibilities in the absence of minimum wage or standard rate obstacles, it will almost certainly be because of their preoccupation with personnel harmony. The dread of upsetting good morale among the whites and arousing fears of the ultimate consequences of racial justice upon white privileges has, admittedly, influenced employment policy. But if the nonwhites (or other unprivileged group) were in a position to discount such disadvantages, even *this* barrier could be broken through.

Direct discrimination in recruitment (forced on managements through white proletarian prejudice and union policy) is experienced in another form under duress-imposed wage rates because of the rationing problem created. Entrants must be selected according to some different criterion from prospective efficiency when the decision is no longer made through the bidding process of the market. It is not surprising that, in these circumstances (as Alchian and Kessel have put it):

> Admission will be easier for people whose cultural and personal characteristics conform to the interests of the existing members. And admission will be especially difficult for those regarded as potential price cutters in hard times or not to be counted on as faithful members with a strong sense of loyalty to the union. Minority groups and those who find they must accept lower wages because of some personal or cultural attribute, even though they are just as productive in a pecuniary sense to the employer, will be more willing to accept lower wages if threatened with the loss of their jobs. But these are the very types who will weaken the unions' monopoly power. All of this suggests that young people, Negroes, Jews, and other minority or unorthodox groups will be underrepresented in monopolistic unions.[55]

We have noticed that sole proprietors and partners may, if they wish, sacrifice profit in order, so to speak, to purchase the objective of favoring preferred employees. But it is impossible to be certain in most cases whether apparent instances of such discrimination are actual instances. However, certain Chinese sole proprietors or Chinese partnerships in the United States are believed by some deliberately to recruit only from their race or, at any rate, to give their own people preference. And we actually do find evidence which may be so interpreted in the small (allegedly "sweated") industries in the Chinese quarters of some big cities. Although the Chinese businessmen are typically represented as *exploiting* their own people, they are more likely, I

183

believe, to be discriminating in their favor. The explanation seems to be that minimum wage laws and the standard rate, combined with the proletarian prejudices of white unionists, have excluded Americans of Chinese ancestry from opportunities elsewhere, creating an "incidental contrived plenitude" (see pp. 93 et seq.) There may indeed have been collusion between Chinese managements and workers to avoid the more oppressive consequences of minimum wage enactments and the labor-pricing policies of the white-dominated unions. But that is a quite separate issue.

Concern for customer disapproval may be a factor, especially in white working-class districts when employees and customers come into contact.[56] It could be argued that, in these circumstances, the market is simply serving consumer preference, in the sense that it is when airlines discriminate against ugly women in appointing hostesses.[57] But even members of the KKK are color-blind outside the sphere of personal services; and they seem never to object to being served by Negroes who are acting in what they regard as the Negroes' traditional role.

Adequately to cover all possibilities, we ought really to make a distinction between *prejudice* as such and *genuine misjudgment*, based on lack of knowledge. Judgment about the abilities of underprivileged groups may be distorted by prejudice, but genuine error has not always been a negligible factor. Thus, some managements in the American South may have sincerely believed at one time that the Negro was incapable of anything more difficult than put and carry work. But let us, as economists, see that we are not a prey to equally mistaken judgments. *Where managements have underrated Negro (or other nonwhite) potentialities, their mistaken judgment has always been contrary to the pecuniary interests of the shareholders to whom the managements have been responsible.* And in the United States the lesson was learned with fantastic speed in the most obvious case, namely, in professional sports where, once the door was opened, color prejudice in recruitment could soon be financially disastrous.

There are some aspects of "fair employment practices" legislation which may work in the opposite direction from the minimum wage—discouraging or eliminating racial discrimination instead of fostering it. As Gary Becker puts it, "through litigation, fines, unfavorable publicity, imprisonment," and so forth "the cost of not hiring some disadvantaged groups" is increased.[58] But he does not, I think, bring out the crucial point, namely, that because antidiscriminatory policy pressures in this form are *not* in fact used effectively against the unions (at least in the United States), managements have to balance the disadvantages of having to appease proletarian cupidity and prejudices—supported by the unions—on the one side, with the disadvantages of not buying labor in the cheapest market *plus* any penalties which might be imposed on them for appeasing proletarian prejudices on the other side.

The requirement under the Fair Labor Standards legislation that firms shall be "reasonable and just" in hiring does not sufficiently protect managements from the unions. It is certainly possible, however, that the course of U.S. politics *may* eventually lead to enactments which insist upon some percentage sharing of jobs. This could, at any rate, insure a nonracial sharing of privileges and injustices. Many years ago, I challenged the South African labor unions by suggesting an arbitrary quota system which would have had such an effect. I pointed out that the "Coloureds" (that is, the half-castes) of the Cape industrial area were approximately equal in number to the whites. I reminded the unions that the Coloureds had, half a century previously, supplied most of the skilled labor in the area. But there was then, as they knew, a very small proportion left in well-paid, artisan work.[59] As the unions typically claimed that the purpose of standard rates (including legally enacted minimum wage rates) and other labor protective laws was to prevent the exploitation of the Coloureds as well as the whites, my challenge was that they should agree to enforce a gradually introduced quota system under which the Coloureds could be assured 5 percent of the better paid employment openings in the first year, 10 percent in the second year, and so on, so that after a couple of decades the privileged occupations (if they were privileged) would be shared equally between the two groups. Naturally the challenge was ignored.[60]

Federal policy in the United States has not yet begun to move clearly and efficiently toward enforcement of civil and human rights for nonwhites in the labor field. If the aim of minimum wage legislation, and government tolerance of strike threat-determined standard rates had honestly been to protect the poorer races from exploitation, any compulsions applied would (as Demsetz has insisted in the case of the United States)[61] have been accompanied by quota provisions. But some effort has had to be made to give a semblance of meaning to election promises, and quiet pressure upon the union executives appears to have been exerted, with a hint of a quota. During Lyndon Johnson's presidency, hesitant administrative pressures in the quota direction appear to have been exercised. This occurred, I understand, with secret assurances to the AFL-CIO that only token disturbance of the status quo would be required. Under Nixon's presidency, rather more tangible token concessions *appear* (as this is written) to have been asked for. It seems that white labor unionists are now being advised that their unions are expected to make small concessions toward the equality of opportunity which the standard rate has prevented, in order to avoid larger concessions later. Veiled references to a Federal takeover of recruitment and apprenticeship, the withholding of federal funds in construction projects in which an insufficient proportion of Negroes is employed, and suits by the Department of Justice against certain locals, on the grounds of race discrimination—these moves (under both the Johnson and the Nixon administrations) *have* been compelling officials of national unions to veer toward abandoning the traditional excuse that they cannot interfere with the autonomy of their locals. Executives of the parent bodies seem to be shifting therefore from a tongue-in-cheek acceptance of or lip service to the principle of equality of rights, toward recommending some sort of sharing of their privileges—hopefully with just a few from the minority races. If this trend develops, the eventual outcome is likely to be a quota type of arrangement, reserving

185

ultimately (through successive concessions) jobs for, say, Negroes more or less according to the proportion of Negroes in a district. Even the president of the almost wholly white Plumbers Union, told the executives of his locals, in March 1968, that although "we" (the officials of the parent union) "carried the fight about as far as we could," it was now essential for the locals to stop "pussyfooting" and allow blacks in. "You cannot legitimately blame the whole affirmative action on us," he said.

The result of a trend toward racial quotas, if carried to the point at which monopolistically valuable wage outlets come to be shared in proportion to racial numbers, will merely *substitute social injustice for racial injustice*. Apart from continuing unfairness toward those excluded from the bargaining process by the standard rate, the quota system would *necessarily* discriminate against the more efficient or valuable in one or other group, on grounds of race alone.

We are forced to the conclusion that the *racial injustices* due to the standard rate can be mitigated through resort to the quota system only at the cost of creating less conspicuous *social injustices*. Nevertheless, the substitution of social injustices for racial injustices does not *aggravate* the evil and may help in drawing attention to it. For that reason the "libertarian" may, perhaps, welcome the quota device.

In 1937, Dr. Abdurahman, the most influential leader the "Coloureds" of South Africa ever had,[62] surprised everybody by asserting, in a reservation to the *Report of the Cape Coloured Commission*, that ". . . until equality of opportunity in the matter of education and technical education has been established, and until a greater measure of equality of consideration has been won, minimum wage legislation will generally work as an effective barrier to the advancement of the Cape colored people."[63] Had there been any suspicion that Dr. Abdurahman would have spoken so unequivocally about this reality, I do not think he would ever have been appointed to the Commission. As things were, his reservation was ignored, and it has been completely forgotten by the "Coloureds" for whose advancement he was pleading in vain. There are as yet few signs that a leader of equal enlightenment is about to arise among the Negroes and the other underprivileged races of the United States.

I have so far illustrated my argument by reference to nonpreferred groups where color, race or ancestry are the origin of prejudice. But women nearly everywhere fall into the nonpreferred category for many employments. Psychosociological considerations complicate the issue rather differently but, I judge, even more powerfully where women's employment is concerned. Some of the resulting complexities are recognized by writers who seem to think that restraints on the free pricing of their services can rectify the injustices. But in the light of what *principles* could wage-rate fixing by private coercive power or legal enactment assist? There are so many obstacles to equality of opportunity for women and so many reasons why, in a wide variety of tasks, women are less suitable than men, and so many special costs of employing them in such tasks, that *justice for women often demands their right to accept less than their male competitors*. Is not the basic problem simply: How can one effectively secure them that basic human right?

Now one would expect that in the lower paid kinds of work, for example, "put and carry work," women's general physical disadvantage in respect of muscular strength would be greatest, and that in work demanding skills, their physical disadvantages would be least or nonexistent, for example, in typesetting. In fact, however, it seems that the higher the average hourly wage rates, the greater the discount women must offer or accept (in relation to men's remuneration) in order to compete on equal terms.[64] This *may* be accounted for of course by quality differences, for example, the normal inability of women to attend work with the same regularity as men, a factor which is, presumably, more important in the higher-paid types of work.[65] But on the whole one would have expected the discount needed to have declined as the development of mechanization in industry has reduced the importance of muscular power, and as the decline in male prejudice has reduced the costs of employing women. Moreover, in some cases, for example, as tellers in banks, pretty girls in their teens and twenties are probably more valuable than men; and their employment as tellers seems indeed to have been forced through interbank competition. But in industrial operations, because the proportion of women employed in the kinds of skilled work of which they are capable tends to be very small in most countries of the world, it is hardly possible to doubt that the inability of women to offer their services at lower wage rates has served as the most effective means of discrimination against them.

Studies of divergencies of earnings between men and women in the same or comparable work are very difficult to interpret; for while a tendency for the range of differences to narrow has undoubtedly been to the advantage of women when it has been due to the gradual success of entrepreneurs seeking least cost labor, it has had the opposite effect when the narrowing has been due to legal enactment or when it has been due to strike-threat pressures. It is then almost always evidence of discrimination *against* women. Admittedly, the small minority of women who do manage to be allowed skilled employment, without bearing the discount which can mitigate inequality of opportunity, are obvious beneficiaries; and once in, they are often the strongest defenders of the system and likely to claim the source of their privilege as the achievement of equality between the sexes.

In stressing here the manner in which the standard rate can be used to trample on the prospects of advancement for the low-grade or "nonpreferred" worker, I am incidentally drawing attention to the rights of *every* individual who tries to smash through privilege-protecting walls. And here I must refer again to my argument in Chapter 4. Among the nonpreferred, we must include *nonstrikers*—those persons who believe that their future is likely to be harmed if a strike in which they refuse to participate is successful, or who oppose the method on moral grounds. We must include *strikebreakers* also. *Their* great opportunity may happen to occur through a strike. Accepting the employment which the strikers abandon often gives would-be interlopers their solitary chance of getting round the standard rate barrier from which they have suffered in the past.

If this argument at first sounds outrageous, let us look at the issue in this way. Can we even *begin* to approach the necessary conditions for ·social justice until *every person's right to improve his condition (without exploitation or theft on his part) is unconditionally and unequivocally guaranteed*? If our answer is that such a right *should* be guaranteed, it means that *we must recognize and explicitly protect the rights of the "scab."* For the "scab" is no moral leper just because we have allowed a loathsome name to be pinned on him. We ought indeed to attach to the *use* of the word "scab" all the opprobrium that is rightly attributed to the word "nigger." The strikebreaker is simply saying, "That job, at the wage rate and prospects it offers, is for me better than any alternative society is offering. This strike creates *my* opportunity and my hope. I wish to accept the offer." For him, it is indeed the chance to slip past *the most unscalable wall to equality of opportunity that society has ever allowed to be erected*.

But (as I contended earlier, pp. 51-54) largely through the degradation of democratic representation, public opinion has come to applaud those who seek their individual betterment through the repression of their competing fellow men, and to condemn and despise persons who seek their betterment, *without exploitation*, at the expense of the privileged. In other words, people have been indoctrinated into an admiration of the striker and a contempt for the "scab" or "black-leg." To such an extent is this the position in the United States that the would-be nonstriker or strikebreaker, engaged in perfectly legal (and for the enlightened, praiseworthy) action, can today seldom expect *effective* protection from the police or district attorneys. And in place of laws expressly designed to protect the underprivileged, there are laws designed to protect the privileged. In some states and towns the employment of strikebreakers has been made unlawful.

It is essential to repeat that under free market determination of wage rates, *equality of "net advantageousness"* for work of different types *tends* to be established. The forces which exert this tendency are not instantaneous but powerful. "Equal pay for equal work" within each labor market sheltered only by the costs of spatial mobility is the early *consequence* of true market freedom. Enforced uniformity of wage rates, instead of promoting the achievement of this ideal, frustrates it, and is often deliberately used to frustrate it; whereas *market freedom itself determines minimum real wage rates* in respect of every area for every set of workers the value of whose product does not fall below the minimum so determined. In the case of *any type of labor*, this minimum will be the highest that is compatible with the availability of the most favorable employment opportunities for them, *given the nonavailability of better employment opportunities*. By this I mean that a market-imposed minimum may well reflect an "incidental contrived plenitude." But that could never be through some defect in the free market

188

which determines it or some defect in other free markets.[66] The cause in such cases is to be found in restraints on freedom in other labor markets. The reader is reminded of our conclusion in Chapter 7 that if wage rates in an occupation are "too low" in any meaningful sense, it is because persons in that occupation have been shut out from more productive and better remunerated employments, and often from training for such employments.

Empirical evidence of free-market enforced minima is not lacking in spite of so great a part of the economic system being dominated by wage rates influenced by the strike threat. In districts in which no statutory minimum wage rates (or union standard rates) apply to any occupation, a very effective *market-imposed minimum wage rate is usually observable*, for example, for domestic servants in many parts of the world. Both Pepys and Defoe (in the seventeenth and eighteenth centuries respectively) commented on the phenomenon in this occupation.[67] No household can acquire the services of persons seeking employment at less than the local market rate (and the more than normally competent can command a premium). The knowledge of market conditions among unorganized domestic servants can, indeed, create an illusory appearance of oligopoly (tacit monopoly) among them. Even in the case of girl juveniles, there seems to be a known market-determined minimum. George Shultz quotes this typical assertion: "The girls talk a lot among themselves about salaries and when jobs in firms paying lower salaries are offered, they refuse them."[68] Moreover, summarizing the effects of "the upward pressure" on wage rates for girls taking up clerical work, Shultz draws attention to the fact that "some firms followed a policy of raising their rates in anticipation of this competitive struggle. Firms with lagging rates of pay felt the pressure most strongly."[69]

Market-enforced minima are incomparably kinder to minorities who, by reason of some physical, mental or moral defect, or by reason of such things as inability to serve for regular or conventional hours, are less productive than the majorities. *The free market takes better care of these unfortunates than any form of social security in the way of handouts*. In preserving their *right to earn*, which exemption from the standard rate maintains, it preserves their pride, their independence, their sense of social usefulness and their awareness of purpose in life. The question of the *supplementation* of their earnings by handouts is a separate issue, and must not be allowed to cloud thought about the ideal pricing of their labor.

Among the injustices which are unavoidable when the standard rate is enforced over an industry or area is *discrimination against the smaller firms*. In the free market, relatively small enterprises tend to be burdened—not unfairly—with higher than average labor costs per unit of output, although by reason of the different *type* of labor they usually require, the average earnings per head of workers employed in the small undertakings will be typically rather less than in big concerns. When the standard rate is forced on them, however, it means that these costs are raised more than proportionately to the costs of their larger competitors.

Moreover, (a quite different case) it sometimes happens that investment in the smaller enterprises occurs *because* the standard rate proves to be enforceable on the larger undertakings only. The small firms, if not under strike-threat coercion, can mitigate the situation and provide an extremely important form of social security. They can offer a source of earned income for the outcasts of the collective bargaining process—the excluded or displaced labor from the larger firms. But they can only provide this form of social security when each increment of the labor they employ costs less than the prospective marginal value of its output. Hence the minimum wage can exclude the disadvantaged class by denying them—temporarily or permanently—the right to an earned income, possibly offering them instead unemployment compensation or relief handouts.

Since the beginnings of the industrial revolution, the process I have called "economizing-displacement" (of labor and assets) has been causing the *real* price of labor to be rising (just as, since the 1930s, inflation has been causing the *money* price of labor to be rising in *addition*). Looking at the course of this experience in the United States since 1938, the increasingly rare market-set minima seem to have risen more continuously and steadily than duress-imposed or statutory minima. Market-set wage rates have risen *at least* as rapidly as far as trend is concerned, *when allowance is made for any tendency of the growing strike-threat influence to aggravate the process through which underprivileged groups have been confined to occupations of relatively low productivity and earning power*. The enforcement of nonmarket rates has had the effect of maintaining an inegalitarian wages structure. Yet the available statistics suggest that wage rates generally have risen *in proportion to statutory minima* during the period since 1938.[70] Nonmarket minima tend, it seems, to rise in jumps, and what I have termed "market-set minima" move evenly.

A point of major importance must now be stressed. The harm wrought by the standard rate, whether enforced through the strike threat or legal enactment, is not to be perceived *mainly* in the lay-off of workers, still less in the actual unemployment of labor, although I do not minimize in any way the sociologically harmful consequences of unemployment when it does occur. *The main social detriment is borne through distortions in the composition of the stock of assets and in the specialization of labor for kinds of work which make a lower contribution to productivity and have in consequence a lower earning power*. The standard rate is continually causing the relatively poor *employed* persons to be poorer and the relatively affluent to be more affluent. Of course, on occasion, actual displacements of labor caused through the forcing up of "the rate for the job" (or its maintenance despite an adverse change in consumer preference or other demand transfers) are responsible for obvious and avoidable distress, because the adjustment period is both prolonged and characterized by many unemployed. But abnormal unemployment of labor is a minor economic burden, although, because it is a visible phenomenon, it is politically important.[71]

Reformers who wish to see the erosion of time-strengthened bulwarks against equality of economic rights among different races, castes, classes, individuals and areas must face realistically the general principle. Neither legislative restrictions of the free market nor use of the strike threat can offer effective protection for the minorities to whom equality of opportunity has been denied; whereas legislation to *foster* the free market could be effective if it were tried.[72]

NOTES

[1] Nationwide standard rates are found, for instance, in the United States in such industries as coal, pottery, hosiery, and certain types of glass and glassware. They have been imposed either through industrial unions, covering the nation, or through the use of the "whipsaw" or "strike in detail" (see p. 47) with the objectives set by acceptance of a common standard.

[2] See Sidney and Beatrice Webb, *Industrial Democracy* (London: Longmans Green and Co., 1920), Chapter V.

[3] H. Demsetz, "Minorities in the Market Place," *North Carolina Law Review,* 1964-1965, p. 276.

[4] Joan Robinson, "A Fundamental Objection to Laissez Faire," *Economic Journal* (1935).

[5] W. H. Hutt, *Economic Journal,* March 1936, pp. 61-62.

[6] Ibid., pp. 78-79.

[7] This is because *collusive* monopsony can be directly tackled. See the following paragraph.

[8] It is not *"true* discrimination" if persons of different ability *or differing costs of employment* do not receive the same remuneration.

[9] That is, almost every firm is in a position to increase its earnings in the short run (raising its prices or—much less likely—forcing down its costs) by reliance on this small degree of "natural" monopoly or monopsony. But it may be able to do this only at the expense of adverse reactions (losses or perhaps disaster) later on. See pp. 117-118.

[10] This may be because of prejudice (color, race, sex, creed) against working side by side with them on the part of the general body of workers (a prejudice which raises the cost of their employment), or it may be because their *initial* qualifications for the work are inferior.

[11] The reader is reminded that the word "displaced" refers to workers laid-off. The word "exclude" refers to workers denied entry.

[12] When a formerly existing standard rate is further raised by duress, the earnings or prospects of those who had been earning more than the new standard rate must tend to fall for similar reasons.

[13] That is, the net effect will not be egalitarian. Some redistribution at the expense of workers who would have avoided displacement at higher wage-rates under the free market may occur.

[14] A fall in demand for the services of *all* labor in an occupation implies

a downward shift in the demand schedule. A fall in demand for the services of a *grade subject to the minimum* implies a movement along a curve representing a demand schedule for that grade of labor.

[15] See H. A. Turner, "Inflation and Wage Differentials in Great Britain," in J. T. Dunlop, ed., *The Theory of Wage Determination* (London: Macmillan, Ltd., 1957), p. 129.

[16] Demsetz, op. cit. p. 276. The "nonpreferred can be plain women or physically deformed persons as well as Jews or Negroes." (Ibid., p. 278).

[17] For example, through "equal pay for equal work" laws or "laws which confer a high degree of monopoly power on unions" (Ibid., p. 276).

[18] Ibid., p. 277.

[19] Ibid., pp. 277-78.

[20] Ibid., p. 278.

[21] Ibid., p. 279.

[22] Gary S. Becker, "Comment," *Aspects of Labor Economics: A Conference of the Universities—National Bureau Committee for Economic Research,* A Report of the National Bureau of Economic Research (Princeton: Princeton University Press, 1962), pp. 178-179.

[23] Ibid., p. 179. Becker points out that, theoretically, even income tax could have this effect.

[24] See W. H. Hutt, *Economics of the Colour Bar: A Study of the Economic Origins and Consequences of Racial Segregation in Africa* (London: Andre Deutsch, Ltd., 1964), p. 173, *et seq.*

[25] Yale Brozen, *Journal of Law and Economics,* October 1962, p. 103. This example refers, of course, to what I have called "displacement." But as I have shown, "exclusion" (under my definitions—see p. 97, note 4) is an even more serious cause of "incidental contrived labor plenitude," and of the avoidable low earning power of the workers affected.

[26] This excellent illustration is from Henry Simons.

[27] When former farm workers are being introduced to industrial work, for instance, work attitudes are often particularly important. Factory employments require not only the acquisition of skills but of habits of regularity, responsibility and discipline that are largely alien to those whose background has been work on the land, or whose home environment has been that of humble agricultural laborers.

[28] H. C. Simons, *Economic Policy for a Free Society* (Chicago: University of Chicago Press, 1948), p. 140.

[29] The ratio was 2.4 in 1967, but the figures are not strictly comparable. See Yale Brozen, "The Effect of Minimum Wage Increase on Teen-Age Unemployment," *Journal of Law and Economics,* October 1969, p. 118.

[30] Ibid., p. 119.

[31] Ibid., p. 121.

[32] Ibid., p. 122.

[33] Labor may be comparatively plentiful in certain districts by reason of such things as local differences in living costs; or the availability locally of sub-

sidiary, "moonlighting" employments; or race attitudes which, allied to the standard rate, restrain the effective availability of competing employments in those parts; or an exceptional rate of growth in population of working age.

[34] On the general question of wage-rates imposed to cover wide areas, see John Van Sickle, "Geographical Aspects of a Minimum Wage," *Harvard Business Review* (1946, No. 3), especially pp. 277, 280-81; and M. R. Colberg, "Minimum Wage Effects on Florida's Economic Development," *Journal of Law and Economics*, October 1960.

Of course, in the United States, in those cases where the minimum applies only to employment in the manufacture of products which enter into interstate trade (that is, where similar minima are not imposed by the state legislatures), the relative poverty perpetuated or created will be less serious.

[35] See pp. 172-173.

[36] A partially countervailing factor is that some of the states in the South have availed themselves of their rights under 14 (b) of the Taft-Hartley Act and adopted "right to work laws" (see Chapter 18).

[37] There were of course other obstacles to the rapid progress of the South. The low initial *per capita* income meant a lack of lucrative markets for its industrial products except at high freight costs; and land in the South is, on the whole, very much less fertile than land in the North. John Van Sickle refers in this connection to a Department of Agriculture survey which shows that "there was more first-grade land in the single state of Iowa than in the 11 southern states." See his "The Wage Problem in the South," *Georgia Review* (1947), p. 496.

[38] Demsetz, op. cit., p. 284.

[39] Simons, op. cit., p. 135.

[40] Ibid., p. 136. Since 1938, the minimum set, beginning at 25 cents per hour, has been continuously raised (as technological progress has raised the *real* value of labor and inflation its money value) in order to preserve the protective effect of the minima; and a minimum of $1.60 has been reached as this is written.

[41] L. G. Reynolds and C. Taft, "Union Influence on Wage Differentials," in E. Wight Bakke, Clark Kerr and Charles W. Anrod, op. cit., pp. 596-599.

[42] Ibid., p. 598.

[43] Ibid., p. 598.

[44] Ibid., p. 598. They seem to have conceded, in the passage quted above, that the standard money wage-rate is a means of forcing certain firms in certain districts to pay more than those in other districts.

[45] Ibid., p. 599.

[46] Ibid., p. 596.

[47] That is, the releasing of competitive forces—the *intended* purpose of anti-trust.

[48] Reynolds and Taft, op. cit., p. 596.

[49] It does so by reducing any current exploitation (a) of consumers, (b) of previously excluded workers, and (c) of workers who have previously suffered

from an insufficiency of complementary assets (tools, machinery, factories, etc.) because high standard wage rates have been reducing prospective yields to investment in such assets.

[50] Clark Kerr, "Wage Relationships. . . . ," in, Dunlop, op. cit., p. 183.

[51] A similar effect will follow if a plentiful and cheap labor supply in an area can leave to undercut in high wage areas (that is, where the stock of assets is more plentiful). This reaction (which I judge to be less common) will also cause a leveling-up in the one district and a leveling-down in the other.

[52] See Henry Simons' comments, quoted p. 177.

[53] The assumption here is of course that the circumstances discussed on pp. 163-166 do not apply.

[54] Most often, however, racial prejudice *is* least powerful among the better-educated classes, which include the managers. Today, most business executives can see how preposterous discrimination on the basis of skin-pigmentation or cultural inheritance is.

[55] Armen A. Alchian and Reuben A. Kessel, "Competition, Monopoly, and the Pursuit of Pecuniary Gain," *Aspects of Labor Economics*, pp. 173-4.

[56] The question here is more complex than some readers are likely at first to perceive. About 30 years ago, I tried to persuade a big retailer in South Africa to employ "Coloured" (half-caste) shop assistants in shops serving mainly the "Coloured" people. He said that previous attempts in that direction had failed because—strange though it might seem—the "Coloureds" greatly preferred to be served by whites. A "Coloured" cooperative retail society which I encouraged and of which I was a member failed, I think, largely for that very reason. (See my *Economics of the Colour Bar*, pp. 23-27.)

[57] Some economists describe such preferences as "noneconomic," but they have exactly the same *economic* status as all other preferences.

[58] Becker, op. cit., p. 179.

[59] A coalition formed in 1924 between a rather extreme radical or socialist party and a nationalistic party representing mainly Afrikaans-speaking whites had applied a *Wage Act,* an *Industrial Conciliation Act,* an *Apprenticeship Act* and other legislation to perpetuate rather than to secure this situation.

[60] Actually, my challenge in South Africa was made in the form of a quota proposal purely for polemical purposes. I thought it would be an effective way of exposing how unjustly the standard rate (and indeed the whole system of wage-rate determination) was working. On other grounds, we must recognize how the quota system could itself be used for discrimination against a race with good traditions whose people had been more successful than those of another race *by reason of the virtues of their traditions.* For instance, a quota restricting the number of Jewish medical practitioners according to the proportion of Jews to total population in the United States would be grossly discriminatory.

[61] Demsetz, op. cit., p. 284.

[62] On Abdurahman's death the largest funeral procession (on foot, as is Moslem tradition) ever experienced in his country formed spontaneously. It

included Christian "Coloureds" as well as Moslems. ("Coloureds" means "half-castes" in South Africa.)

63 U. G. 54, 1937.

64 At the lower end of the wage scale, minimum wage enactments may prevent women from offering the relatively small discount which would maximize their earnings (and their contribution to output) in the low productivity operations.

65 The probability of the relatively able younger women marrying and then withdrawing is also a factor because it reduces the profitableness of investing in the development of their skills.

66 The phrase, "free market" (which is an explicit assumption in this paragraph), implies of course the absence of the monopsonistic exploitation discussed in Chapter 8.

67 See W. H. Hutt, *The Theory of Collective Bargaining* (Glencoe, Ill.: Free Press, 1954), p. 33.

68 George P. Schultz, "A Nonunion Market for White Collar Labor," *Aspects of Labor Economics*, p. 140.

69 Ibid., p. 142.

70 One difficulty about such statistical comparisons is that a rise in union-enforced wage rates in an industry *might* cause wage rates in competing non-union firms to rise. Relevant statistics in respect of statutory and market minima have been recently set out and cogently explained by Brozen, op. cit., pp. 110-113.

71 Unemployment of labor is politically important because its magnitude tends to be roughly correlated (inversely) with fluctuations in real income (fluctuations in "prosperity"). But the phenomenon with which I have here been concerned has reference to the *magnitude* of income, not the *fluctuations* to which that magnitude is subject.

72 For a rigorous general treatment of this issue, see Demsetz, op. cit., passim.

13
Established Differentials

ANY STUDY of the empirical contributions which deal with the labor market must leave the student with an impression of the great complexity of that market and its even greater disorder. We find a value chaos due to the inherent arbitrariness of "exploitation" and merely private resistance to it or avoidance of it. Wage rates and earnings for different occupations within the same industry, and for different industries and different districts *for the same occupations*, often differ widely. Even between one group of workers and another *doing virtually the same work for the same working day*, the divergencies are sometimes large. The arbitrary factors can be classified, I suggest, as follows: (a) disparities in the ability to exploit consumers through different elasticities of product demand (that is, the possibility of foreign competition may, in some cases, cause product demand to be rather elastic and limit exploitative power); (b) differences in the willingness and power of unions to shut out would-be interlopers or witness the lay-off of members; (c) differences in the elasticity of substitution of labor-economizing assets for labor; (d) differing degrees in which earlier investment decisions have failed to allow for prospective strike-threat possibilities; and (e) psychological factors which influence the *will* to resort to strike-threat duress, especially when historically determined *relative* wage rates (whether fixed through the earlier expression of free market forces or the earlier exploitation of the strike threat) tend to be disturbed.

Under category (e) we must notice the very human attribute of envy, often indistinguishable from feelings of injustice. It is at times a headache-creating influence for the union leaders as well as for the managements of firms. Because particular groups of workers may and do have their wage rates raised through their unions' pressures, members of other unions naturally and normally expect *their* elected leaders to achieve more or less proportional gains for them. Should their leaders not be successful in this aim, the rank and file are apt to believe that their officials are poor bargainers, or perhaps appeasers. Even if the members do not blame their leaders, they still usually feel that they have somehow been unjustly treated. The continuous depreciation

196

of a currency seems to aggravate discontent as a result of this cause. But such attitudes exist, it should be stressed, regardless of inflation.

"Differentials" so determined are at times difficult to distinguish from (a) those resulting from differences in the inborn abilities of people to acquire valuable knowledge, skills and powers and (b) those resulting from differences in individual willingness or opportunities to invest time, effort and savings into improving their capacity to render valuable services. Under free labor market conditions, it would be *these* factors which would tend to bring about differences in relative remuneration. The initial differentials would then in turn create incentives for reactions which would tend constantly to change them. The direction of the changes would always be toward bringing the prices of the heterogeneous types of effort and skill which are incorporated in outputs into consistency with their natural scarcity prices (see pp. 92-93).

We notice for instance that, when duress-imposed agreements do not prevent it, managements often find it expedient to develop some more or less automatic system of insuring that employees shall be retained at what they are worth as their efficiency grows—especially efficiency due to experience. As the *likelihood* of their ability to command higher wage rates elsewhere—their "bargaining power" in the sense of their "opportunity value" (see pp. 64-67)—increases, their remuneration is raised without the need for their bargaining. Salary and wage increments are one (although the crudest) method of allowing for growing "opportunity values" as experience is acquired. Much more selective are systems of "job evaluation" and "merit rating." Such methods can assist not only in affording a rough guide for the promotions needed for staff retention, but they can help to build a formal wage structure which insures that the less aggressive, modest individuals who never ask for promotion shall not be overlooked when concessions are made to pressures from the less modest. It is a system which can engender general confidence that favoritism and prejudice are not leading to discrimination. But quite apart from the achievement of justice and good morale by such methods, they are conducive to efficiency in the acquisition, retention or lay-off of personnel and they can mitigate the consequences of nonmarket pressures which force relative wage-rate rigidity.

Differentials arrived at through "job evaluation" and "merit rating" are exactly the opposite of those imposed through duress. The former aim at justice. The latter negate it. Free market pressures tend to bring relative wage rates into consistency with one another.

Strike-threat resistance to market disturbance of any existing relationship between wage rates for different labor categories is today variously described as insistence on "established differentials," "established parities," "established relatives," and "due relatives." Once accepted, "established differentials" may be blindly enforced in certain industries for decades; be subject to change only after grievous harm has been caused; and even then, all too frequently, only following the failure of a strike, with a lingering aftermath of bitterness. Some "established parities" in Britain have lasted more than a half a century. So strongly does *the notion that what is customary is "fair"* bear on

197

today's situation, that managements may feel forced to preserve existing *relative* wage rates simply in order to avoid the *appearance* of injustice, however unfounded that appearance may be. Thus, H. A. Turner reports of Britain that "a large part of the strikes . . . turns out . . . not to consist of actions for wage increases as such, but of attempts to maintain a relationship the workers concerned regard as established by custom,"[1] an observation which suggests that "peaceful bargaining" (the mere *threat* to strike) is *also* frequently concerned with the maintenance of such relationships.

These problems of maintaining "due relatives" appear to have been much less important in the United States than in Britain, although they are by no means absent in the former. Changes in the relative remuneration of differently defined groups within an industry occur, I think, more frequently or easily in American industry, possibly because the economy is still more dynamic and fluid than the British. But the issues are the same in both countries, particularly in respect of the relations between the remuneration of craft skills on the one side and unskilled or semiskilled work on the other.

The sort of comparisons which give rise to what may be called "me-too" demands can be classified as interpersonal, interoccupational, interindustry, interarea and between unionized and nonunionized labor in the same industry. If one employee gets a "raise" his colleague will, as we have seen, expect a like gain. And wage-rate increases secured by the members of one union typically call forth demands for similar increases by other unions. If the wage rates of unskilled laborers in an occupation or industry are raised (say because those in this category happen to become *relatively* scarce), the higher-paid skilled artisans will feel that they have a moral right to preserve their former *relative* advantage; and the strike threat will be used to defend their interests in this sense. Again, when there are observed increases in the wage rates of nonunion workers, including most white-collar workers, one of the strongest inducements for insistence on the maintenance of "parities" arises. Union officials tend particularly to think it unfair that the earning power of any group of workers should rise conspicuously when the beneficiaries do not incur the expense of unions, that is, when, protected against exploitation only by the market, their earnings increase more rapidly than the increases the unions can show they are securing. But different abilities exist to avoid the displacement (and perhaps temporary unemployment) of workers in particular firms or occupations as labor costs are forced up for these reasons; and such considerations must in some measure affect the determination to maintain parities.

The phenomena produced through the purposeful maintenance of established differentials—a certain permanence or rigidity in the proportions of different categories of wage rates to one another—are today often referred to under the rather misleading term of "wage structure." The term *could* be used, of course, as a synonym for "frequency distributions of wage rates," however that frequency may be caused. But if there *is* a "structural relationship" among such categories in the sense of "*a complex of rigidi-*

ties''[2]—rigidities which hinder the stabilizing and coordinative mechanism of the value system—it can hardly be regarded as a "structure" ordained by Providence! It must be seen as the outcome of a set of institutions capable of being refashioned.[3]

Now the wage rates in an industry determine, *ceteris paribus*, the numbers employed in it and its contribution to aggregate income. It follows that in so far as the strike-threat system perpetuates earlier-determined "parities" for occupations *in different industries*, in a situation in which demand and supply conditions are changing, or if for that reason the proportions between the prices of different grades of labor within industries are frozen, it must be preventing the adaptation of the productive process to the changing relative scarcities of those grades. Clearly, then, the maintenance of "established differentials" militates against ideal resource use; but the deliberate use of union power to prevent the "leveling-up" tendency which is inherent in free market pressures, appears also as one of the clearest evidences of the inequalitarian consequences of the strike-threat system.

These consequences are, I judge, magnified during inflations because, with noninflationary expectations, managements are less inclined to capitulate. Again, when the value of the money unit is stable, although unions may sometimes be (in H. A. Turner's words) "more fearful of their members' wage rates falling below those of other industries than of the less determinate effect of a wage increase on employment,"[4] a situation of serious labor shortage can be caused at the one extreme and displacement of labor at the other. The latter reaction will, however, tend to create incentives for the unions to permit more coordinated relationships (or rather, less *dis*coordinated relationships) in interindustry or interoccupation differentials than occurs when inflation acts as a shield against competitive pressures.

In times of full scale war, the emergency situation often forces governments (as quietly as possible) to override the unions and insist upon "dilutions" which narrow the range of differentials. The aim is a more productive use of manpower. But greater equality of opportunity and earnings seems to be an almost invariable indirect result. Nevertheless, "dilutions" insisted upon during war emergencies are usually accompanied by promises that the unions' right to reimpose and perpetuate inequalities will be fully restored as soon as possible after the cessation of hostilities.[5] (See p. 227.)

Any satisfactory explanation of wage-rate frequency distributions must of course take into account the rigidities so enforced, *with their concomitant instabilities*. So powerful are the psychological pressures for maintaining custom-based proportions between different grades of work that, in Britain, unions sometimes submit their demands in the form of equal percentage increases for each grade. And in cases (exceptional cases) in which equal *absolute* increases to different grades have been requested or conceded (a procedure probably adopted where it has been difficult completely to flout market pressures toward a "leveling-up"),[6] serious friction has often followed. The arbitrariness is blatant. If all wage rates must rise because par-

199

ticular wage rates rise, then all prices should rise because a particular price rises. But, *ceteris paribus*, if inflation is absent, a rise in one set of wage rates must entail a fall in another unless displacement of labor is to occur and aggregate income to contract.

Dunlop touches on the consequences of *envy* or *irrationalities* which influence the use of the strike threat to preserve "established parities" but does not describe the influences as "envy" or "irrationalities." He says that, "for a variety of reasons," differentials once established "are not readily altered in a looser labor market."[7] He does not explicitly refer to factors such as those I have listed above (p. 196) as the chief determinants of the "parities" which are maintained. He simply argues that "the differentials are not transitory; they are not to be discussed as imperfections. . . ."; they "are not basically to be interpreted as a range of indefinite or random rates;" they "reflect the basic nature of product and labor markets."[8] Such phrases, I submit, mean nothing whatsoever. The truth is that the defense of established differentials against the competition of interlopers is a defense of privilege and a defense of inequality of incomes. This assertion is true whatever the motives of those who defend them, whether or not the wage rates protected were originally set under free market conditions or as a consequence of strike-threat power, and however human or understandable the moral weaknesses responsible may be.

Figures presented by Dunlop show that wage rates for truck drivers in Boston were (in 1951) about 54 percent higher in building construction trucking and oil trucking than in laundry and scrap iron work. But he appears to deny that these differentials were due to use of disparate monopolistic power. He holds that "each wage rate reflects a contour. Each is a reflection of the product market. Within any one contour the wage rates will tend to be equal. . . . But there are sharp differences in rates as among contours," due to historical factors which have "conditioned the labor supply so that the relative rates among contours are regarded as proper." He continues, ". . . Teamsters hauling oil and building materials come in contact with high-paid employees in their work operations, while laundry and scrap drivers have more contact with lower-paid employees."[9] But this discloses only the reasons why truck drivers in industries in which they have been relatively highly-paid in the past, feel it right that the competition with them of less-privileged workers in other fields should be held off; and that those who work in industries in which they associate with highly-paid workers (possibly because the latter can exercise monopolistic power effectively) would *like* to have higher earnings too. Admittedly they may have a stronger motivation for the exploitation of the community than others not subject to the same temptations. But surely, because one truck driver is an almost perfect substitute for another, the main reason why one such driver may have a wage rate almost double that of another (for example, between scrap metal and magazine trucking in Dunlop's examples) is that the magazine trade happens to be more exploitable than the scrap metal trade.

200

A quite separate suggestion to explain the anomaly, mentioned by Dunlop almost as though it were a minor qualification, is that "a larger emphasis is to be placed on the fact that competitive conditions permit higher pay" in the industries in which the truck drivers in fact command higher pay.[10] But by "competitive" he means "monopolistic." He mentions inelasticities of demand due to wages forming a smaller proportion of sales where truck drivers' remuneration is highest. But what does this all amount to other than an admission of what he has seemingly been trying to avoid saying, namely, that the wage-rate differences are largely explained by differing exploitative power against consumers, or different motivation to exploit that power in different industries? He even suggests that the union may be acting like a discriminating monopolist among different industries, exploiting each according to what it will bear.[11]

It would be wrong, however, to leave the impression that frozen relationships between wage rates in different categories of employment are not often subject to thaw, at least over long periods of time. Concrete experience suggests that, although some established differentials have persisted during more than half a century, the process of substitution we call "competition" can seldom be *wholly* suppressed in the absence of governmental edict. Attempts to *suppress* competitive forces very often simply *divert* them—as a rule into less economizing channels. Responses to changes in taste, to changes in preference for alternative products, to changes in production techniques, etc., sometimes give scope for the avoidance of customary rigidities in relationships and make possible changes in the relative speed with which revised wage rates in different industries and occupations are brought about;[12] and less frequently (as successive wage contracts are negotiated), they lead to changes in the ratio of earnings between skilled and unskilled work, even in union-dominated industries. It seems therefore that competition has, in one way or another, been tending to break through the restraints of duress-imposed costs and, in the course of successive wage negotiations, creating greater equality of earnings and reducing the range of differentials. For instance, attempts to maintain the wage rates of whites in a rigid ratio to those of nonwhites,[13] and wage rates for men in a rigid ratio to those of women, appear to have succeeded in most cases only in *slowing down*, not in completely suppressing, a gradual trend to greater equality.

The trend toward industrial unions has apparently strengthened the maintenance of established differentials in some ways and in other ways to have weakened it.[14] When powerful craft unions have found it profitable to merge with the larger, industry-wide organizations, the craft members have usually been careful to insure that any threat to their privileged position shall be minimized. The threat *is* often there—competition with them of "unskilled" ("unqualified") workers who might take on such of their operations as can be learned with little training by seizing opportunities of learning on the job. But the skilled usually have the power which attaches to prestige. The break-away of a craft would be felt to weaken an industrial union seriously, and when the craft sector can capitalize on its power to secede, union officials typically find it expedient to insist upon equal percentage increases for skilled workers when demanding increases for the unskilled. It all seems "only fair." This appears at times to have been the position, for instance, in the British cotton and steel industries.

There are some cases where crafts which have found it expedient to work through industrial unions have been able to raise the proportion of craft wage rates to those of the unskilled or semiskilled rank and file. Operating through an industry-wide organization, the crafts seem to have been able, in certain circumstances, to hold back competitive pressures from the unprivileged more successfully than they could have done if they had operated from separate craft unions. Compositors in the American printing industry have apparently been much more successful in preserving their differential earnings by maneuvering within an industrial union than have the builders operating as an independent craft organization.[15] The evidence is inconclusive; but there is no doubt that the crafts within an industry-wide union can sometimes exploit the charismatic force of the "solidarity of labor" slogan for their sectional advantage.

H. A. Turner suggests that the lower-paid workers acquiesce in established differentials because, if there is no apprenticeship barrier, they have the chance of promotion to the higher grades.[16] The situation could, of course, still appear unjust to those of the "unskilled" workers who have the least chance of admission to the privileged ranks, even where the unions have forced terms which compel promotion from within—that is, which prohibit the recruitment of skilled from outside present union ranks. This is one of the situations in which managements all too often act with what some have charged is cowardice (see p. 50). In Turner's words, "the employers have generally preferred to accept the situation rather than provoke disputes about differentials."[17]

It was pointed out above (p. 197) that free market forces are continuously tending to eliminate such differentials as are not reflections of the relative scarcity of different abilities and valuable attributes; and in industrial unions, because the unskilled often possess the greater voting power, the evidence suggests that they have at times been able to use that power to reduce the craft-imposed restraints on their competition. Where the votes of the lower-paid members are dominant, the union officials have found it a useful compromise to put forward their demands, not as requests for equal *percentage* increases but for equal *absolute* increases. Such concessions to free market pressures to equality of opportunity are, to be sure, very small concessions. But the assurance the lower-paid receive that they have been awarded a larger percentage rise than the higher-paid is probably enough, in most instances, to insure their acquiescence.[18] On the whole, the internal voting strength of the unskilled or semiskilled in industrial unions seems likely to serve as a very indirect method of weakening *some* of the restraints. A less inequitable use and remuneration of labor could result. It is in this respect alone that there is

202

any justification whatsoever for the suggestion of Reynolds and Taft that "the eventual development of trade unions in the lowest-paid industries may enable those industries to pull up closer to those which now stand at the top of the wage structure."[19] That claim can be defended solely if the workers' organization in unions somehow permits them to evade or smash through barriers created by the better-paid groups.

In so far as the general growth of union power in any country *has* been accompanied by greater equality of wage rates in an industry, this has almost certainly been due (a) to managerial initiatives leading to the substitution of semiskilled jobs for unskilled jobs, (b) to the voting dominance of the unskilled in industrial unions tending to mitigate craft exclusiveness, or (c) to the impossibility for other reasons of suppressing all competitive influences. These three factors are not independent.

Competition does, then, succeed at times in eroding, unobtrusively, one restraint on equality of opportunity after another, changing thereby the relative prices of different kinds of labor, and causing a narrowing of the range of wage differentials. But over long periods a straight-jacket of "due relatives" still obstructs the most productive deployment and development of human resources.

R. S. Morrison, a United States businessman, perceiving (a) the damage done to the community in its consumer role by the strike-threat system, (b) the arbitrariness and injustices of its bearing on relative wage rates, and (c) its responsibility for chronic inflation, has put forward a plan for fundamental reform.[20] He proposes, among other things, the elimination of the arbitrariness we have been discussing in this chapter via the application on a national scale of the techniques developed in connection with job evaluation within firms (see p. 197). The purpose of this part of his plan (which he calls the "Contax Plan") can be said to be to eradicate duress-imposed differentials.

The adoption of such a procedure could certainly do much to mitigate injustices *on its first application*. But the plan fails to allow for the coordinative function of divergencies of relative wage rates (for labor inputs of standard content and quality) among different firms, occupations, industries, and areas. An expanding firm will find it profitable to offer a wage premium to attract the labor it needs, while in a firm confronted with declining demand, wage cuts can (a) minimize the harshness of consumers' democracy and (b) provide an incentive for a sufficient number of workers to leave for activities in which their remuneration or prospects are higher (a reaction which will minimize the magnitude of mutually beneficial wage cuts).

Job evaluation within firms is defensible only when its purpose is to discern values which the free market is tending to determine but which managements (through neglect or defective judgment) have somehow failed to perceive, or to impose such values in cases in which managements have allowed favoritism, nepotism, or appeasement of personnel or unions to influence them in discriminations between individuals, sexes, races or age groups.

203

Similarly, to be defensible on a national scale, as under the "Contax Plan," the authority to which the task was entrusted would have to try to discover those cases in which monopolistic or monopsonistic influences were causing the wage rates of particular groups to diverge from free market values. And in the labor market as a whole, this can be incomparably more efficiently achieved through removing restraints than through the enactment of the values which the responsible authority judges would have resulted under those conditions.

NOTES

[1] H. A. Turner, in J. T. Dunlop, *Theory of Wage Determination* (London: Macmillan, Ltd., 1957), p. 123.

[2] The reader is reminded that by "rigidities" here is meant restraints imposed by man-made law ("controls") or man-made contrivance (that is, the enforcement of the standard rate). "Immobilities" due to, say, costs of movement; or costs of training (otherwise than costs due to such things as union barriers to investment in human capital); or custom which is not perpetuated by legislation or collusion, etc., these things are not here regarded as "rigidities," although they will have to be included among the determinants of the *frequency distribution* of wage-rates. They are no more "rigidities" than are mountain ranges. See Chapter 8, pp. 102, *et seq.*).

[3] A different kind of rigidity, which is not to be specifically discussed in this chapter, involves fixed relationships between *numbers* of journeymen and apprentices, or between *numbers* of skilled and unskilled, or in the relative *numbers* of those engaged in a variety of specified tasks in an industry.

[4] Turner, op. cit., p. 129.

[5] In South Africa, an attempt by the mines to preserve the right they had acquired during World War I to allow simple skills and simple responsibilities to be entrusted to Africans led to the most bitter and bloody strike in South Africa's history, in 1922. Two years later a Labor Party shared power, through a coalition with the Nationalists, and the Mines and Works Act of 1926 was passed to freeze previously established differentials through prohibiting skilled or responsible work by Africans. The leader of the ultimately successful strike of 1922 became the secretary of the Communist Party of South Africa almost immediately afterwards. Later, he became and remained its president until that party was outlawed. (See Hutt, *Economics of the Colour Bar,* pp. 61-2, 68-70.)

[6] Because equal *absolute* increases must cause greater equality.

[7] John T. Dunlop, *The Theory of Wage Determination* (London: Macmillan, Ltd., 1957), p. 22.

[8] Ibid., p. 22.

[9] Ibid., pp. 21-22.

[10] Ibid., p. 22.

[11] In the light of this notion, an interesting proposition would be the Teamsters' Union exacting the spoils of exploitation, achieved through discriminat-

ing monopoly power exercised on behalf of *all* its members, and dividing the spoils equally (or according to some other principle of equity) via private taxation and handouts, among *all* the truck drivers!

[12] For instance, in the 1950s, strike-threat destruction of prospective yields to replacement eventually forced the acceptance of low wage rates in the British cotton industry (relatively to those in other industries).

[13] The maintenance of such rigid relationships between the wage rates of whites and nonwhites has been achieved most successfully in South Africa, but only because union-enforced standard rates have been supported by the government-imposed economic *apartheid* policy. In periods in which there has been an temporary relaxation of collectivist policy, a trend toward a gradual diminution of inequality of opportunity and earning power has manifested itself.

[14] The situation in which the industrial union form of organization tends to weaken established differentials is to be discussed shortly.

[15] See Reynolds and Taft, in Bakke, Kerr, and Anrod, *Unions, Management, and the Public* (New York: Harcourt, Brace and World, 1967), p. 599.

[16] Turner, op. cit., p. 133.

[17] Ibid., p. 134.

[18] Even so, the resentments of the higher-paid groups are often aroused.

[19] Reynolds and Taft, op. cit., p. 602.

[20] R. S. Morrison, *The Contax Plan* (Morrison Publications, 1970). Mr. Morrison should be forgiven for believing that forcing up particular costs and prices forces up the general scale of prices. In the absence of *inflationary policy,* however, it means that other costs or prices must fall or that the economy is forced into a cumulatively worsening depression. But economists of world reputation are guilty of the same fallacy. What ''cost-push'' does, as we shall see, is render inflation politically expedient.

14
Fringe Benefits

IF THE strike-threat system has failed to transfer income from investors to workers, has it not at any rate insured that the general "conditions of labor" were improved? I propose to show (a) that the costs of all amenities enjoyed by employees at their place of work and such pecuniary perquisites as "severance pay," "vacation pay," pensions, and so forth simply represent certain uses to which labor's remuneration is (with or without the individual worker's approval) devoted; and (b) that managements (representing investors) had never to be fought to secure permission for the workers to devote their earnings to such objectives.

We have noticed that, apart from rising real earnings, the chief ways in which the "working classes" benefited during the industrial revolution were *firstly* in the form of an amelioration of the general working environment (as well as an equally noteworthy improvement in domestic living conditions), and *secondly* (although often via confused and irrational motivation) the choice of greater leisure in preference to a more rapid growth in *material* well-being (that is, in food, clothing, shelter, and so forth).

The process of distributing part of the fruits of rising real earning power in other forms than "wages" (in the narrower definition of that term) has grown steadily down to the present age. Wage rates in the sense of labor costs per unit of labor input have been increasingly offered as amenities which are purchased, so to speak, *for* the worker out of his earnings, by decisions which he is unable *individually* to influence. The kinds of things acquired for him in this manner cover a wide range, and the proportion of his earnings (that is, of labor costs) of which the utilization is removed from his personal discretion seems to vary widely. At one extreme, deductions for "fringe benefits" can cover a large proportion of the taxes for which the employee is liable. They might include, for instance, health, accident, disability, and other insurance premiums for himself and his dependents (that is, for maternity benefits or family endowment, pension contributions, "saving-up" for vacations ("vacation pay"),[1] unemployment compensation ("lay-off pay"), certain minimum savings allocations on his behalf, "profit-sharing" rights, etc.

Sometimes deductions for specified benefits are stipulated by legislation, but most often it is the union and not the government which dictates or overrules individual preference in these matters.

The growth over the years in the proportion of wages enjoyed in non-monetary terms, I judge to have been *chiefly* an automatic consequence of rising working-class affluence. As the real value which consumers have bid for labor's inputs has risen, the appropriate standards of conditions of service have seemed to rise more than proportionally. It is this which creates the chief justification for *the imposition* of the "choice of benefits" purchased through deductions from the full cash value of labor's contribution. Rising earnings during the present age have made it possible to argue somewhat confidently that the workers can now *afford* these new objectives, especially in so far as they have concerned indirect provision for the future. As economists put it, the immediate future on the workers' scales of preference has fallen in relation to the more distant future. That is, perhaps, one reason why union members have not come to cry more often, "wages, not fringes."

The partition of labor's remuneration between pecuniary and non-pecuniary forms is obviously independent of the factors which determine labor costs. The profitable employment of labor in any field is a function of total costs. Always it is the contractual price of work done, which includes any noncash rights, that is offered, "collectively bargained" and conceded. The value of fringes *could* have been received as money earnings had that been preferred. They do not, in themselves, entail any *superimposed* cost burden.

Yet the unions have created the impression that the worker's share of income can be effectively devoted to things like provision for retirement and disability only through aggressive union pressures! The truth is precisely the opposite. The payment of part of contractual remuneration as amenities or rights of money's worth, instead of in money itself has, on the whole, been encouraged by normal entrepreneurial incentives. Managements have had an obvious interest in the health, efficiency, comfort and contentment of personnel, and generally in the wise use of wages; and the fact that the advantages for which the worker is called upon to sacrifice money earnings *are* usually of a kind that contribute sensibly to his and his family's general well-being (including their security) is recognized as tending to discourage avoidable labor turnover. Hence although firms have mostly been averse to offering payment of wages in kind, except in the form of maintaining safe and pleasant working conditions as the best way of retaining or attracting staff, the profit incentive has, especially during this century, encouraged recourse to what has been termed (not very appropriately) "nonprice competition" for labor. Often the method is, indirectly, that of deductions from wages to meet "employers' contributions" to insurance, pension or other "benefit" funds. Money wage rates *in the narrow sense* have for this reason risen less rapidly than would otherwise have occurred.[2] But managements would never have resisted the acquisition of things like health or medical insurance, retirement contributions or other nonmonetary disposals of labor's remuneration *out of*

207

an unchanged aggregate labor compensation. On the contrary, managements have had every incentive themselves to offer the security and stability which the market for thrift and insurance can guarantee when such an offer has been judged to be an effective competitive inducement. (And managements can usually provide at least cost the administrative machinery required for group savings and insurance.) They have equally had an interest in offering all the amenities which make industrial or commercial enterprises safe, healthy, and happy establishments. The executives of this generation know that it is as important to achieve a harmonious atmosphere among personnel as it is for universities and colleges to strive for such an atmosphere among staff and students. Often they find it profitable to invest in objectives which, in some cases, can create the tone of a friendly club; although their efforts can hardly succeed if infiltrators instructed to sabotage the attempt are tolerated or unidentified (see pp. 50, *et seq.*, 87-89).

That managements (on behalf of investors) will tend generally to favor any system under which what amount to deductions from money wages finance "fringe benefits" is seldom perceived. This is in part because it is in the interests of the union hierarchies to represent fringe benefits as *something additional to wages*—an element wrested by negotiation or struggle from investors. But managements also (as we have seen, pp. 69-71) typically feel it to be strategically advantageous to allow it to appear that the benefits *are* essentially "employers' contributions," wrung from "profits" through the "bargaining power" of concerted action. Large concessions in money wages can then be avoided by small but showy concessions in fringe rights. It can be said, I think, that the psychological value of fringe benefits has frequently been greater than their cost under strike-threat bargaining. While union officials can say to their members, "Look at what we have won for you," managements can say, "Look at what we are doing for you."

Moreover, partly because public opinion is a factor in strike-threat strategy (see pp. 47-48), unions find it expedient to negotiate for additional compensation in fringe benefit forms, which tend to stand in a good light with the public. When they do so, they naturally encounter normal managerial resistance, not to concessions *in that form*, but to additional labor costs imposed by duress. The intended purpose to which the increased *per capita* claim on the value of the product is to be devoted is of subordinate importance in relation to labor's input costs.

We must recognize, then, that "the workers" have never had to *fight* to win the right to invest part of their earnings in provision for their future, or the right to devote some part of their wages to chosen amenities. Empirical studies on this topic are complicated because legal enactment (mainly in respect of health and safety) often removes the workers' (or the managements') discretion.[3]

I am inclined to think that the developments we are considering would most likely have gone further and had even more far-reaching consequences had it not so often been union tactics to maintain an atmosphere of veiled antagonism toward labor's partners (see pp. 50, *et seq.*, 87-89). The psychological warfare strategy, which is the inevitable concomitant of aggressive unionism, has militated against managerial incentives and initiatives to educate the worker to a wiser choice of ends as his means have grown. The scornful cry of "paternalism" has, in large measure, frustrated the *not disinterested* benevolence and leadership of managers. An enlightened use of labor's share (where managements can persuade labor to accept it) is universally to investors' advantage. In particular, the allocation of revenues to the creation of a pleasant atmosphere in the work-place can be more effective than "generous" wage rates as a means to the achievement of a contented and loyal staff with low labor turnover.[4]

The only real opposition which might be expected to fringe remuneration *as a mere deduction from money earnings*, that is, after contractual labor costs have been determined, is from the rank and file of union members. One can understand the workers wishing to express their own preferences. Indeed, only if the unions' pressures for partial payment in that form can be regarded as *educative* of their members, or if the inclusion of all members in an objective enables material economies from which all may benefit[5], is the removal of the decisions from voluntary choice (of workers remunerated) defensible in a free society. And whether the disposal of such withholdings from the worker's pecuniary earnings has been genuinely educative or a restraint on his freedom is not easy to judge. In my own judgment, fringe benefits *have* been on the whole to the advantage of the bulk of the union members.[6] Artisans and laborers tend notoriously to be improvident; and the illusion that "the employer" has been meeting the cost may alone have persuaded the workers to allow the use of part of their earnings in so sensible a manner. In other words, the unions may, partly as an incidental consequence of the tactics of strike bargaining,[7] have imposed a beneficial educative compulsion upon their members.

Some readers may feel, however, that it is by no means certain that free market pressures could not have achieved a far more rational choice of leisure and nonpecuniary forms of remuneration. Some libertarian scholars would claim, I think, that through the unhindered substitutions which constitute the competitive process, more efficient health, sanitary and safety conditions, and cheaper, less discriminatory insurance and retirement benefits might have been attainable. And it is indeed true that, *provided the objectives which make up noncash remuneration would actually have stood high in the workers' scales of preferences*, negotiations uninfluenced by fears of strike-threat compulsions could have brought forth a more satisfactory response to demands for these objectives. Had such ends *really* been individually demanded, they could have been met as effectively as demands for beer, baseball, and television, and often at a lower cost. With rising real incomes, and commercial incentives to offer and publicize endowment, health and disability insurance, many workers might well have decided, quite voluntarily, to make their own provision for old age and security. Obviously, every employee *could* arrange independently for investment of some part of his earnings in these objectives if he wished.

On the other hand, there are economists who insist that social justice requires a certain measure of forced thrift upon those persons who, if they do not make their own provision for the future, are apt to become a burden on others. This is a judgment which some "libertarians" question but which cannot be lightly dismissed. In so far as remuneration in the form of insurance or pension benefits has effected a guaranteed provision for old age and against the unpredictable contingencies of life, it has imposed a wise use of income on the worker. Nor can we reject the *possibility* that, through the bargaining strategy of the unions, a "beneficial" influence may have been indirectly exerted upon the composition (as distinct from the value) of labor's compensation—an influence which managements themselves may have been unable alone to exert.[8]

In using the adjective "beneficial" here I must insist that it is based on a challengeable but not necessarily wrong philosophical premise. John Stuart Mill argued that the overruling of an individual's preferences and actions for his own good (by the tyranny of public opinion or indoctrination and private or government compulsion) is never justified. The individual's "own good," he contended, either physical or moral, "is not a sufficient warrant." But as I see things, a compulsion intended superficially to protect an individual from possible future distress may force him to pay for the provision made and protect others who might otherwise be called upon (through their charitable feelings or through taxation) to support him when things go wrong. That is, the confiscation of wages for investment in insurance against employment hazards or retirement pensions may be held to protect others rather than primarily assist the wage receiver whose free choice is overruled. Certainly an improvident person or a drug addict is likely later on to become a burden on the charitableness of the provident or the taxpayer and the ethical consensus surely does make it appear desirable that the charitable should be protected from the full cost of having to shoulder support of those whose earlier thriftlessness or other irresponsibility has landed them (and perhaps their dependents) in destitution.[9] Again (a less obvious point), any compulsory thrift element is likely to improve a worker's morale and productivity.

Nevertheless, with certain kinds of benefit, such as costly seniority privileges in respect of "employment security," it seems as if many adversely affected would object vigorously if they had any say or if they understood; and this could apply in other circumstances also. F. A. Harper has aptly illustrated the difficulty by means of an imaginary letter to management from a worker, referring to "paid vacations," saying that his family needed the extra income more than he needed the extra week of leisure. "Please reconsider this fringe detriment you have imposed on us."[10] Managements could, of course, specify the contractual remuneration as, say, $400 per month, of which $325 is the monthly pecuniary wage, $20 pension or provident fund contribution, $15 health, medical and workmen's compensation insurance benefits, $20 provision for "paid vacations" and $20 for all other fringe benefits, including health and safety costs. But most managers would feel that to attempt to enlighten their staff in this manner would do more harm than good.

Opposition to fringes sometimes does occur among the rank and file in the unions. They have been known to refer to nonpecuniary benefits as "jam on the pudding," "gravy on the meat," or "trading stamps instead of cash discounts"; and such cynicism often has more than an element of shrewd justification. Yet as we have seen, it is indeed possible—and the possibility must not be minimized—that the *educative persuasions* needed to induce the typical artisan or laborer to sacrifice cash wages for such things as contributions to group medical insurance or provident and pension funds, have been achievable only through reliance upon the illusion that the "employer" can be made to pay. The very term "employers' contribution" itself perpetuates the probably beneficial delusion (see pages 206-209). Noncash compensation, however advantageous for the worker, may not otherwise have been regarded as an effective competitive inducement in the attraction and retention of labor. But although the illusion may have been indirectly to the worker's advantage, *the student* of these things ought not to be left under any misapprehension. Fringe rights and benefits are an alternative to cash receipts, while cash wages *plus* such rights and benefits are in general met by consumers, not by stockholders.

I have referred to the incidental advantages which the reduction of pecuniary wage rates under union pressure, to pay for *noncash* or fringe compensation (sometimes called, misleadingly, "nonwage" benefits), may be held to have achieved. But we must beware of assuming that such advantages are universal and automatic. Most often they are mere mitigations of the strike-threat system. What must always be kept in mind is that every duress-imposed rise in the cost of labor inputs, as distinct from every change in the relative cash and noncash portions of labor's remuneration (which need not raise labor costs), reduces the flow of wages and renders the distribution of the flow less equal and less equitable. And certain forms of fringe benefit seem to be particularly likely to be sought (by way of the strike threat) only when the price of labor can be forcibly raised for the advantage of those who retain their jobs at the higher labor price, or who can monopolize the occupation in face of a rising demand schedule for the product.

Consider, for example, "job security" as a "fringe benefit." There *have* been successful strikes to prevent announced dismissals. But this is one of the ways in which the disinvestment of the assets in an undertaking can be accelerated and the mere prospect of which can destroy wage-multiplying developments on a great scale. The security of *all* workers is clearly reduced thereby. The same objection applies of course to job security in the form of "severance pay" or "lay-off pay," or of contractual discrimination on the grounds of seniority (length of service in the industry or firm) in the event of dismissals when labor comes to be priced out of employment.[11] And when the right of managements to dismiss redundant workers in general is not challenged, the inclusion of "job security" provisions in an employment agreement *almost necessarily* means greater security for some at the expense of lessened security or reduced earning power for others.[12]

When simple guaranteed employment for a stipulated period is offered without discrimination and in a free market, it is an indication of great managerial confidence in demand and supply conditions in the industry, and especially of trust that those employed will not resort to the strike threat to destroy investors' security. When such a contract is offered, it is nearly always one-sided, that is, with no "lock-in" provision. It is offered simply as a type of competitive labor attraction through which managements believe that they can buy the services of certain people at least cost. But contractual employment security as a competitive inducement is rarely found. Typically, it is forced on managements by strike-threat duress, and accompanied by a substantial rise in prospective labor costs at the time of its imposition. This *can* be so even when it takes the relatively reasonable form of long dismissal notice requirements. The enhancement of costs brought about for that reason must curb the rate of growth (or cause the decline) of any undertaking or industry compelled to accept it, not because the unions prefer their members to sacrifice pecuniary earnings for it (the reduced cash incomes providing, so to speak, premiums for employment insurance), but because, in those circumstances, labor costs as a whole increase and cause thereby a greater degree of contrived scarcity. Moreover, any benefits achieved are likely to favor specially powerful interests within the unions, particularly when discrimination on grounds of seniority with the firm or industry is required for lay-offs; and there are several other ways in which noncash forms of remuneration (in Bowen's words) "permit a rather subtle, yet a profitable form of wage discrimination."[13]

When the magnitude and form of the noncash part of labor's remuneration are a matter of governmental decision, the danger of the politically weak being sacrificed is very real. And sheer arbitrariness—a consequence of the workers' preferences being ignored—is an even greater danger. Politicians are hardly likely to worry very much about the *wantedness* of the objectives purchased through the reduction of pecuniary wage income.

There are indications for instance that, in underdeveloped countries, progress toward higher material living standards is being slowed down seriously through the imposition of conditions of employment which might be appropriate for the affluent proletariats of the United States and Western Europe but not for such "backward" populations as have been unable yet to price their services to attract wage-multiplying assets, and provide the investment security necessary. What may be a wise composition of labor's remuneration in highly industrialized regions can be a grave burden on peoples whose initial penury demands different priorities in purchases and in the form of productive effort. The influence of the International Labor Organization in this respect has probably been a major factor in maintaining the huge gap which has been observed to have arisen in the industrially backward countries between the real earning power of the emerging artisan class and the traditional agricultural and unskilled laboring class. The full incentives of market inducements to orderly modernization may have been lost through the failure to perceive that costly factory amenities are "paid for" by the workers who live under them. The profit motive to bid workers away from low-paid laboring jobs to relatively well-paid semiskilled and skilled jobs, under (for them) better working conditions, has almost certainly been weakened because too large a proportion of labor's remuneration has been absorbed in environmental costs. That is, the "labor-cost mix" is not what appeals most to rural laborers. There is no suggestion here, of course, that the workers in countries which are beginning to industrialize should not make the fullest use of what the world has learned over the last two centuries about industrial health, safety and environmental considerations generally. Moreover, as such workers progress, the larger will be the proportionate share of noncash wages they may be expected to prefer. But their preferences (or the choice of benefits delegated to their trusted advisers) ought to be rational, in the sense that the full implications of any choice are among the determinants of that choice. And if they are wise, they will perceive among other things that it is in the interests of their competitors in the developed areas of the world represented by the ILO to advise or "educate" them in a manner which reduces their ability to compete and slows down their rate of material advancement.

There is another rather ominous feature of the growing proportion of labor's remuneration which is coming to be received as "welfare" services. The contributors are increasingly tending to receive, not the actuarial value of their compulsory contributions to insurance or pension schemes, but benefits more or less adapted according to their "need." Thus, not all sickness benefit payments are being made in proportion to an individual's scale of contributions, as under "commercial" schemes. Certainly, any redistribution from high premium to low premium contributors for standard benefits, if voluntarily accepted by the former, may be regarded as laudable—just as would be a voluntary redistribution of the pecuniary earnings of the better-paid workers for the benefit of their less fortunate comrades. But no one ever argues *explicitly* that pension benefits should be based on "need," while contributions should be based on earnings ("ability"). The traditional attitude of the higher-paid workers under typical labor-union ideologies hardly suggests that altruism—concern for the interest of their poorer comrades—can provide an explanation. Presumably, therefore, the development has been tolerated because the aggregate sum involved has so far been small, or because the more productive and higher-paid workers have not perceived a forced redistribution in which they have been the losers.

It may help us to view these questions in due perspective if we constantly remind ourselves that managements have no more right to be *generous* to the workers (with fringes or anything else) than the managements of stores have the right to be generous to their customers, or banks to be generous to borrowers with their depositors' capital. (See p. 113.) All have the duty not to indulge in any form of sharp practice and to be strictly honest in their dealings. Managers are in the position of trustees in their relation to stockholders. Moreover, it is rather absurd to regard generosity on the part of one or other party to a bargain as a factor determining the terms of the bargain.[14]

For instance, in time of war, managements have often interpreted correctly the wishes of stockholders when they have paid honoraria to those of their staff who have served in the armed forces. Sometimes, with the same justification, honoraria have been paid to amateur sportsmen who have attained prominence of which the firm has been proud (although that is often profitable personnel or publicity policy). When sheer misfortune has hit a member of the staff—particularly one who has served the firm for many years—managements have often rightly interpreted stockholders' wishes in giving noncontractual financial assistance. And during inflation, with a similar justification, managements have been known to increase the pensions of former employees—victims of the monetary policy that the strike-threat system has made expedient. But even if we can assume that, in such circumstances, there is no ulterior motive for *ex gratia* payments—like the goodwill of the firm—this does not affect the issue raised here. In any realistic assessment of the nature of collective bargaining about the price of labor, the notion of *generosity* on either side ever entering into the picture can hardly find a place. When a corporation poses as "generous" to its workers, it reminds one of the sort of "generosity" implied when "free gifts" or "three for the price of two" are offered by a store.[15]

An economic system which develops under free market institutions is likely to give unstinting opportunity for expression of those "other-regarding" emotions and conations which are manifested in generosity and altruism. For contrary to what is usually assumed, avarice, greed and envy are aroused, and the sources of charitableness and generosity quenched, when people are allowed, by restraint of the right of substitution, or via voting-power under corrupt democracy, to enrich themselves at the expense of others. Benevolence and unobtrusive charity are characteristic of societies in which the relatively successful or fortunate feel secure from depredations (governmental or strike threat). But these virtues are expressed *in the use made of individual incomes and not in the process of determining those incomes*, that is, not when arriving at the value of the product of labor or the value of the services of assets. An understanding of this truth by those who presume to be the world's moralists could, I sometimes think, work with unparalleled success toward achieving the ideals which they champion and we all accept.

The ethical issues are impressively treated in two recent books—*Envy*, by Helmut Schoeck,[16] and *The Modern Corporation and Social Responsibility*, a debate between H. G. Manne and H. C. Wallich.[17]

NOTES

[1] We can regard leisure (including "paid vacations") as a "fringe benefit," but as having been purchased in a way which leaves a reduced compensation out of which *other* fringes can be acquired.

[2] There appear to have been other reasons for the recent trend toward a rise in fringe benefits. During the inflationary decades since World War II,

direct wage-rate increases have at times been frowned upon, and entrepreneurial competition to retain or attract labor has tended therefore to take the form of nonpecuniary offers. Another special stimulus to nonpecuniary compensation has been due to pension contributions and the like being accorded specially favorable tax treatment.

[3] Someone has pointed out that the conditions of cowsheds and stables generally have improved enormously over the century with no union pressures to bring about the improvement!

[4] The courtesy of businessmen toward their staff and toward their clients is not *hypocrisy,* simply because they know that lack of courtesy would be harmful to them. Such relations still often lead to genuine friendships. And the inculcation of loyalty to the firms with which employees have wage contracts ought not to be deplored.

[5] The circumstances envisaged are those which the economists describe as "externalities" (see pp. 272-273).

[6] If the income withheld *is* more wisely used for the workers's benefit than would have resulted from his own decisions, a strong argument can be made out for it. I discussed this difficult and controversial issue in Chapter 17 of my *Economists and the Public* (Jonathan Cape, 1936).

[7] I say *partly* because I am not suggesting the absence of any enlightment about income disposal on the part of union officials.

[8] But nonunion firms *have* often found it profitable to offer pension schemes and similar benefits, both as an aid to recruitment and as a method of maintaining stability of personnel.

[9] We cannot of course talk of "ethical consensus" when governments seek to enrich majorities of voters at the expense of minorities of voters or the unenfranchised. See W. H. Hutt, *Politically Impossible. . . . ?*, Part IV.

[10] F. A. Harper, *Why Wages Rise* (Irvington-on-Hudson, N. Y.: Foundation for Economic Education, 1957), pp. 92-93.

[11] I have not read of any explicit "agreements" in which age as such (as distinct from seniority in the firm or industry) constitutes the basis for discrimination in lay-off.

[12] There are of course exceptions. The offer of what is called "tenure" in public service and university circles *can* be a particular kind of wage inducement.

[13] William G. Bowen, *The Wage-Price Issue: A Theoretical Analysis* (Princeton: Princeton University Press, 1960), p. 96.

[14] This is not to deny that an act of altruism may *follow or accompany* a bargain or that a voluntary transfer of income may be the sequel to or the accompaniment of a bargain. Nor does the assertion imply a denial that a gift may be tactfully hidden in the terms of a transaction.

[15] On the question of generosity expressed by participants in a free market system, see p. 113.

[16] Helmut Schoeck, *Envy—A Theory of Social Behavior* (New York: Harcourt, Brace and World, 1970).

[17] H. G. Manne and H. C. Wallich, *The Modern Corporation and Social Responsibility* (Washington, D.C.: American Enterprise Institute, 1972).

15
Labor's Share

IN CHAPTER 3 I referred to the widespread conviction that, through the "bitter struggles" of more than two centuries, unions managed to acquire a larger share of aggregate income for the workers. This quite general belief that history records a redistribution in favor of the working class as a whole, through victorious strike-threat warfare (whether defensive or aggressive), is a formidable, illusory stereotype. In this and the next chapter we shall be concerned with changes in the *proportion* of income accruing to labor.

Some economists have wondered why anybody could be interested in such a question. If it should happen that, in the absence of the strike-threat, aggregate nonlabor income would rise proportionately to labor income, while aggregate income was greatly increased *and more equally distributed* (and I have tried to show that a more equal distribution *would* be the consequence of a strike-free economy), why should a possibly smaller percentage of wages to aggregate income be a matter of concern? The actual flow of wages would be much greater; and given the greater real earnings, why should not the individuals making up "labor," *through that very process*, have become owners of a greater proportion of assets, receiving an additional income in that manner? Why then worry about labor's share?

The answer is that the strike threat system is applauded, or respected, or tolerated because it is believed to bring about a more equal or a more "just" distribution of income between labor and capital. From the standpoint of the unions and their apologists, the "prime objective" of the system is, according to Golden and Ruttenberg, to exercise "constant pressure for a larger share of the nation's annual income,"[1] or, as Mathew Woll puts it, "organized labor's obligation to its members is to pursue wage increases until . . . the national income is distributed equitably and stays so distributed."[2]

Moreover, *the growth in labor's absolute real income during the period over which unionism was growing has left an impression that a rising relative share of income was gained for labor*. It is important that this stereotype be disturbed. I have found from personal experience that academicians of distinction—open-minded in the spheres in which they are expert—believe, almost without exception, that the higher standards of living (real wage rates and working conditions) which the working classes enjoy today, in comparison with, say, 1880, or 1900, or 1930, were won against reluctant "employers" after years of strikes and strife. They are nearly all convinced that a large gain was gradually achieved at the expense of "property." The illusion has had a profound influence on the attitudes of sociologists and scientists with a smattering of economics, to say nothing of judges, schoolteachers, clergy, journalists, and union officials. The fact is that, in a country like the United States, real income per head has been growing so rapidly that, *even if labor's proportion had fallen materially this century, the average real wage rate could still have risen prodigiously*.

The causes of the phenomenal rise in working-class affluence since the industrial revolution have been summarized in Chapter 3. It will suffice here to stress that income redistribution has been a factor in raising the material condition of *the poorer workers* only insofar as a reduction of inequalities in the natural scarcity values of the workers' powers (their efforts and skills) has been brought about; and this has been a process in which union pressures have played a negative role. But the results contribute to a general illusion that a rise in labor's proportion of aggregate income has been achieved.

There are grounds for holding that the *most important* consequences of (a) the better use of the qualities of the people (via upward mobility), and (b) the better use of a growing stock of assets (which we have seen are the true origin of growing working-class well-being) must have been to cause the remuneration of *both* income categories to rise more or less in the same proportion *even if not always in exactly the same proportion* (because the one can hardly be expected perfectly to balance the other). I have, I maintain, already explained why the unions' conventional influence on wage rates must necessarily fail to bring about any lasting net redistribution in the "private" sector if they rely on the strike-threat weapon. But I must be in a position to answer critics who may say, "Well, that's all theory! What are the facts? The henchmen of the strike-threat system hold that it *can* change the proportions in a socially defensible way. Can you prove them to be wrong? Can you show that income has not been redistributed from the rich to the poor, or from investors to workers, during the period in which the strike threat has been increasingly used?" I certainly *can* show this; but no one can *prove* from the findings of statistical inquiries alone that labor's share would not have been still smaller in the absence of union pressures!

In his great study of human action,[3] Von Mises has explained why the *type* of reasoning on which the foregoing analysis has relied does not *require* the type of empirical confirmation to which I am about to appeal. If statistical evidence seems not to confirm the conclusions, that is presumably proof that the data, or the treatment of the data, must in some way be defective. But the economists' logic has never been infallible: still less have empirical or political assumptions at the stage at which inferences are made (to put it mildly) always been unchallengeable. Hence in the following chapter

(Chapter 16) I shall submit my general conclusions to the test of broad consistency with statistical studies.

The matter of labor's share in income is among the topics to which several distinguished statistical economists have directed ingenious studies. Through analysis of income, production and pricing data, they have tried to discover what change there has been in this share over various time periods. I shall in due course quote their verbal summarizations of what I regard as their most relevant conclusions. Unfortunately, the difficulties met with in such investigations are formidable, and in spite of all the ingenuity the investigators have exercised, the significance of their findings is perforce sometimes rather limited.

My reference to these difficulties implies no criticisms of those statistical economists whose inferences, including policy inferences, are conditioned by efforts at reconciliation with the conceptual clarity of "orthodox" analysis. This is exactly what Schultze and Weiner are attempting in their scholarly introductory essay to *The Behavior of Income Shares*, an important symposium of statistical and econometric studies of the determinants of the relative shares of labor and capital.[4] And it is what Tibor Scitovsky also is concerned with, in respect of the whole field of "empirical" contributions on this subject, in the learned article with which that symposium opens.[5]

During the last quarter of a century there has been a remarkable interest shown by economists in the visible income redistribution consequences of strike-threat policy—indeed, we have witnessed what Gregg Lewis has called "an outpouring of empirical research on unions and wage differentials."[6] This "outpouring" reflects, indirectly, widespread misgivings about the labor movement. Nevertheless the investigations have been carried out with a scrupulous objectivity and the researchers have mostly allowed their figures to speak for themselves. But partisans of the unions seems to be uneasy about it. Dunlop almost suggests that the statistical economists are showing a morbid or unhealthy interest in the unions as determinants of wage rates and labor cost! He says, "The persistent concern with the impact of unionism as an institution perhaps reflects a preoccupation with defending or condemning the institution as a whole." But, insists Dunlop, "the institution is here and is likely to stay,"[7] as though to suggest that whether the determination of labor's remuneration under duress is beneficient, innocuous or pernicious is hardly a matter which should worry the serious scholar. It will happen anyway!

At the same time, Dunlop thinks it worthwhile to refer to some of the limitations of empirical investigations, as though they must necessarily invalidate such studies. But only if, which I do not think is true, the investigators are blind to the pitfalls do his warnings have applicability. In some fields, admittedly, there is no way of bringing the categories and concepts which economists have found useful into close correspondence with the cruder categories and concepts with which the statistician must be content. Yet it *is* possible to attempt to determine how the *relative* shares in aggregate income of "labor," variously defined, on the one side and *all other factors* lumped together on the other appear to have changed over periods in which the strike-threat influence has been growing. And it *is* possible to compare movements of wage rates in the unionized and nonunion sectors. For such studies to be done satisfactorily, however, there are conceptual problems which must be faced.

What I have just termed "all other factors" are usually described as "capital" or "property." A better term for this would be "investors," for *all* assets have been invested in. We sometimes talk, not misleadingly, of "human capital" and of the "investment" in it of time, effort and resources. But the yield to capital in such a form is conventionally treated as the remuneration of labor. Fortunately, this usage does not greatly hinder our present task.[8]

At one time, in discussions of income distribution, economists classified agents of production as "land, labor, capital and enterprise." Today, "land" is classified as "capital" and the remuneration of "enterprise" is classed as part of the yield to "capital." Such a classification is justified simply because a certain division of labor in respect of the risk-taking or entrepreneurial function realistically links enterprise with property ownership. *But properly visualized, entrepreneurial remuneration is neither remuneration of capital nor remuneration of labor. It may accrue to either (positively as profits or negatively as losses) according to which assumes the risk of the entrepreneurial decision turning out to have been wise or lucky (or unwise or unlucky).* Those earlier economists showed real insight who classified entrepreneurship separately, as "enterprise," an agent of production distinct from the other three agents—land, labor, and capital. For the yield to "enterprise," namely, "profit," is payment by results for the most important function that is performed on behalf of the community—prediction and responsible action to determine the composition of the stock of assets and/or valuable skills. Through this function, entrepreneurs determine the form of economic activity. In the vast majority of cases, however, it is the owners of capital who assume most of the risk which the entrepreneurial factor involves; in empirical studies there is no satisfactory way of isolating either the interest element or the labor element in the owners' income; and hence for practical reasons it *is* usually appropriate to classify profits (positive or negative) together with interest as nonlabor income. Under this classification, the part of income with which "labor's share" is usually compared is the whole of the remainder, in other words, that earned by "property" or "capital" *and* "enterprise." It is all nonlabor income (as I have said) "lumped together," and consists of interest (which includes rent) *plus* profits and *minus* losses. Nevertheless, we must remind ourselves that there are no legal or institutional barriers to contractual arrangements under which labor becomes the residual claimant and takes the profit.[9] A rather different complication is that the worker, in seeking the most remunerative fields for acquiring skills or for selling his services, is acting as an entrepreneur; and the yield to his shrewdness or enterprise, although received as "wages," is in principle a form of "profit." This is a matter of small importance in the present context, although it will be of great importance in another (see pp. 223-224).

In some studies, "labor's share" covers the earnings of artisans and laborers only. In others, it covers all "employee compensation," that is, all forms of contractual remuneration for services rendered by people, and it is this connotation that has been most often used. "Salaries," which are conceptually distinguishable from "wages" only in the most nebulous way, and statistically distinguishable only by arbitrary definition,[10] have usually been reckoned as part of the remuneration of labor in the broadest sense, and regarded as part of "labor's share." But this share covers, as we have seen, a yield to investment in human capital.

And we have another conceptual difficulty to face. To the extent to which investors who have not anticipated or adequately evaluated strike-threat consequences are exploited, it is, as we have seen (pp. 135-137), *through the seizure of some part of investors' property and the income stream which that property yields*. There is clearly no way in which empirical studies can isolate this element and count it as part of the yield to property.[11]

Before referring to the findings which meticulous statistical investigations have reached about changes in the income distribution pattern, as reflected in the relative shares of "labor" and "investors," it is important to consider, in the background of the analyses presented in the earlier chapters, *what we should have expected to find has been happening to these two great statistically defined magnitudes since the beginnings of this century*.

Firstly, we have certain "observable circumstances" (including the *unpredicted* use of the strike threat) which would have led us to expect that, in the United States, since the 1880s, and especially since 1935, labor's share would have been increasing (circumstances discussed on pp. 226, *et. seq.*).

Secondly, we have certain other "observable circumstances" of an offsetting nature, which we should have expected more or less to have neutralized those tendencies.

I hope to show that these discernible determinants of relative shares are *probably* responsible for the rough constancy for labor's share that empirical studies have established, despite continued efforts to raise that share, and in spite of illusory evidences that those efforts may have had some success.

All economizing displacements, *considered in isolation*, tend to reduce the *percentage* share of those whose assets or labor provide the services economized. For example, every time unskilled or unprivileged workers manage to sneak through the fences and work their way into a skilled or privileged occupation, their entry tends, *ceteris paribus*, to reduce the *relative* share of labor in any activity affected. But we cannot validly draw inferences after merely considering the consequences "in isolation." For *firstly*, the cheapening of any kind of labor tends to attract in additional assets to cooperate with it, and this may be expected, over the whole economy, to work toward restoring the former proportions. That is, the more easily capital can be attracted by relatively low labor costs in any activity, the weaker will be the tendency for the better use of labor to reduce labor's proportion. And secondly, the more easily labor can move into fields in which the tools of

220

production are increasing in efficiency, the weaker will be the tendency for technological progress to raise labor's proportion.

The point can be explained in more general terms. In every productive activity the workers are, so to speak, demanding the services of complementary assets and of risk-taking, while investors (as owners and entrepreneurs) are demanding the services of the workers. Both invest inputs (services embodied into outputs), the value of the resulting outputs being shared according to a contract (influenced by free or restrained market forces). In each case, any economization of labor expresses an increased demand for the services of the complementary assets used, just as any economization of such assets expresses an increased demand for the services of the labor used. Each economy tends therefore to raise the opposite party's relative share.

Exactly the same principle is relevant with diseconomies (such as an earthquake, or the raising of a wage rate by a strike threat, or a collusively enforced output restraint). The reduced contribution of a factor will mean a rise in its percentage share in the value of the output. *The general principle* can be stated as follows.

Given unchanged knowledge, the application of further increments of any factor of production to a fixed "amount" of any other factor of production, or to a fixed "amount" of any unchanging combination of other production factors will, in the absence of any economies of scale, yield less than proportionate *average* returns. Thus, a reduction in the number of man-hours worked,[12] *the volume of complementary assets being assumed unchanged in magnitude and composition*, must mean a rise in labor's share. A growth in the stock of assets in an industry, with the number of man-hours unresponsive, must have a similar effect. To put it differently, if the quantity of services rendered by any factor of production rises or falls *relatively* to an assumed fixed quantity of services which owners of complementary factors of production find it profitable to retain or bring into a particular productive activity, the proportion of the value of the product which accrues to those who provide relatively larger or smaller inputs will fall or rise respectively.[13]

Such are the basic factors determining the division of aggregate income between investors (property) and labor. We are concerned, that is, with changes in the relative supplies of productive services rendered by assets and those rendered by labor; and various changes in these magnitdes (and in other factors) can be observed to have been occurring over history—changes which, superficially considered at any rate, could have been expected to be affecting the proportions. The following changes are relevant:

(1) in the size, race and sex distribution of the population;
(2) in society's valuation of leisure, including changes in (a) the ages at which different classes of juveniles are allowed to compete with their elders and enter various remunerated employments, and (b) the ages at which people are encouraged or forced to retire from remunerated activity (generally or in specified sorts of occupation);

(3) the extent to which certain kinds of work are regarded as properly reserved for a particular class, sex or race;

(4) in the extent to which the fixing of wage rates under duress occurs (that is, the extent of deliberate contrivance of labor scarcity in that manner);

(5) in saving preference schedules (that is, in people's desire to provide for the future);

(6) in the rate at which (given saving preference) the process of economizing displacement assists the net accumulation of assets (through raising prospective yields to investment) and thereby increases investors' bidding (as intermediaries) for labor, which in turn multiplies the yield to labor;

(7) in the extent to which the economizing-displacement process tends to be neutral, or to cheapen either labor or assets *relatively* to one another;

(8) in consumer preferences as between outputs of labor-intensive and capital-intensive production.

It should be noticed that (1), (2), (3) and (4) (empirically representable by the number of man-hours actually worked *and* the distribution of those hours over tasks of different degrees of productivity) represent *labor's bidding for the services of the tools (that is, of the assets) which multiply labor's yield*, while (5) and (6) represent investors' bidding for labor, a bidding which actually expresses the multiplication just referred to. Changes (7) and (8) bring in a different kind of influence.

Now superficially this notion of labor's bidding for the services of complementary factors may appear to involve a paradox and scope for confusion in other ways. The composition of the great complex of demands for the productive services of both men and assets is determined, as we have seen, by people in their consumer role. That is, consumers—the ultimate employers—demand the joint product. Hence when investors (as intermediaries) demand services for incorporation into assets (work in progress), theirs is a derived demand. That demand is expressed *through* their initiative when they are residual claimants, as they virtually always are. But because labor hardly ever takes the residual share, *this does not mean that the workers are not entrepreneurially involved*. The wage system relieves the workers from the greater part of the risk burden; but they are still buying the services of assets, and profiting or losing from the wisdom or unwisdom *of their policy* in so doing. The wage terms on which they work in any activity are a major determinant of the rate of flow of services into replacement and growth of the assets they use. *Ceteris paribus* the cheaper their services the greater will be the investment their "bidding" calls forth.

It is through interpretation of this empirically observable complementary relationship between assets and labor that we can perceive, I suggest, the main reason for the constancy of proportions. Assets (of all degrees of physical or economic perishability) are the tools of labor, and increases in their quantity and quality (their cheapening) mean increases in labor's earnings. An overwhelming proportion of the value of assets is in constant process of consumption and replacement at various rates, and the costs of replacement as well as of growth are borne jointly (out of the realized value of the output) by the workers and the owners of the assets. Hence, a general cheapening of labor will mean the cheapening of assets;[14] the magnitudes (a) aggregate real value of the services of assets and (b) aggregate real value of the wages flow, are not wholly independent of one another; and some tendency to stability in the relative value of their shares is therefore to be expected. It is true that a general cheapening of labor would otherwise tend to reduce labor's relative share (while raising its absolute share); but because cheap labor means cheap tools, there will be a countervailing tendency to maintain the relative shares which other factors have determined.

What may *at first* seem to be a separate reason for the hardly changing proportions (in spite of strenuous efforts to transfer income from the one sector to the other) is put forward in a rigorously argued contribution by Lebergott. On the realistic assumption that wage rates in the industries which *produce* capital goods will in practice change more or less in the same proportion as wage rates in the industries which *use* capital goods, he infers that this explains why in practice the price of capital service tends to "bear a long-term proportionality to that of labor."[15] This long-term proportionality, he shows, "derives from the fact that the supply forces working to fix the price of capital are dominantly wage costs in the capital-producing industries and those that supply them. In the competitive market these wage costs parallel wage cost changes in capital-using industries because wage changes for identical occupations must bear a parity with one another in all employing industries."[16] G. Garvy restates Lebergott's conclusions as follows: "In ultimate analysis, the cost of capital goods can be reduced in essence to wage costs incurred in previous periods. Therefore, in the long run, the price of capital goods must bear constant long-term relation to that of labor."[17] As I see the issue here, it is that rising labor costs of supplying and replacing relatively long-life assets (which are assumed to rise more or less proportionally to rising labor costs imposed on industry generally) affect labor adversely in the industries which must use such assets and meet the interest, depreciation charges and upkeep costs. Lebergott is, I think, envisaging labor in what I have termed its "entrepreneurial role." He sees it as I do, as continuously demanding the services of capital equipment—demanding with the value of the services the workers contribute as inputs. Duress-imposed real labor costs tend therefore to recoil to labor's disadvantage and bring about no gain to the workers as a whole.

The lesson is perhaps clearest if we think of labor costs in the iron and steel, the construction and the machinery-manufacturing industries. Rising output prices in these activities adversely affect yields to labor of all kinds. But the rising costs of supply of assets which labor has to bear in the circumstances imagined are simply the consequence of a smaller real value of assets being retained, replaced or added to in the industries which manufacture fixed assets. This is the reaction to the strike-threat system explained in Chapter 10. It may be that Lebergott's way of stating the principle assists our understanding of the simple reality that "assets are labor's tools," while duress-imposed costs of manufacturing the tools are against labor's advantage.

The services of assets and those provided by labor can, then, be envisaged as demanding one another, the *relative* values being, in each case, market-determined. The fact that the market is seldom "free" but constrained by various contrived scarcities and plenitudes creates no tendency for the *relative* values of the two broad kinds of services as a whole to change *in the long run*, especially when the argument of Chapter 7 and the dynamic factors referred to above are given due weight.[18] For instance, if we imagine a reduction of the "labor supply" in existing employments through widespread collusive action, we can hardly usefully assume the survival of an unchanged stock of assets. A reduced real value of complementary assets will be profitably replaceable or accumulable in each activity affected by contrived labor scarcity. Not only will the costs of replacing or adding to the stock of assets *as presently composed* be higher than previously, but the real value of assets which compete with labor (that is, noncomplementary) will tend to expand and *ceteris paribus* reduce labor's share. In addition, the assets structure (the composition of replacement and growth) will be molded to suit less productive employments; for some labor will be diverted to less productive (that is, less income-generating) employments (including, perhaps, unemployment). Demands for labor and demands for services of assets will tend to contract in correlation.

A reduction of man-hours supplied in relation to the capital stock can be relied upon, then, to bring about a rise in labor's share only while the composition of the stock of assets can be assumed *still to be in process of becoming fully adjusted*. If we assume that no such adjustment occurs, and for the short run an assumption of that kind may at first seem to be reasonable, union policies which have the effect of reducing labor inputs must indeed tend to raise labor's percentage share (to labor's absolute disadvantage). But over a period as long as a decade, the effect of contrived labor scarcity can certainly be realistically expected to bring about compensating changes in production functions.[19]

We are in practice concerned, however, not only with the substitution of factors in the production of a defined bundle of outputs, but also with the substitution of one kind of output for another, that is, for a changing composition of outputs in general.[20] Every time the price of one input rises, the other complementary inputs become less profitable; and as time passes, the providers of the inputs will tend to divert them to different kinds of output. Any increased share acquired at first by the contriver of a scarcity is likely to be gradually whittled away through reactions from the great society outside (that is, external to the firm or industry in which the contrived scarcity is imposed). *Ceteris paribus*, the real value of complementary factors used in the activity will gradually diminish.

The fact that capital can sometimes substitute for labor is of course a vital consideration. Such a substitution is one of the most conspicuous ways in which assets take on less exploitable forms. It tends to reduce labor's share. Admittedly investment in labor-economizing plant may sometimes itself be highly exploitable, although vigilant entrepreneurs will avoid the trap. For this reason, however, other reactions upon the composition of the stock of capital resources may be more important. But in my judgment, labor-economizing developments must have had a formidable influence in reducing labor's share.

To recapitulate. To the extent to which assets are initially mainly complementary in their relation to labor, the burdening of activities which produce such assets with strike-enhanced labor costs will be a self-defeating way of trying to augment labor's relative share. Not only must labor incur higher costs for the assets they have to use (which will ultimately offset, at least partially, any immediate transfer at property's expense), but even more important, it will induce a change in assets structure through which investors will be able to avoid continued exploitation. In other words, while strike-threat pressures *statically considered* must tend to raise labor's proportion (as distinct from its absolute earnings), *dynamically considered* the process can be expected to have a neutral effect upon relative shares. Labor's tools will assume a less wage-multiplying form while the workers will be driven to cooperate with different assets, in employments which will, on the average, be less remunerative.

Assuming now that the community's savings-preference schedule remains unchanged, any former rate of growth in the real value of the aggregate capital stock must fall (perhaps become negative) following a wave of duress-imposed labor costs. For prospective yields must decline and the value of profitable investments in inputs must shrink. This also will tend to offset any tendency for labor's percentage to rise. On the other hand, rising thrift, especially if accompanied by autonomous capital-economizing developments, in accelerating the rate of additions to the stock of complementary assets, will tend to raise labor's share.

My own interpretation of the data of United States experience is that *if* (and I must place strong emphasis on the *if*) the rate of growth in the stock of assets which has been witnessed this century had taken a form determined under *free* market incentives (the proportion of complementary to competing assets being an important consideration), yet reached the magnitude in relation to man-hours to which reference was made above, *there would have been a very large increase indeed in labor's share for this reason alone.*

In fact, I suggest, we have found the reverse. Technological and managerial ingenuity has, for instance, been canalized toward labor-substituting, automating forms. *Growing recourse to the strike threat has biased the form of economizing displacement.* Undoubtedly, this is one of the most important factors explaining why labor's relative share has been kept down. Certainly we should have found *some* tendency toward growing automation and the assembly-line and mass-production methods of the western world, even had history been different and a relatively strike-free economy been experienced. But far more effort would then have gone into developing machines which increase demands for labor than into those which have the opposite effect.

I have throughout been occasionally reiterating the deliberately challenging yet accurately descriptive term, "wage-multiplying assets." The more cheaply *complementary* assets may be replaced or accumulated in any activity, the greater will be the relative yield to effort and skill in that activity and the greater its share. But even such assets as compete with labor are still wage-multiplying in the sense that *economies achieved in their production* tend to multiply the *absolute* wages flow, although they must (subject to the important qualifications we have just noticed) tend to reduce the *relative* value of wages as a component of total income. That is, while the cheapening of labor-economizing assets is not wage-multiplying for the workers in any occupation directly affected, it does have this effect for workers in all the other occupations which stand in a noncompeting relationship. It tends equally, of course, to multiply yields to capital in noncompeting fields.

Some economists hold that a rise in the demand for leisure (not uninfluenced by strike-threat influences) over the past century must have been tending to raise labor's percentage of the value of the product—a reduced aggregate physical product. These economists feel that (1) the subsidization of early retirement in various ways; (2) prolonged schooling for such young people as do not benefit therefrom, and who are often deprived in some measure thereby from training in wage-multiplying skills;[21] and (3) a reduction in the hours of labor in privileged occupations, must have been contributing to an augmented relative share for labor (although at the expense of labor's absolute share). Certainly a general enforcement or subvention of a preference for leisure (against the alternatives of greater material well-being and security) combined with all the other relevant factors, including the age distribution of the population, can be observed to have been causing the number of man-hours worked (in terms of "efficiency units") to increase less rapidly than the stock of assets.[22]

In considering this issue, we must remember that the aggregate number of man-hours supplied is influenced not only by voluntary or duress-imposed demand for leisure but by every contrived labor scarcity. Greater leisure may well be one of the products purchased by the private beneficiaries of the scarcity contrivance. But more important, once man-hours are measured in "equal productivity units," it becomes clear that their number is reduced whenever the price of labor is raised by force. Even if there had been no change in conventional working hours in any occupation, the raising of wage rates above the natural scarcity level must have meant a withdrawal of labor supply in terms of "equal productivity units"; for *ceteris paribus* a larger proportion of the workers must have been confined to work of lower productivity. Hence there is no *special* problem due to the reduction of labor supply via abnormally early retirement, prolonged useless schooling or shortened hours of labor.

226

Let us now consider the United States where it has been estimated that the volume of physical capital has increased this century more than three times as much as the aggregate number of man-hours has increased.[23] One would have expected (relying solely on static assumptions) such a relative growth in the productive power of assets to have raised labor's share in a marked degree. *But this expectation is always subject to the crucial qualification enunciated on p. 221, namely "the volume of complementary assets being assumed unchanged in magnitude and composition."* It is just this assumption which we cannot make. The real value and the form of assets are in process of constant adaptation to the price and type of labor available. That seems to be why no increase in labor's share is discernible.

In continually insisting that what happens in the short run is no necessary indication of what will happen in the long run, I have so far only briefly referred to the business cycle, over the period of which changes in relative shares certainly do occur. During the downturn, costs tend to be more rigid than prices, and fixed assets become underutilized, leading to a rise in labor's share; while during the upturn, labor's share declines. Thus, when a reduction in man-hours worked occurs during a developing recession (mainly through unemployment due to the maintenance of wage rates), there is a discernible cyclical redistribution in favor of labor's share. Labor's percentage is increased to labor's disadvantage.[24]

During wars in which public opinion strongly supports the war effort, it is possible to increase the relative flow of labor inputs because the workers agree, so to speak, in some measure to sacrifice leisure for the common good, or in return for high "overtime" payments. Further, in these circumstances, the unions often permit (voluntarily or otherwise) a measure of "dilution" (unprivileged workers doing privileged work). But recognition of the anticyclical movement of labor's share must not lead the reader to the conclusion that during a period of growing prosperity, *it is essential* for labor's percentage to decline. Demands for labor are derived from prospective yields from investment in labor's inputs. Hence the optimism and feeling of entrepreneurial security which would exist under boom conditions if strike action were ruled out would almost certainly cause most demands for labor to increase, and this would tend to preserve labor's proportion. Entrepreneurs would strive to increase their activity ahead of their competitors. Nevertheless, in considering a long period with an inflationary trend but covering several cycles of recession and boom about the trend, we should expect a tendency for labor's share to decline unless we must give much weight to what has been called the "ratchet" effect (see pp. 229-230). But two contrary factors are likely to offset this tendency: (a) price controls intended immediately to reduce predicted residual claims and (b) the fact that wages and salaries in the armed forces are paid out of income transferred via taxation, while the wages and salaries of those employed in producing for the war effort are also remunerated from this source. Empirical studies do, indeed, seem to confirm such conclusions (see Chapter 16).

I have been discussing the tendencies which (allowance made for cyclical disturbance) appear to be stabilizing labor's relative share, despite factors which one might at first think would be inclined to change it. There are indeed six possible reasons why, *if we did not take account of the reactions which I have just been discussing*, we should have expected[25] labor's share to have increased during the last century and to be clearly discernible in empirical studies.

1. The first has already been dealt with, namely, the enormous growth in the stock of assets in relation to labor supply (in the sense of the number of man-hours of standard productivity).

2. The second possible reason is that this century unions have been growing in aggregate membership and becoming expert in strike-threat techniques, while investors have, one would have thought, been adjusting their expectations to the use of these techniques only gradually. Hence, substantial temporary exploitation of investors *could* have occurred. As I have insisted, in the short run, during a period in which entrepreneurial anticipations are gradually being molded by experience of the emerging aggressive unionism, some redistribution at investors' expense may well happen, everything depending upon how wisely entrepreneurial predictions of the future private use of coercive power cause early changes in the composition of the community's stock of assets.[26]

3. A yet stronger reason why we should expect an increase in "labor's" proportion of aggregate income is the remarkable increase in government employment, and resort to various kinds of "welfare handouts" which form part of "labor's share." Public services tend to be labor intensive, while public servants are remunerated via direct transfers, that is, via taxation.[27] A very large part of the community's income has come to be redistributed in this way, and much of it is in the form of what really amounts to relief work. For this part of the redistribution, however, the strike-threat is *not* the cause except in so far as government employees are permitted to use this method in order to force redistribution through taxation. The limitations to strike-threat power which were discussed in Chapters 1 and 10 do not, as we saw, apply to government employments. There is no clear limit to the "soaking" of taxpayers by governments when the bulk of the visible taxes are paid by a political minority, except the ability of entrepreneurs to export capital; and even that door may be obstructed or completely closed by exchange control (including "interest equalization"). Taxation by *local* governments (states, provinces, counties, municipalities) may of course divert some investment to other areas within a country. But because the actual use of strikes in the government sector has been increasing in recent years, in what I feel has been a largely unpredicted manner and degree, one would have expected "labor's share" to have grown.[28] There *is* some evidence that this may be the explanation of a very small rise in that share which certain empirical investigations disclose.

4. A further reason why we should expect to find evidence of a larger share accruing to labor is the growing governmental exploitation of the provident otherwise than by overt taxation. Politicians often find it expedient to mulct

228

those *rentiers* who have not correctly predicted the speed and duration of inflation, while the debasement of a currency implies a redistribution which seems likely *on balance* to cause the share of property to decline. This is because wage contracts are short term, and labor shortage at initial wage rates caused by inflation pulls up the money price of labor with a relatively short time lag, while bonds are long-term contracts. Of course, the losses borne by interest receivers are offset in some measure by the gains to residual claimants. But through the presence of the strike threat, what would otherwise be *"restorative" entrepreneurial yields* due to inflation (see p. 229), *may* be successively seizable through the exercise of union power. When the inflationary process is recognized as having been built into the economy, there may be no countervailing gains against the losses imposed on interest receivers. In these circumstances, however, the *rentiers'* expectations must be brought into the reckoning. As soon as *they* come to anticipate inflation, market interest rates rise sufficiently to prevent their further exploitation. Nevertheless, over the years for which most of these statistical comparisons have been made, one would have expected the exploitation of the *rentier* class to have been reflected in the figures, and therefore to have caused some increase in labor's share.[29]

5. Another reason why one would have expected, *ceteris paribus*, to find evidence of a rising trend in labor's *relative* share, is sometimes described as "intersector shifts" of labor. It has reference to transfers of consumer preference toward the outputs of more labor-intensive types of occupations.[30] For instance, labor's share in agriculture is lower than it is in nonfarm occupations as a whole and there has been a shift—indeed a substantial shift—away from agriculture in most Western countries.[31] Moreover, in an increasingly affluent society, we can observe a rising preference for "life-enrichment" activities, toward the service occupations generally, toward the constructional industries, and toward commerce (as distinct from physical manufacture). These occupations tend to be more *labor intensive* than the average, and in them the proportion of wages in relation to the value of output is well above the average. Growing mechanization may have reduced the significance of this trend, but it has by no means offset it.

6. The final reason for expecting to find that labor's share has been increasing is what has been called the "ratchet" effect. It is concerned with the phenomenon noticed on page 227, namely, the expansion of labor's percentage during periods of depression and unemployment. The "ratchet" effect is operative when that gain is not wholly offset during the shrinkage of the percentage (normally to be expected) as the flow of wages recovers and fuller employment is achieved. Because wage rates are more rigid downward than they are upward, this *could* mean a gradual increase in labor's proportion (at the expense, of course, of a reduced rate of recovery in the aggregate wages flow) through the seizure of what I have called the "restorative" element in the residual yield. (See pages 229 and 253-255.) If such a redistribution does tend to occur, however, it must be classed as a special case of the situation in which investors have failed to perceive their exploitability. And

this is relevant to another circumstance, also connected with cyclical effects, namely, eventual recourse to "disinflationary" policies which are not accompanied by government action to protect the wages flow.[32] In such circumstances, investors may be exploitable by continued labor union pressures to raise wage rates, and labor's share will tend to increase as long as entrepreneurial expectations underrate the probability of exploitation in this form.

In addition to the above-mentioned reasons for expecting evidence of *actual* transfers from yields to property in favor of yields to labor, there are five reasons for expecting the statistics to reflect merely *apparent* (that is, illusory) redistributions in the same direction.

1. Income statistics seldom include nonpecuniary yields to property, yet this kind of income has obviously been growing in importance as the general level of material well-being has been rising. An increasing proportion of real income has tended to be received in the form that Marshall called "gratifications" from investment in consumer capital goods. In the United States, this must be true in some degree of all income groups except perhaps the poorest; but the higher the income, the greater the importance which must be given to the yield from consumer durables. The propensity of well-to-do persons with expanding incomes to hold a large proportion of their assets in "luxury" property forms like mansions, country estates, mountain lodges, seaside dwellings, yachts, and so forth, as well as costly jewelry, antique furniture, valuable pictures, and the like, is an obvious manifestation of the phenomenon. No doubt the incentive is largely demand for status symbols, which the political trends of the last half century have encouraged. But any such "conspicuous investment" must be regarded as yielding a nonpecuniary income that normally exceeds the interest which, capitalized, represents the pecuniary value of the assets.[33] The tendency is likely to have been reinforced by the growing recourse to the strike threat. It is one of the ways in which attempts to avoid exploitation can cause assets to take on a less wage-multiplying form (see pp. 143-144). Moreover, for reasons connected with the growing tax burden over the present century, other yields to property have tended more and more to take the form of nonpecuniary benefits; and such benefits are seldom reckoned as part of "national income." The remuneration of property in this "invisible" form must therefore tend to raise the *apparent* proportion of labor's income to all income.

An important special case is the "gratifications" in which we mostly share in some degree from *collectively owned assets* the services of which are "free," or sold to us at prices which are insufficient to cover interest and depreciation. The growing proportion of labor's remuneration as a result of government employment is *not* balanced in income statistics by the yield to the growing stock of property which is owned by *the state* (that is, supposedly by the people). The illusory element from this cause can be regarded as unimportant if collective ownership of assets is judged to result in an egalitarian distribution of the services rendered by those assets. But as with most consumer durables, they tend to be in the nature of luxuries—things which one would think satisfy the priorities of the rich in income use rather than those of

230

the poor. It is doubtful whether free preferences expressed in the market would lead to the people who form the category "labor" voluntarily paying for such things if their cost in interest and upkeep had to be met out of, say, handouts of equivalent value in the form of a "negative income tax." On balance, then, it seems that income data must reflect an illusory redistribution in labor's favor from this cause.[34]

An offsetting factor may be the growing proportion of fringe benefits in relation to pure wage income for which the statisticians may not have been able to make full allowance. This is a rather recent phenomenon, and I do not think it can have had more than a negligible influence over the greater part of the periods which empirical studies of income distribution have covered. Such influence as it has had, however, may have led to an *understatement* of labor's proportion.

2. A further consideration which cannot be ignored is the effect of corporation taxes on the form of income declaration. Whenever the managers themselves are the owners of a large proportion of the capital, minimization of the tax burden has an important consequence. If the income of such managers is classed as a yield to labor, their total tax is less than if it is classed as a yield to capital. Hence as taxation of corporations has increased, the remuneration of managers has been less likely to take the form of stock options or stock allocations; for the identical remuneration can be offered, with identical incentives, at a smaller sacrifice of income to the tax collectors. It becomes profitable to remunerate executives through commissions, bonuses or salary increases. Again, what would have been declared as "profit" in earlier periods has been increasingly declared as salaries—that is, yield to "labor." And resort to the device of undistributed corporate profits as a reaction to inflation, *while actually increasing*, is a quite likely additional cause of an illusory rise in labor's share.

3. A possibility which should be mentioned is that underdeclaration of profits due to attempts to minimize the rising taxation burden may create an unduly low declaration of income from property. Such underdeclaration could be inadvertent. Growing investment in research, including market research, pilot schemes, models and prototypes, or even advertising expenditures ought at times to be treated as investments, although actually treated as current costs.

4. Another very important reason why we should expect recorded statistics to show an illusory growth in labor's share is the fact that the proportion of income accruing to small businesses has declined gradually in the course of technological progress. Services which were formerly remunerated by income returned as "profit" have been increasingly remunerated in the form of income returned as "wages." For instance, last century we found a much larger proportion than we do today of people who were serving at shop counters, yet owned their own businesses. They gained a modest return which was described as "profit." Today the same class of people will be wage-earning shop assistants, but enjoying considerably larger real incomes as "wages" than their forebears earned as "profits." Again, housewives and other mem-

bers of a family who perform services in the home will be remunerated by a share of, say, the husbands' wage income. But their remuneration is not reported as a contribution to income. Last century and early this century far more women fell into this class than today, when their counterparts are largely performing paid work. Such women have been released from providing services for the family directly, and provide instead services for the community generally. Families are being increasingly served through the preparation and cooking of food in factories, while manufacturing provides, replaces, repairs and services washing machines, vacuum cleaners, dishwashers, central heating apparatus, mechanical can openers, etc. The labor employed in this field is remunerated. When it had been performed domestically no remuneration was recorded. The proportion of privately owned assets directed by the "self-employed" or in the form of unincorporated undertakings (industrial, agricultural and commercial) in the United States has declined substantially since the beginning of the century (from 41 percent in 1900 to 23 percent in 1956).[35] The consequences upon the *description* of incomes must have been far from negligible. Again, self-employment has always been important in agriculture (although agriculture has tended more and more to become a corporation-directed activity). Much of the real earnings of farm operators (including their families) does not get reported as income.[36] Hence because the relative share of agricultural income in national income has been declining, we have a particularly important example of the growing tendency for income of a kind which was earlier returned as profit to be returned as wages.

5. A factor of some importance is that in an area as vast as that of the United States, considered over a period in which average incomes and standards of living in different districts differed widely at the outset but which, with the passage of time, were gradually becoming less unequal, the shift of workers from areas of relatively low productivity and low earnings to areas of relatively high productivity and high earnings, must have meant that the money earnings of those who moved increased by a greater proportion than their real earnings increased. The relatively lowly paid regions are typically low cost-of-living areas. For the same kind of reasons the movement of labor from agriculture to higher paid industrial or urban pursuits must have meant that any increase in *money earnings* which the statistics record was substantially greater than any increase in real earnings. This is because of the relative cheapness of living on farms and the perquisites available in that occupation.[37]

Through the operation of these eleven factors, six concerned with *actual* redistributions and five with *illusory*, we should have expected to find, from studies of income statistics, that during the last century at least, an indisputable and substantial redistribution of recorded income from investors to labor could be discerned. *In fact we find nothing of the kind.* Although some such studies have seemed at first to show that small transfers of aggregate income in the expected direction have indeed been experienced, further investigation into the validity of the methods or significance of the data

232

appear nearly always to have established that the proportions in which aggregate income is divided between the two broad groups "property" and "labor," far from having changed discernibly, have remained disconcertingly constant!

Theoretical economists and statisticians have long been fascinated with the ultimate constancy that is discovered, which Schumpeter (reviewing the course of empirical inquiry in this field) termed "a remarkable fact"[38] and other economists have described by words like "miracle," "mystery," "amazing," "Medusa-like," and so forth. Yet the fixity of the proportions which has prompted such descriptions might be, Solow has suggested, merely "an optical illusion" or a "mirage,"[39] or, as Samuelson has suggested, "an interesting coincidence."[40] If my argument on pages 220 et seq. is valid, however, the constancy is neither a "miracle" nor a "mirage." There is some justification, I think, for Samuelson's phrase, "an interesting coincidence," although there is more to it than mere coincidence.

The thesis presented above certainly does suggest that a fairly constant ratio will be established between the value of the efforts of men and the value of the services of the tools men make. My reasoning in these passages is simply a special exposition of the "classical" marginal productivity theory of the valuation of the services of men and of assets. On this issue, Bronfenbrenner has referred to what he calls the "considerable constancy" implied by "conventional marginal distribution theory" . . . "provided only that the elasticity of substitution between capital and labor is not well below unity,"[41] and he is here, I think, touching on what is fundamental. My own argument in Chapter 10 can be interpreted as an explanation of why elasticities of substitution will be less than unity in the short period, but move in the direction of unity in the long period (see also pp. 233 et seq.). Reder has concluded (in a review of thought and empirical inquiry on the subject) that "the mechanisms of product and factor substitution have been such that whatever pressure unions have been able to bring to bear upon wage rates has been offset in so far as any effect upon relative shares is concerned."[42] If this explanation is acceptable, an important causal factor in the constancy cannot be appropriately described as merely coincidental. At the same time, we cannot hold that the elasticities and substitutions which appear to have been bringing about the balance over the periods investigated must necessarily be operative under all conceivable institutions or policies. One "control" imposed (by unions or government) on the valuation of the services of men and of assets appears always to set more or less countervailing reactions going; but the measure of the permanence of proportions which results *is* a chance phenomenon. There is no reason to expect an exact restoration of disturbed ratios. Indeed, during a time span in which strike-threat pressure in each period, as we have seen, has been greater than entrepreneurs had expected in the previous period, some evidence of redistribution in favor of labor would be a reasonable expectation. Hence if my suggested explanation of why no such redistribution has indeed occurred is sound (namely, that labor—in an entrepreneurial capacity—had to incur higher costs for the services of assets, while the stock of assets assumed a less wage-multiplying but less exploitable form), the rough balance in proportions brought about *does* seem to justify the word "coincidence."

In a strike-free regime, the reduced risk involved in capital-economizing investments could have increased entrepreneurial demands for labor from the assets side by more than it increased demands for the services of assets from the side of the providers of labor. If this judgment is valid, we must accept that it *is* a coincidence—although an explicable coincidence—that, during the nineteenth and twentieth centuries, the *strike-threat system has everywhere been permitted to prevent labor's share from rising* (as well as reducing the absolute wages flow) and has throughout *just happened* to maintain that share constant.

In my opinion, there can be few surviving "optical illusions" due to the pitfalls of statistical investigation. It is true that the researchers have been unable to discern the weights of the many heterogeneous factors which are unchallengeably the determinants of income distribution. And there are certainly illusory data. But these tend almost entirely to show a spurious rise in labor's share (at least if the argument under headings (1) to (5) (pp. 230-233 is acceptable). It is indeed only after adjustments have been made to offset such "optical illusions" as can be identified that investigators have discovered the hardly changing long-term ratios. But, although it must certainly be stressed that "an appearance of inevitableness" in relative shares does not mean "an inevitableness" unqualified, *the fact* of the constancy found, under different definitions of the aggregates compared, cannot be described as a "mirage." It is an undeniable reality.

APPENDIX TO CHAPTER 15.
Note on a Recent Contribution.

Just after this book was prepared for publication, I noticed an important article by Professors H. G. Johnson and P. Mieszkowski (hereinafter referred to as "the authors"),[43] which relates to the topics here discussed, and reaches conclusions which are similar, although arrived at by very different methods.

It begins with a rigorous geometric examination of a model in which labor is regarded as homogeneous and two commodities only are produced, one with capital-intensive methods and the other with labor-intensive methods. It is pointed out that, through the influence of unionization, "the allocation of factors among industries" and "the allocation of production and consumption among industries" will be rendered inefficient.[44] *Making abstraction of such repercussions* it is argued, however, that if unionization occurs only in the capital-intensive sector, "unionized labor must gain, while nonunionized labor must also gain"; for "unionization is in effect a tax on the labor of the unionized industry, and therefore has the effect of shifting demand away from that industry." Such a tax results in "a fall in the demand for and price of the

234

services of capital and an increase in the demand for labor, from which both sections of labor may gain.''[45] For similar reasons, it is argued, if unionization occurs only in the relatively labor-intensive industries, the capitalists will gain and labor will lose in both sectors.

It is true that the end-products of capital-intensive activities can be rendered less preferred at the prices which result from a labor tax on them and hence the end-products of labor-intensive activities (on which no labor tax is levied) rendered more preferred. But this merely illustrates a particular case with very unrealistic assumptions under which labor's *relative* share may be raised (the issue to which this chapter has been devoted).

If the labor tax is levied in capital-intensive activities only, and the reactions on resource allocation (which the authors stress on p. 543) are brought into the reckoning, then given the losses caused thereby in aggregate real income, any conceivable increase in labor's *absolute* income is extremely difficult to imagine.

If we now drop the two commodities assumption and suppose that a very important source of demands for labor-intensive activities is the incomes of those who own assets—the capitalists (a highly realistic assumption), we can see that a labor tax on capital-intensive activities may cause labor's *relative* share to fall as well as its *absolute* share. Capital-intensive activities contribute to the real wage flow just as labor-intensive activities do. And their outputs contribute to the source of demands for *all* noncompeting productive services, those of labor as well as those of assets.

In turning from geometric analysis to algebraic, with arithmetic illustrations, and using data based on empirical evidence, the authors draw attention explicitly to the limited practical relevance of their conclusions. Their methods here, they warn, "do not allow for the long-run effects of unions on the distribution of income and the real wage." Their findings, they say, "err to the extent that the formation of unions changes the level of investment."[46] Even so, they find that, given other plausible assumptions, any gains of unionized labor are largely or wholly at the expense of nonunionized labor.[47]

Later, dropping the assumptions that labor is homogeneous and all labor in capital-intensive activities is unionized, the authors substitute the assumption that all blue-collar workers are unionized and all white-collar workers are nonunion. This change in assumptions is shown not to affect the conclusion that "unionized labor gains primarily at the expense of nonunion labor." It is shown further that the tendency for a "tax on labor" (duress-imposed wage gates) to benefit unionized workers at the expense of nonunionized, may be limited by "a substitution of capital for labor in the union sector."[48]

I mentioned above the authors' warning that "the formation of unions changes the level of investment." In the long run, they say, "the level of capital formation will fall."[49] Now it is true that labor costs raised by the strike threat must reduce prospective yields to investment in general. Hence, *ceteris paribus*, given any propensity to save, the rate of interest must fall. Exactly how it will affect the magnitude of achieved savings or dissavings (that

235

is, the rate of net accumulation or decumulation of output-yielding assets) will depend upon a variety of considerations. But what is most important is not the *magnitude* of the savings flow (the *"level of investment"*) but *its composition*. It is *the form* assumed by the stock of assets in their replacement or net accumulation which matters most—the extent to which assets acquire more "wage-multiplying" attributes, irrespective of whether new methods induced are capital-intensive or labor-intensive (or, alternatively, capital-economizing or labor-economizing).

If the penalization of investment by duress-imposed wage rates in an industry causes (through its bearing on end-product prices) demand for the output of that industry to fall, it will become unprofitable to replace fully (or maintain a previous rate of growth in) the stock of complementary assets. The workers remaining in the industry may well gain, but marginal workers will be laid-off and potential recruits to the industry will be forbidden access to the bargaining table. In my judgment, however, *the vital consequence will be the reduction of the real value of labor's earnings in noncompeting activities* and the reduction of yields to previously invested capital in noncompeting activities, *because the offer of outputs from the protected field for the non-competing inputs will contract*. Labor in general must certainly suffer detriment. The authors cover this reality only through their warning (mentioned above) that their methods do not allow for reactions upon *real* wage rates.

Nevertheless, the authors reach the final conclusion that, for "a partially unionized economy, . . . most, if not all of the gains of union labor are made at the expense of nonunionized workers, and not at the expense of earnings of capital."[50] Such "unionization of labor does not in fact benefit labor at the expense of capital."[51]

Turning then to a wholly unionized economy, the authors find that even if *all* labor were unionized and the "bargaining power" of the unions happened to be equally spread (*presumably* meaning by this use of the term "bargaining power" that the threat to disrupt by strikes happened to reduce prospective yields to investment everywhere and in all activities by an equal proportion),[52] unless the unions could somehow offset any monopsonistic purchase of labor, or unless the unions could thereby seize some share of the monopolistic gains of complementary parties, "the distribution of income (would) be essentially the same as the distribution in an economy in which unions (did) not exist."[53] That is, the *proportional* shares of capital and labor in the reduced aggregate income would be more or less unaffected.

236

NOTES

[1] See S. Golden and H. J. Ruttenberg, *The Dynamics of Industrial Democracy* (New York: Harper, 1942), p. 151.

[2] M. Woll, *Labor, Industry and the Government,* p. 146, quoted in P. Sultan, *Labor Economics* (New York: Henry Holt, 1957), p. 383.

[3] Ludwig von Mises, *Human Action* (New Haven: Yale University Press, 1949), Chapter 2, passim.

[4] C. L. Schultze and L. Weiner, eds., *The Behavior of Income Shares,* National Bureau of Economic Research (Princeton: Princeton University Press, 1964).

[5] Tibor Scitovsky, "A Survey of Some Theories of Income Distribution," in ibid.

[6] H. Gregg Lewis, "The Effects of Unions on Industrial Wage Differentials," *Aspects of Labor Economics: A Conference of the Universities—National Bureau Committee for Economic Research,* A Report of the National Bureau of Economic Research (Princeton: Princeton University Press, 1962).

[7] John T. Dunlop, "Comment," Ibid., p. 343.

[8] R. M. Solow holds, however, that if we could identify the part of the wages flow which is a yield to investment in human capital, it would materially affect our conclusions. "A Skeptical Note on the Constancy of Relative Shares," *American Economic Review*, 1958, p. 630.

[9] In the actual world, of course, we do not find such arrangements, for reasons which have already been discussed (see Chapter 6). Hence no serious difficulties arise for this reason.

[10] Attempts to distinguish "wages" from "salaries" involve so much arbitrariness, it seems to me, that any significance of inferences relevant to the apparent constancy of "factor shares" is destroyed.

[11] Nor can effective allowance be made for changes in the proportion of income from property generally accruing to the group of persons envisaged as "labor," or (as we noticed above) the proportion that properly should be isolated as yield to labor in income returned as "profits."

[12] Theoretically, it is essential to assume man-hours of unchanged average efficiency or productivity.

[13] While this is true in each particular activity, the principle cannot be safely transferred to the whole economy without encountering the lurking danger of the fallacy of composition.

[14] That is, in reducing the cost of services flowing into the replacement or net accumulation of assets, a cheapening of labor is enabling a given sacrifice of consumption by savers (i.e., a given flow of savings) to go further.

[15] S. Lebergott, in *The Behavior of Income Shares*, pp. 53-100, especially p. 66.

[16] Ibid., p. 66.

[17] G. Garvy, in *The Behavior of Income Shares*, p. 96.

[18] We saw in Chapter 7 that a contrived scarcity in one activity, in increasing labor's share in that activity, creates an "incidental plenitude" of labor for the benefit of investors in other activities, so that labor's share elsewhere will tend to be reduced and to restore therefore aggregate proportions.

[19] W. J. Fellner has drawn attention to these important considerations, *American Economic Review, Proceedings,* 1953, p. 491.

[20] Under the relative austerity imposed on consumers by the restriction of inputs in general, different preferences will be expressed, and both the composition of the stock of assets and the form of skill acquisition will adjust to the expectations created by *the changing demand situation.* Because this kind of reaction can be reasonably expected in practice, the likelihood of any increase in labor's percentage for such a reason is reduced.

[21] Solow thinks that one assumption here is factually wrong. He suggests that improving investment in human capital through "education, training, public health, etc . . ." may have been sufficient to cause "the measurement in man hours" to underestimate "the rate at which the labor force grows as properly measured in efficiency units." (Solow, op. cit., p. 630.)

[22] The tendency for such a situation to raise labor's percentage will not be weakened if resort to the shift system enables a plant to be worked by two or more sets of workers during the 24 hours. For such a capital economy is expressing an increased demand for complementary labor.

[23] Samuelson accepts that the stock of physical capital in the United States has grown six-fold since the beginning of the century, whereas population has only doubled. The number of man-hours has increased much less rapidly than population.

[24] This phenomenon forces one to ask again whether it is not really rather foolish to be concerned with percentage shares instead of with absolute shares. It *seems* indeed that, in a strike-threat age, labor in general is best off when its percentage share of aggregate income is least!

[25] Solow (op. cit., p. 619) has warned about the fuzzy use of the notion of "what one would ordinarily expect." I hope that my use of the notion absolves me from suspicion of sloppy thinking on the issue.

[26] I do not include here the much less likely, but theoretically possible reason that, before the emergence of powerful unions, labor had been exploited for the benefit of investors through monopsony, while, as the exploitation was overcome through union resistance, a redistribution of income could have been expected. My reason for not again referring to this possibility here is that the argument presented in Chapter 8 has shown the improbability of more than negligible monopsonistic exploitation occurring in the actual world.

[27] See M. Reder, "Alternative Theories of Labor's Share," in M. Abramovitch, *Allocation of Economic Resources* (Stanford, Calif.: Stanford University Press, 1959), p. 196.

[28] I say "unpredicted" because strikes in governmental employments are illegal in most countries. But as the people of the United States have learned recently, illegality does not amount to much if law enforcement and the judiciary have been allowed to fall into political control.

[29] In referring to the *rentiers'* expectations, it is important to refer to the relative time-lag in the expectations of the low-income *rentiers* who, for other reasons also, are in an inferior position when it comes to escaping exploitation through inflation. Humanitarians should never forget that *rentiers* with incomes below the average include many relatively poor people who, largely in order to avoid having to rely upon public assistance or charity (for themselves or their dependants), invest in savings and loan associations, life insurance, endowment insurance, pension funds, etc. Income transfers at the expense of the real value of the savings of the thrifty poor seem to benefit mainly union members whose incomes are above the average of all incomes.

[30] This possibility must not be confused with the vastly more important shifts from work of low productivity to work of high productivity (noticed above, pp. 220-221), which would (in itself) increase only labor's absolute (*not* its relative) share.

[31] "Contrary to what one might expect, agriculture is a capital intensive industry utilizing relatively large amounts of capital (includi g land) per worker." (D. Gale Johnson, "The Functional Distribution of Income in the United States," *Review of Economics and Statistics*, 1954, p. 181.

[32] I. e., not accompanied by governmental action (a) to permit or facilitate market-selected wage-rate adjustments or (b) to protect or raise the profitability of production (profit prospects) via the crude remedy of wage-rate "controls."

[33] That part of the yield which exceeds interest is "consumers' surplus."

[34] Collectively-owned assets which produce an income for government, thereby lightening the tax burden, give rise to no problems.

[35] R. Goldsmith, *A Study of Saving in the United States,* quoted by I. B. Kravis, "Relative Income Shares in Fact and Theory," *American Economic Review*, December, 1959, p. 920.

[36] See Reder, op. cit., p. 197.

[37] This point is made by Kravis (op. cit., p. 934) who, estimating from data in a U.S. Bureau of Labor Statistics publication of 1945, suggested that a dollar of nonfarm income was roughly equivalent to 70 percent of a dollar of farm income.

[38] Joseph A. Schumpeter, *History of Economic Analysis* (Oxford: Oxford University Press, 1954), p. 1042.

[39] Solow, op cit., pp. 618-619.

[40] Paul Samuelson, *Economics* (8th ed.; New York: McGraw-Hill Book Company, 1971), p. 719.

[41] Martin Bronfenbrenner, "A Note on Relative Shares and the Elasticity of Substitution," *Journal of Political Economy*, 1960, p. 287.

[42] Reder, "Alternative Theories" p. 196.

[43] H. G. Johnson and P. Mieskowski, *Quarterly Journal of Economics,* November 1970, p. 539.

[44] *Ibid.,* p. 543.

[45] *Ibid.,* p. 547. A tax on unionized labor, the proceeds of which accrue to that labor, is only one way of envisaging the income-distribution consequences of any fixing of the price of a particular supply of labor under strike-threat duress.

[46] Ibid., p. 548. My own analysis has stressed the *composition* rather than "the level" of investment, as I am about to reiterate.

[47] Ibid., pp. 554-558.

[48] Ibid., p. 559.

[49] Ibid., p. 548.

[50] Ibid., p. 560. In practice workers laid-off because of duress-imposed labor costs often find employment in less well-paid *unionized* occupations, as may "excluded" workers, never admitted to an activity they could enter under market freedom.

[51] Ibid., p. 561.

[52] Actually, the authors use the phrase, "If . . . the bargaining power of all unions is the same in all industries . . ." (Ibid., p. 561.)

[53] Ibid., p. 561.

16
Empirical Studies of
Labor's Share

IN THIS chapter I propose to quote, and where it seems helpful to comment on, the crucial findings, expressed verbally, of the statistical economists who have conducted meticulous investigations into recorded experience of changes in income shares.

The most famous (perhaps "notorious" would be a more appropriate adjective) was a thorough and ingenious pioneer effort by Pareto. Publishing his findings in 1897, as the emerging strike-threat system was causing deep misgivings among the prescient, but before it had developed as the strong influence it is today, he summarized the results of his own statistical studies in what is known as "Pareto's law."[1] He maintained that if income sizes and the number of persons receiving incomes are plotted on logarithmic scales, the result is an approximately straight line, and that "at all recent times the slope of this straight line" had been constant. But he claimed further that the law holds "in all countries and at all times."[2] In a later treatise, Pareto himself warned against hasty deductions from his finding. "Empirical laws," he wrote, "have little or no value outside the limits for which they were found experimentally to be true."[3] Moreover, I do not think that any economists today accept his apparent suggestion that what his studies *seemed* to prove *had* happened over a wide scale would necessarily be repeated under different institutions in later periods.

In any case, Pareto's statistical procedures (not the data he used) were questioned in the 1930s by Yntema, Gini, and other statisticians. Through visual illusion due to representation on logarithmic scales, his curve suggests a rigidity of the proportions which is today recognized as misleading. But the phenomenon which he sought to illustrate, and for which he was trying to find an explanation remains. His work certainly did demonstrate that, for a variety of reasons which it is difficult to identify empirically, any existing market-determined distribution of income is very difficult to change.

Bowley, making careful studies of income distribution in Britain, and discussing such changes as were discernible over the period 1880 to 1913, remarked: "The constancy of so many of the proportions and the rates of movement . . . seems to point to a fixed system of causation and has an appearance of inevitableness."[4] This has been termed "the Bowley law," although that rigorous and meticulous statistician certainly intended the words "seems" and "appearance" to bear their full meaning.

In 1928, studies by Cobb and Douglas[5] brought out the fact that the ratio of aggregate wages *plus* salaries to aggregate value added in manufacture has proved tenaciously stable over time. Many authors have tried to explain or to explain away this relationship (which has become known as "the Cobb-Douglas function"). But a long chain of subsequent painstaking statistical inquiries, assisted by theoretical analysis, has failed to disclose convincing evidence that labor's share has increased in relation to the nonlabor share. Despite the enormous costs the unions have incurred (in the form of wages foregone, equality of opportunity in the labor market destroyed and social cohesion sacrificed) in efforts to change the proportions, they have seemingly remained obstinately fixed.

Covering the period 1850 to 1910, when the strike-threat influence was relatively unimportant, a pioneer study by W. I. King suggested that the proportion of income enjoyed by labor had fallen from about 78 to about 76 percent.[6] But even had the data available for that long period been adequate, the imponderables are so many that the seeming decline in labor's share can hardly be regarded as significant.

Simon Kuznets, in a famous study, presented data showing a rise in labor's share between the periods 1919-28 and 1929-38 from about 73 to 78 percent.[7] But the comparison is, of course between a boom, full employment, period in which, as I have insisted, labor's share can be expected to be well below the average and a period marked by the most disastrous depression of American history, with chronic unemployment, during which, as I have also insisted, labor's share can be expected to be well above the average. In the case of Kuznets' figures, this tendency is magnified because he included relief payments in labor's income.

In another impressive investigation into income shares, D. Gale Johnson, building among other things on the earlier investigations of King and Kuznets, constructed tables which indicated a rise in labor's proportion over the course of five decades. The data he analyzed suggest that labor's share of money income *in the economy as a whole* had increased from 68 percent in 1900 to 75 in 1952.[8] But Johnson himself pointed out that nearly half of the apparent increase occurred prior to 1929; and that was a period in which the strike-threat influence, although growing in the nonagricultural sector (spasmodically and with some setbacks), was still exerted over a relatively small portion of the United States economy.[9] Moreover, for the earlier period, Johnson was working with inadequate data. From 1929 onward the data become more plentiful and more reliable. Comparing the period 1930 to 1939 and 1940 to 1949, Johnson's findings show that labor's share fell;[10] yet it was in the middle of the first period that the Wagner Act seemed suddenly to enhance strike-threat power by more than any other event in the history of labor.

These findings, says Johnson, "can be explained, in part at least, by the failure of our national income data to record the income produced by government property" (see page 230), "by the effect of increased urbanization . . ." (see page 229), and "by the transfer of labor from relatively capital intensive to capital extensive industries"[11] (see page 229).

It seems that, as soon as we make due allowance for the illusory factors discussed above (pages 230-232, 1 to 5), we find that, in Clark Kerr's words, "labor's share of national income has remained more nearly constant than any other economic variable in society";[12] "there is little apparent increase since 1929 in labor's share; and it is since 1929 that the great growth in unionism has occurred in the United States. . . . employees are better off to the extent that all income recipients are better off."[13] Kerr's position in respect of constancy of shares seems to be confirmed by the results of all other serious inquiries. Some of these have independently examined the data and tested the inferences of other investigators, as well as having brought out the consequences of different definitions of the categories compared. Thus J. Alterman has shown that, *in the corporate part of the economy*, the proportional shares of capital and labor were virtually the same during the periods 1922-1929 and 1947-1959.[14] S. Lebergott, whose critical review of earlier statistical work in the field Alterman is discussing, confirms the finding of long-term stability in the proportions (for which he suggests "a market mechanism" is responsible).[15] Dealing with *the manufacturing field* (in which one would have expected strike-threat transfers to be most effectively achieved, by reason of the typical short-term specificity of the assets), he shows that wages as a percentage of value added (in the United States) had long-term stability over the whole period 1889 to 1954; and he quotes in support the findings of Wooden and Wasson, for the period 1929 to the early 1950s, as also showing "an approximate constancy," and as being "a more precise measurement."[16] A study for Canada, by S. A. Goldberg, presents data which suggest at first that the share of wages in aggregate income had risen there between 1926-1930 and 1954-1958.[17] But this impression is dispelled when the author makes his own essential qualifications, which refer to a rapid shift from agriculture to industry and from unincorporated ownership to corporate organization (both of which factors could, as we have seen, have accounted for a rise in labor's share even if no union pressures had been present).[18] In any case, a critical discussion of Goldberg's careful investigation by M. C. Urquhart leaves the impression that it is doubtful whether even a *moderate* rise in labor's share was really experienced in Canada over the years examined. Thus, "if we include in labor's share of income that part of the unincorporated enterprise income which should be attributed to it . . . the null hypothesis that factor shares have not changed has not been disproved."[19]

I. B. Kravis begins his study with a claim that he will show "the notion of long-run constancy in relative shares" to be false,[20] because he finds "some evidence of a slight tendency to drift downwards"[21] on the part of the property share since 1929, and he attributes this "slight" apparent transfer from "property to labor"[22] to exactly the causes which I myself have suggested would have led us to expect such a transfer.[23] Yet, comparing "averages for overlapping cycles," he finds that the property share since 1929 ". . . has been characterized by near secular stability. . . ."[24] It seems to me that this is his crucial conclusion.

E. F. Denison, examining *the ordinary business sector*, reaches the conclusion that (excluding the depression and the war years, and making the necessary adjustments) there was "substantial stability" in respect of the employee percentage of income.[25] M. Reder, interpreting these findings for the period 1929 to 1952, suggests that is "is tantamount to saying that labor's functional share of private non-farm output was constant. . . ."[26] And independently discussing an apparent rise in the "employee compensation" share which Denison's figures suggest, and directing attention to "labor's functional share" (that is, "employee compensation" after correction for the illusory element due to "self employment"),[27] and allowing for a real influence tending to raise labor's share,[28] namely, "an increase in the relative numbers in industries with more than average employee shares," Reder concludes that "it is quite possible that (this share) . . . has stayed constant in the United States since 1910 or thereabouts."[29] Moreover, he refers to the significant finding that "within individual industries there is also very substantial stability (over time) of the wage share."[30]

Bronfenbrenner's acceptance as proven "the observed degree of constancy in the relative shares of labor and capital in developed capitalist countries"[31] has already been noticed.

Phelps-Brown, asking whether the unions can in fact achieve what their most active members believe is their primary purpose, namely, the winning of "a larger share of the product," says that "the observed stability of the distribution of the product between pay and profit" suggests that such a purpose is "delusive," and he gives reasons for holding "that the profit margin in the selling price is in practice not generally compressible by wage rises."[32] During the last hundred years, "the proportionate share of the product accruing to employed labor has not changed widely or cumulatively."[33] "The trend of the wage-income ratio is conspicuous for its stability." In Sweden, "the wage-income ratio was no different in 1913 from what it had been in 1961."[34]

In his textbook, Samuelson includes among the "six basic trends of economic evelopment" with which he suggests the fundamental "facts of economic history in the advanced nations" . . . can be "summarized," "Bowley's law".(see pages 241-242), relating to the apparent long-term fixity of the proportions. He rightly warns the student that all such empirical laws are "only approximate truths." But after plotting the relevant data, he remarks of the period 1900 to the present, that "labor has kept about the *same* share of total product, with property also earning about the same relative share throughout the period."[35]

Kaldor, who is among those who have stressed the "stability of shares" which, he says, has been experienced "in the advanced capitalist economies over the last hundred years or so, despite the phenomenal changes in the techniques of production, in the accumulation of capital relative to labor and in income per head,"[36] *should have added* (in the context of the word "despite"), "and above all despite the enormous increase in the strike-threat influence."

There are indeed studies which indicate not only the apparent constancy of labor's proportion of income over long periods of time, but suggest that the strike-threat influence does not cause the percentage share of wages or of employee compensation in occupations subject to that threat to be higher or to increase more rapidly[37] than in fields not subject to it. For instance, in 1930 Douglas drew the attention of economists to the fact that, contrasting six highly unionized industries with eight nonunionized industries, and referring to the period between 1914 and 1926, "wages in the nonunion manufacturing industries have risen at least as rapidly as have those in the union manufacturing trades. . . ."[38] This finding was accepted with respect but obvious reluctance and skepticism.[39] However, later investigations have tended to confirm Douglas's tentative conclusions. Thus, P. Sultan who, like the rest, finds that "over time, labor's percentage has remained amazingly constant,"[40] demonstrates also that the ratio of wage and salary payments *plus* supplements to income in unionized and nonunion industries between 1929 and 1956 followed "a remarkably similar path." His conclusion is that, in the absence of runaway inflation or deflation, "union wage/income ratios are likely to approximate those in the nonunion sector, union wage pressures notwithstanding."[41] That is, movements in labor's proportion of income in unionized and nonunion industries appear to be *correlated* over minor cycles of boom and depression.[42] Moreover, interpreting data presented by Levinson, Sultan shows that while unionized workers were most successful in avoiding wage-rate adjustment during the great depression, during the recovery from 1933 onward, the nonunion workers caught up and during 1934 "received extraordinarily large wage increases."[43] And referring to the fact that, from 1934 to 1937, unorganized workers gained nearly twice as much as the organized workers, he remarks: "It is surprising that at the very moment in history when unions enjoyed tremendous power and influence, the relative wage differential accruing to the union sector should appear to diminish."[44] "The mushroom growth of unionism since the mid-thirties has not produced any upheaval in distributive shares."[45] Sultan rightly insists, however, that "it is impossible to determine what the distribution of income would have been in the absence of union pressures."[46]

Simler reaches almost identical conclusions. Dealing with the period 1929 to 1954, he finds that in the private sector "labor's share in unionized industries has generally not increased more than in nonunionized industries";[47] and he comments further that, if other years had been chosen for comparison, it would look as though unionism must have had adverse effects on labor's share! His conclusions are unequivocal. Using Levinson's data he finds that, between 1919 and 1929, "the influence of unionism on labor's share had been non-existent," and that between 1929 and 1947, a tendency for the figures to indicate a rise in labor's percentage (from 56 to 59.3 percent) is to be explained by "factors other than unionism."[48] He finds further that "the hypothesis that there exists a positive and significant correlation between the strength of trade unionism and labor's relative share of income is not confirmed by the available data for the manufacturing sector of the American economy. . . . The hypothesis originally asserted by Dobb and since advanced by others, that 'where wage earners are strongly organized in trade unions, one might expect labor to succeed in obtaining a larger share of the product than elsewhere' is contradicted by the experience in the manufacturing sector of the American economy in the first half of the twentieth century."[49] And yet it is in this particular field, the manufacturing sector, in which the importance of fixed, nonversatile assets are most important, that I have shown the *possibility* of exploitation of investors to have been greatest.

Kenneth Boulding, concluding an essay in which he submitted "a partial rehabilitation of the wage fund doctrine," and advancing the thesis that the distribution of income "is largely independent of what happens in the labor market," comments (without reference to the empirical studies with which he obviously expects his readers to be aware) on "the evident impotence of trade unions in increasing the share of labor in national income";[50] and Clark Kerr, weighing up, together with his own investigations, a whole range of independent inquiries in the field, finds that "labor's share, . . . industry by industry, has fared no more favorably in unionized industries than in nonunion industries."[51]

Again, among those who have reviewed previous investigations into labor's share, we find Albert Rees, who is satisfied that "no effect of unions on labor's share . . . can be discovered with any consistency,"[52] that is, that when adjustment of the data to allow for some of the illusory factors which I have listed above (pp. 230-233) has been made, there is "a remainder that shows no particular relation to union power."[53] Whenever the aggregate output of the community is increasing more rapidly than the population of working age, the unionized and the nonunionized sectors of the economy enjoy intermittent increases in real earnings, and during inflations' intermittent increases in money earnings, for exactly the same reasons. That is, Rees insists, the union gains "would . . . have taken place even without the union."[54]

Bradley also, summarizing the findings of post-World War II empirical investigations conducted by some of the economists whose work I have been quoting, and by other authorities, says that, over the periods studied, "wage gains did not occur entirely or even largely in those industries and trades where most workers were represented by unions. Nor were wage losses restricted entirely or largely to the industries or trades where most workers were not represented by unions. In terms of real wages the two groups did about equally well."[55]

The same considerations apply to wage rates fixed under legal enactment. In an important article from which I have already quoted, Yale Brozen has concluded, from a careful study of United States data, that such wage-rate increases as have been gained via successive amendments of the minimum wage statute "would have come anyway in most cases within two to five years" because "the wage rates of low-paid employees in non-covered occupations have been rising at 4 percent per year since 1949. . . . What successive amendments to the minimum wage statute have done is to jump rates in the year of application. *Very slow rates of increase then occur* in the following years . . ."[56] (My italics.)

Experience under inflation gives special emphasis to the point these economists are making. If there were no strike-threat influences present, and any measure of inflation occurred, prices would increase and the demands for all kinds of productive services (in terms of money) would increase *more or less* in proportion to the prospective prices of final products. Inflation makes it profitable for entrepreneurs to bid up *the money price* of labor in the same way that the growth of real income similarly makes it profitable for entrepreneurs to bid up *the real price* of labor. Strike-threat pressures have never been needed to bring about such revaluations.

But what does remain true is that, when the extent of the use to be made of the strike threat has not been fully anticipated, and its consequences not allowed for, investors are exploitable. This truth has been constantly stressed since the earlier chapters. But the corollary has been equally stressed that expectations of exploitation will not continue to be wrong indefinitely. Hence, any redistributive tendencies due to this cause will be temporary. Evidence of such temporary influences on income shares is discernible in empirical studies. These influences have, however, obviously been insufficiently important, in relation to others, to show in most of the aggregate figures. What empirical investigations *have* apparently established is that workers in newly organized industries may gain through the strike threat, sometimes appreciably;[57] although after a while the unionized workers cease to gain further in relation to workers in nonunion occupations. This is, of course, direct confirmation of the thesis I have just reiterated.[58] I conclude that if all the other determinants of the relative shares can be assumed to have been tending to establish a near constant ratio, the failure of the strike threat system discernibly to change that ratio can be attributed to the factors discussed in the previous chapter.

We have noticed, however, yet other reasons why labor's share could be expected to have been increasing. Hence, the observed constancy of its share (except through cyclical factors) suggest that *strike-threat activity, while it has undoubtedly greatly reduced the flow of wages, has not only failed to transfer income from investors to workers, but everything points to its having worked as a contractionist force on labor's percentage*. (See above, p. 234.)

The passage quoted from Kaldor (see page 245) reflects the general surprise of economists that an apparent big "accumulation of capital relative to labor" has not brought about a rise in labor's percentage. The most plausible explanation is, I think, the one I suggested above (pages 144-145), namely, that the more exploitable forms of investment, which tend to be the most wage-multiplying, have been avoided. A less wage-multiplying *composition* of the stock of assets appears to have come into being. *The effect of strike-*

threat pressures may, I repeat, have been not only greatly to reduce labor's absolute income below what it could otherwise have been but even to reduce its relative share in some measure.

In case any reader should still be under misapprehension on the point, the demonstration in this chapter that, in an era in which the strike threat is an established institution, wage rates in unionized industries do not increase more rapidly than those in nonunion activities, does not mean that the strike threat has not succeeded in winning for labor unionists (as distinct from labor) considerably higher real wage rates on the average than they could otherwise have gained (out of the aggregate real income which the distortions of the system must have greatly reduced). There is no important controversy about this. H. Gregg Lewis has estimated that the unions in the United States have been able to raise the wage rates of their members, *relatively to nonunion workers*, by between 10 and 15 percent.[59] However, as the forcing up of wage rates in one field forces down wage rates in other fields,[60] any *absolute* gain to the average union worker would have been less than his *relative* gain, *even if there had been no adverse effects upon the aggregate wages flow*. But, in the light of the effects of the strike-threat system upon the magnitude and composition of the assets stock, "organized labor" must have shared a much smaller cake. Hence, when the costs of organization to achieve strike threat power and the costs of the occasional exercise of that power are allowed for, a net absolute advantage is *probably* enjoyed by a very small proportion only of the workers who confidently believe themselves to be beneficiaries. *This consideration has an important bearing on the political practicability of reform aimed at the establishment of a nonstrike era. The overwhelming majority of labor unionists would almost certainly benefit.*

NOTES

[1] Vilfredo Pareto, *Cours d'Economie Politique* (Rouge, 1897), Vol. II, pp. 304 *et seq.*

[2] These words are the summarization of "Pareto's law" as presented in the National Bureau of Economic Research, *Income in the United States* (1922), p. 344.

[3] Vilfredo Pareto, *Manuel d'Economie Politique* (Giard et Brière, 1909), p. 391.

[4] A. L. Bowley, *The Division of the Product of Industry* (Oxford: Clarendon Press, 1919).

[5] C. W. Cobb and P. Douglas, "The Theory of Production," *American Economic Review*, supp. (March 1928).

[6] W. I. King, *Wealth and Income of the People of the United States* (New York: Macmillan, 1915), p. 160.

[7] Simon Kuznets, *National Income and Its Composition, 1919-1938*, Vol. I (New York: Macmillan, 1938), Tables 22 and 64.

[8] D. Gale Johnson, "The Functional Distribution of Income in the United

248

States, 1850-1952," *Review of Economics and Statistics*, May, 1954, p. 178. Johnson recognized that labor's share in money income had increased more than its share in real income. (Ibid., p. 180.)

[9] By the end of the period nearly one-third of the nonagricultural workers were union members.

[10] D. Gale Johnson, op. cit., p. 178.

[11] Ibid., p. 175.

[12] Clark Kerr, "Labor's Income Share. . . ," in *New Concepts in Wage Determination*, eds. G. W. Taylor and F. C. Pierson (New York: McGraw-Hill, 1957), p. 260. See Kerr's Table I, column 4, p. 280.

[13] Ibid., p. 281.

[14] J. Alterman, in *Behavior of Income Shares*, (National Bureau of Economic Research, 1962), p. 93.

[15] S. Lebergott, in *Behavior of Income Shares*, p. 57 (see above, p. 223).

[16] Ibid., p. 85.

[17] S. A. Goldberg, *The Behavior of Income Shares*, pp. 189 et seq.

[18] In the employment shift to agriculture, a *real* factor (see 5 on p. 229) and an *illusory* factor (see 5 on p. 232) are involved. In the shift to employment in corporations, the factor is *illusory* (see p. 231, number 4).

[19] M. C. Urquhart, in *The Behavior of Income Shares*, p. 272.

[20] I. B. Kravis, "Relative Income Shares in Fact and Theory," *American Economic Review* (1959), p. 917.

[21] *Ibid.*, p. 931.

[22] *Ibid.*, p. 918.

[23] He says, "The number of man-hours worked has not expanded as fast as population . . . , while reproducible capital (in constant prices) has nearly doubled in relation to man-hours." "The greater responsiveness of the supply of capital to the demands of a growing economy has led to price-induced substitution with existing techniques and probably also to capital-using innovations." (Ibid., p. 918.) And finally, "a change in the industrial composition of employment and income" was a factor. (Ibid., p. 946.)

[24] Ibid., p. 931.

[25] E. F. Denison, "Distribution of National Income Since 1929," in *Survey of Current Business*, 1952.

[26] M. Reder, "Alternative Theories of Labor's Share," in M. Abramovitz, *The Allocation of Economic Resources* (National Bureau of Economic Research, 1959), p. 197.

[27] See p. 231.

[28] See pp. 229-230.

[29] Reder, *op. cit.*, p. 197.

[30] Ibid., p. 200.

[31] M. Bronfenbrenner, *op. cit.*, p. 284.

[32] E. H. Phelps-Brown, *Economics of Labor* (Oxford: Oxford University Press, 1962), pp. 184-5.

[33] Ibid., p. 220.

[34] Ibid., p. 222.

[35] Paul Samuelson, *Economics* (7th ed.; New York: McGraw-Hill, 1967), p. 719.

[36] N. Kaldor, "Alternative Theories of Distribution," *Review of Economic Studies*, 1955-56, p. 84.

[37] On *private* gains achievable by unions (at the expense of consumers and laid-off or excluded workers) see p. 248.

[38] Paul H. Douglas, *Real Wages in the United States, 1890-1926* (Boston: Houghton Mifflin Co., 1930), p. 592.

[39] Consider, for example, the discussion by H. A. Millis and R. E. Montgomery, *Labor's Progress and some Basic Labor Problems* (New York: McGraw-Hill, 1938), pp. 212-3.

[40] P. Sultan, *Labor Economics*, (Henry Holt, 1957), p. 73.

[41] Ibid., p. 389.

[42] During World War II, the proportion enjoyed by the unionized industries did increase relatively, probably because price controls were more important in the unionized industries (see above, pp. 000-000) and because war demands for the output of the unionized industries increased relatively to demands for the output of nonunionized industries, involving overtime payments in the former as well as a larger proportion of demand not subject to market rationing.

[43] Sultan, op. cit., p. 191.

[44] Ibid., p. 393.

[45] Ibid., pp. 384-5. Could it not be that entrepreneurial anticipations had already caught up?

[46] Ibid., pp. 384-5.

[47] N. J. Simler, *The Impact of Unionism* (University of Minnesota Press, 1961), p. 41.

[48] Ibid., pp. 40-41.

[49] Ibid., p. 11.

[50] K. Boulding, in David McCord Wright, ed., *The Impact of the Union* (New York: Harcourt Brace and Co., 1957), p. 148.

[51] Kerr, op. cit., p. 283.

[52] Albert A. Rees, *The Economics of Trade Unions* (Chicago: University of Chicago Press, 1962), p. 94.

[53] Ibid., p. 95.

[54] Ibid., p. 81.

[55] P. Bradley, *Labor Unions and Public Policy* (Washington, D.C.: American Enterprise Association, 1959), p. 63.

[56] Y. Brozen, "The Effect of Minimum Wage Increase on Teenage Employment," *Journal of Law and Economics* (1969), pp. 121-122.

[57] For example, Arthur M. Ross, "The Influence of Unionism Upon Earnings," *Quarterly Journal of Economics*, February 1948, pp. 263-286.

[58] A neat statement of the empirically-based principle is that "new unionism has been the source of relative wage advantage . . . whereas continuing unionism has not." Arthur M. Ross and William Goldner, "Forces Affecting the Inter-industry Wage Structure," *Quarterly Journal of Economics*, May 1950, pp. 254-281.

[59] H. Gregg Lewis, *Unionism and Relative Wage Rates in the United States,* (Chicago: University of Chicago Press, 1963), p. 193.

[60] Every "contrived scarcity" entails an "incidental plenitude". (See Chapter 7). I am not overlooking here the frequent tendency of nonunion undertakings which are competing with union undertakings to match duress-enforced wage-rate increases, in order to discourage the spread of unionization to their activities.

17

The Strike Threat
and Inflation

I⊤ IS common to lay part of the blame for inflation on the unreasonable use made of the strike-threat system. The forcing up of wage rates more rapidly than productivity rises is supposed to bring about the "cost-push" as distinct from the "demand-pull" type of inflation. The notion *has* indirect justification, yet is seriously misleading. I propose to argue that the notions of "price-induced," or "cost-induced," or "wage-induced," or "cost-push," or "wage-push" inflation have meaning only if they are based on *a tacit political assumption*.[1]

The assumption is that governments must react in a certain way to the fixing of particular prices and wage rates at levels which reduce prospective yields to "investment" (replacement *plus* net accumulation). That is, the inflation of the contemporary world is a government reaction to the setting of costs and prices at levels which reduce the community's ability or willingness to purchase previous outputs. But, the pushing up of particular wage rates and prices under duress does not *cause* inflation. An inflationary monetary reaction may be usual—perhaps almost universal in the present age—but it is not a *necessary* reaction.

H. G. Johnson, objecting to the suggestion "that in modern economics the wage rate is autonomously determined by collective bargaining and the money supply is automatically adjusted to it," says that this "would be the case if government were formally committed to the maintenance of full employment, whatever happened. . . . But governments have not," he maintains, "been prepared to accept this sort of unlimited commitment; they have instead been prepared to tolerate a varying amount of unemployment. . . ."[2] This not only insists that inflation is not a *necessary* reaction but implies that too rapid an inflation to offset strike-threat consequences may be as politically disadvantageous as the unemployment caused.

Fruitful study of what we now tend to call "wage-price" policy demands that we be crystal clear on this point. Can the raising of *particular* prices or costs itself be inflationary? My contention is that it cannot. Whether the prices or costs that are raised are a consequence of factors expressed through free market forces, or due to collusive or political action to create a contrived scarcity is immaterial.[3] The real explanation of any labor union responsibility for the inflationary era is simply that strike-threat pressures *cause inflation to be politically expedient*. Any decline in the real value of the money unit of the kind sometimes termed "wage-inflation" is not *caused by* duress-imposed wage rates any more than inflation generally is *caused by* duress-imposed product prices.

Let us suppose that, as the result of a strike threat, wage rates in the footwear industry are raised, *or* that the price of leather (wholly imported) rises, causing the price of shoes to increase. Then, *in the absence of inflation*, either *some other prices* must fall or a *cumulative* decline in activity (that is, in other outputs) must occur (a) until any price or wage-rate rigidities which prevent other prices from falling are broken, or (b) until wholly new ways of using the displaced labor and other resources—probably ways less subject to value rigidities—have been discovered.[4] But inflation may "validate" the discoordinative pricing which is causing the decline in activity. Only when one or more of these reactions has followed will the cumulative decline cease. An equilibrium at a lower real income will then have been established unless thrift (possibly aided by current technological progress and managerial ingenuities) happens to have been compensating or bringing forth growth. In other words, every upward pressure on costs in an industry has adverse effects on the magnitude of profitable output; the enhanced costs reduce thereby the possible contribution of that industry to the source of demands for noncompeting outputs; and hence, unless the upward pressure on costs has been caused by an expansion of other outputs, or unless the price-cost effects are "validated" by inflation, it must inevitably set going a cumulative tendency to recession.

Admittedly, the decline in activity caused when certain prices are forced up by private or governmental duress will *automatically* bring about some inflation *if monetary policy is rigid*;[5] just as improved coordination in any society (expressed *ceteris paribus* in price and cost reductions) will *automatically* be followed by deflation if monetary policy is rigid. A contraction or expansion of real income requires monetary contraction or expansion if the purchasing power of the money unit is to be maintained constant. Any inflation or deflation which follows individual price changes is fully explained therefore by monetary *policy*—usually deliberate, even if often reluctant in the present age.

Exactly the opposite idea is reflected in the confusing notion that high economic activity generates inflation. In reality, high activity means high output; and that implies a deflationary outcome (in the sense that deflation will follow under monetary rigidity). The common reversal of cause and effect which I am here trying to expose is one of the most deplorable intellectual consequences bequeathed by the Keynesian ara; and it arises because inflation *is* (when not fully expected and discounted) a method (albeit a very crude method) of generating activity—that is, of reducing costs relatively to prospective prices; while those responsible for inflation find it expedient to place the blame on the stimulated activity rather than on the stimulant.

Thus, when expectations begin to catch up with the rate of planned inflation, *a slowing down of the rate of inflation* becomes expedient. The authorities like then to talk euphemistically of aiming at "*a slowing down of activity*" or "*a slowing down of growth*." The absurd implication is, of course, that the discoordination is somehow due to "over-activity," or "too rapid growth," or "overheating." The notions of "over-activity" or "too rapid growth" are meaningless in such context,[6] as are the even less rigorously conceived ideas of an "overheated" economy or, of a "straining of existing capacity."[7] The term "activity," if rationally used, is synonymous with "output;" and (as was insisted above) an increase in output is the reverse of inflationary. Of course, the tacit (but preposterous) assumption is that aggregate output *cannot* grow in the absence of inflation, so that any actual growth is proof of inflationary pressures. A phrase of the following kind in a newspaper report illustrates how seriously confused public discussion of the issue has become: "A discouraging development in the inflation fight is the Commerce Department's report that orders for durable goods . . . are marching again."[8] (I return to this subject on pages 255-256.)

The fact that wage-rate increases conceded under strike-threat pressure "require higher payrolls" in particular cases, or cause increases in the money cost of given inventories, or induce investment in labor-saving machinery (all of which require "financing"), does *not* imply that they have any inflationary effect. If, under such circumstances, borrowing occurs more rapidly than noninflationary monetary policy would permit, it can only be because policy is *not* noninflationary!

Nor are such things as transfer payments (for example, unemployment compensation or relief expenditures), or the reduction of tax payments in developing recession, inflationary or disinflationary in any meaningful sense, although they *have* been regarded as of a stabilizing nature in such circumstances. Only if inflation maintains a certain money valuation of income (a certain "disposable income" as it is often put) when real income would otherwise fall, can any mitigation of the price discoordination which causes a general decline in activity be brought about by fiscal or monetary means.

It is equally wrong to regard "escalator clauses" as inflationary; for if any inflation ceased, so would the "escalator." Such clauses do not increase the *flow* of money wages. If the volume of deposits *plus* money in circulation is maintained in a more or less constant ratio to real income,[9] the flow of money wages can rise solely through a rise in output, irrespective of what proportion of those employed are remunerated on an "escalator" basis. In fact, monetary authorities responsible for inflationary policies hate "escalator clauses" (and often dub them "inflationary") because they destroy the rational purpose of inflation, which is to achieve such coordination of relative prices as results when costs lag in relation to final prices. *Universal* resort to "escalators" would force abandonment of the inflationary remedy!

But all these factors may be *termed* "inflationary" if we have previously made it perfectly clear to our students or our readers that all we mean is that the factors concerned are *assumed to make it expedient for the monetary authorities to set inflation going or keep it going*. If we do so we are, however, under an obligation to emphasize that the *inflation is then deliberate and planned, however reluctant*. And students and readers should be left under no misconception about the fact that a monetary authority which accepts such an aim must make use of all the difficult and highly expert techniques by means of which the real value of the money unit can be forced to depreciate without causing a general expectation of the speed and duration of the inflation planned. A universal demand for "escalator" valuation or other private action to escape inflationary burdens would defeat the objective.

An equally misleading yet influential idea is that inflation is due to something called the "over-all level of demand" being "in excess." Such phrases have meaning only when they describe a situation which monetary and fiscal policies have created. But some economists who write in this sort of way do perceive that, if inflation is to be avoided *and* full employment objectives sought, policy is, in Melvin Rothbaum's words, forced to "focus on either reducing the power of wage-setters and price-setters or on changing their behavior. . . . [and]. . . .[this] may include attempts to change the structure of business and labor organizations, to devise economic penalties and incentives that will induce the desired wage-price performance, to request voluntary changes in purpose, or to compel the desired performance through a system of controls."[10] Yes, but if "the structure of business and labor organizations" is changed in the manner required,[11] neither "requests" nor "controls" will be necessary; and the "penalties and incentives" to which Rothbaum refers will not need to be *devised*. They are already there—waiting to be released from the chains in which they have been shackled. They are expressed through the loss-avoidance, profit-seeking discipline which forces entrepreneurial decision-makers constantly to determine the form and use of productive resources through comparison of objective and prospective input values (including interest) with prospective output values, under careful and continuously revised estimates of marginal yields.

A similar notion, also due to a wrong discernment of cause and effect in the interpretation of inflationary experience, has led superficial observers to believe, or careless expositions to assert, that only a state of unemployment is capable of preventing inflation. In my judgment, it has been the present generation's tolerance of virtually unrestrained resort to the strike-threat system which has been responsible both for this belief and for the corollary that a money unit of defined value is impossible in any society which wants to avoid the curse of chronic unemployment. Hansen expressed the notion in 1949, referring to the United States, in the words, "to secure stable prices it is necessary to have several millions unemployed."[12] The truth is diametrically opposite. Employment of labor means output, and each output contributes to the source of demands for all other noncompeting outputs. No one would question the possibility that, *in a strike-threat era*, only unemployment (of men and assets) may be capable of forcing "reasonableness" on the part of unions, and creating an incentive on the part of managements to resist duress-imposed cost increases and so make a slowing down or cessation of inflation politically conceivable.[13] But this is never said in such simple terms that everyone will understand what is meant. The possibility is the justification of the "Phillips curve."[14]

In my judgment the semantic confusion of "wages" with "wage rates" (that is, of a share in the income flow with the prices of different qualities of labor), in phrases like "high wages make for prosperity," has had an enormous influence. It is of course true that "prosperity" is characterized by a high flow of wages and other income; but the source of "prosperity" is coordination through the price system, under which the utilization of productive power is adjusted to the magnitude of income and expressed preferences in the market. I forecast that the ultimate verdict of economic historians will be that the most disastrous economic phenomenon of this century, the Great Depression, was due to the pricing of output in the unionized sector at first beyond the reach of uninflated income, later inconsistently with price expectations, and *mainly* in consequence of strike-threat power in key sectors of the major countries.

The old "classical" teaching pointed to the remedy, namely, the restoration of the flow of wages and income *via* the repricing of inputs so as to make full potential outputs profitable. But this teaching was spurned through the accelerating influence of Keynesian notions; and those notions were plausible because, even in the 1920s and 1930s, the labor unions stood in the path of the most urgently needed market-selected price and wage-rate adjustments. In the circumstances, unanticipated inflation seemed to have become the only politically acceptable way out and the public was indoctrinated with the idea that the depression had been essentially a monetary phenomenon—as a result of the defects of the supposedly outmoded gold standard system.

It is truly astonishing how successfully blame for the Great Depression was transferred from defective human organization (in the determination of wage rates and other prices) to the gold standard. For that monetary standard was the foundation of a simple, straightforward system under which—as long as the contract in it was honored—the measuring rod of value had been removed from political tampering. This is not the appropriate context in which to discuss the attributes of the very imperfect credit and currency institutions which had arisen while currencies were fully convertible into gold. But the Keynesian and other attacks on the gold standard were directed as much against the virtues as against the vices of the system. It is obvious that Keynes was, throughout his contributing life, hostile to the notion of *any* kind of money unit with a defined value. Although he changed fundamentally from time to time the arguments on which he based his opposition, he wanted the money unit's value to be a matter of government discretion.[15] But the origin of his position lay in his recognition that, if there is a money unit with the attributes of a satisfactory measuring rod, it bars resort to the process of increasing the money valuation of a given real income; and the latter seemed

256

to him to be necessary in order to enable the community to purchase output without far-reaching reform of the pricing system.

Admittedly, under widespread wage-rate rigidity and price rigidity, the cessation of a period of inflation or even a reduction in its speed, will cause a displacement of labor and wasteful idleness, especially in nonversatile capital resources. The question is, however, are we bound to accept rigidities of this kind as inevitable? *A policy which deliberately aimed at preventing any reduction of the wages flow and income while inflation was being gradually but finally brought to an end, could insure continuous normal activity.* But any such policy would have to protect managements from the overruling, by strike-threat duress, of social pressures (market forces) in their task of revising wage-rate offers.

If this were understood, it would be perfectly possible, I suggest, to fashion institutions under which there are effective incentives to the pricing of all productive services (of men and assets) so that the full potential flow of output is continuously consumed or utilized, no matter what value for the money unit policy happens to dictate. But the maintenance of some *defined value* for the unit (such as that of a constant "real value" or a given weight of gold) will *assist* the coordinative process under which price changes permit not only the *uninterrupted use* of all productive factors but, what is even more important, their *optimal use*.

While union spokesmen are unquestionably right, then, in their contention that it is monetary and fiscal policy alone which is responsible for inflation, and not the pressure of their demands on wage rates, when they make this claim *they cannot honestly deny their responsibility for the political attractiveness of inflation*. Union officials must admit that if inflation does *not* follow the consequent continuous rise in labor costs from which their profession benefits, cumulative displacement of labor will be unavoidable and multiplied through the decline in the wages flow (and contraction of the income-flow generally) which *their* policies bring about.

To blame the strike-threat system for increasing the political expediency of inflation is not to deny that inflation itself creates the "need" for upward adjustments of wage rates determined under union "negotiation" if the real value of those wage rates is to be preserved; but as the coordinative effect of inflation depends upon its reducing that real value, through "restorative" increases in end product prices, any policy which allows the restoration of duress-increased *real* wage-rate levels must be self-defeating.

Whereas the influence of the strike threat is to cause critical money wage rates to be rigid downward during deflations, during inflations it appears to have the opposite effect. It prevents the full benefit which wage-rate inertias can exert in maximizing output and income when inflation tends to rectify duress-imposed price distortions. The "vicious circle" of wage rates chasing prices originates when inflation begins to bring about the intended[16] rise in the cost of living. As soon as the consequences become generally obvious, the policy tends to prompt pressures (first in one occupation and then in another)

257

at least for the restoration of former real wage rates; and if these claims are generally conceded, the whole *raison d'être* of attempts at inflationary validation of the situation is eradicated. The perception of this has led to some recognition of the folly of the whole process—the purposelessness implied in the term "vicious circle" itself.

Nevertheless, unless the strike threat *is* continuously exploited, money wage rates which have earlier been determined under that threat will tend to remain relatively undisturbed, while wage rates not fixed under union coercion will tend to rise. The effect will be that customary differentials, based on privilege, will be upset. Should any union then fail to maintain the degree of exploitation from which its members have been profiting, they will lose *relatively* to other groups, privileged or unprivileged. And as we have seen (in Chapter 13), the feelings of envy or of injustice which are aroused when the comparative earnings of different kinds of workers are changed, bring formidable irrationalities into the wage-rate determination process—a consideration to which we must shortly return.

The discoordination caused by the strike-threat influence in wage-rate determination, and its crude recoordination via "fiscal-monetary" policy (that is, inflationary policy) have created a succession of "short-term" problems. Typical of these are chronic balance of payment deficits, or (when entrepreneurs are trying to assist the avoidance of inflation by avoiding price increases) "shortages" due to inflation-financed demands. Such situations have seemed to call for what it has become usual to term "temporary economic policies," based on short-term expediency. And most economists would claim, I think, that the policies adopted have not all been altogether ineffectual. When values raised under strike-threat influence have been tending to bring about a slowing down of economic activity, inflationary "validation" in one form or another *has* always been satisfactory enough, they suggest.

That is one reason why continuous recourse to wholly pragmatic solutions has superficially come to appear inevitable today. Deliberate reform of the pricing system—the only alternative—is ruled out, even by majority opinion among economists, because modern politics demands inhibition of any *frank* recognition of the strike-threat influence in causing uninflated "aggregate demand" to contract. Economists who have wished their writings or their explicit advice to be regarded as sophisticated or "operational" have mostly felt expected simply to take the strike-threat system for granted. It would be as purposeless, they think, to be critical of that system as to be critical of earthquakes. The world just happens to have both. *But the inherent contradictions of inflationary "validation" of duress-imposed wage rates when all come to expect that "validation," yet some parts of the economy remain free from coercion, have never been solved*. And the contradictions are, I maintain confidently, insoluble. All efforts to solve them *have* failed miserably.

Consider, for example, attempts in recent years to make the working of the price system depend upon "guidelines," admonitions, exhortations, prayers, entreaties, dissuasions, persuasions, threats, appeals for "moderation," appeals for "voluntary restraint," appeals for explicit "voluntary wage freezes," appeals for "voluntary wage ceilings" or "stops," appeals for "concern for the public interest" and the like, and ultimately wage and price "freezes" followed by discretionary "controls," through pay boards, price commissions and cost of living councils. All these things are *intended*, of course, to weaken the strike-threat factor in price determination. They are apt to be described, however, as "supplements" to or "adjustments" of demand and supply forces! It is, I suggest, obvious why governments were driven first toward rather pathetic pleas, persuasions, half-hearted threats of compulsion, and later to the political determination of wage rates and prices. They were confronted with two causes of unpopularity: the alternatives of recession with unemployment, and *increasingly ineffective inflation*. They felt bound, therefore, to apply at any rate *some* curb or discouragement on the activities which precipitated their dilemma.

But what sort of coordinative principle is disclosed in policies so fashioned? And what incentives are favored in such policies? Let us remember that the *purpose* of "incomes policies," whether "persuasive" or mandatory, is to *mitigate the tendency of wage rates fixed under duress to reduce the current and prospective flow of wages and income*. If the labor market can be protected in any measure or for any length of time from strike-threat pressures, it is thought, the speed of the inflation required for crude recoordination of the economy and restoration of the income flow can be reduced and, while the restraint lasts, even brought to an end. Unfortunately, campaigns to obtain general acceptance of voluntary restraints, and threats (in practice, idle threats) of politically unpopular action unless there is "voluntary" submission, seem so far to have been almost completely unsuccessful. Perhaps the most promising attempt was the request for a wage freeze in Britain, tried in 1950. Although accepted by the Trades Union Congress, this initiative lasted a record nine months. Factors which we are about to consider then became too strong and strike-threat demands again became general.

In the United States, an attempt during the Kennedy administration to persuade the unions to limit demands for wage-rate increases to proportions which did not exceed the rate of growth in productivity, tended (in spite of a few exceptions) to induce unions which might otherwise have hesitated, for fear of adverse reactions, to feel justified in pushing up costs (and managements to feel justified in acquiescing). Provided the proportion of the increase did not exceed the level which had supposedly been officially pronounced as reasonable, there were few inhibitions. Publication of the statistically determined rate of increase in productivity seemed to become an invitation to all and sundry to defeat any hope of achieving real wage rates conducive to noninflationary prosperity. Certainly "guideline" pressures appeared not to slow down the rate of inflation or check the chronic weakening of the dollar (although of course things might have been worse had there been no "guideline" initiative). The hope had been that unions which ignored the government's exhortations would arouse *the disapprobation* of the other unions. In fact what happened was rather for them to arouse *the envy* of the others. Failure to comply provoked no denunciations from the union camp.

259

The complete uselessness of persuasions seemed to become even more obvious as the exceptional union militancy under the Johnson administration developed. And the Nixon administration, probably with less optimism, persevered for two years in attempts to inculcate "reasonableness" in the use of the strike-threat weapon before finally resorting to wage and price restraints.

There are five good reasons for the failure of these and all other experiments in moral suasion, cajolery or compulsion in general wage-rate freezing or imposition of wage-rate ceilings—reasons which explain why governments have acted so hesitatingly, inconsistently and ineffectually.

1. Suppose that all unions decided to behave exactly as governments wished, that a complete wage and price freeze was imposed; and that (a most unrealistic assumption) the freeze was applied with no concern for the vote-controlling power of different groups affected. All that would have been achieved would have been a freezing of one arm of the coordinative process, which depends upon *relative* prices and *relative* wage rates continuing to reflect changing relative scarcity. Quantities—outputs—would become the sole variables. "Prices have work to do. Prices should be free to tell the truth," said Benjamin Anderson. The maxim is as true of the prices of labor's input as it is of the prices of materials and the prices of final products. And *wage freezes have one of the chief defects of inflation as a means of rectifying the tendency to force real wage rates "too high"*: They penalize those whose real wage rates are *too low* precisely because other real wage rates are *too high*. There is no discrimination between the innocent and the guilty.

2. When the initiatives in question are merely "persuasive," although the voluntary aspect reflects perhaps some recognition of the absurdity of freezing *all* wage rates, insufficient account can be taken of the irrationalities and envies which play so important a part in motivating resort to the strike threat. When reliance is placed on "reasonableness," the members of those unions which regard governmental entreaties seriously or sympathetically must come off worst. Unions which treat appeals for a modicum of altruism with contempt can win larger gains at the expense of the rest. Indeed, do not such appeals offer an exceptional yield to those who cynically but realistically ignore all the exhortations? Are not "voluntary" policies tailor-made to assist those who have no concern whatsoever for the public interest? At their best—that is, in so far as they do succeed in mitigating the lurking influence of strike fears on the coordination of the economy—*they permit procrastination in seeking a fundamental solution to the problem of how to protect the flow of wages from depression through strike-threat pressures*. At their worst, the policies are an incitement to extortion.

Suppose a great political leader could persuade at least some of the more public-spirited union officials to dissuade their members from insistence upon blindly perpetuating the wage-price spiral. Could that set in motion the dynamic reactions needed to maintain the wages flow during a gradual cessation of inflation? It could not, I suggest, largely because *the reasonableness of some must raise the yield to defiant avarice on the part of the rest.* In any tendency to recession, as Simons pointed out (*apropos* the Great Depression):

> No single group, able to hold up its own price or wage, could advantage itself by reductions unless other groups acted similarly and simultaneously. Even if general reductions were in prospect, each single group could advantage itself by holding back. . . . They naturally all sat tight, cutting their own throats and all losing absolutely in order to preserve their relative position.[17]

3. When the politically necessary condition for the (nominal or genuine) acceptance of reasonableness in strike-threat pressures is that "profits" shall be limited in some manner, the whole purpose of the price-cost coordination sought in that crude manner is defeated. The sole defense of inflation is that it raises predicted yields to replacement and accumulation of capital, and thereby moves forward to greater magnitudes the planned outputs at which marginal prospective yields are equated with the rate of interest (thereby restoring the flow of wages and income). The politicians have no way out of this dilemma. The expediency of an incomes policy (persuasive or mandatory) is due primarily to the scope it gives for misrepresentation of its immediate objective. To the extent to which it is justifiable at all, the aim is, as I have just insisted, to improve profit prospects. But the workers' leaders could never openly approve of that. It would mean admitting that the larger the profits flow the larger the wages flow; and any such admission would be damaging to their profession. Hence a bluff of limiting profits (as an accompaniment of wage-rate ceilings) may create an aura of justice. The snag is that it is unlikely to remain a bluff and the economic system will find itself enmeshed in totalitarian shackles, with the politically powerful feathering their nests at the expense of the people as a whole.

4. The insistence as a parallel condition for "wage restraints" or "wage ceilings" that the prices of final products shall not rise has a *further* defect in that it fails to take into account the reality that wage rates already conceded under strike-threat pressures have been conditioned by the expectation of both managements and union leaders that the wage rates established will be gradually "validated" by subsequent inflation. The awkward truth is that any really effective correction of the situation must *appear* to be grossly unfair to labor. Logically, even if wage rates are frozen or wage ceilings imposed, final prices have to be left to determination under market discipline if the crudely coordinative reactions are to be realized.

The inclusion of dividends and product prices in guideline persuasions has probably always been pragmatic—to provide an apparently satisfactory answer to those who would otherwise shout that not to include prices and profits would be unfair to labor.[18] But if policy is sincerely aiming at wages equity and wages-maximization, booming *profits* ought to be encouraged, never restrained or exploited. Accelerating demands for labor, of which rising prospective yields to replacement and growth (that is, rising dividend forecasts) are the manifestation, should surely never to be curbed as a quid pro quo to satisfy the rank and file of unions whose rulers who shrink from the task of leadership.[19]

5. Probably most important of all, the officials of the labor union movement have correctly felt that the very purpose of the "voluntary restraints" arises from the dawn of an understanding of the indefensibility of strike-threat pressures as such. Under a Labor Government in Britain, when the alternative was a government likely to be even more critical of the system, it was expedient for the Trades Union Congress to be cooperative, even to recommend "no-strike bargaining" and exhort its members to think in terms of real wage rates. But for the logic of "wage persuasion" to be explained, an important concession toward the principle of free market determination of wage rates would have had to be made. It is unthinkable that union officials would be capable psychologically, even if intellectually, of communicating such a notion to their members. This, together with the influence of the other factors mentioned above, appears to have caused all attempts at wage rate "restraint" to have been of little or no effect. And when resort is finally had to compulsion, it remains "politically impossible" to use the "controls" effectively.

From the standpoint of the politicians, the press and other makers or leaders of public opinion, there has never been anything more than a groping toward an understanding. The issues which have activated appeals to the unions for "wage reasonableness" have often been described as "political dynamite;" governments and their spokesmen have undoubtedly fought shy of discussing them with the clarity which candor could have thrown upon the subject; and the terms we discussed above, like "wage-push" or "wage-induced" inflation, seem to have been coined by "sophisticated" economists—experts in semantics—to serve as the politicians' currency. At any rate, those terms have been eagerly borrowed by politicians and political journalists, and they have been, I think, largely responsible for the survival of the idea that inflation can be held in check in spite of an increasing volume of bank deposits and currency in circulation relative to aggregate output.

In a sense, the object of an incomes policy may be said to be that of superseding the chaos and arbitrariness of political or private restraints on the competitive mechanism. The method is, as has been suggested, the enactment of values—directly or via ceilings and floors—which the executives entrusted with the policy judge *would* have been established under unhindered competition. But it is extraordinarily difficult, even for experts, *to guess* what the valuation results of the unhampered pricing mechanism would have been. All that any controlling authority could know with any certainty is that, in the presence of abnormal unemployment, wage rates as a whole fixed under duress are too high for the achievement of the maximum wages flow. But if some wage rates are too high, that means that certain other wage rates will be too low. For as we have seen (pages 92-93) every "contrived scarcity" involves an "incidental plenitude." Even wage rates determined under strike-

262

threat influences may be too low. Workers excluded from more profitable employments may themselves be exploiting other, even less privileged workers. Any rectification under an incomes policy is likely to be just as arbitrary as the confiscation of increases in real wage rates by means of rising prices, which is the "full employment" policy that it is the purpose of an incomes policy to supplant. Worse still, in practice vote-procurement incentives will almost inevitably come to dominate the administration. Henceforth, wage rates will be politically determined.

Moreover, because the objective is enhanced realized outputs, downward adjustment of certain product prices initially may be essential. Hence it might seem that there could be no harm in guaranteeing this outcome (via price controls) in order to overcome opposition. Even so, it is difficult to imagine the officials entrusted with the task of insuring that wage-rate cuts are accompanied by cuts in end-product prices understanding the *raison d'être*, as I have explained it. But an incomes policy having been adopted, it is incomparably better to be perfectly frank about the purpose—restoration of profit prospects by the cheapening of such labor as has been priced to cause its prospective profitable output to be beyond the reach of uninflated income. That will reduce, but certainly not eliminate, the political dangers to which I have just referred.

Naturally the union officials and their spokesmen make casuistic use of the argument which the Keynesians once gave them. They are apt to argue, with apparent authority (for effective answers from press, radio, television, pulpit, statesmen, and other opinion-makers are lacking), that the forcing up of costs is the path to economic growth. "Higher wages increase consumption and aggregate demand," they echo. And reasoning from this major premise of what was once confidently asserted to be "the new economics," they claim that acquiescence in "guideline" limits, for example, can be the cause of a slowdown and recession. The fact that most of the economists who once used this argument would now like to forget that they ever gave it any support, does not prevent union spokesmen from continuing to rely upon it. (See p. 256.)

It is essential also to reject the notion (also a consequence of Keynesian influence) that "demand in general" ("the overall level of demand," "aggregate demand," etc.) can become "unbalanced," or that one or other influence held responsible for inflationary or deflationary tendencies needs "moderating" or "adjusting" by order of a government official who can somehow perceive just what is wrong. The only magnitude which can be said to be "too great" in an inflationary condition is the number of money units[20] in relation to the demand for monetary services. But that is, as we have seen, wholly a matter of monetary policy. And properly the "policy" in this case *ought* to be purely interpretative—the choice of the least-cost method for adhering to some monetary contract with the world or some acceptable real value of the money unit: for example, the maintenance of the value of the money unit in terms of gold, or in terms of foreign currencies, or in terms of a price index (as when a government *claims* to be "fighting inflation" although wanting the monetary freedom permitted under floating exchange rates). There is no country in the world in which the treasury and central bank between them cannot cause the volume of deposits *plus* currency in circulation to change in any direction they wish.[21] When inflation occurs, then, it is because it is the duty of these agencies to bring it about—sufficient of it to achieve some objective like full employment or full activity (with no explicitly enacted or enforced restraint on collusive action to raise particular wage rates or prices, which will set the whole "vicious circle" going again).

The suggestion that strike-threat pressures divert income from "saving" to "spending," thereby ensuring prosperity, because the poor are less provident than the rich, is based on the same invalid assumption. There is, as we have seen, no net redistribution in favor of the poor so caused. But through the inflation which the tolerance of strike-threat anarchy makes politically expedient, *together with the differential taxation which usually accompanies it*, there may be a short-run redistributive effect. Even so, there is no *stimulus* to the economy due to this redistribution (as there is from the consequences of inflation upon prospective cost-price ratios). I have dealt elsewhere with the Keynesian notion which suggests that there *can* be such a stimulus.[22] The fallacy lurks in the idea that consumption is a *source* of people's demands (as distinct from the ultimate *purpose* of their demands) whereas the real source of demands lies in *production to replace consumption* or to add to the stock of assets. If, however, such a redistribution *does* cause the consumption of a bigger proportion of an income which has been rising at a given rate, it reduces any rate of increase in the volume of assets; and assets are, in general, wage-multiplying. The confusion of the stimulus of rising prospective yields, due to an accompanying inflation with the supposed stimulus of increasing consumption has been disastrous to clarity of thought.

I sometimes think that the tendency for official pronouncements to attribute the blame for inflation to "cost-push" influences (via strike-threat pressure on wage rates) is due to a mistaken judgment that it is the most tactful way—perhaps the only politically feasible way—in which to draw the attention of the public to the persistently discoordinative pressures the unions impose on the economy. The aim has certainly been to bring public opinion into operation as a dissuasive factor. But the weakness of such an "anti-inflationary" strategy lies partly in the plausible fallacy on which it relies. A cumulative decline in output—due to worsening unemployment, or to capacity diverted to less productive uses—and not inflation could conceivably be the politically preferred alternative following the forcing up of costs, as we noticed on pages 000-000. It could be preferred because it would focus the blame for discoordination and unemployment upon those responsible for it. Fundamental reform would then cease to be politically inconceivable. Blaming strike-threat pressure for *inflation* merely diverts attention from the fundamental causes of discoordination. The cumulative withholding of productive capacity which becomes profitable ("profitable" in the sense of minimizing losses), when one wage rate is forced up by the strike threat in the presence of general price rigidity, itself creates *pressures* toward coordinative adjustments; and if governments resumed their "classical" planning and coordinative functions (and such a step would constitute the fundamental reform needed), these pressures could select the particular adjustments needed.

The only remaining justification for the belief that market-selected wage-rate reductions may fail to restore employment and the full wages flow in incipient recession arises from the possibility that the initial adjustments may be too small to bring wage rates and prices into harmony with expectations. This brings up the general problem which can arise under what I have called (in another work) "unstable price rigidities."[23] Thus, if reductions are made in certain long-term wage agreements, entrepreneurs may feel that subsequent agreements are likely to facilitate planning at even lower labor costs. In the meantime, then, they will tend to invest to an abnormal degree in liquid assets. They *may* indeed judge that even normal replacement, let alone net accumulation, of fixed assets and inventories (of materials, work in progress and stocks of end products), is likely to prove unprofitable until further cuts in wage costs have been secured.

Such a reaction will, some economists fear, reduce the money valuation of a given real income and hence cause another round of downward price and wage-rate adjustments to be necessary for recovery. But the monetary deflation implied need not follow. It is solely a question of monetary policy; and that policy, if correctly discerned by entrepreneurs, is *assisted* by their speculative activity.[24] Hence, unless deflation is purposeful, to rectify a previous inadvertent period of inflation, or adopted as a collective objective,[25] it is impossible to contemplate its ever being deliberately adopted. Thus, we can assume the absence of any deflationary effect and eliminate it as a causal influence in respect of unemployment or underemployment of resources. This implies that any idleness of labor or capital assets will be due to particular wage rates and/or particular prices being *too high*, and possibly too high in the sense that certain wage rates or prices, *even if they have been reduced*, are still too high in relation to expected wage rates and prices.

This may be the position, as I have just suggested, when there are *unstable* rigidities present in the pricing mechanism. It is the belief that these rigidities will eventually break down which temporarily causes the prospective yield from money to increase relatively to the prospective yield from nonmoney, and hence the aggregate real value of money to rise. Under a flexible but noninflationary monetary policy this will call forth monetary expansion. But if outputs generally are declining in consequence of duress-imposed labor costs, a recessionary effect must emerge through the real income contraction. At the same time, of course, the recession itself—manifested in the slowing down of activity—will be creating powerful incentives for coordination, that is, for the rigidities to be overcome and the flow of income to be restored. Unfortunately the incentives, in spite of their strength, may be frustrated.

In the circumstances just discussed, if the unions acted as entrepreneurs on behalf of their members, they would at once approach any corporations which were working at below full capacity to bargain for the reemployment of all their members who did not have better openings at the full employment wage rate. They could do so by agreeing to accept wage costs judged to be sufficiently low *in relation to expected wage costs*. If such a policy were *generally* followed, very small wage-rate reductions would be necessary in most cases. Through the operation of Say's law, the point would soon be reached at which labor shortage began to create pressures for the restoration of former real wage rates. The increased outputs in any one industry would be adding to the source of uninflated demands for the outputs of noncompeting industries. And if, at any time, the required fall in labor costs had not been achieved in any industry, enlightened unions would bargain further for the full employment of their members.

It seems to me that, in the psychological atmosphere created by prolonged depression in the 1930s, when entrepreneurs had again and again been disappointed, incurring losses through wage contracts influenced by unfounded expectations of recovery, it was essential (in the interests of full and optimal employment) that they should have had iron-clad guarantees of freedom at any time to reduce, if necessary, their wage-rate offers. It was, in my judgment, because such guarantees could not be given that the Great Depression of the 1930s was so prolonged. But the power to reduce wage rates would have been limited, of course, by what I have called "market-established minima"—the wage rates at which firms would lose essential labor, not through strikes, but through their workers leaving for better paid employments (see pp. 188-190).

The vital condition for optimal employment is that managements, as representatives of the residual claimants—the providers of the assets—should be allowed untrammeled discretion in their interpretation of market commands and hence in making wage offers. We should remember that the result would be not merely to *restore* the flow of wages and full employment; it would set in motion a trend toward the *maximization* of the wages flow, and the *minimization* of inequality in the distribution of that flow.[26] It would draw people from the unskilled ranks for training in semiskilled or skilled work, as well as promote a fructifying net accumulation of wage-multiplying assets.

I conclude that incipient depression caused by duress-imposed labor costs and expressed as the depletion of wages and income generally, is incapable of being held off except by inflation. And ultimately it is due to the fact that union officials have been allowed to acquire immense political power. The textbooks of labor economics ought to be drawing the students' attention to this reality. But because rising prices are now universally expected and hence bereft of their former coordinative ability, *the sole purpose of inflation has become political*—to satisfy the many vested interests which have come to depend upon it. The profession of union officials may well be the most important. But all those organizations of persons who have used the remnants of the market system to protect themselves from the policy will now be confronted with serious difficulties if inflation really threatens to come to an end; and they will constitute a formidable obstacle to the emergence of any noninflationary era. They have been forced to gamble and they have—so

266

far—forecast the continuance of inflation. They will have lost if inflation comes to be recognized as economically purposeless simply because everybody expects it to continue.[27] Yet all great steps in the progress of mankind have created difficulties—especially problems arising from disappointed expectations and requiring drastic readjustments.

Today's problem of inflation is, however, unique in history in some of its aspects. Unless it can be solved, the survival of the freedom which the West has enjoyed in increasing measure is in jeopardy. And the solution is not to be found in monetary policy alone but in the reform of a chaotic, private pricing policy which—until the present, emerging era—has made inflation inevitable for any government which has wished to remain in power, but at the cost of increasing instability, perpetuated inequality, social injustice, and worsening chaos in the international monetary sphere.

We must be clear on two important practical points. First, the difficulties created by the abandonment of inflation are less likely to promote civil strife than inflation itself. The inflationary policy of the period 1960 to 1971 in the United States was accompanied by growing and successful incitement to disorder—a phenomenon which, I think, no recession period has witnessed. Secondly, while recession *can* act as a harsh discipline forcing the unions to make the concessions needed to raise the wages flow, wise policy would make it clear to the unions and the community that the pains of that type of adjustment are avoidable. Policymakers could tactfully explain that if strike-threat entrenchments against the maximization of the average wage and the minimization of inequalities in the distribution of the wages flow were abandoned, a stable money unit would not only be compatible with, but conducive to, "full employment," higher wages and greater security than have ever been realized in the past.

Inflation was the scourge of the masses under the monarchies. The invisible taxes it levied accorded the princes resources which they could never have obtained openly without violent opposition. That it has survived in the world's totalitarian countries is not surprising. It helps to finance the ruling groups in dictatorial regimes as it formerly helped to finance royalty and the court. But its survival under representative government is something of a mystery, despite the inconspicuous way in which—for long periods of time—it takes its toll. Public tolerance of inflation under democracy is paradoxical because of its blatant regressiveness, the distortions of the production structure for which it is responsible, and the sapping of incentives (for enterprise and for thrift)—vices which seem to be its necessary concomitants. Admittedly, inflation remains a device through which elected governments can raise funds without parliamentary authorization. But that alone would not account for its survival. I venture the following diagnosis.

While (as I have insisted) the strike-threat system does not directly cause prolonged inflation, the link between them is close. Governments have accepted responsibility for the maintenance of prosperity but have abdicated from their duty to remove observable obstacles to prosperity when those obstacles have been erected by groups with great voting strength. *Inflation*

267

has become chronic because, when not fully discounted, it works as an antibody to duress-imposed costs. In other words, it acts as a continuous (although partial) rectifier of the discoordination which the overruling of the market mechanism persistently causes. But what is so worrying today is that *"the antibody" is losing its ability to preserve the apparent health of the body economic.* For creeping inflation *is* being more and more expected and more fully discounted. As I write, *the advisers of governments do not appear anywhere to have drawn the attention of politicians effectively to this disconcerting and worsening phenomenon. Perhaps the almost anarchical relations between the world's currencies which have been created, despite the cold-shouldering of the IMF through the ill-fated "Smithsonian" initiative, may bring opinion-makers in the "democracies" to their senses.* [28]

NOTES

[1] This thesis is developed at greater length in my *Politically Impossible. . . ?* , already cited.

[2] H. G. Johnson, "The Determination of the General Level of Wage Rates," in J. T. Dunlop, ed., *The Theory of Wage Determination* (London: Macmillan, Ltd., 1957), p. 37.

[3] Defining *inflation* as the loss of value in some defined sense in a money unit, and illustrating by the case in which value is measured in abstractly conceived "real terms," we can say that inflation occurs when monetary policy allows the aggregate value of money *in actual money units* (that is, in dollars, pounds, francs or marks) to increase more rapidly than the same aggregate value *in real terms*. We are concerned in the text with how *autonomous* changes in particular prices affect this relationship.

[4] Under minimum wage legislation, this last way of mitigating the discoordination may be seriously restrained.

[5] Monetary policy may be defined as "rigid" when, in terms of the "quantity theory identity," $MV \equiv PT$, M does not rise or fall in proportion to changes in aggregate demand for monetary services (which demand changes in proportion to changes in T and/or in $1/v$.

[6] The notion of *wrong* activity is not meaningless. An activity which yields the largest flow of *final products* in the short run may be "wrong" in the sense that it is being achieved through a sacrifice of the rate of replacement or net accumulation of productive capacity—that is, because there may be unobserved consumption. But aggregate thrift—the net accumulation of income-yielding assets—can never be "too great" except insofar as any preference can be judged on purely ethical grounds.

[7] Unless what is meant is the condition referred to in the above footnote, and I do not think that *is* ever what is intended by the phrase.

[8] Report in *San Francisco Examiner*, October 26, 1969.

[9] I say "more or less" in order to envisage monetary policy as reacting to those sources of demand for the services of money which are not correlated

with the magnitude of output (i.e., not correlated with T in the quantity theory identity).

[10] Melvin Rothbaum, "Wage-Price Policy and Alternatives," in Lloyd Ulman, ed., *Challenges to Collective Bargaining* (Englewood Cliffs, N. J.: Prentice-Hall, Spectrum Books, 1967), pp. 135-136.

[11] That is, so as to exclude the power to fix wage rates and prices above the free market level and thereby reduce the flow of uninflated wages and income.

[12] A. H. Hansen, *Monetary Theory and Fiscal Policy* (Norton, 1941), p. 101.

[13] It can create also a collective incentive to eliminate by law the strike-threat in the interests of a stable, well-coordinated economy with full employment.

[14] The "Phillips curve" is designed to represent the empirically established relationship between the magnitude of "unemployment" and the rate of inflation.

[15] His position may have seemed rather equivocal until 1936. It became most explicit in his controversy with F. D. Graham and F. A. Hayek (*Economic Journal*, 1943, pp. 185-7, and 1944, pp. 429-30). See W. H. Hutt, *Keynesianism, Retrospect and Prospect* (Chicago: Henry Regnery Co., 1963), pp. 95-105; *Politically Impossible . . . ?*, Part V.

[16] "Intended" because no one really doubts that monetary and fiscal policies aimed at "maintaining aggregate demand" cause the money valuation of income to rise more rapidly than its real value increases.

[17] H. C. Simons, *Economic Policy for a Free Society* (Chicago: University of Chicago Press, 1948), p. 128.

[18] It has no other justification unless there has been a failure to use antitrust (or similar) initiative against contrived scarcities achieved through managerial collusion.

[19] It should be noticed that if policy is framed with main focus upon the greatest advantage of wage earners *collectively,* the benefits which accompany the general increase of profits in a coordinated economy are likely to be enjoyed by labor as much through a shift in employment from low-paid to high-paid categories of work as through increases in the real remuneration of different kinds of work. Free market influences are, as I have several times insisted, intensively egalitarian.

[20] The "number of money units" may be taken to mean, for this purpose, the volume of demand deposits *plus* currency in circulation. For full accuracy, the "pure money equivalent" of "money substitutes" or "near money" would have to be included. See W. H. Hutt, *Keynesianism*, pp. 90, 92, 96, 417.

[21] This does *not* mean that such changes in demand for the services of money as some economists envisage under the misleading term "velocity of circulation" can be ignored in attempts to maintain money income in a planned proportion to real income.

[22] See Ibid., Chapter 10 to 12 and especially pp. 195, 233-240, 250-51, 256-59, 295-96.

[23] See Ibid., pp. 25, 64, 170-76, 242.

[24] See Ibid., pp. 40, 100-101, 106, 169-70.

[25] As it was by Britain after 1920, as a means of keeping faith with the world from whom she had borrowed cheaply during World War I through her promise to return to and maintain the gold standard at the 1914 parity.

[26] For any such policy of maximizing the wages-flow to succeed, however, it would be essential that unemployment compensation should not be allowed to sabotage it.

[27] On the difficulties which long perseverence with Keynesian-type policies has created for governments, see F. A. Hayek and Sudha Shenoy, *A Tiger by the Tail* (London: Institute of Economic Affairs, 1972).

[28] On the general subject of strike-threat power in relation to inflation, see *Inflation and the Unions,* by G. Haberler, M. Parkin, and H. Smith (London: Institute of Economic Affairs, 1972).

˙18

The Closed Shop

THERE ARE economists (as we have seen—pp. 15-16) who feel that there would be little harm in groups of workers agreeing among themselves about what remuneration they are willing to accept, provided only that certain admitted abuses of this process could be eliminated. They believe, that is, that the right to exert strike-threat pressures can be tolerated as long as those who organize for this purpose have no right or power, under any conditions whatsoever, to restrain the employment of others. Such economists maintain that, if the rights of nonstrikers or other strikebreakers were *effectively* guaranteed, the right to strike could (on wholly pragmatic grounds) be permitted. All that is required is that the "closed shop" or the "union shop" shall be forbidden and the use or threat of bodily violence stamped out. No other major limitations on union activities would be then necessary. This was, for instance, the broad view of Herbert Spencer of the last century.

Now the ability to withhold at any one moment a large volume of labor employed in any firm, or in any group of competing firms, can be seriously disruptive even if there is no restraint on the recruitment of substitutes to fill the vacated jobs. And the private coercion used in such a case, although weaker than it is when the civil rights of nonstrikers need not be respected, may still compel the acceptance of wage contracts which gravely harm minorities (those *within* a union and potential employees outside it). Yet it must be admitted that the path toward a socially coordinated labor market will be at least *partially* cleared by reforms to protect the interloper, including what have been called "right to work laws" in the United States, authorized for individual states by Section 14 (b) of the Taft-Hartley Act. The incorporation of the 14 (b) clause in Federal legislation *would* be a move toward what has been called "the emancipation of labor" and the democratization of the wage determination process. Such a reform would need supplementation, of course, by other reforms to remove all those immunities and privileges before the law (discussed on pages 51-52) which have virtually conferred upon the unions the right to intimidate, assault, or slander executives or nonstrikers in the course of a trade dispute or during preparations for a dispute.

271

What is needed (on the assumption that *physical* violence has been eradicated) is the explicit abolition of any right to compel any person to join a union as a condition for permission to accept or retain any employment, unless the union member is left clearly free, if he wishes, not to strike on the motion of a majority or on the command of an elected official. The present chapter is devoted to an examination of the objections which have been advanced against reforms in this direction.

In the United States a trend toward the closed shop regime was powerfully fostered by the Wagner Act of 1935. Congressional critics of this legislation feared that it would indeed lead to compulsory union membership. "Nothing could be more false," said Senator Robert F. Wagner reassuringly. But after 38 years of lobbying expenditures and electoral pressures, the "closed shop" form of organization now dominates the American labor movement. In 1935, less than 3 percent of union membership in the United States was "involuntary." Today, union membership is an essential condition for the individual's employment in the overwhelming majority of unionized occupations. We are supposed to have had, as someone has put it, "a voluntary acceptance of involuntary unionism."

The case for compulsory union membership (whether in the form of the "closed shop," the "union shop," or some variant thereof) is primarily based on appeal to a principle which, *if applicable*, appears unchallengeable to many economists. When a union, in providing valuable services for its members, necessarily provides these services also for nonmembers, the latter are getting a "free ride." They share in benefits provided from others' pockets, efforts, enterprise and risk—benefits which would not be provided at all, or not in the same degree, unless all prospective beneficiaries contributed to the costs. The *assumption* is, however, that representation by the union is synonymous with benefit from the union, or that the nonmembers really do want the union's services but shrewdly rely upon others paying for them.

The problem raised by this possibility is an all-pervading phenomenon in economics generally—an aspect of the problem of "social cost" or "externalities." I myself always illustrate the issue by the example (not original) of lighthouses. The providers of lighthouses do not allow any shipping lines to claim that their captains are such skilled navigators that they do not need guidance by light, and that therefore they should not be called upon to pay "light dues" (levied for this purpose on users of ports and harbors). In this case, there is no serious controversy. Not all economists agree that compulsory charges in these circumstances are defensible; but for the purpose of the present controversy, I propose not to argue the point.

The question to be considered is then as follows: *Is* the "closed shop" (or the "union shop," or some other variant of compulsory union membership) an acceptable parallel? In our kind of society, groups of people invest effort and capital in ventures that benefit not only themselves but obviously others also. In general, persons who put work or capital into a project under such conditions do so either because they think that they will benefit *sufficiently* (in spite of any "free riders") or out of some sense of social duty. Their recognition that others will reap some part of the reward for the activities they have provided does not deter them. For instance, party political organizations work for certain legislation and support the candidatures of certain aspirant legislators; but if the parties have any sincerity at all they expect their activities to be for the benefit of all, including even those who work against them! The political parties cannot be charged with assuming that all the finance and effort will be not worth while unless the advantages accrue to their due-paying members only. No one thinks that the party political system will cease unless all persons can be forced to contribute to one or other of the political parties. But one of the arguments used in defense of compulsory unionism is that all workers benefit from the legislation or administrative action of the political parties which the unions finance, even if some may not believe they benefit. But the controversy largely arises out of the conviction that minorities are compelled to finance the organization of their own detriment.

Perhaps an even better example is the Conference of American Small Business Organizations (not to be confused with the official Small Business Administration!). This body exercises a general vigilance regarding legislation which may affect its members. Presumably these members believe that they get good value for their subscriptions. But there is no doubt that the services the conference performs benefit many more small businesses than contribute to the costs. Yet the conference does not press for compulsory membership to compel all beneficiaries to pay their share. The reader will be able to think of innumerable other examples. However, the question is far too important to be summarily dismissed on grounds such as these, and I propose to examine the case for the closed or union shop from all angles.

It is obvious that not all members or potential members of a union will attach the same value to the prospective benefits which membership offers. Some may expect to get good value for their contribution; others may genuinely feel that any prospective benefits are not worth the dues; while others may feel that union pressures actually work to their disadvantage. Even those who would admit that they get some *gross* benefit may feel that the cost is too high.[1] Hence the possibility of a potential unionist quite genuinely judging membership to cost more than it is worth to him cannot be dogmatically dismissed.

Moreover, we must consider those who will almost certainly feel that they are more likely to be harmed than helped by union activity. They will fear that, if wage rates are pushed too high for current outputs to be absorbed, they will be the first to be displaced. Their misgivings may exist because they feel—realistically—that they are not quite so well qualified as the majority; or because of some seniority or other rule which a union has imposed concerning "lay-off"; or by reason of their race, religion, sex, political opinions and so forth, they may expect to be the ones most likely to have to suffer in bad times—unless they can count on being allowed to bargain with greater freedom than a union is likely to permit.

It has been ruled in the United States, however, that a union is not "barred from making contracts which may have unfavorable effects on some members of the craft represented." (323 U.S. 203)[2] Then is it really morally defensible that those who believe that they are the ones who will experience the "unfavorable effects" shall be forced to finance the operations which threaten to harm them? The fact that what may benefit a majority can well be to the disadvantage of a minority cannot be ignored.

The argument *against* the closed shop is in part based on concern for the rights of any such minority. Bradley has put the point in terms of the question, "Can the exploited be compelled to finance their exploiters? . . . It might be urged that Congress lacks the power arbitrarily to select unoffending citizens and to compel their own self-destruction."[3]

The relevant general principle here is that there are many reasons why there should be a conflict of interest among the different groups which form a union's membership. We find it as between the skilled and the unskilled; between those paid by time and those paid by piece; between those in expanding branches of a firm or industry and those in a contracting branch; between those employed in areas with a high cost of living and those in areas in which living costs are low; between those in developed areas and those in underdeveloped areas; between those who prefer more leisure (and would like to sacrifice pecuniary earnings in order to obtain it) and those who prefer the opposite; and between the young and aggressive members and those (often a small but older minority) who feel that the relative certainty of continuous employment is of greater value to them than a wage-rate increase (more accurately, that such an increase might prove incompatible with the survival of their present source of income). This last kind of minority tends to consist of those who, because of their special obligations, value employment security high in their "scales of preferences."

In so far as court decisions confirming the unions' right to compel membership have been based, not on the principle that minorities may be legitimately *harmed*, but on the incompatible belief that nonunion workers gain unfairly from the protections won by the unions, the effect has been either to deny the individual the right to make his own judgment on the matter or to *accept as proven* the thesis that nonunionists are shrewdly relying on the "free ride." But what imaginable *meaningful evidence* could be brought on this last issue? In one case the court invited employees who did not believe themselves to be beneficiaries from compulsory membership to come and give evidence. But under the existing power of a union to deprive them of their livelihood, naturally few would dare to appear. In that very case the Solicitor General had argued bluntly that those who thought a union did not benefit them should give up their jobs![4] If the courts had been permitted to hear the evidence of unwilling union members *in camera*, and with effective arrangements to prevent the disclosure of their identity to the union rulers, they might well have reached different conclusions.[5] As things are, individuals who might have the courage to fight are unlikely to possess the resources needed and it would be very difficult for them to find philanthropists prepared to take up their case on principle.

274

The mere fact that a union may provide unemployment compensation for members who are displaced does not imply that the recipients are net beneficiaries of the strike-threat system. This would only be so if the levies on the employed members were sufficient to provide full compensation for those who are laid off. And "full compensation" here means sufficient to bring their earnings in alternative occupations up to the net earnings (wages *minus* the unemployment levy) of those retaining employment. But in practice, as I pointed out in my *Theory of Idle Resources*, the "displaced workers get . . . a mere sop. They appear to consent because they do not understand. . . . It is nothing but their ignorance which prevents them from insisting upon an *equal* sharing of the spoils in return for their agreement to refrain from 'black-legging.' "⁶

Others may feel such confidence in the free market value of their services that they judge their income prospects to be more favorable if the prosperity of the firm they are serving is assured by low labor costs. They may fear, for instance, that the firm's growth, or even the industry's growth, may be held back by aggressive union activity; and they may therefore view any forced membership with great distaste. Exceptionally able or skilled workers in an industry-wide union may sometimes form the minority which believes it is harmed by union policies.

Some minorities may disapprove of union policy on moral grounds, through an intuitive feeling or ethical perception that the private use of coercive power is indefensible. And in the case of certain unions, minorities may object because they believe that the union leaders are unprincipled demagogues or utter scoundrels whom they cannot, in good conscience, finance voluntarily. Ought private coercion, and on occasion the threat of bodily violence, be allowed to force such people into membership?

Again, some reluctant union members feel that the funds to which they must contribute are used for the support of political causes which they oppose. Mr. Justice Black gave one view of the present position in this respect, in a famous 1961 judgment. He found that "the union shop . . . is being used as a means to exact money from these employees to help to get votes to win elections for parties and candidates they are against. If this is constitutional, the First Amendment is not the charter of political and religious liberty its sponsors believed it to be." Nevertheless, the Supreme Court ruled, by five to four, that such a use of funds is not unconstitutional. But what is now constitutional may yet be intolerable. It must be remembered, however, that a union shop or closed shop *could* be restrained by law from using its funds in this manner without the right to compulsory membership being abolished.

The union leaders and their academic and political allies sometimes deny that a minority has the right to endanger or destroy what they like to call the "freedom" of the union they serve to protect the income and conditions of work of its members. But the controversy turns largely on whether that word "freedom" is used to mean "privilege." Support for 14 (b) is motivated by the wish to *preserve* the freedom of minorities who feel that union policies withhold opportunities from them, or have objectives which they (the minorities) reject. Superficially, at any rate, it would appear that the minorities who must be coerced into membership are most often the weakest members of the group—those for whose protection society *ought to be* most solicitous. Admittedly, this minority may possess considerable power when the individuals who make it up are free to bargain independently and seek the most remunerative employment opportunities. But their power is capable of harming others only when there exists some privilege which their competition can erode.

A possible objection is that the unions can be trusted to deal fairly with minorities, in spite of the protection of majorities by compulsory membership, and that divergencies of interest tend to be adjusted through mutual agreement. Undoubtedly internal adjustments *are* made from time to time in response to representations or pressures from within. But generally speaking, the less well-qualified workers whose prospects are damaged are regarded as an expendable minority. It seems to be less infrequent for a *skilled* minority successfully to demand autonomy within a union and to be conceded the right to negotiate separately. And sometimes local groups, perceiving the conflict of these interests with those of other groups in different areas, have revolted against the exclusion of their competition via "the rate for the job." Such a revolt occurred some years ago in the United States meat packing industry when, under bargaining on a national scale, one local group perceived that their source of income was being shrunken or exterminated by the general forcing up of labor costs. But although a minority group within a union *can* in some circumstances break away and form its own organization in this manner, the possibility of doing this appears to occur but rarely. We cannot hope therefore for any weakening through spontaneous fragmentation of the arbitrary power structure which has been fashioned. The divergencies of interest which we are here considering do not seem powerful enough to be effective. In general, passive acceptance of the union's authority is *normal*. Active opposition from exploited groups within is *abnormal*. (See pp. 201-203.)

Let us now return to the case of those who object to union membership, not on the grounds that they are directly *harmed* by the policies pursued, but simply on the grounds (already mentioned) that they do not think the benefits are worth the cost. An important general proposition is relevant here. When some people want a good or service very strongly (that is, when it ranks high on their "scale of preferences"), and others want it only moderately (when it stands low on their scale of preferences), while others want it so slightly that they would only make use of it if it were provided free (that is, when they will use it if they have to make no sacrifice of other things to get it), economists have recognized that there *may be* a case for "price discrimination" (see pages 163-167). It is recognized that those people who value the good or service highly can benefit by agreeing to pay more for it than others are called upon to pay. The principle involved, sometimes known as "charging what the traffic will bear" has, in my opinion, often been seriously abused. *But the conditions under which it can be accepted are perfectly clear, namely, that the parties discriminated against obtain thereby a good, service or other objective*

276

which they would otherwise be unable to obtain at all, or else that they obtain it cheaper than they could in the absence of discrimination against them. And, in the extreme case, one class of possible beneficiary may be called upon to pay nothing at all. For instance, toll roads are not rendered unprofitable investments for the community because passengers in excess of one per car are normally allowed to use them free. Hence the mere fact that those beneficiaries of union activity who do not value the benefits sufficiently to agree to buy them voluntarily may, unless forced to contribute, succeed in getting "a free ride," does not ipso facto justify coercion.

The unions' answer to this objection is that *the great majority of those employed obviously do believe and know that they benefit materially from union protection or aggression.* That being so, all may justly be called upon to contribute. Employees in any craft, occupation or industry who refuse to do so have no integrity. They simply accept the benefits knowing that they can get them for nothing.

The unions argue further that the marginal employees who are harmed—those who would undercut if permitted to do so, or those who might disapprove—are a minority who, like all minorities, must *expect* to be overruled. When the unions rely on this argument, they are reasoning in the manner in which the age limit principle is usually justified. Forced retirements at a certain age in certain occupations may mean that some who are still highly efficient may have to be dismissed; yet the rule can be defended and is generally accepted as not unjust. Similarly, we are all prepared to approve a certain age limit before the right to vote in a democratic society is conferred, in spite of the fact that some young people may be better qualified than most adults to assume the responsibilities of citizenship. The same argument has been used also to justify *Apartheid* in South Africa. The authorities there claim that their discriminations are not really based on color or race but on grounds of civilization. Most nonwhites, they hold, are relatively uncivilized; and when asked why, then, they deny rights to highly educated Africans which are enjoyed by some virtually illiterate whites, their answer is exactly that which we have just noticed; and official policy in South Africa does, indeed, explicitly rely upon appeal to the age limit parallel.

Now this age limit principle is acceptable as a voting qualification only because age *is* a rough evidence of responsibility and because youth is a handicap out of which one grows rapidly. Age-retirement limits are, perhaps, justifiable on the grounds that they enable administrations to avoid invidious decisions which might entail telling one air hostess that her youthful charms have faded while another's of the same age have survived, or telling one pilot that his judgment can no longer be trusted while another's of the same age is believed to be unimpaired. The suspicion of favoritism or nepotism is also avoided when an inflexible rule is applied. But similar circumstances certainly cannot be used to justify the discriminations of *Apartheid*, or forced membership of a union for those who claim or believe that they do not benefit from membership, or that the policy is likely to harm them, or that the policy is ethically indefensible.

The unions are apt to argue that, without compulsory membership, the efforts of their staff must, to some extent at least, be diverted from more important activities to the process of selling their policies, in order to insure continued membership. But would the continuing necessity to justify the use made of funds collected voluntarily, in order to maintain membership, be such an undesirable thing? Would it not be an advantage if the administrations were called upon regularly to account for their stewardship in detail? The voluntary subscription (like any other unenforced payment) is the most democratic form of voting. Would not the voluntary principle alone tend to mitigate some of the actual or alleged abuses that I have been discussing? And could not every producer of goods and services say, with equal justification, "Give our firm a monopoly and we can eliminate all the advertising and other selling costs for the community's advantage"? Would we contemplate such an argument for a single moment if it were used on behalf of any institution other than a labor union?

Certainly legislation has conferred on unions the privilege as well as the duty of representing both their own members and their nonunion competitors in the same undertaking. But there is no obvious reason why, because they have been given the privilege of pleading their rivals' case, their position should be further strengthened by the right to extort financial support from their competitors—from those who will contribute under duress only.

Up to this point in the present chapter I have not again challenged the assumption that the services supplied by labor unions are really services for the benefit of "labor." But this assumption cannot be upheld if the argument of the previous chapters can be sustained. For I have tried to show that if by "labor" we mean the whole body of artisans, laborers, clerks, shop assistants, etc., the gains secured by the unions via the strike or strike threats are for the benefit only of a section and always against the advantage of the whole.

Yet it was, ostensibly at least, acceptance (on intuitive grounds, unsupported by evidence presented or recorded) of the thesis that strike-threat pressures bring about a redistribution in favor of "the workers" that labor policy (in parliaments, administrations and in the courts) has almost everywhere been based—in the United States, especially since the 'thirties. And the tolerance of compulsory membership has, in particular, been justified on the grounds that, because all workers share in a redistribution at the expense of "capital" brought about by union activities, all beneficiaries can be properly forced to contribute to the costs of those activities. But as we have seen, no such redistribution is actually achievable.

There may be many functions which can be usefully undertaken by an organization which negotiates a wage contract on behalf of wage earners whom it represents but does not coerce, and in so far as such an organization is concerned solely with these functions, there may be some justification for compulsory membership. But this is a possibility which does not need further discussion in the present context.

It may of course be claimed that even if strike-threat activity can benefit sections only, it is still just that all those who enjoy the unjustly-gained benefits should contribute toward the cost of their achievement (in the sense of honor among thieves). Moreover, in a society in which general union pressures are accompanied by monetary and fiscal policy to insure full employment, it is possible that any group which does not have an aggressive union to push its wage rate up ahead of the average is likely to come off worst. Thus regarded, the use of union power in each instance is *defensive*—defense against the aggression of all the other unions. That being so, may there not be additional grounds for insisting that all those who benefit from the defense shall be called upon to contribute? To answer this question satisfactorily we must recognize that the abolition of compulsion will weaken the power of aggression as much as it weakens the power of defense. To forbid the closed shop and the union shop will be to take one positive step in the direction of economic disarmament. There is little doubt that acquiescence in forced union membership tends to perpetuate rather than weaken the present internecine system or expose its malignance or absurdity.

An argument *against* compulsory membership which I have not yet mentioned is that, in a racially mixed country, it facilitates race discrimination. I have explained above why the simple enforcement of the standard rate—"the rate for the job"—constitutes everywhere by far the most important color bar in racially complex communities. But there have been union shops in the United States which (in practice although not in principle) have (until recently at least) refused Negroes membership. The result is an *explicit* color bar. This source of racial injustice is easily recognizable. It is, however, *relatively* unimportant. The really serious injustices stem from the standard rate, the force of which would be lessened under effectively enforced "right to work" laws. For under such laws, Negroes would at least be able to *bid for entry* into the more remunerative kinds of employment.

It is, I suggest, in the context of the above discussion that the question of compulsory union membership (as a facet of the general problem of the private use of coercive power) must be considered. Let us bear in mind that every argument used for it can be appealed to with equal validity in support of compulsory membership of cartels. But in the case of cartel type action, government policy aims most frequently not only at preventing *obligatory* membership of any organization to price output or limit output collusively, but even to prevent any form of purely *voluntary collusion* with that end in view. The purpose of antitrust is rightly *to rely upon the conflict of interest among producers—their lack of solidarity—to insure that the interests of the public are paramount in the pricing process*; and there is no valid reason why unions should be treated differently from cartels. Defenders of the closed shop or the union shop are claiming the paramountcy of sectional interests over the community's interests.

During the controversies which led to an abortive House of Representatives' resolution to repeal Section 14 (b) of the Taft Hartley Act, it was alleged that the purpose of that section was to destroy the unions. But justly stated, the object was to weaken the private use of coercive power in a man-

279

ner which was denying the civil rights of minorities. And that infringement of what we have come to accept as a basic freedom of modern man has no compensatory benefits. For as we have seen, the pricing of labor and output through economic warfare has throughout tended to reduce the aggregate flow of wages and render the distribution of income less equal and less equitable. And this result would have been unchallengeably obvious had not technological progress ("economizing displacement") and creeping, crawling, chronic inflation crudely mitigated the burdens and obscured the inegalitarian consequences.

The erosion of civil rights by way of compulsory membership of unions can well foster further erosion. It is notorious that in the United States union members have been expelled for openly supporting a "wrong" political party or "wrong" causes (such as for the retention of 14 (b)). When the president of the International Machinists' Union of California can defend the expulsion of a member on the grounds quoted below, is it surprising that those who are vigilant in the cause of human freedom feel that they must work for the universal adoption of "right to work laws"? The union president's ruling was: "While it is agreed that the right to express one's views is a privilege guaranteed by the Constitution, this does not mean that a member is entitled openly to denounce the considered position of the labor movement."[7]

But the "considered position of the labor movement" may be indefensible! Actually, it is difficult to avoid the conclusion that it is precisely because that "considered position" is felt to be vulnerable that the suppression of its critics is attempted with such determination. And does not the union president's ruling stress one of the most disturbing phenomena of the present era, namely, the recrudescence of the idea that nonconformity may be suppressed?

In Chapter 4, I suggested that the union leaders have acquired what many regard as illegitimate power by methods which amount to a process of revealed corruption. There are at least some grounds for holding that Mr. Justice Black was justified when he held, a few years ago, that it is compulsory membership "which has enabled corrupt union officials to entrench themselves in the organized labor movement and exploit the working man for their own purposes."[8] And for this reason alone, I suggest, a case can be made out for the repeal of the right to compel membership where this right exists. In the United States the required repeal could be achieved simply by the incorporation of 14 (b) into Federal law.

It is no argument against Section 14 (b) that, considered in the light of the *other* privileges before the law which the union managements enjoy, it cannot provide any adequate defense against oppression by the union rulers. Admittedly the clause cannot eradicate *all* the injustices of a despotic system, but it *can* mitigate them. In particular, it can protect the actual or potential marginal workers in a trade, who feel they will suffer from the curtailment of employment outlets if labor costs are raised by strike-threat pressures.

The fact that most managements have acquiesced in the closed or union shop is irrelevant to the thesis advanced in this chapter. With public opinion, the consensus of current moral teaching, the majority of university economists, and virtually every teacher of "labor economics" against them, managements have (as we have seen on pages 50-51) mostly lost sight of their moral duty, namely, to fight on behalf of consumers and for a minority they could profitably put into contact with consumers if wage rates and prices were socially determined, instead of determined through economic warfare.

NOTES

[1] After all, the cost is not negligible. If the typical unionist invests throughout his life, at compound interest, a sum equal to what he pays out in union dues, he will have a substantial capital sum at retirement.

[2] P. D. Bradley, *Labor Unions and Public Policy* (Washington, D.C.: American Enterprise Association, 1958), p. 81.

[3] Ibid., p. 82.

[4] Ibid., p. 84.

[5] Such evidence could then have been available for rebuttal in spite of the identity of witnesses not having been disclosed.

[6] Hutt, *Theory of Idle Resources* (Jonathan Cape, 1939), p. 131. This example brings out one of the biggest difficulties involved. Many who are harmed by union policy *believe* themselves to be beneficiaries. (See ibid., pp. 128-140) But law and the courts ought to protect the ignorant, not connive to facilitate their exploitation.

[7] Quoted from *14 (b), the Key Issue* (Washington, D.C.: Free Society Association, 1966), p. 14.

[8] Quoted from Ibid., p. 16.

19

Conclusion

THE BROAD conclusion of the analysis presented above is self-evident and hardly needs reiteration. The strike-threat system is an intolerable abuse of economic freedom. The strike is a type of warfare under which privileged groups can gain at the expense of the unprivileged. The system provides no acceptable shield against monopsonistic exploitation. In an era in which it has become an accepted institution, wage rates imposed through it cannot transfer income from investors in general to workers in general; nor can it redistribute income from the rich in general to the poor in general. On the other hand, it can and has greatly reduced the community's aggregate income wherever it has been tolerated. Hence, because it has failed to raise labor's proportion, it must have materially reduced the absolute aggregate wages flow. Moreover, it has rendered the distribution of the wages flow more unequal—a *regressive* consequence which is *aggravated* because labor costs enhanced through duress exploit all the people in their consumer capacity and harm the poor differentially.

Strike strategy demands the creation and fostering of a war psychology on the workers' part. The system has tended therefore to frustrate attempts to achieve good relationships between employees and the managers who coordinate their activities and who act for the providers of the assets which multiply the yield to labor. It has militated against the fashioning of more effective procedures to protect the worker from the possibility of managerial tyranny—a possibility which must always be present whenever the right to command is required by orderliness in cooperative effort. Equally seriously, the strike-threat system has caused the worker often to feel that, through the wage contract, he is selling himself instead of selling his contribution to the common pool of output. For that reason it has been destroying the worker's dignity, his joy in work, his sense of belonging to the great society and, above all, his faith in the justice of an order—the free market order—which can (if allowed) maximize his earning power and security as well as promote satisfaction or pride in simple or skilled achievement.

In tolerating the right to disrupt through the concerted withdrawal of labor,

282

society has acquiesced in the private use of coercion. Society has unwittingly allowed government to abdicate regarding its traditional duty to protect the individual from spoliation by others. There is no more reason to suppose that use of the strike weapon will have a just outcome than to assume that the private use of firearms will have this result. But acceptance of the system by public opinion has appeared to validate resort to disruptive tactics by "activists" in other spheres as well; and the traditional supplementary devices of the system—physical intimidation and sabotage—have accompanied the extension of strike-threat practices.

The spirit of the "activists" is expressed in the phrase, "You do as we insist or else. . . ." Resignation to such demands seems to have allowed a deplorable emasculation of the intellectual and social life of famous universities in the United States. In some cases, *esprit de corps* and pride of membership in the most illustrious institutions of learning have been virtually trampled under. And, accompanying this phenomenon, a contempt for freedom of expression has emerged which is the direct antithesis of age-old university traditions. On controversial issues, dialogue is rejected for vituperation. It may seem rather far-fetched to blame all this on the influence of the strike-threat system. And yet it is the widespread conviction that the power to disrupt may be properly relied upon by those who are in a position to organize disruption (to secure whatever objectives they believe are good, or for their own advantage), which has precipitated the humiliating situation in which some of the leading American universities find themselves today.

I want the reader to consider whether the survival of the democratic system may not be dependent upon a general recognition of the illegitimacy of privately motivated coercion *in all forms*. But if the withdrawal of the right to coerce by the threat to strike is to become politically acceptable, a truly great leader—of exceptional eloquence, intellectual courage and pertinacity—will have to arise. I expect to be told, however, that I am hoping in vain for a Messiah, that only the intervention of heaven could break through the barrier of "political impossibility" which excludes any effective curbing of strike-threat power. My reply to critics who would advance such an objection is that, if they wish the joint institutions of representative government and freedom of enterprise to survive, they may soon be forced to perceive that the right to strike—*under any circumstances*—must be denied. I have discussed some of the issues at greater length in my recently published book, *Politically Impossible . . . ?* But I can here refer to emerging circumstances which, it seems to me, will make an early attempt to grapple with the problem inevitable.

The strike-threat system must accept main responsibility for the political expediency of inflation in modern societies. In tending to repress yields to investment and hence yields to effort (the aggregate wages flow), duress-imposed labor costs are persistently tending to generate a cumulative contraction of the source of demands for the services of men and assets, causing thereby a slowing down of economic activity, with short-term unemployment. It is to reestablish or preserve price-cost relationships (and hence profit prospects) consistent with normal outputs and sales, and hence to restore or maintain the flow of wages (as wage-push influences are constantly tending to repress the flow) that governments have restored to the chronic, creeping, crawling inflation of the current era. But as we have seen, anticipated inflation tends to become purposeless inflation. Moreover, because it seems absurd to expect any agreement among the nations on the rate of inflation, uncoordinated national initiatives in currency depreciation sabotage international monetary order.

Thus, the position today is that legislators are already beginning to feel compelled to accord the restoration of profit prospects a higher political priority than the union hierarchies' vested interest in the strike-threat system. They are moving toward the raising of prospective yields to investment via wage-rate "controls," whether in the form of "incomes-policies" or extralegal coercions ("persuasions"), with of course the politically expedient bluff of price and profit "controls." But as soon as governments take over the market function (except as a crude, once for all rectification of a disastrous situation), free enterprise is on the way out. Wage rates will before long become determined either by vote acquisition prospects or by corruption, or both. And because I do not judge that (even in the politician-dominated United States) public opinion could be persuaded to accept the abandonment of free enterprise, the reasonableness of achieving the maximization of the wages flow, equity in income distribution, and employment security via market-selected wage-rate (and price) adjustments may not be so unlikely to receive early recognition as might at first be thought.

It has been a growing awareness of the fact that the traditional economic freedom of the British people has been threatened by an "incomes policy" that, as this is written, a long experiment in that direction has been temporarily abandoned in Britain.[1] But incipient unemployment in that country has caused continued inflation still to be regarded as the lesser evil from the standpoint of vote acquisition; hence, as long as wage push is allowed to continue threatening the wages flow and full employment, I feel that the "inevitability" of a return to wage-rate "controls" will remain. Admittedly, through the Industrial Relations Act, 1971, what appears to be the first effective step toward curbing strike-threat power (in Britain or indeed anywhere[2]) since 1824 has been adopted. But whether this legislation will prove to be much more than a gesture is by no means certain. In my own present judgment it is unlikely to prove an adequate restraint on the right to disrupt for private gain. I fear therefore that a relapse into a more drastic incomes policy will soon again be regarded as politically expedient, even by the Conservatives, at least as a transitional measure. But the alternative—a coordinated labor market (that is, a freed market) with the greater security and distributive justice it guarantees, will again have to be considered. I cannot avoid the inference that, *if economic freedom and democracy are to survive in Britain*, sooner or later a policy of labor emancipation, that is, freedom achieved in the market for effort and skill—for labor's benefit—must necessarily win through.

284

It seems distinctly paradoxical that the dilemma of recession or inflation and international monetary disorder presently confronting governments should be the source of a ray of hope. But threatened disaster has often inspired wise reforms; and if political wage-rate determination is to be avoided yet chronic inflation is to be eradicated, the strike-threat system cannot survive. In asserting this proposition, I am giving full weight to the fact that the intelligentsia—the opinion-makers—of this age have been so deeply indoctrinated that even those who are critical of the use made of the strike-threat power are mostly convinced of the legitimacy of that power; and that the majority of intellectuals have been conditioned to feel contempt for "free enterprise," largely because they have been more aware of the excrescences of the system than of its inherent virtues. It may well be, indeed, that the revolutionaries will be allowed to impose totalitarian regimes. But the prospects are not, I think, as black as they sometimes appear superficially to be.

I have tried to justify a guarded optimism in my *Politically Impossible . . . ?* , to which I have just referred. In that book I lay the blame very largely on my own profession. I charge economists with having been thrown off their intellectual balance by their virtues—warmth of heart, humanity, sheer kindness. Like their fellow intellectuals whom they have influenced, their sympathies have all too often ruled their minds.[3] Stigler has charged that Marshall's great work was vitiated for this reason. I have charged that Adam Smith (whom I venerate) initiated a tradition of woolly thinking on the subject of the present book because he allowed his deep sympathy for the workers inappropriately to color his judgment. But in my *Politically Impossible . . . ?* I have accused economists also with having tried to be influential in the easiest way, obscuring their political assumptions, and thereby destroying scientific unanimity, especially on the subject of labor's share in income. And I have gone even further and charged that many "economists," seeking fame and power, have observably swum with the tide, carefully pandering to current popular stereotypes. The most influential textbooks of "labor economics" seem to me to be reprehensible in this respect.

I recently asked a very influential American economist, who described himself as a "left-of-center" liberal, why the government's advisers failed to recommend a drastic cut in the federal minimum wage rate—a step which, he agreed, would rapidly reduce the unemployment figure and especially multiply employment openings and "training on the job" opportunities for non-white juveniles and women. He replied that we had "as much chance as seeing a snowball in hell" as seeing any step which might seem to threaten the interests of the AFL-CIO hierarchy. But if he and other "liberal" economists would only speak out unequivocally and with pertinacity against measures and institutions which they perceive are responsible for easily avoidable poverty and insecurity, quite different policies would become politically expedient.

Exactly how the first effective moves toward *fundamental* reform are likely to occur, I make no attempt to forecast. Nevertheless, the aim of the required legislation is as simple as it could be, and capable of clear, truthful description. Lying preambles are all too common in acts of Congress and acts of Parliament. But we can at least *imagine* a bill with a truthful preamble, designed to rescue the labor market from duress-imposed restraints, and introduced under the title, say, *The Emancipation of Labor Bill*. Its preamble could honestly read, "to promote the maximization and most equitable distribution of the wages flow and, in particular, to protect the right of every person to accept any lawful employment." The basic aim should be to entrench the individual's right to agree to any wage terms offered which he believes will enable him to better his condition or prospects, whether in respect of pecuniary remuneration or other benefits.

Subject to three important conditions, provision could be made in the bill itself for its automatic repeal, after a stipulated period of years, if a marked increase in the aggregate real wages flow and greater equality in its distribution had not in fact resulted. The three conditions necessary are first, the suspension during the testing period of all minimum wage provisions; secondly, reasonably effective enforcement of the bill's provisions—in other words the absence of unofficial strikes or other forms of duress in the labor market; and thirdly, the stern application of the principle of less eligibility in any government-provided unemployment compensation or relief. For the purpose of the statutory comparison, the aggregate wages flow could be defined as all real income other than interest, rent, royalties, dividends and profits. Analysis of tax collection figures could provide adequate comparative data.

The provision for automatic repeal and restoration of the status quo in the event of the failure of the "experiment" might, I think, overcome much of what would otherwise be sincere although mistaken opposition. But a quite separate step to improve justice in income distribution could usefully accompany labor market reform and help remove resistance to it. What are widely felt to be inequities *resulting from inherited wealth* could, in my judgment, be materially mitigated without harmful repercussions. The case against progressive taxation is partly that it is seriously detrimental to incentives while the additional revenues governments obtain through it are almost negligible;[4] and more important still, it is held that, through progressive taxation, part of the people's stock of wage-multiplying assets is being continuously squandered in the vote-buying process. But even steeply progressive inheritance taxes (the height of the tax in each case depending upon the sum inherited by the individual, not the sum bequeathed) accompanied by an enactment (preferably constitutional) to the effect that the proceeds must be maintained intact in the form of collectively owned capital, would exclude the capital squandering possibility. The yields could then be employed to reduce the level of taxes.[5] Under such circumstances, one objection to the progressive principle would fall away. I have discussed this possibility elsewhere and need not elaborate the possibilities here.[6]

Except in references to occupational licensing, I have not referred to parallel abuses for which the organized professions—particularly of medicine and law—are responsible. The sole reason is that the professions hardly ever resort to any practice resembling the strike threat or the strike. This does not necessarily cause collusively arranged scales of charges or restraints on entry to be any the less exploitative. But as I have insisted that justice requires antitrust initiatives to protect the workers as consumers—especially when the workers' own power to contrive scarcity is being dissolved—so must I insist on the importance of reassuring the workers that the highly paid professions are not to be exempted when their (the workers') right to exploit is withdrawn. Each individual practitioner needs to be accorded the fullest freedom in pricing his services and in communicating his charges to the public. He must be protected from any disciplinary control exercised by *practitioners* acting in concert. But nonpracticing members of his profession, appointed by government, could be entrusted with the enforcement of appropriate codes of professional conduct (with appeal to the courts).

The chief transitional difficulty which can be predicted during the assimilation of the economy to a strike-free era concerns the severity of a disturbance to "established expectations" which may be experienced in those occupations which have been enjoying the greatest private benefits from "exploitation". A wide gap may well be disclosed initially in some cases between previous, union-enforced wage rates and the alternatives in such other employments as will be *immediately* available for the workers affected. Within the range of this gap, formerly privileged workers may truly be "at the mercy of" managements. But the paucity of well-paid alternative employments available at the outset will itself have been a consequence of the strike-threat system. The more appropriate alternatives will have been shut off through union-imposed restraints on entry. The whole purpose of the "Emancipation of Labor" enactments would be that of permitting *the emergence on all sides of better-renumerated employment outlets, which relief for investors from strike-threat exploitation risks would call into being.* As soon as the providers of wage-multiplying assets can be guaranteed that prospective yields will not be robbed by duress-imposed costs, a phenomenal stimulus to the provision of such assets will follow.

Unfortunately, the response to that stimulus could hardly be instantaneous. It might take some time before entrepreneurs generally grasped the full significance of the new régime. Hence provisions for protection of a minority of workers against catastrophic change would have to be considered. For instance, a provisional rule could be that, during the first few years of operation of a strike-free régime, managements could not reduce their wage offers by more than (say) 10 percent per annum. Such a rule would enable employees adversely affected (with the assistance of their unions) to search for alternative employments without a *disastrous* shrinkage of their source of income. But at the end of any such period, every person should have the unrestrained right to improve his earnings or acquire access to training by accepting any employment on any terms whatsoever, except for unauthorized "lock-in" terms (see pp. 101-102).

There is another *possibility* that might have to be guarded against. Attempts could be made to engross the fruits of the better use of men and assets for the benefit of favorably placed investors (with special facilities for the collusive fixing of prices or outputs). Such an outcome could be avoided through the inauguration of exceptional antitrust vigilance and (if necessary) speedy action. The objective would have to be recognized as that of facilitating the cheapening of all productive processes, including the marketing process. But provided this objective is sought with a clear understanding that the evil to be eradicated is "the contrived scarcity" (or "the contrived plenitude") and not that of high profits, it is an attainable objective.

In thus stressing this objective, it should be explained that a general *cheapening* of outputs does not imply deflation. Certainly the advent of a strike-free era could mean the advent of an inflation-free era. But a vital concomitant reform to the *Emancipation of Labor Act* would be the explicit acceptance of monetary flexibility. Thus, in the United States, the Federal Reserve Board could be placed under the obligation to maintain a dollar of constant purchasing power. That would mean that the further any current scale of prices diverged at any time from the norm set, the smaller would be the probability that it would diverge further in that direction and the greater the probability that it would soon move toward the norm. The rapidly rising wages flow due to the abandonment of strike-threat influences would then permit the parallel abandonment of attempts to use monetary policy to maintain full employment (or other "national objectives").

I remarked above that "we can at least imagine" legislation such as I have sketched. But I have never ceased to be aware of the historical reality that most great *peaceful* changes in human institutions seem to have occurred through the emergence of a new reality while old forms have remained. Maybe much less drastic reforms might be expedient during a transition to a more just and humane economic order. But my object in referring to this imaginary *Emancipation of Labor Bill* has been primarily to set minds working on the topic. At the same time I am confident that, if attempted, a wholehearted experiment with a strike-free régime would win *almost unimaginable* benefits.

I diagnose the repeal in 1824 of the ancient common law proscription of "conspiracy" or "combination" as having created the most burdensome institutional defect from which the British "free enterprise system" has subsequently suffered. Whether that repeal was due to misconceived sympathy for poor workers apparently struggling against rich, avaricious "employers," or through cynical politicians who had perceived the command over electoral decisions possessed by union leaders, its consequences have been gravely detrimental to the vast majority of those who are believed to have been the gainers. *And a similar weakness plagues the whole western world.* The elimination of this weakness must, as I have already suggested (pages 282-285), come to be recognized as *the major economic problem of the present generation.*

I know that it will be very easy for economists with an axe to grind or other vested interests to misrepresent both my arguments and my motives for writing this book. I even expect the allegation that I am a paid lackey of the capitalists. But I was born in the last century and I am much too old to have any personal ambitions, within or without the academic field. And I shall never have to ask anyone to vote for me. To critics who think they have heard the goose-step in my contribution, my reply is to ask them to consider the unchallengeable truth that, with a few honorable exceptions, the capitalists of this century conspicuously refrain from giving financial support to the classical liberal school, to which I obviously belong. Moreover, there is no discernible academic group concerned with achieving justice for the classes whose thrift (or that of their forebears) has provided the assets which multiply the real wages flow, and whose entrepreneurial acumen has determined the form those assets have taken. There have been several able defenses of the corporate system against misconceived—sometimes demagogic—attacks. But I know of no attempt whatsoever to show that the investors' share has been unfairly mulcted. I certainly do not suggest that there *ought* to have been.[7] But the phenomenon is significant.

The loss-avoidance, profit-seeking system receives scant effective defense in academic circles today. In some degree this is due to "the workers" being presumed to be poor while "the investors" are presumed to be rich. But the bias is less toward the workers than toward the labor union hierarchy. In reality, *"the workers" are the victims of the strike-threat system*; for unparalleled prosperity and improvement in material well-being awaits them in any country which, through suppression of private duress, once again permits the social discipline of the free market to be the ultimate determinant of the wage rates it will be profitable for managements to offer. That is what I believe this book to have shown.

NOTES

[1] This page was written in 1971. My forecast of a return to wage rate controls has since been borne out (November, 1972).

[2] The U. S. Taft-Hartley Act, at any rate as administered and adjudicated, has had little effect.

[3] The best treatment of this important sociological and political phenomenon is John Van Sickle's *Freedom in Jeopardy—The Tyranny of Idealism*(New York: World Publishing Co., 1969).

[4] See F. A. Hayek, *The Constitution of Liberty* (Chicago: University of Chicago Press, 1945), Chapter 20; W. J. Blum and H. Kalven, *The Uneasy Case for Progressive Taxation* (Chicago: University of Chicago Press, 1953); David McCord Wright, *Democracy and Progress (Kelley, 1951),* pp. 94, *et seq.*; L. von Mises, *Human Action*, pp. 803, *et seq.*; F. C. Benham, in *Agenda for a Free Society,* ed., A. Seldon (London: Institute of Economic Affairs, 1961), Part VI.

[5] In the beginning, the proceeds would be appropriately applied in liquidating the community's "collectively owned *negative* capital," which is my realistic description of the national debt, instead of accumulating a fund of

"collectively owned *positive* capital." This would of course reduce the level of taxes needed in the same kind of way.

⁶ Hutt, *Politically Impossible . . ?* , Part IV.

⁷ For one thing, I have shown that, as soon as the strike-threat system has become accepted as an institution, investors as a class have become unexploitable by it.

Index of Authors
Cited or Mentioned

Index